# FUNDAMENTALS
# OF
# EXPERIMENTAL
# PSYCHOLOGY

# FUNDAMENTALS OF EXPERIMENTAL PSYCHOLOGY

## A Comparative Approach

**P. W. Robinson**

BRIGHAM YOUNG UNIVERSITY

Prentice-Hall, Inc., *Englewood Cliffs, New Jersey*

*Library of Congress Cataloging in Publication Data*

ROBINSON, PAUL W   (date)
  Fundamentals of experimental psychology.

  Bibliography:   p. 367
  Includes index.
  1. Psychology, Experimental.   I. Title.
[DNLM: 1. Psychology, Experimental   BF181 R663f]
BF181.R62        150′.1′8        75-17950
ISBN 0-13-339168-X

© 1976 by Prentice-Hall, Inc., Englewood Cliffs, New Jersey

PRINTED IN THE UNITED STATES OF AMERICA

10  9  8  7  6  5  4  3  2  1

Prentice-Hall International, Inc., *London*
Prentice-Hall of Australia, Pty. Ltd., *Sydney*
Prentice-Hall of Canada, Ltd., *Toronto*
Prentice-Hall of India Private Limited, *New Delhi*
Prentice-Hall of Japan, Inc., *Tokyo*
Prentice-Hall of Southeast Asia (Pte.) Ltd., *Singapore*

*To*
*Julia Ellen Robinson*
*Millie Weeks Spackman*
*Elizabeth "Bessie" Swain*
*Velta Wright Robinson*
*who have shown so many people the true meaning of mother love.*

# Contents

## 9
## Two-Group Designs   186

## 10
## Multigroup Designs with One Independent Variable   209

## 11
## Factorial Designs   235

## 12
## Small N Designs   259

## 13
## Contemporary Experimental Psychology   287

# Preface

As the manuscript draws toward completion, I begin to reflect in a serious vein on whether these long hours of writing have produced what others will consider a unique addition to the field. In looking over the final product, I think there are several aspects of the text that make it a functional contribution.

First is the approach. Experimental psychology texts can be grossly divided into three types. First, there are content oriented texts, which concentrate on theoretical and empirical concepts in specific areas of psychology, such as perception, learning, motivation, and cognitive processes. Second, there are methodologically oriented texts dealing mostly with the role of experimental designs in research and important statistical concepts. The third type of experimental text is also methodologically oriented, but it emphasizes procedural, rather than statistical dimensions of psychological investigations. This text falls into the third category. It emphasizes procedural aspects of psychological investigations such as selection of independent and dependent variables, means of controlling secondary variables, criteria for selecting subjects, and so on.

This text is distinguished from other texts on several other points also. It is geared for a contemporary experimental psychology course in which a large portion of the students are headed for applied psychology careers. All types of psychological investigations are covered, from clinical case studies in the field to the use of factorial designs in controlled laboratory experiments. Similarities and differences between analytical approaches, such as two-group designs, baseline designs, case studies, and quasi-experimental designs, are presented in an easy-to-understand manner. Experimental dimensions are organized into simplified categories (for example, four primary types of psychological investigations, six basic steps in conducting an experiment, five main ways of measuring a dependent variable) to help the student master the fundamentals involved. To avoid a long explanation of statistical theory (usually required to ready the student for correctly analyzing experimental data), I have provided with every type of experimental design covered complete step-by-step examples of how to statistically analyze data. (Unfortunately, these examples make the book look highly statistical to anyone just thumbing through.)

Although experimental investigations involving one or two subjects have been employed in psychology since its inception (Wundt's experiments on introspection, Pavlov's on classical conditioning, to name just two), only in the last twenty years with the growing use of behavior modification has the valid use of a small-N analytical approach begun to grow widely. One of the chapters in the text shows not only what the basic parts of a small-N approach include, but also what the similarities and differences are between large-N and small-N designs. This type of comparative coverage is not available in any other experimental psychology text.

Most experimental psychology courses require students to perform an experiment and write a report on their findings. Instructors must either prepare handouts on how to write a report or require their students to purchase a separate manual. This text, in Chapter Fourteen, gives detailed instructions for writing a report in the APA style and provides many examples. A section on how to look up articles in *Psychological Abstracts* is also included.

Every instructor has his own research interest and special area of expertise, be it learning, perception, psychophysical scaling, sensory processes, or some other area. This text does not include speical-interest content material, so that each instructor can flavor the content in the course according to his own interest by combining this text with other readings. No attempt is made to slant the text toward animal-versus-human or behavioral-versus-cognitive research. The procedures presented are general and can be employed in almost any subfield of pscyhology. My overall purpose is to present general analytical approaches rather than specialized research techniques.

The publication of any book is the product of many people's work. I would like to express appreciation to some of those who played a role in this one. As the major sources of my undergraduate and graduate intellectual stimulation, Peter C. Wolff and David R. Stone deserve first mention. Being one of possibly many who left their tutorship without letting them know how much their association meant, I am grateful for the opportunity to express my debt and gratitude to them. I am indebted also to the Prentice-Hall staff for effectively completing this project, including Neale Sweet (subject editor), Margery Carazzone (production editor), and Dwight Osborn, who prompted the writing of the text. Thoughtful advice and suggestions regarding the manuscript from Geoffrey Keppel (University of California, Berkeley), Jay M. Finkelman (City University of New York), Frank B. McMahon (Southern Illinois University, Edwardsville), T. S. Krawiec (Skidmore College), Ron Norton (University of Winnipeg), and James J. Jenkins (University of Minnesota) are appreciated. Less obvious, but equally important, is the patience and forbearance shown by my wife, Carol.

P. W. ROBINSON

# 1

# An Overview

*Often a student of psychology goes through his undergraduate program without gaining an overall perspective of what his psychological training entails, what the field of psychology includes, and what he should know when he completes his training. The purpose of the first four sections of this chapter is to help the student gain an idea of what the field of psychology involves, what skills the psychologist needs, and what role an experimental psychology course can play in developing those skills. The fifth section provides a brief résumé of each chapter so that the reader can visualize how a particular chapter fits into the overall scheme of the text. The sixth section lists the steps involved in conducting an experimental investigation. This is possibly the most important part of the chapter—and the book, for that matter—for that is what the text is all about—how to design and carry out an appropriate psychological investigation.*

## PSYCHOLOGY IN PERSPECTIVE

Psychology is most commonly referred to as "the study of behavior and its correlated processes." Its goal is generally expressed to be the "identification, explanation, and prediction of the behavioral principles and processes by which man operates." Although correct, these statements are somewhat misleading, for they imply that psychologists spend most of their time on basic research geared toward isolating new behavioral principles. The definition does a satisfactory job in representing psychology as a scholarly and scientific discipline, but the field is more than an academic area of investigation. It is also a profession concerned with offering guidance on and assistance with everyday problems. In fact, only about 18 percent of the profession's time is spent in basic research; the rest is given over to providing services for intrapersonal problems.

Defining psychology as an area of scientific investigation was more appropriate in its formative stages. As psychology has progressed, the proportion of psychologists involved in laboratory research has declined. This has not been due to lack of interest in research, however, for research is a prime area of concern for all psychologists. There are three interrelated reasons for this decrease in the percentage of psychologists involved in laboratory research. The first is the development of psychology into an applied science. In the late 1800s the field of psychology was in its infancy. Like all other applied sciences in this stage of development, the emphasis had to be on basic research. One of the objectives of psychology was to become a functional part of everyday life situations. In order to adequately develop an applied psychology, however, the proper groundwork had to be laid in terms of devising appropriate analytical techniques and empirically based theoretical structures. As the years passed, more behavioral principles and analytical procedures became available, and with increased confidence and new techniques came programs for training applied psychologists.

This development generated the second major reason for the decrease in the percentage of experimentalists. The demand for applied psychologists went beyond all expectations. With society taking over a greater responsibility for ensuring the health and physical welfare of its members, individuals began concentrating more on inter- and intrapersonal problems. People became more concerned with juvenile delinquency, peer conflicts, mental retardation, learning difficulties, phobias, compulsions, and other such problems. As a result, psychology was inundated with requests for professionals knowledgeable in the dynamics of behavioral relationships. The demand significantly stimulated the increased production of applied psychologists.

The third reason for the increased proportion of nonexperimentalists was the limited job opportunities for experimental psychologists. Most psychological research projects have been funded by the government and carried out at institutions of higher learning. Unfortunately, the number of universities with adequate research facilities has not kept pace with rising needs and student populations. Junior colleges and small four-year colleges without adequate research facilities were built to meet increased enrollments. Consequently, only a few students will have the opportunity for a career in psychological research. Most students who expect to enter graduate school in psychology should plan on a career as an applied psychologist rather than as a laboratory experimentalist.

With these points in mind, we can more appropriately classify psychologists as a group interested in contributions to knowledge about human and animal behavior, the communication of such information, and its applications. Figure 1–1 presents psychology in terms of its various subfields. The percentages represent the proportion of psychologists in that area. It is apparent that psychology has proliferated along many dimensions. Psy-

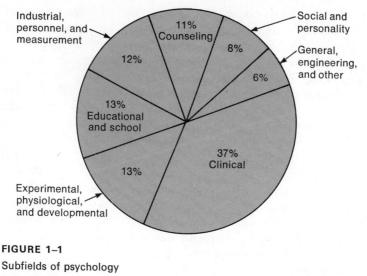

**FIGURE 1–1**

Subfields of psychology

(Adapted from Ross & Lockman, 1963, p. 8. Copyright 1963 by the American Psychological Association. Reprinted by permission.)

chologists specializing in a particular subfield, such as social, developmental, educational, and physiological psychology, have become welcome additions to the profession.

## PRIMARY WORK ACTIVITIES OF PSYCHOLOGISTS

With psychology's diversity of interests has come an increasing range of work activities. A psychologist may be found doing most anything from analyzing the mating behavior of the ground squirrel to arbitrating a labor dispute. Figure 1–2 divides the primary work activities of psychologists in terms of the percentage of time the profession as a whole spends on each. Figure 1–3 shows who employs psychologists. To provide a better understanding of what each division entails, let us take a look at the major activities.

**Clinical and counseling.** As mentioned previously, the largest proportion of psychologists are concerned with the use and application of psychological techniques and principles in face-to-face, individual situations. Psychologists in these categories are frequently concerned with intrapersonal problems involving anxiety, adjustment, motivation, communication, and vocational or educational attainment.

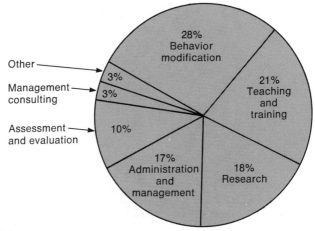

**FIGURE 1–2**

Major work activities of psychologists

(Adapted from Ross & Lockman, 1963, p. 10. Copyright 1963 by the American Psychological Association. Reprinted by permission.)

**Management and administration.** Every year more psychologists are being drawn into industrial administrative posts and other organizations. Psychologists in these executive positions find themselves planning, developing, organizing, and executing various programs. Schools, hospitals, clinics, private businesses, corporations, and research laboratories are a few of their employers. Administration is considered to be one of the most open and lucrative fields for the future.

**Testing.** One of the most widely known areas of psychology to the layman deals with the assessment and evaluation of psychological tests. Psychologists in this area may be involved with the development, administration, or interpretation of tests designed to measure intelligence, achievement, aptitude, interests, vocational suitability, and personality disorders.

**Research.** Psychology, like all other sciences, is actively involved in research. Research carried out to advance our understanding of behavior is accomplished by investigations centered around both theoretical and practical problems. One investigator may be involved with determining the internal processes involved in personality development, while another may be attempting to develop a new technique for eliminating phobias. Psychologists carrying out research can be found in hospitals, universities, and industrial and governmental laboratories throughout the country. They are also found

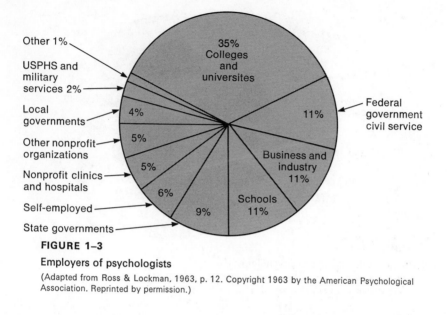

**FIGURE 1–3**

Employers of psychologists

(Adapted from Ross & Lockman, 1963, p. 12. Copyright 1963 by the American Psychological Association. Reprinted by permission.)

outside the laboratory—in supermarkets studying buying trends, in forests studying animal behavior, and in schools analyzing the behavioral patterns of children.

**Teaching.** The main function of one-fourth of all psychologists is teaching. Psychologists work as professors at institutions of higher learning. They are also hired to develop and implement training programs in industry and governmental organizations.

**Consulting.** There are many requests from industry, business, and governmental agencies for psychological expertise on a part-time basis. Psychologists are called to aid in the development of instructional programs, help develop educational toys, and assist in applying laboratory findings to everyday situations.

## ROLE OF AN UNDERGRADUATE
## EXPERIMENTAL PSYCHOLOGY COURSE

With such diversity in contemporary psychology and a smaller proportion of psychologists spending their time in laboratory research, we could question the importance of an experimental psychology course for all undergraduates majoring in psychology. Most psychology majors intend to become applied psychologists. They are interested in training to become clinical, industrial, or educational psychologists, or counselors. They therefore see little value in taking experimental psychology. But psychology is an analytical field, and one of the prime duties of any psychologist is evaluation. He should be able to apply psychological principles and evaluate the effects of these principles in specific situations. To do this effectively, he must have two kinds of training. First, he learns the principles: he takes content courses such as learning, developmental, personality, and abnormal psychology to learn the principles of behavior and what events influence them. The content courses provide the psychology student with the facts as they are currently understood. He learns such things as the stages a child goes through in his development toward adulthood, the perceptual processes people use in dealing with the world, the anatomical divisions of the nervous system and their correlated behavioral functions, the different types of behavioral disorders, the factors involved in personality, and the processes involved in learning.

Second, he takes courses in analysis. Here he learns how to identify problems, how to apply the behavioral principles he learned in content courses, and how to evaluate whether or not the principles are effective in the situation he is concerned with at the moment. A student in psychology requires two types of analytical courses. First, he needs analytical courses that deal with the basic formats used in scientific investigations. These teach the prospective psychologist the alternative types of investigatory procedures that are accepted by professional psychologists and that he may employ as a professional. They deal with what types of investigations a psychologist can carry out, what steps are necessary, and how to implement the various experimental designs. The formats are very general in nature; they are basic investigation types used in all areas of psychology irrespective of the specific area of emphasis. An educational psychologist or a social psychologist, for example, may employ a manipulatory investigation involving two randomized groups. This type of investigation is a common approach used to analyze cause-and-effect relationships, even in disciplines other than psychology.

The second type of analytical course is more related to specific subfields in psychology and is much more restricted in applicability. Psychotherapeutic procedures, for example, are based on general experimental methods that have been modified to deal with specialized case situations encountered by the clinical psychologist. These procedures may not be functional for educational psychologists. A child psychologist may be interested in exploring the ability of children to distinguish between different colors, so he asks his subjects to identify verbally the colors they see. A comparative psychologist interested in animal behavior may want to study the ability of nonhuman organisms to identify colors. Perceptual studies such as this one can be done with monkeys, rats, or pigeons although these creatures cannot talk. Though both the child and the comparative psychologist may use the same basic experimental design, their graduate courses in analysis will have taught them what special modifications are necessary in the experimental procedures to deal with their respective situations.

An undergraduate course in experimental psychology is intended to give the student an understanding of the general types of investigatory methods available to all psychologists. Generally speaking, it is the only course in analysis the undergraduate student will have before entering graduate school, for the emphasis of his other undergraduate courses is on content rather than procedure. This course should provide him an opportunity to develop his general analytical skills and sharpen his ability to diagnose which type of scientific investigation should be used in any given situation.

Unfortunately, many students have difficulty in visualizing the importance of experimental psychology if they plan to be applied psychologists. They cannot see any practical application for experimental design problems in human situations, especially when the instructor consistently uses examples with rats running through mazes and pigeons pecking little plastic keys. I recall an example given in my first experimental psychology course. With a gleam in his eye, the professor began explaining the steps involved in a scientific investigation. He used as his example an investigation concerning rats turning right or left in a maze. Although that gleam over the rats' behavior was initially interpreted as an indication of senility, I later came to appreciate it as an honest effort by an intelligent and sensitive scholar to arouse the students' interest in experimental psychology. The wise student should actively attempt to relate the material in the course to his chosen area of interest.[1] Many graduate students have spent long hours learning principles of scientific analysis they failed to pick up in their undergraduate experimental psychology courses because they saw no relevance to them at the time.

There is also growing pressure for graduate psychology programs to increase students' training in experimental procedures. More and more, society is requiring that the psychologist demonstrate the effectiveness of his programs. Boards of education now expect educational psychologists to document their views on such issues as whether teaching machines are more effective than teachers, whether students do better when graded or not graded, and whether low student-teacher ratios result in better student performance than high ratios. The clinical psychologist in charge of the county mental health program may be required to carry out investigations to show that his innovative group therapy program (which is expensive) is more effective than some less costly program, or that the drug crisis program is worth the money needed to continue it.

It is also important that psychologists stay well versed in experimental procedures so that they may be able to apply various techniques accurately,

1. In an effort to help the student see the relevance, I have attempted to use examples from all subfields in psychology, not just animal experiments in the laboratory.

as indicated in the following story. A psychiatrist was employed by one of the Rocky Mountain states to deal with special behavioral problems that arise in grade school children. One of his cases involved a second-grade girl who had a skill at profanity that would put a sailor to shame. After reading an article on the use of pennies to operantly condition normal talking behavior in certain mute children, the psychiatrist decided to try the same thing on this girl. The following week the girl was brought into his office and seated across the desk from him. His plan was to give her a penny each time she spoke without using profanity, in the hope that he could eventually bring her language under control by paying her to speak nicely.

He sat quietly in his chair with pennies lined up in front of him on the desk and waited for her to speak, just as the psychologist had done in the article he read. "What's wrong?" she asked. Smiling, he slid a penny across the desk to her. She looked down at the penny, back up at him, and back down at the penny. "What's this for?" she asked. A second penny was pushed toward her. "Is this a game?" she asked, while looking at the two pennies in front of her. Again without comment he sent another coin her way. "What the hell's the matter with you? Cat got your tongue?"—no penny. After fifteen minutes of this (and increasing emotion being displayed by the child in response to the "mute" psychiatrist), he told her, "Well, that's all today. I'll see you tomorrow." Quickly the girl got up and started walking toward the door. "Aren't you going to take your pennies?" he asked. In reply she told him exactly where he could stick those pennies.

Later, after recounting the incident at a meeting, the psychiatrist adamantly maintained that his situation demonstrated that techniques currently being used by many psychologists in behavior modification programs were ineffective and potentially damaging due to the frustration and anxiety they may develop in children. There are a number of things wrong with his situation. He should not have drawn that conclusion from such an uncontrolled situation. There are several potential explanations for the results he obtained, other than the one he presented. He used an experimental procedure with which he was unfamiliar, besides not understanding the principles involved. A better background in carrying out scientific investigations would have saved him from making such unfounded claims and from the verbal chastisement he received from his audience.

## SKILLS REQUIRED OF A PSYCHOLOGIST

There is a common misconception held by many students interested in psychology that the only thing a psychologist needs to know is principles. Psychological training is envisioned by these students as a program in which the prospective psychologist is fed facts and figures about behavioral relationships until he knows all there is to know about psychological principles. These principles include such things as the different stages an infant goes through in becoming an adult, how people react in crowds, and what makes the mind work. Actually, psychological training involves much more than learning facts and figures. A potential psychologist must learn more than one skill to become a professional. There are five skills which all psychologists need to develop in becoming a professional, no matter what subfield of psychology they select. These are:

1. Analytical prowess
2. Knowledge of psychological principles
3. Skill in communicating ideas to professional peers
4. Skill in communicating ideas to laymen
5. Ability to evaluate research

### Analytical Prowess

More than anything else, the psychologist is trained to be an analyst. Society presents him with behavioral problems to be solved: Why are there so many divorces? Why are people violent? How do mistakes help a person learn? As would be expected, there is more than one way of answering these questions. Laboratory experiments could be performed, surveys could be conducted, observations could be made, case histories could be reviewed. A large portion of psychological training involves teaching the apprentice psychologist how to answer these questions. He learns what types of investigatory procedures are available, the advantages and disadvantages of each type of procedure, and in what situations each may be used.

The psychologist's role is similar to that of an aeronautical engineer. An engineer may be called in to investigate why a particular plane crashed, or to come up with a better landing device. One of the main reasons for hiring him is that he has been trained to analyze such situations. The engineer knows how to design scientific investigations that can answer these questions. The psychologist is also an expert on how to design a scientific investigation, but in behavioral rather than aeronautical situations.

### Knowledge of Psychological Principles

The medical doctor is our society's authority on physical health. He is the one to whom people turn for solving medical and surgical problems. He either knows the appropriate medicine to give in a particular situation, or he knows where to find out. The same is true of psychologists in regard to the mental health of society. The psychologist spends many course hours learning what is known about the psychological composition of a person in terms of his actions and thought processes. At first, his training consists of a general foundation in all content areas of psychology including learning, thinking, physiological mechanisms, motivation, perception, growth and development, personality, social, and abnormal psychology. Later this training becomes confined to a special area of interest such as child psychology, experimental analysis, psychological testing, physiological mechanisms, or learning. As in medicine, so much is currently known in subfields of psychology that it is impossible for one person to know all areas well. The psychologist selects a certain area of psychology to specialize in and becomes intimately familiar with what is known in that area.

### Skill in Communicating Ideas to Professional Peers

The psychologist needs to be able to communicate with other professionals in his field. Every academic area has its own jargon and style of writing. Special terminology and ways of presenting information have been devised in psychology so that new findings can be presented to other psychologists. Certain formats are considered acceptable for presenting new results, ideas, hypotheses, and theories to others in the field by means of professional journals and presentations at psychological conventions. Learning the proper form and writing style is an important part of psychological training, and it is a skill that should not be taken lightly.

### Skill in Communicating Ideas to Laymen

The psychologist must also be able to develop a good rapport with the nonprofessional. His success as a psychologist is highly dependent on his ability to relate to laymen and explain the solutions to psychological problems in their terms. Although this is especially true of clinical and other applied psychologists, it is also true of research and academic psychologists, who must make their program needs known to administrators and funding agencies.

### Ability to Evaluate Research

Progress is continually being made in psychology. More becomes known every day. New principles are being discovered, new approaches are being developed, and new needs are arising. To keep abreast, the psychologist must spend at least a few hours each month reading professional journals. He needs not only to read but also to be able to evaluate the results of the published research. In many instances more than one conclusion can be drawn from the results of a research project. The psychologist must rely on his training in how to carry out investigations to help him interpret the strong and weak points of a new innovative technique reported by a peer. He also needs to be able to note the strong and weak aspects of articles that show conflicting results.

## OVERVIEW OF THE TEXT

The objective of this text is to introduce the reader to the analytical dimensions of psychology. In the thirteen chapters that follow the reader will be exposed to the various tactics and methods psychologists currently use in carrying out psychological investigations. This may sound like a sizable chore for one textbook, and it is, for there are literally hundreds of different strategies used in psychological investigations. If one were to try to learn all the different psychological investigatory designs individually, it would take hundreds of books and more than one lifetime. What this book attempts to do is show that all the hundreds of designs are derived from a few basic elements or building blocks. Just as the thousands of words in our language are derived from the 26 letters of the alphabet, so the different psychological strategies are derived from a few basic methodological dimensions.

The essence of all psychological investigations is to identify causal relationships between variables. A psychologist, for example, may be concerned with the effect of LSD on people's attitudes and actions. To analyze this relationship, he may devise a scientific investigation in which one group of subjects receives LSD and a second group receives a placebo. The investigator tries to make sure that the two groups are the same in terms of age, IQ, ethnic background, and so on, so that any behavioral differences that show up can be attributed to the LSD, not to something else. A second psychologist may be in a country that does not allow the use of LSD in experimentation. To answer the question "what effect does LSD have," he must resort to an alternative type of scientific investigation. He may interview people who have taken the drug, or he may observe people who have been arrested and are still under the influence of the drug. These are only three of hundreds of different approaches psychologists could use to determine the cause-effect relationship between LSD and behavior.

What would all the different types of investigations have in common? All would be trying to show that LSD and not some other variable present caused some effect on behavior. All would want to be able to state with some degree of validity that LSD has such and such an effect on actions. How could all the alternative investigations differ? They could differ on many variables, such as how much LSD was given and what type of behavior was measured. In terms of validity, however, they will all differ according to how well they control for the possibility that some variable (commonly called a secondary variable) other than LSD may have caused the actions being recorded. Control of secondary variables, then, is the crucial aspect of all psychological investigations and is generally the building block dimension for providing alternative types of investigations. As we shall see in Chapter Four, there are five basic ways of controlling secondary variables upon which scores of alternative types of psychological investigations are based.

The main purpose of the book, then, is to tell the reader what are the basic dimensions of psychological investigations that can be mixed or matched to provide the psychologist with the numerous tactical alternatives at his disposal. The steps involved in carrying out a psychological investigation are presented along with the basic points that must be taken into consideration to design and carry out any investigation or analyze a past investigation. A brief synopsis of the text chapters is presented here to give an overview of what is to be covered. This text is designed for interested students who have no more knowledge of psychology than that obtained in a general psychology course, although a background in statistics would be helpful.

Chapter Two attempts to give the reader some idea of how the general analytical approach used by psychologists originally developed. The major schools of thought are presented along with the methodological approaches they advocated.

Chapter Three categorizes psychological investigations along two dimensions: (1) whether they occur in a controlled laboratory setting or in the natural environment and (2) whether a variable is manipulated (experimental research) or not (ex post facto research). The main steps involved in carrying out these different types of investigations are discussed with strong emphasis on their similarities and differences, advantages and disadvantages. Five reasons for carrying out psychological research are also included.

One of the prime objectives of the book is to get the reader to understand that scientific investigations center around analyzing variations brought about by variable fluctuations. Variation and its causes are initially covered in Chapter Four in the comparison of the terms *variation* and *variance*. Total variation is then divided into *systematic* and *secondary* components to emphasize the fact that an investigator is concerned with different sources of variation. Five methods for controlling unwanted variables in an experimental investigation are presented. These are elimination, constancy, randomization, making the unwanted variable a second independent variable, and statistical control. The advantages of these five techniques are compared. After defining variation and the different ways of controlling it, the general sources from which unwanted variation may arise are covered. Chapter Four is an important chapter, for it presents the rationale behind all psychological investigations that involve the actual manipulation of some factor.

Chapter Five discusses several important facets of scientific investigations that do not have to do with how the investigation is designed. Issues such as selecting appropriate independent and dependent variables, experimenter bias, and instrumentation problems are presented.

As mentioned in Chapter Four, not all scientific investigations involve the manipulation of some variable where one group is given something (e.g., LSD) and a second group is not. Chapters Six and Seven introduce the reader to nonmanipulatory (ex post facto) research designs and alternative methods of data collection. Although manipulatory investigations are preferred over ex post facto analyses, the psychologist is often confronted with a situation that does not lend itself to experimental manipulation. He would, for example, have a difficult time carrying out a manipulatory study to find out why people commit suicide. Several types of ex post facto investigations are presented that are as scientifically sound as experimental investigations, yet are less powerful for identifying cause-effect relationships.

Chapters Eight through Eleven present sixteen of the most commonly used experimental (manipulatory) designs in behavioral research. All sixteen designs involve performing statistical tests such as a $t$ test and an F test to aid the investigator in determining whether the manipulated factor did have an effect. Not all readers will at this stage of their training have had a course in statistics. Although a course in statistics would be beneficial, it is certainly not necessary. The main purpose of these chapters is to show the student how these designs are used, where they are used, and when to use them, rather than emphasize the importance of statistics. A logical analysis of the statistical computations is provided, however, for the students with and without a statistical background who may be interested in the reasoning behind the statistics. Mathematical examples of each design are presented in a step by step fashion so that the reader may in fact carry out the statistical computations needed without knowing statistics. The numerical examples are also included for another reason. The student should keep this book as part of his personal reference library. When he later needs to carry out a certain type of investigation and has forgotten how the statistical computations are done, he can turn to the appropriate example and carry them out in cookbook fashion.

The use of small $N$ experimental designs in basic psychological research and applied behavior modification therapy is generally considered to be one of the most significant innovations in analysis since the implementation of statistical tests in research. Chapter Twelve presents the experimental analysis of behavior based on operant conditioning procedures using a small number of subjects rather than larger numbers of subjects, as is the case with the experimental designs presented in Chapters Eight through Eleven. The rationale behind such investigations, plus examples, are included. The development of experimental analysis procedures that can be carried out on as few as one or two subjects has provided the practicing psychologist with the opportunity to carry out sound manipulatory investigations unthought of years ago.

Another main objective of the text is to familiarize the reader with the variety of interests of present-day psychologists. Some of the important studies carried out in the last twenty years in psychology are presented in Chapter Thirteen to make the reader aware of what is currently going on in research and to attempt to kindle an interest in some area of research.

As previously mentioned, writing skills are important to a psychologist. Students are generally expected to develop their technical writing skills in the undergraduate experimental psychology course. Chapter Fourteen presents the principles required to write in the style approved by the American Psychological Association. The reader is also introduced to the various journals in psychology and their main areas of concentration.

## STEPS IN CONDUCTING
## AN EXPERIMENTAL INVESTIGATION

Students in an experimental psychology course generally find themselves in a contradictory situation. On the one hand, they are told that they need to finish the course to be able to carry out experimental investigations, and on the other hand they are told they must design and conduct an adequate experiment before the course is over. To help the student in this situation, the basic steps involved in a scientific investigation are presented here so that he may have some idea of how to plan and properly carry out an investigation. If a particular step is unclear after this brief discussion, the reader may turn to one of the later chapters for a more in-depth coverage.

How many steps are there in a scientific investigation? That depends on which experimental psychology text you look at. If you were to ask twenty different experimental psychologists "How many steps are there in carrying out an investigation?" you would probably get twenty different answers. Although they would all agree basically on what needs to be done, they would not agree on how many steps into which to divide the overall task. The situation is analogous to asking three chefs how many pieces there are in a pie. Though they would agree on what the whole pie is, they might disagree on how to divide it up. The important point here is that there are no universally accepted specified steps for carrying out research. This text will divide an investigation into six steps. Actually, the number of steps varies somewhat depending on what type of investigation is carried out (experimental or ex post facto). The steps presented here are for experimental types of investigations because most courses require students to carry out an experimental rather than an ex post facto investigation because experimental investigations are superior in determining cause-effect relationships, and students should have the experience of carrying them out. If the student does happen to carry out an ex post facto investigation as a class project, Chapter Three will provide him with the steps involved in such studies.

The six basic steps in planning and carrying out a psychological research project are:

1. Selecting a research topic
2. Classifying variables
3. Selecting an appropriate design
4. Planning the method for carrying out the project, and carrying it out
5. Analyzing the results
6. Drawing conclusions about the relationships involved

First, the student decides what he wants to investigate. At the end of this step he writes down exactly the phenomenon he is interested in analyzing. Second, he identifies the variables and divides them into three categories: the independent variable, the dependent variable, and the important secondary variables. Third, he chooses a research design. A research design is simply a way of setting up the experimental situation that allows secondary variables to be controlled by applying one or more of the five control procedures that form the basis of all research designs. Fourth, the exact steps in carrying out the investigation (e.g., the subjects are seated in a classroom, shown a film, and fill out a questionnaire) are specified and carried out. Fifth, the results obtained are analyzed. (Normally this involves performing some statistical test.) Sixth, he draws conclusions about what happened in the experiment and makes generalized statements regarding the value of this project to situations other than the specific experimental situation. Perhaps an example will better illustrate the role of these steps in conducting an investigation. The following is an account of a former student who had to select and conduct an independent research project for course credit.

Sid was a junior when he enrolled in an undergraduate experimental psychology course. Although listed as a psychology major, he was not sure whether he wanted to become a physiological psychologist or go into the medical profession. Like most of the other students in the class, he had no idea what he would do for the independent research project assignment, which was due at the end of the term. After having had no luck thinking of something to do, he asked the instructor for suggestions. The instructor then asked him what his interests were and what professions he was considering. Sid mentioned he was interested in physiological psychology and the problem of drug addiction. He was told to look through the *Psychological Abstracts*,[2]

---

2. *Psychological Abstracts* is a reference journal published monthly that summarizes every psychological research investigation published in any journal that month.

especially the sections dealing with the use of drugs. He found from his readings that very little had been done in actually working with people while they were under the influence of a drug. Some articles had even suggested that it was impossible to work with persons under the influence of certain drugs (e.g., LSD, apomorphine) that caused them to act in seemingly uncontrollable ways. After going through the *Abstracts* and having a few more discussions with the instructor, Sid decided on a project.

He proposed injecting rats with apomorphine and trying to get them to work at some task. Why did he select rats for subjects and apomorphine as the drug? Like all research situations, there were restrictions. Drug research on humans by students is not ethically acceptable, and most addicting drugs are not available for experimental use. Drug research on animals under supervision was acceptable; and apomorphine was available. Apomorphine is commonly used in hospitals in large doses to make a person vomit. In small doses it causes infants to chew compulsively, and rats to gnaw. In previous articles rats had been observed to chew wood, sandpaper, and even their own tails under the influence of apomorphine.

Sid wanted to carry out a research project on the effects of apomorphine. Rather than merely observe rats given the drug, he wanted to get a measure of how strong a motivational state apomorphine caused. He took 12 rats and divided them into two 6-rat groups. All the rats were put in individual metal restraining tubes 2 1/2 inches in diameter, which allowed the rat's head to protrude at one end. They were then trained to swing their heads to the right and to gnaw on a block of wood for 15 seconds as reinforcement. When a head turn was made, the block was presented to the subject by means of a retractable bar. Six rats were given an injection of apomorphine during the sessions; the remaining 6 were not. After 10 daily one-hour sessions, the drugged rats were averaging 114 head turns per hour, while the undrugged rats were only averaging 3. From the results, Sid concluded that apomorphine did have a motivational effect and that subjects under the influence of the drug could be conditioned to respond to what was going on around them.

When doing an experiment, you should fill out a planning form on the proposed experiment. Figures 1–4 and 1–5 show an example of such a form for Sid's project.

### Defining the Problem

Selecting a research problem is difficult for most students. Generally, they are unfamiliar with what is currently going on in terms of psychological research. Consequently, they do not know what to try and they do not know what has been done. One solution is for the student to skim through *Psychological Abstracts*. A second source for research topics is the instructor. He is usually full of ideas, especially feasible projects. Frequently, students decide on a project that is too large or complex to be handled by the novice

RESEARCH PLANNING FORM

I. Definition of Problem

  A. General reason for the study  *To determine whether an organism under the influence of a strong drug could be made to attend*

  B. Operationally defined hypothesis *To determine the effects of apomorphine on the gnawing behavior of the rat, and to see if the rat could be conditioned to turn his head while under the influence of apomorphine*

II. Classification of Variables

  A. IV  *Apomorphine*

  B. DV  *Head turning*

  C. Secondary Variables  *Concentration of drug, how it is applied, species of rat, weight of subjects*

III. Type of Investigation

  A. General type of investigation *Laboratory experiment*

  B. Specific type of design  *Randomized two-group design*

IV. Method  *(See reverse side)*

V. Type of Analysis  *t-test*

VI. Conclusions

  *1. Apomorphine does induce a compulsive gnawing syndrome in rats.*

  *2. The effects of apomorphine can be empirically quantified.*

  *3. Subjects under the influence of a powerful drug can be worked with and conditioned to emit behaviors.*

**FIGURE 1–4**
Sid's research planning form, front side

IV. Method

A. Subjects *Twelve female Long-Evans hooded rats, three months old and weighing 240 to 290 grams*

B. Instrumentation *A steel restraining tube 2¼ inches in diameter, and 7 inches long, was used to hold the rat during experimental sessions. Two bolts, one at each end of the tube, ran through the diameter of the tube to keep the rat in. A photoelectric cell was placed 1 inch in front of the tube and 1½ inches to the right of the center of the tube.*

C. Procedure

1. *Each rat was run for a one-hour daily session for ten consecutive days.*

2. *During each session a rat was placed in the tube with his head protruding at one end.*

3. *Every time the rat turned his head far enough to the right to break a photoelectric beam, a wooden block was presented in front of him to gnaw on for 15 seconds, by means of a retractable bar.*

4. *Six rats were placed in the tube each day without being injected with a drug, while the other six were injected interperitoneally with 2.0 mg/kgm of apomorphine 20 minutes prior to being put in the tube.*

5. *The number of head turns each subject made per hour was recorded.*

6. *A t-test was run on the data using the following formula:*

$$t = \frac{(\bar{X}_A - \bar{X}_B)}{\sqrt{\frac{SS_A + SS_B}{(n_A - 1) + (n_B - 1)} \left(\frac{1}{n_A} + \frac{1}{n_B}\right)}}$$

**FIGURE 1–5**

Sid's research planning form, reverse side

experimenter. The instructor will usually help steer the student away from such situations.

The step of selecting a research project actually has two parts: (1) deciding on what the general intent of the investigation is and (2) defining exactly what is to be analyzed. In Sid's case the general problem was to determine whether subjects could be made to attend to environmental conditions while under the influence of a strong drug. Notice that this is a broad statement and indicates what general area the investigation involves. To carry out an experiment, however, the investigator must specify clearly how it is to be analyzed. This is the reason for the statement of an operationally defined hypothesis. The hypothesis in Sid's situation was "to determine the effect of apomorphine on the head-turning behavior of the rat." Why are two statements made, one general and one specific? The general statement tells what the basic area of concern is. As in the example, however, there is more than one way to study drugs and behavior. The specific statement pinpoints more closely how it is going to be studied.

### Classifying Variables

After stating a hypothesis, the investigator takes stock of exactly what variables are involved in the project. First, he defines the variable he is going to investigate. This is called the *independent variable* (IV), which in Sid's situation was apomorphine. Then he decides what variable he will measure to determine whether the IV had an effect. This is generally called the *dependent variable* (DV) and in Sid's case it was head-turning behavior. Sid was not really so interested in head-turning behavior, he simply chose that as one means of measuring the effect of the drug. All other variables (secondary variables) in the situation that could influence the head-turning behavior were then listed. This is an important step in carrying out research, for the objective of an investigation is to determine the influence some IV has on a DV. To do this, the investigator's main job is to make sure the secondary variables in the situation were controlled so they could not have caused changes in the DV. Chapter Five elaborates on the selection of the IV and DV of an experiment. Chapter Four discusses secondary variables and ways to control them.

### Selecting the Type of Investigation

Over the years psychologists, like other scientists, have learned that there is more than one way to analyze a given problem scientifically. Some investigations involve the manipulation of an IV; others do not. Some are carried out in a controlled laboratory situation; others may be carried out under everyday conditions. Psychological investigations can be divided into four types:

1. Controlled laboratory experiments (IV manipulated in controlled setting)
2. Field experiments (IV manipulated in everyday setting)
3. Ex post facto laboratory studies (IV not manipulated in controlled setting)
4. Ex post facto field studies (IV not manipulated in field setting)

Why have psychological investigations been divided into these four categories? There are a number of different ways investigations could be categorized—for example, dividing them according to whether they are carried out on animals or humans, or dividing them according to their content area of investigation (e.g., perceptual, developmental, social). Whether an IV was actively manipulated or not and whether it is carried out in a controlled laboratory situation or in the field were chosen because they are so important in determining what conclusions may be drawn about cause and effect relationships. Scientists feel safer in concluding that cigarette smoking causes cancer after carrying out a manipulatory investigation (e.g., raising some mice in a smoke-filled chamber and raising other mice in a smoke-free chamber) than after carrying out a nonmanipulatory study (e.g., observing more smokers get cancer than nonsmokers). In a nonmanipulatory study there is a greater chance of drawing incorrect conclusions because the cause in question is not actively applied and removed. There is a greater possibility that some secondary variable is responsible for the effect.

Whether an investigation is carried out in the laboratory or in the field is also an important dimension in determining whether a cause and effect relationship may be concluded. In a laboratory situation the investigator has much greater control over the secondary variables, making it less likely that an incorrect conclusion will be drawn about what caused what. Chapter Three divides psychological investigations into the four categories listed and and compares them in terms of similarities and differences, advantages and disadvantages. The student should decide which of the four types of investigations he is going to carry out (notice that Sid decided on a laboratory experiment).

After choosing the general type of investigation to be used, the investigator selects a specific design. A design is a way of setting up the investigation, a procedure for arranging the situation to analyze a certain problem. There are two-group designs, factorial designs, randomized one-way ANOVAR designs, and many more. If an investigator wants to determine whether drinking influences driving ability, he may randomly select two groups of people: one is given alcoholic beverages before driving and the other group, nothing. This investigator has chosen a randomized two-group design to compare the two groups on how they drive and determine whether alcohol has an effect. If an investigator wished to determine which of three types of teaching machines was most effective in the classroom, he might select a three-group one-way ANOVAR design; a two-group design would be inappropriate.

How many different designs are there? There are scores of designs from which a researcher may choose. Chapter Eight lists sixteen basic designs, and the wise student should at least look over this chapter before deciding to use a specific design.

### Planning and Carrying Out the Method

After the appropriate design has been selected, the investigator plans the method. Method may sound like an inappropriate word here, but it is the accepted term in professional journals, so we will use it. If you look in any experimental psychology journal, you will find a section labeled "Method." This section lists step by step exactly how the investigation was carried out. The section is usually divided into three parts: subjects, apparatus, and procedure.

**Subjects.**   In the subjects portion the investigator lists all the pertinent information about the subjects used, such as the species, sex, age, IQ, their number, or anything else that may be relevant.

**Apparatus.**   If any elaborate equipment, such as timers, test chambers, and so forth, is used, the investigator briefly describes it in this portion of the report.

**Procedure.**   In the procedure subsection the investigator lists all the things done in carrying out the experiment. For instance, in Sid's experiment he listed how the rats were divided into groups, what concentration of drug was used, how it was injected, how the head-turning behavior was conditioned, how long the reinforcement was presented, how many sessions were run, and so on.

The method section is important because the investigator must know exactly what he needs to do before starting. The method section is also important after the project is finished, when the investigator writes up a report. If anyone wants to replicate the experiment, he can read the method section and reproduce exactly the research investigation. Replication plays a prominent role in research, so the investigator should be sure the method section of his report is complete.

Deciding just how the investigation is to be carried out is also a difficult step. Like someone planning a vacation, the investigator may find he has forgotten to consider some important points after the project has begun. How can a student guard against this? There is no way to guarantee that the investigator will not miss some important point, but there are things he may do to make it less likely. First, he should look in *Psychological Abstracts* and see how investigations similar to his were carried out. The authors of such published articles are professionals and have thought out their research carefully. Use their experience to your advantage by reading their articles and noting the procedures they used.

Some students try to design and set up an experiment without first reviewing related published material. The student taking this position is doing his project the hard way. Reviewing literature first can make carrying out a project much faster and easier, besides helping the student select a higher-quality project. Looking over previously published studies can help the student pick an appropriate problem; it will also tell him what design to use, the procedural steps, what to look for, and what statistical test to use. In fact, not reviewing the literature first is the worst mistake the beginning investigator can make.

### Analyzing the Results

After the results of the investigation have been recorded, they are analyzed. Analysis usually involves performing some sort of statistical computation to determine whether the IV had an effect. Isn't it possible simply to compare the means of the two groups in the investigation and if they differ conclude that the IV had an effect? No, because it is highly unlikely that the means would ever be exactly equal even if the IV had no effect on the group of subjects it was given to. Suppose an investigation was carried out to see what effect displacement prisms[3] would have on a subject's accuracy in throwing darts at a bull's eye on a dartboard. First, a subject throws three darts at a board without the prisms, then he throws a dart with the prisms on. Theoretically, the three darts thrown without the prisms should hit the target in the same place. Actually they do not, however, because the conditions are not exactly the same each time he throws. He may stand just a little differently; wind conditions may change; or he may hold the darts differently each time. The variation in the distance the three darts landed from the bull's eye is termed *error variation*, for it is due to small error-like fluctuations in the situation that cannot be controlled. If there was variation in the accuracy of the three throws without the prisms, then we should hardly expect the

---

3. These may be a specially ground pair of glasses that makes everything look 10 degrees farther to the left than it actually is.

throws with the prisms on to be exactly the same as those without, even if the prisms did not distort the visual field at all.

At this point the reader may be saying to himself, "Well, if there is always variation in scores between groups, how do you determine whether the IV had an effect?" The answer to this question is simple and is discussed at length in Chapter Four. Briefly, what is done is this: a measure of variation without the IV present is obtained along with a measure of the variation with the IV present. Table 1–1 presents theoretical scores of the dart situation as an example. First, a mean of the three throws without the glasses is calculated $\left(\bar{X} = \frac{4 + 6 + 8}{3} = 6\right)$. The average absolute amount each dart "varied" from the mean is calculated $\left(\frac{|4 - 6| + |6 - 6| + |8 - 6|}{3} = \frac{4}{3}\right.$ $\left. = 1.33\right)$.[4] Then the distance the dart thrown with the prisms on varies from the mean is calculated $(14 - 6 = 8)$. The amount of variation found with the prisms on is then divided by the amount of variation without $\left(\frac{8}{1.33} = 6.01\right)$ to give a rating of how many times larger is the variation from throws with the prisms versus without the prisms in contrast to variation in throws just without. Putting the glasses on causes over 6 times as much variation as without the glasses. Can we conclude, then, that the prisms did influence accuracy? After the ratio is calculated, the investigator looks up 6.01 on a table which states the probability that a ratio this size could occur by chance. If there is a 5 percent possibility or less that 6.01 could have been obtained by chance, then the investigator concludes the IV (prisms) did influence accuracy.

What has just been covered is the basic idea behind a statistical analysis. Because scores will naturally vary due to chance, the investigator carries out

**TABLE 1–1**
*Distance (in inches) from the bull's eye for each dart throw*

| Without prisms | With prisms |
|:---:|:---:|
| 4 | 14 |
| 6 | |
| 8 | |
| $\bar{X} = 6$ | |

4. The straight lines in the numerator indicate that absolute values should be used. The mathematical calculations performed here are designed to serve as an illustration and do not represent the exact procedure used in such cases.

statistical computations to obtain a ratio of the amount of variation found when an IV is applied divided by the amount of chance variation found when no IV is present. He then takes this ratio and turns to a table that tells him the probability such a ratio would occur by chance. In this text the student will be shown exactly how the statistical computations are carried out for each type of design. Once a student selects a design, he should look up the type of statistical analysis it involves and record it in step five. Then, after his data are collected, he may turn to the chapter containing the type of design he used and follow the example given for how to perform the computations required.

Students seem to dread the statistical analysis of an experimental investigation more than any other part, perhaps because they do not understand how statistics are derived. It is not the objective of the book to teach statistics, but to show the student where statistics are used in scientific investigations, a bit of the rationale for their use, and step by step examples of how they are used.

### Drawing Conclusions

Drawing conclusions is the reason for carrying out investigations in the first place. The investigator wants to make some statement about the problem he is concerned with that he could not make without conducting his research. Sid was interested in finding out what effect apomorphine had, and if it was possible to get subjects under the influence of the drug to attend to things around them. From his analysis he now can draw these conclusions: (1) apomorphine does induce a strong gnawing compulsion; and (2) even though the subjects did not seem to be aware of what was going on around them while they were under the influence of the drug, conditions could be set up so that they would attend to external conditions. In Sid's case this meant they would emit some behavior to get the chance to chew on a block of wood.

Injecting rats with a drug and having them turn their heads in order to get a block of wood to chew on may not sound like an investigation that would have any value in solving human drug addiction. It is an important addition to scientific knowledge, however, because it shows that you can get subjects to respond under the influence of a powerful drug. It suggests that it may be possible to interact with humans who are under the influence of strong drugs, and this is an important step in understanding how strongly drugs may control people's behavior. Studies are currently being carried out on alcoholics to determine how much control alcohol has over them by seeing how hard they will work to get alcoholic beverages.

The ability to perceive the value of a seemingly trivial investigation is a skill which the psychologist develops. The more research he has been involved in, the better he usually is at determining how valuable projects are. Having students evaluate the results of investigations is an important part of psychological training.

## SUMMARY

Psychology has expanded during its hundred-year history to become both an academic and an applied discipline. The various subfields of psychology include learning, experimental, developmental, clinical, counseling, social, industrial, physiological, educational, personality, abnormal, and perception. The primary work activities of psychology include clinical work, counseling, management and administration, testing, research, teaching, and consulting.

Most undergraduate psychology courses deal mainly with content. In a content course the student learns the facts regarding behavioral relationships as presently understood. In contrast to the content course, the experimental psychology course is designed to teach the student how to analyze psychological situations and devise appropriate procedures for answering the questions with which psychologists are faced.

A professional psychologist needs five skills: (1) the ability to devise means for analyzing psychological problems, (2) expertise on the principles of behavior and why a person acts as he does, (3) the ability to write in a professional manner and present his ideas to his professional peers, (4) the ability to communicate with laymen, and (5) the ability to evaluate research.

The last section of this chapter presents the steps involved in planning and carrying out an experimental investigation. These are (1) selecting an appropriate topic, (2) classifying the variables (IVs, DVs, secondary variables), (3) selecting the design to be used, (4) planning and carrying out the basic steps, (5) analyzing the results, and (6) drawing conclusions about the relationships involved.

# 2

# History of Experimental Psychology and the Scientific Method

*Chapter Two attempts to give the reader some idea of how the general analytical approach used by psychologists originally developed. The scientific method is presented here as the basic format for all psychological investigations. After covering what the scientific method involves, we will take a historical look at man's attempt to understand his own behavior from the earliest times up through the formation of psychology as a separate discipline to study behavior using the scientific method.*

One of the most intriguing puzzles man has tried to solve is the cause of his own behavior. Even with all the technological advances that have taken place, such as going to the moon, few topics arouse as much interest as why people act the way they do; can people read others' minds; can a person be controlled by means of mental telepathy? There is a demonstration you can carry out to see how captivated people are with human behavior. When you are with a small group of friends, relatives, or roommates, tell them you want to demonstrate the ability of one person to influence another by means of mental telepathy. Ask each of them to take a piece of paper and a pencil, and then be seated. After they are seated and you have their attention, say the following:

> All of you should sit comfortably, relax, and close your eyes. I want you to clear your mind of all thoughts and concentrate on my voice. I am not going to hypnotize you, but I am going to try mentally to pass something to you which you are to write down when I tell you. First, to help clear your mind of other thoughts, I am going to give you a few simple mathematical problems to solve in your minds. Do not say the answers to the problems out loud, just say them to yourself.

What is the sum of 5 plus 1? (Wait about three seconds before giving the second math problem.)
What is the sum of 3 plus 3? (Again wait three seconds.)
What is the sum of 2 and 4? (Wait.)
The sum of 0 and 6? (Wait.)
The sum of 1 and 5? (Wait.)
Now, as quick as you can, open your eyes and write down the name of the first vegetable that comes to mind.

About 80 percent of the people will write down the word *carrot*. After you have given them time to write an answer, ask them one by one to tell the others what they wrote down. Then, from your pocket casually remove a card on which you have earlier written the word *carrot*. For the rest of the evening everyone will be asking how you did it.[1]

There is only one thing people enjoy more than a magical trick, and that is knowing how it is done. The same is true in psychology. As much as the layman respects the psychologist for his knowledge of behavioral principles, he holds him in esteem more for his seemingly extraordinary powers of analysis. Patients are continually surprised at the ability of the practicing psychologist to identify the source of a problem that may have been bothering them for years. How was the psychologist able to analyze and solve the situation, while the patient was not? Didn't the patient know as much about his condition—even more, possibly—than the psychologist?

College students are frequently impressed by the writings of well-known psychologists such as Hull, Piaget, Skinner, Kohler, and Guthrie, and wonder what it was that enabled these men to find some of the answers to understanding man and his actions. Too often this question is answered by saying, "These men are unique; they have almost supernatural powers of observation and analysis." There is, however, a much more parsimonious explanation. What all of them have done, in fact, is employ a rather elementary method of analysis that is not unique to the area of psychology at all. Rather, it was borrowed from other disciplines and found quite effective in solving almost any kind of problem. This type of analysis is called the *scientific method*. The reader may be somewhat let down at this point, having expected the answer to be something other than the oft-mentioned scientific method, a sort of objective and empirical approach to looking at things. Doesn't everybody use the scientific method to some extent in solving everyday problems such as what clothes to buy and what would be the best car to buy? Why should psychologists, and especially famous psychologists, be any more

---

1. Why people generally respond with *carrot* is unclear. Carrots are certainly not the most common vegetable. The reason has something to do with the number 6, however, for the demonstration works best when 6 is the answer to each of the math problems.

effective in finding out why man behaves if all they are using is an approach that most people know of and use to some extent?

The answer lies in the fact that psychologists are something like skilled fishermen. Two persons may have access to the same kinds of poles, reels, and bait, yet not catch the same amount of fish. The expert fisherman can take a fishing outfit and catch his limit of trout in a particular lake while the Sunday fisherman may catch one or two small fish, barely large enough to keep. What is the difference between the two? There are two reasons why the expert fisherman gets superior results—his skill from experience and his knowledge of the capabilities of the equipment he uses. The expert knows what type of rod, reel, and bait to use when going after a particular kind of fish. He also knows what the next best outfit would be, if the best is unavailable. He may know brown trout prefer flies. Not having any, however, he knows what type of bait (worms, eggs) is the next best to try. The skill of fishing, like most skills, comes from practice. The expert spent many hours working on the fundamentals of casting, baiting up, and so on. While he was learning he may have questioned why he had to do things a certain way when he saw no relevance at the time. Later, when applying his skills and seeing the results, he learned to value the apparent idiosyncracies he was taught.

Just as the fisherman has basic equipment, the psychologist has the scientific method. Just as the fisherman may select different types of poles, reels, and the like, so may the psychologist employ two-group experimental designs, systematic observation, case study analysis, and correlational designs. The psychologist has learned what the scientific method involves, what variations are possible with it, how to apply it, and when to apply it. The psychologist knows the best approach to solve a particular type of problem; and if it cannot be used, he knows the next best alternative. He knows, for example, that experimental designs involving the manipulation of an IV are a more powerful type of analysis for finding cause-effect relationships than ex post facto procedures. He also knows that there are problems (e.g., suicide) that do not lend themselves to an experimental type of analysis.

Why are some psychologists better than others in their ability to analyze? Mainly because they have more effectively developed their analytical skill by experience and spent more time in learning when, where, and how various scientific procedures should be used. Now, it is true that everyone does not have the same intellectual ability and that part of the success of well-known psychologists is due to better than average intellectual ability. Extra time and effort by the psychologist, however, play a major role in success. B. F. Skinner, for example, once mentioned that many of his research data sheets have entries dated December 25th.

## ASSUMPTIONS UNDERLYING
## THE SCIENTIFIC METHOD

The term scientific method has been used so frequently and in so many different situations that it might be wise to say just what it stands for here. It is somewhat of an elusive term in that its exact definition has been stated differently by various scientists. Generally, however, it may be said to be a method of analysis based on four assumptions: empiricism, determinism, parsimony, and testability.

**Empiricism.** This term has already been introduced, but let us define it further. The empirical assumption simply says, "Let's look and see." Years ago the common belief was that nerves were hollow tubes through which "animal spirits" ran. Then one day someone cut open a corpse and found that this is really not the case. Empiricism dictates that the statement must be proved, that one must look and see. Without it, rampant speculation, superstition, and hearsay have often stood for scientific truth in the past. Even today, scientific authority is sometimes misused to support unverified speculations.

**Determinism.** Another basic assumption a scientist holds is that there is a law and an order to which all events bow. Indeed, without law and order we could not be sure of even the most common, everyday things. We could not assume that the sun was coming up the next morning. We could not predict that the presence of rain and subfreezing temperatures means snow. Scientists are investigators of the laws of the universe and consequently hold that the universe is an orderly place. How does this belief apply to the psychologist?

The psychologist assumes that behavior follows this lawful order and can be linked to causal factors, even if at first they are not readily apparent. Therefore, he observes behavior and every surrounding condition to try to identify these factors. He assumes in the course of his observation that once the causal factors are identified, he can manipulate them to modify or control the behavior to which the factors are linked. Knowing these factors and the degree to which behavior can be changed, the psychologist then may apply the principles and techniques to abnormal behavior and bring about normal behavior in the subject. He can help the mental patient function in normal society, the criminal to learn to control his behavior, or the college student to bring up his grades.

**Parsimony.** When it comes to speculation or hypotheses about the cause of a scientific phenomenon, the scientist is extraordinarily parsimonious. Parsimony is the assumption that the scientist will never hypothesize a complicated or more abstract scientific explanation unless all the simpler explanations have been experimentally ruled out. In the early years of medical research it was supposed to be common knowledge that demons caused schizophrenia and other mental illnesses. Today, more parsimonious causes for mental illness are considered. Extensive investigation into organic disorders is being done as is investigation into the environmental control of mental illness on the assumption that something more parsimonious than demons causes the illness.

**Testability.**   Last, but certainly not least, of the assumptions of a scientist is testability. In order for an event to undergo a scientific analysis, there must be procedures available to the scientist by which he can manipulate empirical observations in such a way that conclusions can be drawn. A scientific approach requires the investigator to use an analytical system that takes all the empirical data available into consideration. In the past there have often been situations in which empirical observations were available, but no method of analysis. Men could empirically see the other planets, but only speculate about what it was like on the surface, how much water they had, and so on. Certain aspects of the stars could be scientifically analyzed (e.g., their movements), but many dimensions could not. Whenever man speculates about a situation without using some empirically based analytical procedure, he has left the realm of science.

In some cases the investigator carries out an analytical testing procedure of some sort, but fails to take into consideration all the empirical data at his disposal. An investigator may consciously or unconsciously attend only to aspects of his data that support his idea, while ignoring contradictory information. Selectively attending to certain empirical observations while discarding others is, in scientific circles, totally unacceptable.

In order to get a better understanding of exactly what the scientific method involves, let us take a look at a situation in which an analysis that violates the assumptions of science was carried out.

### The Two Faces of Jane Green

The first time Jane Green came to my office was late in December of 1959. She pretended to have come to inquire about having her adenoids removed and gave the impression of being upset when I told her I only did that kind of work on weekends. But there was something else about the small wisp of a girl which made me uneasy. Perhaps it was the large skull and crossbones she had tattooed on the back of her right hand or the football cleats she wore on her feet. I could sense that there was something strange and different about Jane. We chatted for a time about this and that, and Jane's husband, who played the piano for a living, but had recently suffered a double hernia when he joined a marching band. After she had gone, I thought about her for some time. There was something weirdly remarkable about Jane Green. I was soon to learn she had a multiple personality.

Most of us have but one personality we can call our own; good or bad, it is ours for life. In some rare instances, however, an individual may develop two or even three distinctly different personalities. In these cases it is almost as if one is dealing with distinct individuals, so great are the changes in behavior, mannerism, and even physical appearance.

There is some discussion concerning the cause of multiple personalities. One theorist contends that these individuals have an unconscious urge to beat the government out of tax money by declaring each of their personalities as dependents. I am certain, however, that the true cause is a web-like growth in the cerebral cortex causing a schism or "split" in the personality.

It was almost six months after her first visit that Jane Two appeared. I greeted her at the door and immediately noticed the familiar skull and cross bones tattoo. It did not take me long to discern that there was something "different" about Jane. She had always been a small girl, barely over four feet tall and weighing no more than 75 pounds. On that day she was at least six feet five and weighed well over 250 pounds. Her hair which had previously been long and blond was now jet black and crew cut. She had a heavy dark beard and a long ugly scar over her left eye. Even the tatoo, which had previously been on the back of her right hand, was now on her left wrist. She spoke in a gruff voice and told me that her name was Ed Molduleski, and she was here to fix the air conditioner. I was both shocked and amused by the drastic change in her personality. I thought it best that I not show or reveal that I had detected the new personality. "How is your husband?" I asked politely. "Is his hernia better?" Jane appeared to become quite upset and struck me swiftly in the mouth with her amazingly large fist. Before I could regain my composure, she had left the office muttering obscenities under her breath.

While I must admit that her rash behavior took me unaware, it is to be expected from individuals suffering from a multiple personality. In such cases there is always one personality whose behavior is entirely unpredictable, unmanageable, and unanalyzable by any scientific methods.

After that incident, I never saw Jane Two again. It was as though that single encounter had obliterated that other half of Jane Green's personality, leaving only the plain, simple girl I had met on that first day in my office. Jane is now doing quite well and has almost fully recovered from her adenoid operation. She, of course, is completely unaware of that other Jane and of the fact that she once suffered from a multiple personality.[2]

The analysis carried out in this somewhat humorous situation was certainly not scientific. Every one of the assumptions of science was violated. The writer of this article violates the attitude of empiricism when he says that he is certain that the true cause of a multiple personality is a weblike growth in the brain causing a split in the person's personality. No empirical observations were mentioned that would support such a conclusion. A scientist must be careful to make sure any conclusive statements he makes are based on empirical observations.

2. From Whaley and Surratt [1968], © 1967, 1968 by Donald L. Whaley. Reprinted by permission. The book is a composite of many such fictional situations constructed and analyzed to better one's basic understanding of what the philosophy of science involves.

The writer suggests that the rash behavior of Jane Two took him by surprise, but if he had thought about it, he would have remembered that such individuals always exhibit one particular personality which is unpredictable, unmanageable, and unanalyzable by any scientific method. In doing so he violates determinism. We must always assume that things are caused and that these causes can be identified through diligent effort, experimentation, and scientific observation. It may possibly happen that we will, at some future date, run into things which we apparently cannot explain in terms of natural causes, but for now determinism is critical to all science.

The writer attributes the vast differences observed on two occasions in his office to the idea of multiple personalities. He assumes that the conversations he had with the individuals he calls Jane One and Jane Two are really the same person. He states that the differences can be attributed to a multiple personality. It is obvious to most readers, however, that there is a simpler explanation for the great differences in appearance and mannerism observed in these two instances. Therefore, the writer violates parsimony. It is obvious from the statement that he has made two serious errors. He uses very slim evidence to conclude that conversations held on two different occasions were with the same person. He then reasons that since the behavior, mannerisms, and appearance of the individual on these two occasions is so different, the individual must be suffering from a multiple personality. The reader has no difficulty in seeing that a much simpler explanation is possible, namely, that the writer was actually dealing with two different people. This error, of course, is not one that most people would make, and great artistic license has been taken in order to stress the point. Psychologists seem to have more problems with parsimony than most other scientists. This is at least partly due to the fact that so much is still unknown about controlling forces; in addition, man has always seemed to enjoy explanations that are more mystical in nature.

The writer makes an error that violates testability when he assumes that two similar tattoos indicate that he is dealing with the same person. The writer observes the tattoo on the individual he labels Jane Green One and observes a similar tattoo on a later occasion. He makes the error of selectively attending to the tattoos and ignoring differences such as height, weight, and hair color. An investigator must be extremely careful when carrying out his analysis that he does not omit potentially relevant empirical data. Because it is so easy to make an honest mistake on this point, it is an accepted procedure that an investigator should report as much of his data as possible when writing his report.[3]

---

3. There are cases when an investigator may omit part of his data, e.g., if he is very sure some of the fluctuations in his data are due to an irrelevant variable that fluctuated in the situation. Suppose an investigator gave a subject the wrong instructions and did not realize it until after data were recorded on that subject. He may then exclude this subject's scores from the analysis.

## PSYCHOLOGY—A SCIENTIFIC APPROACH

### The Early Years

Psychology was founded as a unique discipline in the late 1800s. Its prime purpose was the analysis of man. This in itself was not new, for man had sought an explanation of his existence since the beginning of time. Two aspects of his quest for knowledge that changed over the years stimulated the analysis of man using a scientific approach. The first deals with the explanation of why events occurred. Man has always believed that life is made up of cause and effect relationships. He considered his behavior to be a function of something, though he was not quite sure of what.

Primitive man believed his destiny was in the hands of animistic forces that had the ability to dispense pleasure or pain at will. The initial organization of man into groups or clans generally centered around a supreme object of worship now often called a totem. The totem could be an animal, a body of water, a volcano, or any other natural phenomenon people believed had power over them. Animistic beliefs are still found in today's primitive societies, and in many children's explanations of the reason certain events occur. Though animism was an incorrect explanation, it implied a rigorous determinism that is considered one of the first steps toward understanding, predicting, and controlling behavior.

Later on, the control of man was shifted from forces of nature to deities and celestial beings not subject to terrestrial bondage. Though the new explanation of behavior still placed man at the mercy of supernatural forces, it was a significant change in terms of the control man felt he had over himself. With animism, man devised various magical rites in an attempt to influence good or evil forces. Imitative dances and objects were concocted which, it was believed, could influence these forces. One man could sap the strength of another by the possession of his hair, teeth, or a doll replica. Although most believed deities could be influenced to some extent, mythology involved a more pessimistic attitude toward man's ability to influence his own destiny and more dependence on fate.

Then astrology entered the picture. Man's first attempt to explain his behavior in some sort of systematic fashion is generally credited to the ancient Egyptians. They observed the movements of heavenly bodies and concluded human behavior could be accounted for by the regularity of the celestial spheres. The sign under which a man was born became important, for it determined the course of his life. Although the explanation of behavior in terms of celestial motion was as fallacious as animism and mythology, it was one more step toward a scientific explanation. Both animistic and mythological explanations of man's behavior are metaphysical, in that they go beyond the physical world by defining men's actions in terms of nonphysical entities and deities. This is an important point, for the astrological explanation allowed an opportunity for verification by means of physical manipulation. Unlike animism and mythology, astrological relationships between the stars and behavior could be empirically determined and possibly manipulated by investigators in future years. Unfortunately, the importance of explanations in terms of physical dimensions was not accepted at this time. In fact, man seemed to prefer metaphysical explanations and strongly opposed any attempts at a more parsimonious physical explanation.

In ancient Greece and for centuries after, philosophy was considered the main route to understanding. At the present time philosophy proposes that there are different means to obtain knowledge: rationalism, metamorphism, and empiricism. Each of the three is considered a legitimate avenue to understanding, though each is verified in different ways. Rationalism is based on logic. With logical uniformity, something is said to be true if it is logical and false if it is illogical. It would be false, for example, to say, "Two particular objects are exactly the same along every conceivable dimension, yet they are different." Metamorphism considers knowledge to be a function of symbolic and intuitive cognitions based on an intangible or metaphysical foundation. Empiricism is a source of knowledge dependent on the analysis of physical dimensions that can be observed and measured.

The early Greek philosophers had a strong bent toward a metamorphic, rationalistic approach to knowledge. They believed in empiricism, and even spent time carrying out observations directed at physical relationships. Unfortunately, however, man found himself in a situation in which he believed in an explanation for everything, yet had little empirical data upon which those explanations might be based. The sudden illness and death of a loved one who shared the same food and housing as healthy relatives was difficult to explain in terms of physical events alone. Not being familiar with viruses and bacteria, man found an explanation in terms of a nonphysical spirit more logical. Just as a child might have the superior ability to inflict pleasure and pain on a captive pet, man thought it more rational to explain his actions by taking into consideration the possibility of a supernatural deity. This approach was considered more justifiable than believing in physical events that could not then be observed—bacteria, molecules, electromagnetic forces.

Metaphysical and magical explanations were coined for every situation, including those now considered part of the natural sciences. Wind velocity, like volcanic action, was accepted as being controlled by supernatural forces. The healing ability of certain herbs was credited to their nonphysical characteristics.

As time passed, man explained more and more events in terms of physical relationships. Physicians, sailors, explorers, and tradesmen found themselves making more progress toward an understanding of life that would allow them to predict and control their environment than the educated monks and philosophers. Functionality, then, was the second reason for man's shift to a scientific approach. The simplistic empirical concept of trying something to see if it worked led to meditation and speculation being surpassed by manipulation as the procedure by which knowledge could be obtained and built upon. Philosophers such as Copernicus, Galileo, Descartes, and Newton aided these developments with their stronger dependence on empiricism in their speculative formulations regarding physics and biology.

More scholars turned their talents toward empirical investigations. Better analytical procedures were developed, and empirical information accumulated. The productivity of the empirical approach led men to realize that the prediction and control they sought in most fields of knowledge were possible without relying on metaphysical explanations. This led to the formation of the natural sciences, which divorced themselves from metamorphism and began an exclusive courtship with logical empiricism. One branch of knowledge remained in philosophy's camp. Most people still felt that man's actions must be under the influence, at least partially, of events outside the physical dimension. In fact, even as late as the eighteenth century, anyone advocating that man's behavior was a function of natural laws was met with hostility or violent punishment.

### Formation of Psychology as a Scientific Discipline

Psychology's emergence as a science resulted from the fusion of certain philosophical movements and the rapid advance in experimental physiology during the nineteenth century. Table 2–1 presents some of the more important events since the 1600s that led to the formation of psychology as a separate science.

**Philosophical root of psychology.** It was approximately seventeen hundred years after Aristotle that a significant trend toward an empirical approach to man's mind appeared. In France, the mathematician and philosopher René Descartes proposed a dual mind-body concept similar to Plato's, except that he took a strong mechanistic stand on behavior and urged the use of the empirical method of dissection. This helped stimulate the development of experimental physiology. A push toward an empirical approach to studying the mind was made by Thomas Hobbes, John Locke, David Hartley, and others. They believed, in essence, that man learns through sensation and that the origin of the "mind" comes through experience. They proposed experiences should be broken up and analyzed empirically if man was to be understood. Not all empirical philosophers proposed a molecular analysis, however. John Mill, for example, suggested a molar type of analysis, much like the gestalt psychologists to come.

**TABLE 2–1**
*Roots of psychology*

| Philosophical Root | | Experimental, Physiological Root | |
|---|---|---|---|
| *Date* | *Event* | *Date* | *Event* |
| 1650 | René Descartes proposed a dual concept of mind and body and urged empirical analysis | 1811 | Charles Bell and François Magendie discovered sensory and motor nerves |
| 1651 | Thomas Hobbes presented the idea of associationism | 1833 | Johannes Muller proposed specific energies of nerves |
| 1690 | John Locke extended Hobbes' idea and proposed that an infant mind is like a *tabula rasa* at birth and gains knowledge by experience | 1846 | Ernst Weber derived the first quantitative law in psychology |
| | | 1850 | Marshall Hall pioneered in the investigation of reflex behavior |
| 1749 | David Hartley combined all the previous ideas of empiricism and association into a school of thought called associationsim | 1858 | Charles Darwin proposed his theory of evolution |
| | | 1861 | Paul Broca pioneered in the clinical method of determining brain functions |
| 1860 | John Mill argued that the mind must be considered as a whole unit | 1869 | Francis Galton studied individual differences and began regression analysis |
| | | 1870 | Gustav Fritsch and Eduard Hitzig used electrical stimulation to study the brain |

**Physiological root of psychology.** Due to the fact that dissection was not tolerated by society, even with animals, until the 1800s, the main discoveries leading toward a discipline of experimental physiology occurred in the nineteenth century. The 1800s began with Charles Bell and François Magendie discovering that sensory fibers of the spinal nerves enter the dorsal portion of the cord, whereas motor fibers leave the cord in a ventral root. Johannes Muller developed the concept of specific nerve energies, which basically held that each different sense quality (coldness, warmness, sweetness, sourness, color, and so forth) has its own specialized sensory mechanism that informs the brain of the quality's presence. Ernst Weber took the experimental methods of physiology and employed them in psychological investigations on humans. He developed some of the first quantitative psychophysical methods with his investigations on sensory thresholds. Charles Darwin's presentation of his theory of evolution had a strong effect on the development of psychology as a separate discipline because of its implications about human behavior.

These comments have given some perspective on the events that led to the launching of a scientifically based discipline concerned with understanding man and his actions. While philosophers were drawing toward an empirical analysis of mental processes, physiologists were investigating the neurological basis of behavior and developing objective analytical procedures. Both played an important role in the formation of psychology as a scientific discipline.

### The Era of the Great Schools

Modern experimental psychology began in 1879 with the establishment of the first psychological laboratory by Wilhelm Wundt at Leipzig, Germany. Most agree that Wundt was the first person to be correctly called a psychologist. Born in 1832, Wundt took his degree in medicine and emphasized physiology in his early graduate work. He became interested in human sensation and perception. His conversion to psychology was complete with the opening of the first psychological laboratory. Wundt was an intellectual who wrote not only about psychology, but also about logic, ethics, and scientific metaphysics. Although slowed down somewhat when he injured his sight while experimenting on himself, he published 54,000 pages of psychological material before his death in 1920.

Psychology as an independent discipline, as undertaken by Wundt, was selectively directed toward the investigation of sensation and perception. Even before the end of the nineteenth century, however, the realm of psychology had expanded. Like most scientific disciplines in their early stages of development, psychology had to address two issues: (1) what is the proper subject matter of psychology, and (2) what are appropriate scientific procedures for investigating that subject matter. These two points seemed almost inseparable at first, so for the first fifty years different schools formed around different views of what psychology should be. Table 2–2 lists the major historical schools of psychology, their major areas of interest, and the types of analytical procedures they advocated.

**Structuralism.**   The first major school of psychology began with two men, Wilhelm Wundt and Edward Titchner. Titchner, a bright young Englishman, went to Germany to study under Wundt and later went to America, where he was responsible for the propagation of structuralism. Wundt believed that the primary subject matter of psychology should be the analysis of conscious experiences using a method called introspection. Introspection, as employed by Wundt, was a highly specialized form of self-observation in which a trained psychologist analyzed his own private experiences while they were occurring, or immediately thereafter. Structuralists felt that all the complex higher processes were derived from three basic elements—images, sensations, and affective states. For them, the main objective of psychology was to analyze experience by means of introspection in an attempt to discover how these three elements combine to produce man's complex mental processes.

**TABLE 2–2**
*Major historical schools of psychology*

| Date | School | Investigation procedure | Area of interest | Important individuals |
|------|--------|------------------------|------------------|----------------------|
| 1879 | Structuralism | Introspection | The "structure" of mental processes and their analysis through personal experience | Wilhelm Wundt (1832–1920) Edward Titchner (1867–1927) |
| 1900 | Functionalism | Introspection, objective observation | The utilization of mental processes to fulfill needs | William James (1842–1910) John Dewey (1859–1952) |
| 1902 | Psychoanalysis | Clinical method— free association and dream analysis | Underlying causes of mental disorders, causal determination of behavior in childhood | Sigmund Freud (1856–1939) |
| 1914 | Behaviorism | Experimental method | Analysis of man's overt behavior | John Watson (1878–1958) |
| 1915 | Gestalt psychology | Phenomenology | Organization of perceptual processes | Max Wertheimer (1880–1943) Wolfgang Kohler (1887——) Kurt Kofka (1886–1941) |

Because structuralism was based on introspection, its scope was considered too narrow and restrictive by many psychologists. Introspection required considerable laboratory training before it was believed to produce valid results. This limited its application, for it could not be used by children, animals, or mentally disturbed individuals; only the normal adult human could serve as a subject. Titchner claimed these dimensions could be analyzed indirectly, however, using introspection by analogy. In these situations the psychologist was to carefully observe the behavior of the subject, then put himself in the subject's place and try to interpret what the individual was experiencing. This was considered one of the weakest links in structuralism, and most felt it was the reason interest in the structuralist position waned. Structuralism is generally given credit for bringing the scientific method to psychology and making psychology a science.

**Functionalism.** Psychologists not content with the limitations of introspective structuralism sought alternatives, one of the most popular of which was called functionalism. Functionalism was a form of psychology promoted by a number of American psychologists whose main concern was a study of the mind as it functions in allowing the organism to adjust to its environment. Rather than restrict its analysis to the way higher mental processes were "organized," functionalism stressed the importance of finding out how these processes were "utilized" by man in coping with his environment. The main emphasis was on how a person used the processes of perception, attention, thinking, and emotion to fulfill his needs.

Introspection was accepted as an analytical technique, especially in investigating conscious awareness. The functionalist went beyond introspection, however, and emphasized the use of objective observation. As time went on, functionalists moved away from introspection and relied more heavily on objective observation. Not being restricted to introspection, functionalism was able to increase its area of concern far beyond that of structuralism. Investigations could be carried out on children, animals, and mentally disturbed individuals. Psychologists could pursue their interests in the unique as well as the average adult; the abnormal as well as the normal; individuals of all ages, from conception to death. The impetus toward a functionalist approach to man played a significant role in developing the applied dimension of psychology.

**Psychoanalysis.** Technically speaking, psychoanalysis was not actually a school of psychology. It was not the product of any academic circle within psychology, nor was it considered a complete area designed to explain all the dimensions of psychology, such as attention, perception, sensation, and learning. Psychoanalysis initially was the product of an attempt to deal with the causes, development, and treatment of mental disorders. It was considered a practice involving nonexperimental techniques for treating patients suffering from psychologically induced physical disorders. Its effect on the academic dimensions of psychology became significant with its emphasis on unconscious determinants of behavior and the importance of the formative years in psychological adjustment.

Methodologically speaking, most of the analysis of behavior was carried out using observation. In drawing his theoretical conclusions regarding psychological processes, Sigmund Freud depended on observations of patients' behavior and inductive reasoning. He did use certain methods in applied situations, but did little in carrying out investigations to determine their effectiveness. The clinical analysis of psychological disorders was, however, an important contribution to the advancement of psychology as a science. Psychoanalysis kindled the interest of society in psychological problems as no other development in psychology had before.

**Behaviorism.** Although John Watson graduated from the University of Chicago, which was the center of the functionalist movement after the turn of the century, he did not agree with the strong mentalistic approach upon which both structuralism and functionalism were based. He became interested in animal research during his graduate studies and carried that interest on into later life. Although functionalism as a school of thought came about through the efforts of many psychologists (William James, John Dewey, James Angell, Harvey Carr), behaviorism as a school of thought was conceived and nurtured in its early years mainly by one man—Watson. Watson believed consciousness was an unscientific residue that philosophical psychologists had carried over from the days of mental philosophy. To Watson, concepts such as mind, volition, images, and consciousness were not tangible items open to objective analysis by scientific methods.

Watson felt the real problem with structuralism and functionalism was their methodology. Introspectionists were disagreeing among themselves on basic issues concerning the conscious processes. The results from introspection were not being reliably supported through replication. Although the introspectionist blamed this on faulty training of the investigator, Watson argued introspection was at fault; it was too subjective. A science of psychology had to be based on better analytical techniques than that. From the natural sciences he saw the importance of using controlled analytical situations involving the elimination and holding constant of important factors in the situation that might influence the dimension being investigated. In his animal investigations he controlled the rest, diet, activity, and hereditary strain of his subjects, variables which, if left uncontrolled, could lead to incorrect behavioral relationships. He strongly advocated the use of manipulatory investigations in psychology, rather than the ex post facto type of analysis predominant at the time. His use of experimental procedures in studying emotional behavior in infants was one of the greatest advances in methodological procedures in psychology.

**Gestalt psychology.** While structuralism, functionalism, and behaviorism were busy debating their strengths and weaknesses, a new school was getting underway in Germany. The new movement argued against the approaches being used by the other three schools. Gestaltists said experience and behavior could not be analyzed into elements of consciousness, as claimed by the structuralists; nor could they be broken down into stimulus-response units, as the behaviorists claimed. Behavior and experience were to be analyzed only in terms of wholeness and could not be broken down into basic elements. The new movement began with Max Wertheimer's interest in perceptual illusions such as the phi phenomenon, an illusion of movement typified by the sequential turning on and off of lights on theater marquees or the turning barber's pole. The gestaltists argued such perceptual phenomena demonstrated the patterning of stimuli much as a painting represented something more than its basic parts (canvas and so much paint.) The gestalt method of analysis centered around the use of observation as an evaluative tool. Gestaltists would observe how humans or animals responded in certain situations. They employed phenomenology, which was the analysis of verbal reports given by naive subjects regarding their experiences, in contrast to the trained introspective approach used by structuralists and functionalists.

Although the schools differed in terms of what they felt the subject matter of psychology should be and the procedures by which it should be analyzed, they did agree that psychology should be approached in a scientific way. From these different approaches research data began filtering in. The ideological and methodological differences, originally perceived by most as detriments to a developing science, were a blessing in disguise, for it soon became apparent that the realm of psychology was much broader than any one group had anticipated. With the end of the third decade of the twentieth century, the heyday of the schools had passed. Psychology as a growing discipline outstripped the boundaries of any one school, and in a wise eclectic fashion selected the best of all the differing positions on which to grow. In terms of investigatory methodology, it became apparent that more than one type of analytical procedure was necessary.

Although ex post facto and experimental investigations were both accepted as scientific approaches, psychologists began to realize that experimental investigations were more powerful in identifying causal relationships. If the investigator could apply some IV whenever he wanted, any change in some DV that followed was less likely to be attributed to some other variable. The number of investigations carried out in controlled laboratory situations began to increase. The idea behind these controlled situations was quite simple: by carrying out an experimental investigation, one could eliminate the presence of certain variables present in natural settings that could affect the DV in such a way that the influence of the IV could not be accurately determined. Experimental investigations began to include the use of *control groups*. Control groups consisted of subjects who were not given the IV. The behavior of those subjects given the IV could then be compared to those who had not received the IV. Any difference between the two groups of subjects was then said to be due to the IV. The procedure of equating the two groups prior to the application of an IV to one was begun. This helped ensure that the differences in behavior between the two groups could be more validly ascribed to the IV. Random assignment of subjects to groups began in the 1920s.

## SUMMARY

Psychology as a separate discipline came about as an attempt to analyze human behavior in a scientific way. The scientific method is based on four rules: (1) the investigator carries out measurable observations (empiricism);

(2) he believes relations between events are lawful (determinism); (3) he accepts the simplest plausible explanation of the relationships he finds (parsimony); and (4) he deals only with situations in which some test can be made that includes taking all the data into consideration (testability).

Since his beginnings, man has believed in determinism; empiricism was not originally accepted as the best means to obtain knowledge. Parsimony and testability were not intially accepted either. As time went on, man began turning away from a philosophical explanation of his actions and toward empiricism, testing, and parsimony in solving his everyday existence problems. Some philosophers and medical men did likewise. With some philosophers asking for a stronger empirical analysis of man, and with greater emphasis on testing assumptions in physiology, psychology emerged from a fusion of the two positions.

After the formation of psychology as a separate discipline, different schools of thought arose—structuralism, functionalism, psychoanalysis, behaviorism, and gestalt psychology—each suggesting what psychology's subject matter should be and how it should be analyzed. The methods of analysis they proposed included introspection, systematic observation, clinical analysis, experimentation, and phenomenology. Psychology sifted through all the methodologicl approaches, taking the good points of each. The net result has been the application of various methodological approaches, all of which are based on the scientific method.

# 3

# *Types of Investigations*

*Chapter Three is important because it lays the foundation for all the following chapters. For the psychologist to determine how a particular situation should be analyzed, he must be familiar with the alternative ways of carrying out a scientific investigation and realize their distinguishing characteristics. Psychological investigations are divided into four basic types according to two factors. The four types of investigations are discussed in terms of (1) how they are defined, (2) the steps involved in carrying them out, (3) the main reasons for using a particular investigation, and (4) the advantages and disadvantages of each. Special care should be taken to understand the similarities and differences among the four types of investigations.*

It is apparent from the last two chapters that the area of investigation carried out by experimental psychologists varies from one researcher to another. A physiological psychologist may devote most of his talent to analyzing the role of nucleic acids in learning, while spending little time investigating the shopping habits of housewives. Marketing psychologists may do just the opposite. Though they are both involved in extending man's knowledge of himself and his environment by means of experimental investigation, each has selected a different area of content according to his own individual interests.

Psychologists differ not only in areas of investigation but also in types of investigations carried out. To cite examples of the various types, much recent attention has been drawn to Masters and Johnson, who as researchers have carried out studies dealing with the sexual mores of our society. They have employed questionnaires and personal interviews to obtain information such as how people of varying socioeconomic levels differ in their attitudes on premarital relationships. John Watson (1878–1958), an early founder of behavior-oriented psychology, was interested in the development and expression of emotional behavior. The investigatory procedures he used, however, did not include questionnaires. With his famous Albert experiment, he applied a particular stimulus (a loud noise) to a child's environment and noted deviations in the child's behavior that followed. In many instances the area of investigation one selects will restrict the type of investigation one can employ; i.e., Watson would not have been very productive in his research by having babies fill out questionnaires, and Masters and Johnson would meet with strong opposition if they attempted to manipulate all of society's sexual behavior in an effort to see the effect on a person's values. It may be helpful, then, to try to classify some of the more common types of investigations used in experimental psychology.

There is a common misconception that a scientific inquiry must involve the manipulation of variables for the express purpose of causing some variation in a second variable. Actually, this is only one type of scientific investigation. There are others, less prestigous perhaps but much more common in the social sciences. With the increased diversity in psychological problem areas, psychologists have had to rely more heavily on nonmanipulating investigations. Alternative scientific approaches may be classified as either experimental or ex post facto. Before elaborating on the differences between these two approaches, their points in common should be covered.

A scientific investigation is initiated because of an unanswered problem. A range of variation is observed in some empirical phenomenon. Noting this variation, the potential investigator asks, "Under what conditions will this variation occur?" "What event (the IV) is responsible for the observed variation (the DV)" All scientific inquiries, manipulatory or nonmanipulatory, involve the investigation of situations in which the variation has occurred in an effort to explain the reasons for that variation. What is the importance of maternal love in child development? Why is the suicide rate for prisoners of war higher than for those who have not been prisoners of war? What effect does delay of feedback have on learning? All these questions can be scientifically investigated. For some cases, the variation may have already occurred, while the investigator induces variation in the others. All involve an analysis of variation in which a relationship between some IV and some DV is sought. Scientific inquiry, then, involves the search for conditions to account for variations.

In any situation, a multitude of variables can and may be inducing changes in a DV. A fourth-grade child is doing poorly in class. The school psychologist sets out to determine why. Alternative explanations include poor intellectual ability, family problems, peer pressure, lack of motivation, language problems, and inadequate training in educational skills. What he is initially confronted with is a DV—poor scholastic records—and innumerable variables that may be responsible for these records. The task facing the school psychologist is to weed out all plausible variables that are incorrect and isolate the variable or variables responsible. How does he accomplish this? Like all other scientific investigators, he will rest his analysis on the systematic manipulation and control of the variables involved. There are several methods of scientific inquiry to choose from. All involve the reorganization and, where possible, the rearrangement of the events involved in order that a relationship between the DV and some other variable may be identified. By systematically combining and rearranging the events involved, an explanatory relationship is precipitated. The methods of scientific inquiry differ according to the strategy employed with the type of systematic manipulation chosen. Each method is based on a different way of organizing and rearranging the variables involved. The way events in any investigatory situation are organized determines the type of investigation to be carried out, and concomitantly, the type of analysis to be performed.

Using an experimental approach, the investigator sets out to determine causal relationships by actually manipulating an IV and measuring resultant changes in a DV. He becomes actively involved in the sequence of events. Not all conditions a psychologist wishes to investigate allow his direct involvement: many conditions are historical in nature; others restrict the psychologist's manipulations due to ethical issues or impracticability. What causes the high suicide rate of released prisoners of war? How has man's increased time for recreation influenced his self-concept? Can children raised by animals be rehumanized?

In contrast to experimental investigations, ex post facto investigations do not include IV manipulation. Whereas experimental procedures identify relationships by manipulating IVs and the conditions in which the IVs are presented, an ex post facto approach identifies relationships more indirectly. The ex post facto strategy involves demonstrating causal relationships by deductively eliminating alternative explanations, and applying mathematical techniques to bring out possible correlations between changes in the DV and some other event. Though the ex post facto type of investigation is somewhat restricted by an inability to manipulate situations directly, it is a valuable tool available to the investigator.

Whether the investigator does or does not manipulate an IV is not the only dimension on which investigations may be categorized. A second functional dimension is the situation in which the investigation is carried out. Investigations may be classified according to whether they are carried out in a natural environment (the field), or in an unnatural setting (the laboratory). The situation in which investigation is carried out may influence the investigator's conclusions. With the increasing demands of society for the psychologist to carry out investigations in more applied situations, the field-laboratory dimension becomes more relevant to the budding psychologist.

Table 3–1 represents the two dimensions given above and shows the four types of investigations possible when they are superimposed. The remainder of the chapter is devoted to comparative analysis of these four types of investigations.[1]

**TABLE 3–1**
*Types of investigations*

| | | IV | |
| | | *Controlled* | *Not controlled* |
| --- | --- | --- | --- |
| Setting | *Unnatural* | Controlled laboratory experiment | Ex post facto laboratory study |
| | *Natural* | Controlled field experiment | Ex post facto field study |

## CONTROLLED LABORATORY EXPERIMENTS

### Definition

After the treatise on the basic assumptions of science you may wonder why the subject of controlled experimentation is being covered here. Are not science and controlled experimentation synonymous? Are we not just restating points described in Chapter One? Scientific inquiry need not involve the manipulation of an IV. Investigations that do involve the direct manipulation of an IV are only one type of scientific inquiry. Scientists who use this method may be referred to as control experimentalists.

A scientist deals with the world in terms of empiricism (he carries out measurable observations), determinism (he believes relations between events are lawful), testability (he deals only with relationships that have the possibility of being proven true or false), and parsimony (he accepts the simplest plausible explanation for lawful relationships). The control experimentalist, a special type of scientist, not only accepts these four bylaws of investigation but adds one other—the direct manipulation of the IV. (The reason for the extra bylaw will be discussed in the next section of this chapter.) Now let us define control experimentation. A controlled experiment is a scientific laboratory investigation in which the IV is directly and systematically manipulated.

1. There are other ways to classify types of investigations besides the two listed. Investigations may be categorized, for example, according to the type of subjects used (animal or human), the area of psychology involved (developmental, social, etc.), or the type of task involved. The two dimensions on which investigations are categorized in this text were chosen because they are based on methodological differences, and methodology is the central issue here.

### An Example

To determine whether learning could occur without performance of an instrumental response, Dodwell and Bessent [1960] carried out a controlled laboratory experiment in which a water maze with eight choice points was used (see Figure 3–1). The 16 rats serving as subjects were randomly assigned to two groups, experimental (E) and control (C) rats, and were taught to swim through the maze to the criterion of three errorless trials. The experimental animals were initially propelled through the maze on a trolley. They then learned the maze by swimming through it. The number of swimming trials required to reach the criterion and the number of errors made were recorded. An error was defined as making an incorrect turn at any of the eight choice points. On the average, group E subjects took 5.6 trials to reach criterion, whereas group C averaged 9.6. Groups C and E averaged 96.4 errors and 18.9 errors, respectively. It was concluded that learning could occur without an instrumental response being made.

### Steps

Six basic steps must be included in order for an investigation to be considered a controlled laboratory experiment. These steps are:

1. Formulate a hypothesis.
2. Select appropriate IVs and DVs.
3. Control alternative explanations for variation.
4. Manipulate the IVs and measure the DVs.
5. Analyze the variance in the DVs.
6. Make predictions regarding the relationship between the IVs and the DVs.

The following is an elaboration on these six steps using the previous example of a controlled laboratory experiment as a reference.

**Formulating a hypothesis.** Prior to the actual carrying out of their experiment, Dodwell and Bessent were confronted with a question to which they had no answer. The question was "Can learning occur without some observable behavior being emitted by the learner?" In order for them to answer this question, they had to formulate a statement that could be shown to be either true or false.[2] To do this it was necessary to formulate a statement that would meet two requirements. First, it had to be testable. It had to be

---

2. No statement can actually be proved absolutely true or absolutely false. Instead, a statement is demonstrated to be more probably true or more probably false. Chapter Six deals with this fact in greater detail.

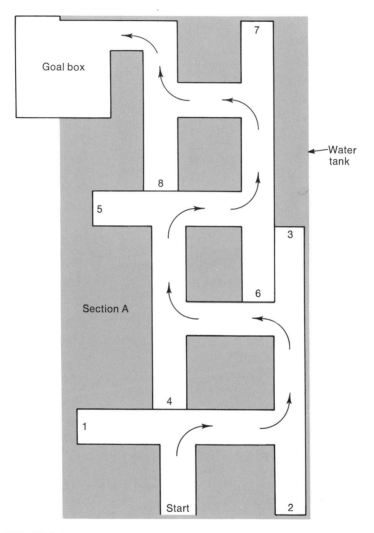

**FIGURE 3–1**

Diagram of the water maze used by Dodwell and Bessant

(Adapted from Dodwell & Bessant, 1960, Figure 1.)

stated in terms of operational definitions, that is, stated in measureable and manipulable terms. For example, in order to formulate a hypothesis dealing with the mind, you would have to define the mind in terms of some measureable unit such as location and rate of electrochemical transmission in the brain. Second, the hypothetical statement must involve a potential relationship between variables. Any hypothetical statement cannot be absolutely true or absolutely false, but have the possibility of being one or the other. "I am on the moon or I am not on the moon" is an absolutely true statement. It has no physical possibility of being false, so it cannot be tested. It inherently includes all alternatives. "I am on the moon and I am not on the moon" is an absolutely false statement. It logically cannot be; therefore, it is untestable. Notice that both are not hypothetical statements, although they deal with operationally definable variables (*I* and *moon*), because they are untestable. In contrast to these two statements, a testable statement would be "I am on the moon." At present, it is possible to take measurements to determine whether I am there or not; therefore, the last statement can be a hypothesis. A hypothesis, then, can be defined as a testable statement of a possible relationship between two or more variables.

**Selecting independent and dependent variables.** After a hypothesis has been formulated, the experimenter begins specifying the IVs and the DVs in terms of events that can be manipulated and measured. In the example, Dodwell and Bessent selected the movement of rats through a water maze without any physical exertion on their part as the IV. The number of trials it took for a rat to swim through the maze three consecutive times without making a mistake and the total number of mistakes a rat made until the criterion was met were the two DVs selected. In more general terms, and to review, the IVs chosen are those variables manipulated by the experimenter acting upon the subject, whereas the DVs chosen are those variables manipulated by the subject himself. IV control occurs when the experimenter varies the IV in a specified course or action to a degree already known by himself. Most psychological experiments measure only one DV, though it is not uncommon for an experiment to measure more than one.[3]

Actually, Dodwell and Bessent could have selected other IVs and DVs to test the same hypothesis. Two alternative IVs could have been (1) putting rats on an elevated platform and letting them watch other rats swim through the maze and (2) feeding RNA brain extract from sacrificed rats who had

---

3. Various areas in psychology differ on the average number of DVs measured in an experiment. Psychophysical experiments most often measure one DV, whereas physiological studies dealing with the polygraph frequently measure four or more DVs (EEG, EAG, GSR, and EMG).

previously learned the maze to naive rats. There are certain problems to overcome, however, if one were to use either of the IVs proposed.[4]

Many things should be taken into consideration when the IV and DV are being selected. For example, if you plan to carry out an experiment with shock as the IV, how long should it be applied, or how intense should it be? The following are some questions Dodwell and Bessent had to deal with in their investigation when selecting their IV and DV: (1) What will be considered an error; (2) how many trials should the group E rats have on the trolley; (3) how fast should the group E rats be drawn through the maze; and (4) are three errorless trials in a row too easy or too strict a criterion? Chapter Five deals in greater detail with the types of problems encountered when selecting the IV and DV. At this point, it is sufficient to say that selection of appropriate IVs and DVs is a crucial step in experimentation and often spells success or defeat in terms of positive results.

**Controlling alternative explanations for variation.** In carrying out an experiment, the researcher must determine whether manipulation of some variable, *A*, has any effect on the DV, *B*. He should keep in mind, however, that there is always more than one variable influencing behavior at any given time. Examine an illustration in which a fisherman wants to know which type of bait is best for catching trout. He selects bait as his IV and number of fish caught in four hours as his DV. During his vacation, he goes to Lake Powell and fishes from 8 A.M. to 12 noon on a Sunday using flies as bait. The following day he goes to White Lake and fishes with worms from 2 P.M. to 6 P.M. He caught one fish at Lake Powell and six fish at White Lake. Should he conclude that worms are the best bait to use? Obviously, variables other than bait could also be the cause of the difference in the number of fish caught. Plausible alternative causes for the variation in number of fish include (1) there are more fish in White Lake; (2) the weather was different on the two days he fished (weather conditions are known to influence the feeding behavior of fish), and (3) the time of day he fished could have caused the difference. It should not be too difficult for the student to suggest changes in the experiment to remove the alternative explanations, or at least the possibility of their influencing the number of fish caught.

In an ideal experimental situation, all the variation in the DVs between the group not receiving the IV and the group receiving the IV should be due to the application of the IV. For an experiment to be ideal, however, both

---

4. For example, if you had rats on the elevated platform, how could you make sure they attended to the rats swimming the maze? In the second IV situation, how could you be sure the extract you fed naive rats could, in fact, influence them any differently than extracts taken from rats who had not previously been taught to swim the maze correctly?

the control and the experimental group should be exactly the same except for the application of the IV. But an ideal experiment is a physical impossibility, for comparison groups will never be exactly the same. Ages of subjects will vary, temperature and lighting will fluctuate, the time each subject is run will vary, and so on. Each variable that fluctuates between the control and the experimental group will influence the DV variation between the groups and, obviously, the amount of influence will vary according to the significance of the variable. In the water maze experiment, temperature of the water, light intensity, and the time each rat was run were not exactly the same for each subject. As you would expect, the amount these variables did fluctuate was so small that their effect on the DV was relatively minor. Variables that could have a much larger influence on the number of trials it took to swim the maze with no mistakes would be past experience with water and past experience with mazes. Notice that Dodwell and Bessent controlled for these two variables by randomly assigning the rats to either the experimental or the control group.

The influence an IV has on the DV in an experiment is often called the primary, or systematic, variation; the influence any or all other fluctuating variables in the experiment has on the DV is called secondary and error variation. The objective of this step of controlled experimentation is to decrease secondary and error variation. One of the values of controlled laboratory experiments is the researcher's superior ability to deal with sources of secondary and error variation. (Chapter Four identifies major sources of secondary and error variation; Chapters Eight through Eleven deal with various means of controlling them when experimental investigations are used.)

**Manipulating the independent variable.**   At the beginning of this chapter types of investigations were categorized in terms of two dimensions, one of which concerned the direct manipulation of an IV. It was also mentioned that this dimension is actually a continuum rather than a sequence of discrete events. Although it is true that there are investigations carried out in which only partial control of the IV is possible, generally one can categorize research investigations in terms of whether the IV was actually manipulated or not. This is one of the most common bases for categorizing research investigations. Cronbach [1957] divides scientific psychology into two main parts: experimental and correlational psychology. He restricts experimental psychology to investigations that actively manipulate an IV; correlational psychology includes all studies in which an IV is not directly manipulated. I have chosen the term ex post facto over correlational because many scientific investigations not manipulating some IV similarly do not carry out any type of correlational analysis. An example is a type of investigation Maxwell

[1970] calls straightforward fact-finding types of studies. The example he cites involved determining the whereabouts and present posts of psychiatrists who had trained at either the Institute of Psychiatry or the Maudsley-Bethlem Hospital. Maxwell noted where these graduates ended up. He then continued his study by asking why some graduates born in one country traveled abroad whereas those born abroad went to other countries to stay. Also investigated was the type of eventual post held by each graduate and the leanings of each (toward teaching, research, and so on) over the years. Thus, Maxwell used a minimum amount of statistical manipulation and no complicated methodology.

The distinction between investigations that directly manipulate variables and those that do not is important for several reasons. First, if one is unable to manipulate a variable in order to note its effects on some DV, there is a greater possibility that changes in the DV were, in fact, due to some other variable that varied simultaneously with the one originally being studied. In medicine, to give an example, it was originally suggested that the red spots present along with measles were the cause of the illness. The simultaneous occurrence of two events in time does not necessarily imply a cause and effect relationship. The ability to present and remove a variable at will decreases the probability that there is some concomitant variable causing the effect on the DV.

Second, when one is able to manipulate variables, certain powerful research techniques and types of statistical analysis are available that are inapplicable with nonmanipulative procedures. An elaborate explanation of this point is beyond the scope of this book, but a thorough explanation may be found in texts by Hays [1963], Keppel [1973], and Winer [1971].

**Measurement and analysis of fluctuation in the dependent variable.** The measurement of change in some variable is an integral part of any type of investigation, from a relatively simple fact-finding type of study to a complex experimental investigation involving a sophisticated statistical analysis. Some events must be measured and recorded before any type of data analysis can be run.

There is a strong misconception about data analysis that is shared by most students interested in doing research: they believe that the more complex the statistical analysis involved, the more controlled the experiment. Actually, the correlation is just the reverse. If an experimenter can directly control sources of secondary variation, he can generally employ a simpler form of statistical analysis because the complexity of the statistical analysis increases as the need to control secondary variation by statistical means increases. Chapter Four deals with this point at greater length; a point to be made here is that students often increase the statistical complexity of their data in an effort to compensate for their lack of adequate experimental control. No amount of statistical manipulation can make up for a poorly conducted project.

**Drawing conclusions about relationships between variables.**  Step 6 is the most important of any experimental investigation; all five previous steps were taken so that an inference could be made about some relationship between the variables involved. First, a testable relationship was formulated between variables. Second, appropriate representatives of these variables were selected. Third, one decreased the possibility of other relationships interfering with the one of intended study. Fourth, intentional manipulation of one of the variables caused fluctuations in the other variables, which in turn could be noted and analyzed in the fifth step. All this was done so that a statement of some cause and effect relationship between two variables would be possible along with the necessary empirical proof to back it up. The basic premise of any scientific investigation involves demonstrating relationships between variables. The kind of relationship can range from no relationship at all to a strong cause and effect relationship. Controlled experiments are not carried out to find some correlational relationship between variables, rather, they are procedures designed to identify cause and effect relationships. In correlational studies one is limited to showing that variable *A* simultaneously occurs with variable *B* to a certain degree. In other words, with a higher correlation between *A* and *B*, the more one knows about *A* the greater one can predict about *B*. Correlational studies, however, do not enable the researcher to make a strong case for a cause and effect relationship between *A* and *B*.

In the water maze experiment previously examined, step 6 dealt with making some statement regarding the cause and effect relationship between learning and the necessity of instrumental responding for learning to occur. After carrying out the experiment, Dodwell and Bessent could state that instrumental responding is not necessarily required for learning to occur. The case for a cause-effect relationship is much stronger in a manipulatory investigation.

### Reasons for Controlled Laboratory Experiments

Why do psychologists conduct laboratory experiments? The standard answer to this question has traditionally been "to test a theory." Theorizing was the main function of psychologists in the past when few principles of behavior were known. It was felt that evaluating a theory was the only acceptable reason for conducting psychological investigations. Over the years that view has changed, however, and now there are several acceptable reasons for conducting experiments. Sidman [1960] lists several reasons besides theory evaluation which the apprentice psychologist should be aware of.

**Evaluation of a theory.** The most common reason by far for carrying out research is to investigate hypotheses and relate them to a particular theory. Experiments that test the adequacy of theories in terms of their ability to provide explanations for relationships between events are important in the scientific community. The basic premise of science, as you may recall, is to identify the relationships between variables. The next logical step up the ladder of experimental sophistication is to identify the relationships between relationships. But before this gets too confusing, let us analyze what has been said so far by means of an example.

If a parent is interested in an individual behavior of his child, i.e., bed-wetting, he might hypothesize the fact that the child drinks a full glass of water each night before going to bed as the cause of the bedwetting. If, after making sure the child no longer drinks water before going to bed, the bed-wetting stops, the parent accepts water drinking as the cause and confirms his hypothesis. Thus, the parent deals with particular facts, simple and exact, and from then tries to discover some singular relationship between the two.

To discover the relationship between relationships would be our next experimental step. If we were to take the relationship of early childhood bedwetting and that of later success in life, ability to adjust, IQ, or any number of other relationships or laws, and relate these to a particular theory or theories, we would be taking that next step. We would no longer be concerned with only one event involving a particular child, but with the relationship between events in a more global framework. We now hypothesize the relationship between bedwetting and its effect on certain situations that may influence achievement later in life. Thus, we are dealing with determining the relationship between previously noted relationships (water–bedwetting, and certain situations–achievement). Theory building involves hypothesizing about the relationship between simpler relationships or facts noted.

**Satisfaction of curiosity.** The second most frequent reason for carrying out a scientific experiment or investigation is to satisfy the researcher's curiosity.[5] This person may be little concerned with integrating the results of his study into some theory, but still may be interested in finding the answer to a particular question or problem, e.g., "Do dogs have ESP?" or "What effect

5. Satisfying one's own curiosity is the most common reason for experiments being carried out in the experimental psychology course, rather than natural causes. One of the standard requirements of an experimental psychology course is to have the student create and carry out an experiment. This places the student in a situation where the instructor may evaluate his ability to carry out the steps involved in scientific research.

does LSD have on memory?" After coming up with a problem to be solved, he then sets out to solve it employing the six steps given in the previous section.

Those who conduct psychological research seem to follow one of two general routes, the first of which involves developing a theory in one particular area or field and with undeviating vigor exploring *only* that area. Ebbinghause was an experimenter of this sort. He developed a theory of memory and explored only those areas directly related to it. The second route is taken by those who are not bound by any particular theory or area. They are interested in problems and solutions utilizing the scientific method in whatever areas those problems may be. Theories, then, become the product of experimentation and data—not vice versa. B.F. Skinner and many others display varied interests and tend to follow those interests wherever they lead. Theories may develop from their explorations, but they are secondary to solving the problem and gathering data.

**Demonstration of a new method or technique.** One of the main reasons for the development of psychology as a scientific discipline in both the applied and research dimensions has been improvement of laboratory methodology and applied psychological techniques. Prior to the development of the Skinner box, for example, it was difficult to carry out investigations on rats that involved more than one type of response from the subject at a time. Generally, the maze was used as the test apparatus, and the only response measured was how long it took for the rat to traverse the maze or which way he turned in the maze at choice points. With the Skinner box, a subject could be given two or more response bars to push at one time. Now it was possible to analyze what effect changing one task might have on a second task which was not changed. A practical everyday example of this type of research would be answering a question such as "Will punishing a child for doing something wrong make him withdraw more from other activities also?" In applied psychology, the application of operant conditioning procedures in mental institutions is an example of an improvement in technique. Certain types of mental problems, such as autism, had not responded very well to therapies based on verbal interaction between the therapist and the patient. Wolf, Risley, and Mees [1964] applied operant conditioning procedures to autistic children and found them to be a welcome addition to other therapeutic procedures.[6]

---

6. Before a graduate student in psychology receives his master's or doctorate, he is generally required to carry out research and write a paper on some topic that will advance the field of psychology. Often this research is in the development of a new procedure or the application of a standard procedure to a different problem area. However, the most important criterion in the resulting data is its quality, not the uniqueness of a technique.

**Demonstration of a behavioral phenomenon.**   Another area in which experimentation is used is in demonstrating a new phenomenon. In discovering what is now called state-dependent learning, Girden and Culler in 1937 demonstrated through their experiments that if a conditioned response was acquired by a dog in a drugged state, that response would thereafter be performed only when the dog was drugged.

The discovery of a new phenomenon is, above all else, a creative activity, though many times accident plays a more important role than most of us would like to admit. The question of how new phenomena are discovered has no set answer. They may be discovered by accident, by prediction, from theories, from casual observation, from systematic experimentation, or by any number of other ways. Many different areas other than psychology may contribute to the discovery of new psychological phenomena, e.g., sociology, anthropology, physiology, and so on. These other disciplines, in which behavioral phenomena are used as tools for investigating other issues, may provide new insights or suggest new avenues for psychological investigation.

**Investigation of conditions influencing behavioral phenomena.**   Following the discovery of a new phenomenon, the next step is to integrate that discovery and its data into what is already known and into acceptable theories. The initial phenomenon then becomes integrated by further experimentation, study, and replication. Following Girden and Cullers' [1937] discovery and pioneer work with state-dependent learning, many others—Heistad and Torres [1959], Holmgren [1965], Overton [1964], Barry [1968], Miller [1961], and Bellville [1964]—tried to analyze the different conditions and effects under which state-dependent learning occurs. They varied the type of drugs, the quantity, and the tasks required, all of which expanded and deepened our understanding of the initial discovery, and by doing so aided in its integration.

### Advantages and Disadvantages

One major advantage of controlled laboratory experimentation over non-manipulatory investigation is the ability to control the application and withdrawal of the IV. One of a magician's basic tactics when attempting a sleight of hand deception is to carry out and accentuate certain irrelevant behaviors while performing the responses required to make a penny disappear. The observer perceives a cause and effect relationship between the accentuated behaviors and the disappearance of the penny. The deception becomes apparent when the observer imitates the magician, only to find the penny unwilling to dematerialize. Nature frequently presents us with similar situations. In 1866 Gregor Mendel carried out one of the first controlled experiments in genetics when he intentionally controlled the cross-fertilization of certain sweet-pea plants and obtained expected colors in the blossoms. The scientists of that day were so duped by nature's sleight of hand that it took until 1900 before previous conclusions drawn from ex post facto research were discarded. Because of the frequency of persons' misperceiving untrue relationships between variables in everyday situations, experimental manipulation of the IV is strongly advocated wherever possible.

A second advantage is superior ability to control secondary variation. There are two ways this is accomplished. First, control procedures may be used in a controlled laboratory situation that are unavailable in ex post facto studies. A variable (which in natural situations would compete with the IV to influence some DV) could be (1) completely removed from the experimental situation, (2) made an IV itself with its effects recorded, or (3) neutralized by randomly assigning subjects to either the control or the experimental group. With randomization, the effects of the variable are equated between the groups, thereby removing the possibility that any difference noted between the groups was a function of the variable in question. Second, control procedures are more precisely applicable in a controlled laboratory experiment.

A third advantage of the controlled laboratory experiment over other types of investigation is the ability of the experimenter to record the DV more precisely. In field investigations there is greater chance for error in measurement. It may not be possible to record some DVs at all outside the laboratory. Brain recordings, for instance, require a polygraph to sense changes that are not visible to the human eye. Also, many responses may occur faster than a person can record them. In addition, individual perceptual differences between experimenters would be a disadvantage in the ex post facto study, whereas in the controlled situation, precise, unquestionable, and agreed-upon measurements are taken by accurate instruments.

Let' us now look at some of the disadvantages of a controlled laboratory experiment. First, some situations—such as mass riots—may not be carried out in the laboratory because of sheer physical impossibility. Second, certain situations may not be carried out because they are not socially acceptable, e.g., it is not permissible in the United States to purchase human infants and raise them in extreme deprivation situations. Third, laboratory experiments may not be carried out because of time limitations. Even if it were socially acceptable to carry out genetic studies on humans, the time required to carry through just a few generations would be way too long. Fruit flies are much more suitable for genetic experimentation in the laboratory since tens of generations can be propagated in a month or so. A fourth disadvantage of controlled laboratory experimentation is cost. Usually other types of investigation are less expensive to carry out because laboratory experimentation requires precision instruments of calculation. It is less expensive to send out questionnaires and ask people what they do than place them in a situation and note their actions.

## FIELD EXPERIMENTS

### Definition

A field experiment may be defined as a scientific investigation carried out in the field which involves the direct manipulation of some IV or IVs.

The field experiment is a scientific investigation carried out in real life. It is similar to a controlled laboratory experiment in that an IV is manipulated, and it meets the criterion of being a scientific investigation. Differences between the field experiment and the laboratory experiment lie in the fact that the field experiment is carried out in a realistic, everyday situation. The importance of this difference is further delineated by the ability of the experimenter to control secondary variation. The controlled laboratory experiment provides the most optimum conditions for control of secondary variation. Field experiments differ from controlled laboratory experiments in degree. Field experiments vary in their ability to control. Some are quite similar to laboratory experimentation and have almost complete control, others occur in a very loose experimental situation that allows little control.

### An Example

In today's urbanized society, with its great city populations, response to police or law enforcement agencies has seldom been passive or readily obliging. The unspoken implication that police are the instrument of power generates a general intolerance of any of their efforts by the populace at large. Yet these agencies, by their very nature defenders of the status quo, are forced into a disadvantageous position as society struggles with disruption and change.

In an effort to understand and possibly avert the tide of citizen resentment, an experiment was recently conducted in which the parameters of police functioning within a common but extremely dangerous situation—the family disturbance—were examined. The project attempted to find out if within an area population of 85,000, a specially trained unit of police (18 men, only a fraction of the usual force) could effect changes in the rates of homicide and assault, two of the most widely found incidents of aggression in present urban society.

The 18 officers were trained in a concentrated course of study that attempted to make the men more psychologically sophisticated, with highly technical skills, while still retaining their basic identity. They then were assigned to work in pairs to provide 24-hour coverage of the area in one radio car for a 22-month period. The core of the program consisted of a consultation period for the officers on a weekly basis with advanced doctoral students in clinical psychology, and in group discussions, also on a weekly basis, in which professional psychologists served as group leaders.

In the final evaluation, dramatic findings were noted. The unit processed 1,375 interventions with 962 families, and indirect sources indicated response to the unit was overwhelmingly positive. It is most interesting that while homicide rates in New York City increased during the period of the project, there was not a single homicide in a family known to the unit. A sharp reduction in assaults in the demonstration area was evidenced, as well as a drop in arrests for assaults. Furthermore, there were no injuries to any of the officers in the unit—a surprising fact since an unusually high risk is involved for officers in an emotionally charged and potentially violent family crisis.

In this investigation one can readily observe the most apparent IV manipulated, the education of the officers as applied to the reactions of that segment of society. The DVs measured included overall reaction of the population as evidenced in homicide level, the number of assaults, attitudes toward police intervention, and injury to the officers. In carrying out a field rather than a laboratory experiment, the researcher had less control over secondary variation, so there was an increase in the possibility of explaining any observed change in the DVs in terms of some variable other than the IV. For example, the increased effectiveness of the officers could have been a result not of their psychological training, but of the fact that they tried harder since they knew they were in an experiment.

### Steps

The steps in a field experiment are the same as those employed in laboratory experiments: a hypothesis is formulated; IVs and DVs are selected; alternative explanations are controlled for; IVs are manipulated; DVs are measured and analyzed; and conclusions are stated about the relationship in question. The differences in these two types of investigations revolve around the ability of the experimenter to control the steps. In many instances the laboratory setting allows more accurate measurements in the application and recording of the IVs and DVs, thereby increasing analytical precision. It is also true that there are usually more control procedures for secondary variation available in the laboratory. In field experiments it is often difficult to hold sources of secondary variation constant or to completely remove them. The investigator must consider the myriad conditions that affect subjects in the field situation more in a field experiment than in a laboratory experiment.

### Reasons for Field Experiments

The reasons for carrying out field experiments are essentially the same as those for carrying out laboratory experiments. Field experiments can be devised to test theories, satisfy one's curiosity, try out new methods, demonstrate behavioral phenomena, and explore the conditions under which a phenomenon occurs. Of the five reasons, the third and fourth are the most common. Field experimentation is more often concerned with problems of practical application than with extensions of theoretical positions. New methods are frequently applied to deal with current problem areas. The previously mentioned study using autism as an area of experimental research is a situation in which little success had been achieved in the past. Field experiments which demonstrate results that have previously been unattainable are also common. For example, Shelley, Keysor, and Robinson [unpublished] demonstrated procedures that can be employed to develop pitch discriminations in people who previously could not tell to what degree two musical tones differ—whether one musical tone is higher, lower, or the same as the one presented before it. After pairing a light with each tone in one octave and then fading out the lights, the accuracy of discrimination improved from 50 to 94 percent.

### Advantages and Disadvantages

In considering one of the values of field experiments, we discover one of the faults of laboratory experiments. With all of laboratory experimentation's advantages of control, it has one great potential defect—the inability to generalize the results obtained in the laboratory setting to the real life situations. This is commonly known as lack of external validity. A scientific investigation may be internally valid (properly controlled to the extent that any change in the DV can be safely assumed to be caused by the IV) but not be externally valid (although the IV is demonstrated to hold a positive relationship to the DV in the experimental setting, the relationship does not hold in everyday situations because conditions in the experimental setting are not analogous to those outside that setting). A juvenile delinquent found guilty of breaking some law may be quite repentant before the judge and vow never to commit the act again. Once outside the courtroom and back in his previous environment, however, he commits the crime again. The pressures on that individual in the courtroom are not the same as those outside; therefore, the behavior emitted in the courtroom is not a valid indicator of behavior outside.

With a little reflection on previous comments regarding superior ability to control secondary variation in laboratory situations, it should be apparent that although laboratory experiments may control for internal validity better than any other type of investigation, this restriction of secondary variation may cause the experimental situation to vary from the real life situation to such an extent that the experiment has little external validity. One of the main values of field experiments, then, is that they involve the manipulation of an IV in a situation that is more true to life than the laboratory setting. So, although the control of secondary variation (internal validity) is less than in laboratory experiments, there is greater possibility that the relationships found are truer demonstrations of what happens in real life situations (external validity). This attribute of increasing external validity makes field experimentation the favorite procedure for social psychologists, clinical psychologists, sociologists, and educators.

Field experiments offer several advantages over ex post facto research. First, the IV can be actively manipulated. Second, control procedures for secondary variation that are unavailable to ex post facto studies (e.g., subject randomization, holding sources of secondary variation constant) can be applied.

## EX POST FACTO FIELD STUDIES

### Definition

Psychologists believe we can gain better understanding of ourselves not only by investigating present and future events, but also by analyzing events of the past. Something good or bad may have occurred, and we are not sure why, so we investigate the past in an attempt to identify the cause of the change. Acts of vandalism on college campuses were noted to be higher prior to World War II than after. The way to study the causes of the increased vandalism would be to carry out an ex post facto investigation. There are two reasons why this problem could only be investigated using this approach. First, it would be impossible to return to the prewar era to carry out a controlled experiment; and second, society would not allow us to intentionally manipulate variables that would induce vandalism. This situation contains the two major reasons for the founding of the particular type of scientific investigations called ex post facto (EPF) research: if some unexpected event occurred in the past, it is obviously impossible to use a controlled experimental approach, and it is too late to manipulate some variable to see if it was the cause of the event. And because society stipulates certain moral codes that cannot be violated regardless of reason or interest, variables that so violate those codes cannot be used—much less manipulated. With this in mind, we can define ex post facto research as any systematic empirical inquiry in which the IVs have not been directly controlled because they have already occurred or because they are inherently not manipulable.

### An Example

Pettigrew [1959] carried out a field study testing whether the widespread belief that white southerners are typically more prejudiced against blacks than are whites in the north was based on (1) more externalizing personality potential for prejudice among southerners, (2) the effects of different cultural norms and pressures, or (3) both of these. Basically, he was contrasting sociological and psychological explanations of prejudice. His test involved administering authoritarian, anti-Semitic, and anti-black scales to randomly selected white adults in four northern and four southern cities.

Pettigrew found that there was no significant difference between northern and southern adults in relation to the authoritarian scale used to measure externalizing personality potential. On the anti-black scale, however, it was found that there was a significant difference between the two regions. Hence Pettigrew reasoned that the anti-black prejudice was based on sociological factors rather than psychological ones.

Notice that no IV was manipulated in this study. Just as a detective might measure the amount of gunpowder residue on various suspects' hands in an effort to relate them to the firing of the gun, Pettigrew took measures of social and personality factors. These measures were taken along with measures of the anti-black attitudes of northern and southern white adults. The issue was whether anti-black prejudice was related more closely to social or to personality factors. If this were a controlled experiment, the social and personality factors would be the IVs to be manipulated and the prejudice would be the DV. Any prejudice that occurred as a result of manipulating social and personality factors would be said to be caused by those factors. Because Pettigrew could not actually manipulate those factors, all he could extrapolate was that when prejudice was found, social factors were "related" to anti-black prejudice.

### Steps

Without the opportunity to manipulate an IV, the functions of the researcher shift to some extent. The role an investigator plays in EPF research is similar to that of a detective who attempts to solve a crime. The event has already occurred, so the opportunity to manipulate some variables and control others has been removed. Instead, one must deal with the situation as it is. All the facts that have any possible bearing are gathered. By a process of elimination, least possible causes are progressively discarded until one explanation is left. The last remaining choice is concluded to have caused the event because it had the greatest probability of being responsible from among all the possible alternative explanations.

In some cases, there is a prime suspect, and the procedure involves gathering data to determine the probability that the prime suspect was the cause. Pettigrew's study is a good example of this type of situation. There were two prime suspects for causing anti-black attitudes, social and psychological. Measurements were gathered and recorded. An analysis was then carried out to determine how strong the connection was between anti-black attitudes and psychological or social factors. The analysis dealt with taking any changes found in the two factors and noting any corresponding changes in anti-black attitudes. The ability to determine causal connections is limited, then, because all that can be shown is that one event occurs at the same time the other event occurs. When an IV can be manipulated, you can show the relationship when $X$ follows $Y$. Showing $X$ can bring about $Y$ is a stronger basis for concluding a causal relationship than simply showing $Y$ is present when $X$ is present.

The steps in EPF research are the same as those for experimental research except that two steps have been eliminated. It is not possible to control actively for sources of secondary variation (step 3) and no IV is manipulated (step 4). The investigation does include forming a hypothesis, defining the possible IV ($X$) and the actual DV ($Y$), collecting and analyzing data, and drawing conclusions about the possible relationship of $X$ to $Y$. Now the most important step for both EPF and manipulatory research is the one dealing with determining a probability that the change in the DV was, in fact, a function of the change in the IV. Actually, neither EPF or manipulatory research can tell you for a fact that the manipulation of $X$ *caused* the changes in $Y$. All either procedure can do is increase confidence that $X$ did by decreasing the possibility that some other variable caused the difference.

### Ex Post Facto Studies and Controlled Experiments

The difference between an ex post facto and a controlled approach becomes more apparent by looking at the application of both to the question of whether cigarette smoking causes cancer. In the well-known post hoc study on cigarette smoking and cancer, the smoking habits of a large number of people were studied. The investigators probed the backgrounds of the people to find out whether they smoked cigarettes and, if so, how many for how long. The study included (1) people presently living who did not have cancer, (2) people presently living who did have cancer, and (3) people who had died. The IV and the DV were the numbers of cigarettes smoked and the occurrence of lung cancer, respectively. It was found that the incidence of lung cancer rose with an increase in the number of cigarettes smoked. The conclusion reached in the study was that lung cancer was caused by cigarette smoking.

A controlled approach to a similar question was followed by Essenberg at the Chicago School of Medicine. Essenberg sought to reproduce in mice the conditions to which human smokers subject themselves. Two glass enclosures were constructed to serve as the controlled environment in which laboratory-bred mice were placed. Attached to the enclosures was a special device that "smoked" a cigarette an hour and sent the smoke to the mice inside. Mice in the second enclosure received ordinary air. Within the year, 21 of the original 23 mice living in the first enclosure had lung tumors. Essenberg concluded that the smoke of the cigarettes contributed to, if not directly caused, cancerous growth in tissues.

### Reasons for Ex Post Facto Field Studies

Ex post facto field studies can be devised to test theories, satisfy one's curiosity, evaluate new methods, identify behavioral phenomena, and explore the conditions under which a phenomenon occurs. These reasons are similar to those for carrying out controlled laboratory experiments, though the approach and the results obtained may vary. The difference lies in the fact that experiments provide greater confidence in any causal relationships found. Ex post facto research is a more indirect approach for testing a hypothesis.

### Advantages and Disadvantages

If the reasons for carrying out all investigations are the same and controlled experiments give one more confidence in one's conclusions, why carry out EPF field studies? There are several reasons. The major ones are found in its definition: The situation happened in the past or an IV cannot be manipulated because of physical or social restrictions. In addition, one may carry out EPF research with limited funds, for controlled experiments generally cost money. EPF research, on the other hand, can be carried out with pencil and paper. Time is another factor. For example, a school board wants to know whether it should hire teachers with bachelor's or master's degrees. Teachers with master's degrees are more expensive. The board could look at past histories of the success rates for both kinds of teachers rather than hire a couple of each and compare. Many times EPF situations will allow more subjects for analysis to be included. In the teacher example, it may not be physically possible to hire more than a few teachers and actually evaluate their ability, whereas past records may provide valuable comparative data upon which to evaluate the teachers.

The limitations of EPF research center around four points, the third of which is a function of the first two. First, no IV can be manipulated; second, inability to control secondary variation sources; third, incorrect interpretation of the results is more probable; and fourth, complicated statistical analytical procedures developed for controlled experimentation cannot be employed.

## EX POST FACTO LABORATORY STUDIES

### Definition

An EPF laboratory study may be defined as a scientific laboratory investigation in which the IVs have not been directly controlled due to the fact that they have already occurred. Often some event that occurs in a controlled laboratory setting is unexpected or noticed for the first time. The investigator may then formulate a hypothesis to explain that event. He then analyzes any data regarding this event and draws conclusions.

### An Example

In the 1950's Joseph Brady carried out a research project at the Walter Reed Laboratories. Some long-term experiments being carried out on monkeys included the application of shock to the subjects, and Brady was finding a high mortality rate among his subjects. No explanation for the deaths was evident, so he attributed the losses to unavoidable circumstances. One day an ulcer specialist, R.W. Porter, asked if he might perform a post mortem examination on the next few monkeys that died. He found small perforated ulcers in the stomachs of the subjects. Since Porter had not found ulcers in hundreds of other monkeys not experiencing the conditions to which Brady had been subjecting his monkeys, an EPF laboratory study was carried out to determine which experimental conditions were most strongly related to the ulcers and the deaths of the subjects. A high correlation was noted between the use of certain types of schedules of reinforcement employing shock and the ulcers.

### Steps

The steps in an EPF laboratory study are similar to those carried out in EPF field studies. A hypothesis is formed, IVs and DVs selected, data recorded and analyzed and a conclusive statement made regarding the relationship found. EPF laboratory studies do not manipulate any variable or control for secondary variation sources as is the case with controlled experiments. As a consequence of these two steps being omitted, the type of statistical analysis employed in EPF research will substantially differ from that employed in controlled experimental research.

### Reasons for Ex Post Facto Laboratory Studies

Laboratory studies are often carried out as a means of selecting an appropriate controlled experiment. After carrying out a particular study an investigator may feel there seems to be a relationship between some variable that is not controlled and fluctuations in the DV. The investigator then analyzes the data for this previously unthought-of relationship and finds a strong correlation. This variable is then selected to be an IV for a controlled experiment. In one particular situation, I was trying to teach kindergarten children a red-green color discrimination using a fading procedure so that the children would not respond to the wrong color. Some children were making many mistakes, while others were making none. With an EPF analysis of the situation, it was noted that the child made mistakes when he or she was left in the testing room alone with the testing equipment but not when an adult stayed in the room. Later, a graduate student decided it would be interesting to carry out a controlled laboratory experiment to investigate the effects of adult presence on discriminations with children.

In many cases EPF laboratory studies are carried out as a trouble-shooting device in controlled experiments. During one semester in an introductory psychology class an indivdual instructional program was used. Students were allowed to go at their own pace throughout the course, and certain days were set aside for testing. Students were to come in and take each chapter exam when they felt prepared to do so. One hour each day the testing lab was open for them to take the exams. After two weeks of class, it became apparent that many students were frustrated. One afternoon, fifteen students approached the assistant and said they were "fed up" with the way the course was being run. They were questioned, and after a while it became apparent that the trouble centered around the fact that many times a student would study to take a test, go in, and wait for his or her turn, and not be able to take it because too many other students had come the same day. After the students left, the teaching assistants were called together and an anlysis of the situation was made. It was decided that sign-up sheets would be posted so that a student could sign up in advance for the day and time he wanted to take an exam. In this way a student would be sure of taking the test when he wanted to. This EPF analysis directed us to a seemingly trivial variable in the program that was severely disrupting our experiment. After posting the sign-up sheets, the frustration dissipated. At the end of the course, seven of the students who initially came in and protested said the course turned out to be one of the best they had ever taken.

### Advantages and Disadvantages

EPF laboratory studies may be carried out as rigorously as other types of investigations. They are commonly employed as a trouble-shooting device for controlled experiments to save time and money in simply trying to find sources of trouble in other controlled experiments.

The limitations of EPF laboratory studies are many. First, no IV can actually be manipulated. Second, secondary variation is not controlled.

Third, it is not generally considered a publishable type of investigation by itself. The information gleaned from it is usually closely related to a later controlled experiment that is of more interest to other scientists. Fourth, some experimenters do not consider it a true investigation, for it is not usually carried out by itself; instead, it is employed in connection with some other experiment that malfunctions. Other experimenters, however, believe one should analyze malfunctioning investigations rather than simply discard them.

Though EPF laboratory studies are not usually covered in experimentation texts, it is an important type of investigation, for its success is related to the skill of the investigator. Applied psychologists differ with respect to their skill in identifying the past sources of problems for which a patient seeks an answer. Those who set up graduate programs in applied psychology have had difficulty determining the exact steps by which this skill is obtained, so they have not yet been able to devise a course the student may take to acquire these skills in cookbook fashion. Instead, students proceed through an intern program in which they work side by side with applied psychologists in an effort to acquire them indirectly by some sort of imitation process.

The same problem is encountered in experimental psychology graduate programs. Some experimentalists are more skillful in their controlled research than others. Many researchers would not have been as perceptive as Brady and Porter in visualizing the potential relationship between the shock situations and the ulcers. Though the exact procedure for developing this sensitivity to potentially relevant relationships in ongoing research is unknown, it is strongly related to the ability to carry through EPF laboratory studies. Many EPF laboratory analyses are in fact carried out only in the mind of the investigator. Nothing is written. An investigator may "eyeball" the data in his ongoing research, mentally note the simultaneous fluctuations in the DV and some potential cause of that fluctuation, evaluate the possible strength of the relationship, and decide whether to carry out a controlled laboratory experiment to increase his confidence that there is in fact a cause-effect relationship there.[7] Most EPF laboratory studies are not published, for whenever there seems to be a strong relationship, it is generally followed up with a controlled laboratory study, the results of which are then published.

## SUMMARY

All psychological investigations may be divided into four categories according to whether an IV is manipulated or not, and whether the investigation is carried out in a laboratory or in an everyday situation (field). Psy-

---

7. "Eyeballing" is a laboratory term for evaluating the importance of the changes in the DV by simply looking at the data. No formal statistical analysis is carried out. More is said about eyeballing in Chapter Eight.

chological investigations that include the manipulation of an IV are called experiments, whereas nonmanipulatory investigations are called ex post facto studies. There are six steps involved in carrying out psychological investigations: (1) formulate a hypothesis; (2) select appropriate IVs and DVs; (3) control for alternative explanations of DV variations; (4) manipulate the IV and measure the DV; (5) analyze the variation in the DV; and (6) make predictions regarding the relationship between the IV and the DV. Controlled laboratory experiments include all six steps. Field experiments also include all six steps, but do not allow for controlling secondary sources of DV variation as effectively as laboratory experiments. Ex post facto studies differ from experiments in steps 3, 4, and 5. EPF studies cannot control secondary sources of variation as well as experiments, do not include the active manipulation of an IV, and require a different kind of variation analysis than experiments. Laboratory situations are more effective in step 3 than field situations, while field situations are more generalizable to other everyday situations.

There are at least five reasons for carrying out psychological investigations: (1) evaluation of a theory, (2) satisfaction of curiosity, (3) demonstration of a new method or technique, (4) demonstration of a behavioral phenomenon, and (5) investigation of conditions influencing a behavioral phenomenon.

The advantages of laboratory experiments include the ability to manipulate an IV, superior ability to control secondary variation, and precision measurements. Disadvantages include: the facts that they cannot be used in certain situations because of physical impossibility, that they may not be socially acceptable in some situations, that they may take too long and be too costly.

Field experiments are inferior to laboratory experiments in terms of measurement precision and ability to control secondary sources of variation. They are superior to EPF investigations in precision, control of secondary variables, and ability to manipulate an IV. EPF studies may be used to analyze past situations and nonmanipulable situations.

# 4

# Variance

*Chapter Four gives the rationale behind carrying out an experimental investigation using two or more groups. Systematic variation and within variation are two of the most important concepts in the whole book. Because the ability to control secondary variables is the crux of all psychological investigations, the five methods for controlling secondary variables presented in this chapter should be memorized. The last section of the chapter deals with problem areas that could invalidate an investigation.*

There are two behavioral trends in which psychologists are interested: what makes people similar and what makes them different. On the one hand, psychologists study what the average child of six can do, what the average homemaker does in her spare time, and so on. On the other hand, psychologists investigate what makes one person's personality different from someone else's, how psychotics differ from neurotics, and so on.

In dealing with these questions, the experimentalist collects two kinds of information, *averages* and *variations*. Averages, such as the mean score or the mean number of attempts to solve a problem, give the psychologist information regarding the similarity of people and events. Suppose an instructor wants to determine how many multiple-choice questions the typical college student can answer in one hour. For the first class exam he hands out a 150-question test, instructing the students to answer as many as they can. The number of questions answered (not just correct) by each of the 15 students in his class are 71, 75, 76, 76, 70, 64, 68, 70, 72, 70, 66, 65, 84, 74, and 69. He takes these raw scores, adds them up, and divides by the number of students to get the mean number of questions a college student can answer in one hour.

$$\frac{1,070}{15} = 71.33$$

He may now use this information to determine the number of questions an exam should have. (Since most students have a fairly good understanding of how to calculate and use means, the point will not be elaborated here.)

There is a second statistical measure, just as important to the psychologist as the mean, which most students have difficulty in understanding. That measure is variance. Generally, a course in statistics is required before a student can enroll in an experimental psychology course. Variance, a basic concept in statistics, is thoroughly covered in such courses. Unfortunately, many students have difficulty in relating the concept of variance covered in the statistics course to the use of the same term in an experimental situation. They have trouble conceptualizing just what variance represents, and consequently, most wonder why researchers are so concerned with it. For this reason, a section on the role of variance and its importance in experimental situations has been included. This section does not cover all types of variation measures; instead, two variance measures will be discussed so that the student gets a feeling for the role of variance in experimentation.

The first measure of variance to be covered, *average variation*, is not a very useful statistical tool, and is presented here only because it is easy to calculate and may aid the reader to understand the second measure by allowing him to compare the two. The second measure, *variance*, is an extremely useful concept in experimentation. The reader should pay close attention to how it is calculated, for it is the very foundation of experimentation.

## WHAT IS VARIANCE?

Technically speaking, variance is a measure of the dispersion of a set of scores. It shows how much those scores are spread out and their degree of difference from one another. The meaning of this may be somewhat hazy to the student at this point, so let us look at a particular situation. As mentioned before, the main interest of researchers is to find cause and effect relationships. To do this, they generally select two groups, experimental and control. The experimental group is administered an IV; the control group is not. The major purpose of the experimenter's efforts is to cause variation between the groups. He wants the IV to influence the experimental group in such a way that the DV measured in the experimental group will vary from that of the control group. The difference between the group scores may then be explained in terms of the influence of the IV initially administered by the experimenter.

Here is a case in point. Eight grade-school children were selected to throw a ball as far as they could. The number of feet each child threw the ball were 11, 10, 8, 7, 5, 4, 2, and 1. It is apparent that all the scores are not the same. Some children threw the ball farther than others. Most people would say that's natural and let it go at that. Not the experimentalist; to him the differences between the scores represent the differential influence of variables in the situation. For each child there were genetic factors (e.g., size, weight, sex, age) and environmental factors (e.g., restrictive clothing, wind, gravity, weight of ball, physical conditioning) that were responsible for the distance the ball was thrown. The difference in distance the ball was thrown indicates to the experimentalist that the children were not all influenced by the same variables to the same degree. Different variables and/or the same variable having different values were influencing each child.

The experimentalist would then set out to get some measure of how much the children were differently influenced by variables related to the situation. He would seek some measure of the average amount of variation between the distance the ball was thrown, thereby getting some indication of how much variability there was in the factors that influenced the distances the ball was thrown. This would give an answer to the question of how much the genetic and environmental factors in the situation differentially influenced the children's behavior.

To get an idea of how much each score varied from every other score, the experimenter could subtract each score from every other score, as shown below.

$$
\begin{array}{llllllll}
11 - 10 = & 1 & & & & & & \\
11 - \ 8 = & 3 & 10 - 8 = & 2 & & & & \\
11 - \ 7 = & 4 & 10 - 7 = & 3 & 8 - 7 = & 1 & & \\
11 - \ 5 = & 6 & 10 - 5 = & 5 & 8 - 5 = & 3 & 7 - 5 = & 2 \\
11 - \ 4 = & 7 & 10 - 4 = & 6 & 8 - 4 = & 4 & 7 - 4 = & 3 & 5 - 4 = 1 \\
11 - \ 2 = & 9 & 10 - 2 = & 8 & 8 - 2 = & 6 & 7 - 2 = & 5 & 5 - 2 = 3 & 4 - 2 = 2 \\
11 - \ 1 = & 10 & 10 - 1 = & 9 & 8 - 1 = & 7 & 7 - 1 = & 6 & 5 - 1 = 4 & 4 - 1 = 3 & 2 - 1 = 1 \\
& \overline{40} & & \overline{33} & & \overline{21} & & \overline{16} & \ \ \overline{8} & \ \ \overline{5} & \ \ \overline{1}
\end{array}
$$

$$\Sigma(X_{ig} - X_{ij}) = 40 + 33 + 21 + 16 + 8 + 5 + 1 = 124$$

The sum total of these absolute differences could then be divided by the number of comparisons carried out to get an average of the amount each score differed from every other score.

$$\frac{\text{sum of differences}}{\text{number of differences}} = \frac{124}{28} = 4.43$$

After you total up the amount each score varies from every other score and divide that total by the number of scores, you have a measure representing the average amount of variation between a particular score and *all* other scores. The *average variation* is an informative statistic in that it is a measure of the dispersion of any set or group of scores that can be seen through simple mathematical arrangement. It tells us how much the scores differ from each other due to the differential influence of variables in the situation.

Another way of getting a measure of score variation may be more familiar to you. In this procedure you calculate a mean ($\bar{X}$) for the group, subtract the mean from each score ($x$), square the difference between the score and the mean ($x^2$), sum up these squared differences, and divide by the number of scores involved.[1]

$$\frac{\Sigma(X_{ig} - \bar{X}_G)^2}{N}.$$

This procedure is shown below using the children's scores.

| $X_{ig}$ | $\bar{X}_G$ | $x$ | $x^2$ |
|---|---|---|---|
| 11 | 6 | 5 | 25 |
| 10 | 6 | 4 | 16 |
| 8 | 6 | 2 | 4 |
| 7 | 6 | 1 | 1 |
| 5 | 6 | −1 | 1 |
| 4 | 6 | −2 | 4 |
| 2 | 6 | −4 | 16 |
| 1 | 6 | −5 | 25 |

$N = 8$  $x^2 = 92$

$$\frac{\Sigma(X_{ig} - \bar{X}_G)^2}{N} = \frac{(11 - 6)^2 + (10 - 6)^2 \ldots (1 - 6)^2}{8} = \frac{92}{8} = 11.5$$

The first variation measure obtained is called the average variation. The second variation measure is called variance.[2] Each in its own right is a measure of how much the scores varied from each other.

It can be seen then that variance is a measure of variation between all the scores. It indicates the degree to which subjects in any experiment were

---

1. $X_{ig}$ is a symbol standing for any score ($i$) in any group ($g$). If you wanted to be specific in a situation and specify the second score of the third group, the symbol would be $X_{23}$. $\bar{X}_G$ stands for the grand mean of all the scores in the experiment. In this case there is only one group; in later situations, the experiments will include many groups. The mean of a group within the experiment is symbolized as $\bar{X}_g$, while the mean of *all* the scores in the study is symbolized as $\bar{X}_G$. $\Sigma$ stand for the sum of, and $N$ is the total number of subjects in the experiment.

2. The common symbolic notation for variance is $s^2$.

differentially affected by factors present while the investigation was going on. Actually, so does the measure of average variation. The variance measure is preferred over average variation because it is quicker to compute, and you may also end up with a measure of central tendency (the mean). This second procedure also allows for certain statistical tests that cannot be carried out with the first approach.

### Division of Variation

A formula for total variance between scores could be written as follows:

$$V_T = V_W$$

Or, the total amount of variation ($V_T$) between the children's scores is equal to the variation ($V_W$) caused by all variables influencing the children. This is a redundant formula so far, since responsibility for the variation cannot be related to any particular variable. We cannot say to what extent any particular variable caused fluctuations in the distance the ball was thrown. This is analogous to the situation in which a detective runs into a room where a gun was fired only to find one dead body, a gun on the floor, and twenty-five people. All he may know for sure is that some person or persons in the room did the killing. He is unable to state empirically how much each person in the room was responsible for the crime.

The psychologist, like the detective, also likes to be able to assign variations in actions to the responsible variables. To do this, he looks over the situation to determine which variables may be causing a large portion of the variation. After deciding on a variable, he may then carry out an experiment to find out how much influence any particular variable (e.g., weight of the ball) had on the distance the ball was thrown. In doing so, he now modifies the formula to read:

$$V_T = V_S + V_W$$

The total variation ($V_T$) is due to the weight of the ball ($V_S$) plus all other secondary variables present ($V_W$). He has now divided $V_T$ into two parts, that due to the systematic manipulation of the IV (in this example, IV would be the weight of the ball) and that due to other variables not controlled for in the situation (see Figure 4–1). He has divided the variation into systematic ($V_S$) and within variation ($V_W$). Now he sets up an experiment in which the weight of the ball is the IV and records changes in the distance the ball is thrown. Before carrying out this experiment and demonstrating how this is done empirically, it may be advantageous to discuss the different types of variation in more detail.

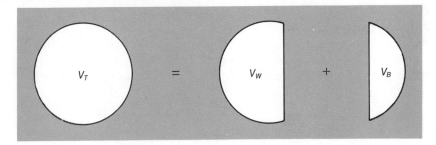

**FIGURE 4–1**
Division of variants in an experimental situation

## Systematic Variation

The role of a professional baseball pitcher is similar to that of an experimenter in that his job involves manipulating variables in an effort to influence other variables. Most of his time is spent refining his ability to cause variations in the flight path of the ball being pitched. He throws fast balls, curve balls, sliders, risers, drop balls, changeups, and knuckle balls. Each type of pitch is related to behavioral variations in his delivery. The better his ability to systematically vary his deliveries, the better his control of the fluctuation in the ball's flight path.

The objective of the pitcher, then, is to choose from alternative ways of delivering the ball and apply that chosen approach in an effort to influence the ball's behavior. In this situation, the delivery used in pitching the ball is the IV; the behavior of the ball is the DV. It may be said that the pitcher is specifically varying his pitching behavior to cause a systematic variation in the ball's behavior. Whenever someone manipulates some IV and a resultant change in the DV is noted, the amount of DV change actually due to manipulation of the IV is called the *primary* or *systematic* variation. Notice that systematic variation is defined as that change in DV *actually due* to the manipulation of the IV, not as *all* the variation in the DV following the administration of the IV. In every experimental situation, variables (frequently referred to as secondary variables) other than the IV (also called the primary variable) are influencing the DV. In the present example, secondary variables would include dirt on the ball, how scuffed the ball is, and changes in the wind while the ball is being thrown. All three of these variables can influence the flight of the ball. Though the pitcher's delivery will be the cause for most of the variations in the ball's behavior, it certainly will not be responsible for all changes in the DV.

In most experiments, two groups are selected. One group is called the experimental group (group E) and has the IV applied. The second group, called the control group (group C), is not given the IV. Any variation found in the DV between the experimental and control groups is due mainly to the systematic manipulation of the IV by the investigator. In this situation, the systematic variation is also called *between-groups variation*. Between-groups variation reflects the effect of the IV; therefore, we say the numerical value of the between-groups variation represents the difference due to the IV.

### Within Variation

As mentioned previously, any fluctuation of the DV in a controlled experiment is a function of the systematic variation of the primary variable, plus variations of the secondary variables involved in the experiment. The variation in a DV caused by variables other than the primary is termed *within variation*. Within variation is the amount of variation between scores due to variables "within" the experimental situation that have not been controlled for. Within variation may be divided into two parts, *secondary variation* and *error variation*. Secondary variation is the resultant fluctuation of secondary variables that could have been controlled by the experimenter but were not, because he did not know they were there, or he was unable to control for them, or he simply did not control for them. Variation in the distance the ball was thrown due to dirt on the ball or wind changes would be examples of secondary variation.

Error variation is a restricted category in which fluctuations in scores are due solely to chance. These are generally small, unsystematic changes in variables that occur in willy-nilly fashion, and over which the investigator has no control. They are the reason no two situations are ever exactly the same.

It is important to note that in experimental situations the exact amount of within variation that is due to error variation cannot be identified and separated from the variation due to secondary variables that could possibly be controlled. For this reason, error variation and secondary variation are jointly represented by $V_W$ in the variance formula. However, keep in mind that it is possible to reduce the effect of secondary variables and thereby decrease $V_W$.

One of the main jobs of an experimenter is to decrease within variation. Because within variation is the result of the influence of variables that were not controlled by the experimenter, it is undesirable. The main objective of any investigation, as you recall, is to demonstrate that manipulations of the IV cause the change in the DV. We can never technically prove some variable caused a fluctuation in some other variable, but we can manipulate the IV and show some high or low correlated change in the DV, and decrease the possibility that any other variable could have caused the change in the DV. Decreasing the influence of secondary variables automatically decreases within variation.

There are three reasons why an experimenter wants to decrease within variation in his project. First, secondary variables responsible for the within variation may interact with the IV in such a way that the change in the DV is not an accurate representation of what influence the IV would have on the DV by itself. To illustrate, a comedian may try out a new joke at a private party before telling it on television. He tells the joke (the IV) to see if people will laugh (the DV). After telling it at the party and receiving much laughter, he tells it to a live TV audience and receives little laughter. In trying to figure out why the TV audience and the party guests "varied" in their amount of laughing, he realizes there was another variable in the situation that he forgot to take into consideration. The people at the party were fairly well inebriated when he told the joke, so their reception of the joke was strongly influenced by a secondary variable. Often, failure to control the effects of secondary variables leads to incorrect conclusions regarding cause and effect relationships. Second, the effect of the IV on the DV may become more apparent by decreasing within variation. The situation is analogous to seeing the effect of a rock on a lake. The waves (the DV) caused by the rock (the IV) will be more apparent if the wind (a secondary variable) is not making the lake's surface choppy. Removing the secondary variable (wind) makes the lake smoother, so the effect of the IV is more visable. Third, decreasing within variation increases the possibility of demonstrating a cause and effect relationship. These last two points will become more apparent later.

### Division of Variance
### in an Experimental Situation

Now that total variation has been divided into systematic and within variation, let us look at an experimental situation that includes both. We will take the ball-throwing example and turn it into an experiment. An investigator wants to know if the weight of a ball will influence the distance a ball can be thrown. He randomly selects 8 children from a particular grade school and randomly assigns each child to either group C or group D as shown below.

| Group C | Group D |
|---------|---------|
| 11 | 5 |
| 10 | 4 |
| 8 | 2 |
| 7 | 1 |

Group C is given a ball weighing 10 ounces, group D, a ball weighing 16 ounces. Each child makes one throw. The results are presented here.

| $X_C$ | $\bar{X}_C$ | $x$ | $x^2$ | $X_D$ | $\bar{X}_D$ | $x$ | $x^2$ |
|---|---|---|---|---|---|---|---|
| 11 | 9 | 2 | 4 | 5 | 3 | 2 | 4 |
| 10 | 9 | 1 | 1 | 4 | 3 | 1 | 1 |
| 8 | 9 | −1 | 1 | 2 | 3 | −1 | 1 |
| 7 | 9 | −2 | 4 | 1 | 3 | −2 | 4 |

$\Sigma X_C = 36$  $\qquad\qquad$  $\Sigma X_D = 12$

$\bar{X}_C = \dfrac{\Sigma X_C}{n} = \dfrac{36}{4} = 9$  $\qquad$  $\bar{X}_D = \dfrac{\Sigma X_D}{n} = \dfrac{12}{4} = 3$

$\Sigma X_C^2 = 10.00$  $\qquad\qquad$  $\Sigma X_D^2 = 10.00$

$V_C = S_C^2 = \dfrac{10.00}{4} = 2.50$  $\qquad$  $V_D = S_D^2 = \dfrac{10.00}{4} = 2.50$

Now that we have calculated the means and variances for each group, let us restate the formula and find the appropriate data to fill in.[3]

$$V_T = V_S + V_W \quad \text{or} \quad V_T = V_B + V_W$$

The total variation ($V_T$) of any particular score from all other scores is equal to variation caused by the IV ($V_B$), plus within variation ($V_W$). $V_B$ was said to be the result of the IV, so the between-group variance can be calculated as follows:

| $X_g$ | $\bar{X}_G$ | $x$ | $x^2$ |
|---|---|---|---|
| 9 | 6 | 3 | 9 |
| 3 | 6 | −3 | 9 |

$\bar{X}_G = \dfrac{\Sigma \bar{X}_g}{n} = \dfrac{9 + 3}{2} = 6$

$V_B = S_B^2 = \dfrac{\Sigma(\bar{X}_g - \bar{X}_G)^2}{n} = \dfrac{18}{2} = 9$

The formula $V_T = V_B + V_W$ so far should read $11.50 = 9 + V_W$.

The question now becomes, "Where do we find a measure for $V_W$?" The answer to that question is to look at each of the two groups individually. Every subject in group C was treated exactly the same, yet the individual scores vary. This is called *within-group variation* ($V_W$). If the experimenter has done all he can to control the influence of secondary variables in the experiment, the within-group variation ($V_W$) should be the result of random variable fluctuations plus variation due to any uncontrolled secondary variables. It

---

3. Note that $V_S = V_B$. The second formula is given because the term $V_B$ (between-group variance) rather than $V_S$ is generally used in statistical formulas. $V_B$ will be used instead of $V_S$ throughout the remainder of the text.

does not include the variation due to the IV, for the effect of the IV was held constant for all subjects in a group. The within-group variance, then, is equal to $V_T - V_B$, which is equal to $V_W$. Notice that the $V_C$ and the $V_D$ calculated in the previous set of calculations equals $V_W$. They should, because the numbers obtained represent the variation between the scores within a group of subjects who all received the same amount of IV. Therefore, any differences between those subjects' scores would be due to uncontrolled secondary variables and random fluctuation. The formula now becomes

$$V_T = V_B + V_W \quad \text{or} \quad 11.50 = 9 + 2.50$$

Now that the amount of variance between the groups is known, the next step is to determine whether the variance between the groups [variance due to the IV $(V_B)$][4] is larger than the within-group variance [variation due to random fluctuations of uncontrolled secondary variables $(V_W)$]. If the between-group variance is equal to the within-group variance, then we can say the weight of the ball had no effect, for the amount of variation between the groups would be equal to the amount of variation between any two scores in which the IV was not varied. To determine whether the IV had an effect, the variance between the groups is divided by the within-group variance.[5] In this particular case, the ratio would be equal to 3.60:

$$\frac{V_B}{V_W} = \frac{9}{2.50} = 3.60$$

What we have just calculated is commonly referred to as the F ratio. We then look up 3.60 in the F table at the end of the book. The table will tell what the possibility is of obtaining this size F ratio by chance alone. Just as fluctuations in variables may influence the DV randomly, so it is possible to obtain an F ratio larger than 1. The more the F ratio differs from 1, the less likely the obtained ratio is due to chance. Generally speaking, an investigator will consider the IV to have influenced the DV if the possibility of obtaining the F ratio he ends up with could have occurred by chance 5 percent of the time or less. Sometimes researchers prefer the cutoff line to be a 1 percent possibility by chance.

4. Remember that the variation between the groups was said to be due not only to IV but also to the uncontrolled fluctuation of secondary variables. The variation between scores within a group reflects random or uncontrolled variation occurring between one score and the next. The difference between the two means from which the between-group variance was calculated also is due in part to these random variations, for they are nothing more than two scores themselves.

5. Note that the within-group variance for both groups is equal. The groups should be equal on all variables except for the IV and any chance variations. In some cases, the within-group variance of one group is a bit different from that of the second, so the general procedure for calculating within-group variance is to add the variance of both groups, then divide by 2.

Now that our illustration is complete, let us summarize what was involved. First, the investigator analyzes a situation to choose a particular variable, about which he then makes a hypothesis. Second, he selects the operationally defined IV with which he plans to bring about between-group variation in terms of some operationally defined DV. Third, he sets about controlling important secondary variance so that between-group variation can be attributed to the IV. This step also includes making sure that the within-group variation is due mainly to random fluctuations in variables so it can be used as a measure of error variance. Fourth, the IV is applied and the DV variations are recorded. Fifth, some measure of between-group variance and error variance is obtained. With these data the probability of the between-group variance being caused by chance is calculated. Sixth, a statement is made regarding a causal relationship between the IV and DV. If the size of the between-group variance could have occurred by chance less than 5 percent of the time, then the IV is said to have influenced the DV.

What has just been covered is the basic plan for almost every experiment the student will ever encounter. The investigator causes variation by systematically manipulating the IV he wants to evaluate. From his data he calculates the amount of between-group variation and that due to chance. He then divides the variance found between his comparison groups by error variation to find out if the IV had an effect. No matter whether he carries out a t test, a one-way analysis of variance, a two-way analysis of variance, or analysis of covariance, the principle behind the analysis is basically the same.[6] The following chapters will deal with alternative experimental designs. Take special care to notice the way the statistical analysis is carried out in succeeding chapters. You will realize that all are dealing with the same comparison (between-group variation versus within-group variation), although the statistical formulas appear to be quite different. Once the student visualizes the similarities between the procedures, the analysis of variance, no matter what type is used, will not seem so awesome and incomprehensible.

## METHODS OF CONTROLLING SECONDARY VARIANCE

In addition to the IV and DV, which are the main concern of any investigator, all experimental situations include other variables that can influence the DV. These variables are often called nuisance variables, side variables, relevant variables, irrelevant variables, and secondary variables.

---

6. All these statistical tests were probably presented in the statistics course generally required of the student before he enrolls in the experimental course. Do not be alarmed if you do not recall how to carry these out. They will be presented and compared later on in the text.

In this book, all variables in an experimental situation other than the IV and DV have been termed secondary variables, with no distinction being made as to whether the secondary variables have a great or relatively little potential effect on the DV.[7] Secondary variables are undesirable sources of variation in an experimental situation that could influence the DV. Though these variables are of secondary importance to the investigator, their potential influence on the DV must be controlled in order for an accurate relationship between the IV and the DV to appear. An important step in any experimental procedure is controlling for potential sources of variation in the DV due to secondary variables. There are five basic procedures for controlling within variation:

1. Remove secondary variables from the experimental situation altogether
2. Hold the effects of secondary variables constant for all groups
3. Make the secondary variables IVs
4. Randomize the subjects and procedures being used
5. Control secondary variables by means of statistical adjustment

Each procedure has its advantages and disadvantages. The remainder of this section will deal with defining the control procedures in detail and indicating the value and limitations of each. In some instances this will include ranking them on effectiveness along certain dimensions. Keep in mind that although it may be true that one control procedure is superior in one situation, it may not be superior in another.[8]

### Elimination

One of the most straightforward methods of decreasing $V_W$ is to remove secondary variables completely from the experimental situation. Since the $V_W$ is the composite effect of all secondary variables, removing any secondary variables from having any possible influence in the experimental situation will automatically decrease the $V_W$. The amount the $V_W$ is decreased depends on how influential the removed secondary variable could have been. A few years ago I was involved in a research project in which pigeons were conditioned to peck a key in total darkness. As the experiment progressed, it was noted that even faint sources of light infiltrating the test chamber seriously

---

7. Some texts label as secondary variables those that may have a large influence on the DV, whereas extraneous variables are those in the experimental situation that have little if any actual influence on the DV. Sometimes the terms *relevant* and *irrelevant* variable are used to make the same distinction.

8. For example, eliminating secondary variables is generally better than controlling them by holding them constant. One exception to this statement would be when the cost of eliminating a variable (e.g., paying $10,000 to soundproof a room) may be more than it is worth.

affected the pigeons' behavior. To eliminate this secondary variable, the test chamber itself was placed in a totally dark room. This resulted in a 40 percent reduction in what was initially thought to be random fluctuation in the birds' pecking. Faint amounts of light allowed in the chambers with pigeons being run with a houselight on have little, if any, observable effect on the birds. It is easy to conclude from this that eliminating the same variable in one situation may not have an equal effect on the $V_W$ in another situation.

Controlled laboratory experiments are better able to employ this type of control on secondary variation than is any other type of investigation. The laboratory situation is often chosen to carry out an investigation mainly because of the ability to eliminate secondary variables. One of the major sources of $V_W$ in scientific investigations is unexpected secondary variables: researchers frequently start their investigation only to find as it progresses that there are important secondary variables in their study which should have been eliminated. Undergraduate students in an experimental psychology course and graduate students carrying out field research are particularly afflicted with this problem. Wise student and professional researchers prefer laboratory situations over field situations where a choice between the two is possible. They realize that by simply moving their study into the laboratory most secondary variables are automatically left outside, and the possibility of being surprised by some secondary variable as the investigation progresses is greatly reduced.

### Constancy

In many experimental situations, important secondary variables (e.g., time, gravity, body orientation, temperature, atmosphere) simply cannot be eliminated, while others (e.g., color, intelligence, shape, sound) may be so difficult to eliminate that it is considered impossible to do so. Since they may influence the amount of variation in the DV, the investigator must find some alternative way of controlling them. One possibility is holding them constant. Suppose you want to try a new abstract method of teaching math to grade-school children. You select two groups of children, one of which will use the standard method. Knowing that IQ is an important influence on the ability to learn, you want to make sure each group is equivalent in IQ. To do this, all the subjects selected for the study are ranked on IQ before being assigned group A or B, as shown in Table 4–1.

Going down the ranking, the first subject is assigned to group A, the second to group B, the third to group A, and so on, until all 20 subjects have been assigned.[9] The experiment could then be carried out with more confidence that the difference in the DV between the two groups was not due to IQ.

---

9. There are other ways of matching the group on IQ than the one shown that would be a little more equitable.

**TABLE 4–1**
*Illustration of matching groups on a secondary variable (IQ)*

| IQ (ranked from highest to lowest) | | Group A | Group B |
|---|---|---|---|
| 128 | 103 | 128 | 127 |
| 127 | 101 | 121 | 120 |
| 121 | 100 | 118 | 113 |
| 120 | 100 | 108 | 107 |
| 118 | 97 | 106 | 106 |
| 113 | 97 | 103 | 101 |
| 108 | 93 | 100 | 100 |
| 107 | 92 | 97 | 97 |
| 106 | 87 | 93 | 92 |
| 106 | 86 | 87 | 86 |

The terms *matching* and *blocking* when used in experimentation refer to holding a secondary variable constant by equating it among the groups.

Notice that the procedure of equating the two groups does not actually remove the effects of IQ from the investigation, it simply distributes it equally between the two groups so that the difference in the DV between the groups does not include IQ effects. The procedure of elimination, on the other hand, completely removes the effect of a variable from the experiment. Elimination has the effect of accentuating $V_B$ by decreasing $V_W$. Normally, elimination is preferred to holding variables constant.

### Making the Secondary Variable an Independent Variable

If a secondary variable cannot be eliminated, it can be made an IV. By making a relevant secondary variable an IV, the formula for total variation becomes

$$V_T = V_{B1} + V_{B2} + V_W$$

The total variation in the DV ($V_T$) is equal to the variation caused by the initial IV you selected ($V_{B1}$), plus the variation of the secondary variable converted into an IV ($V_{B2}$), plus the variation due to all other secondary variables ($V_W$) in the experiment. A good question to ask is "Where did $V_{B2}$ come from?" Is it variation introduced into the experiment that would normally not be there, or did it come from $V_{B1}$ or $V_W$? To answer this question, let us look at an example.

Harry Straightarrow is interested in carrying out an experiment dealing with the effects of alcohol on typing speed. He goes to a typing class at the university and asks for 20 volunteers willing to consume alcoholic beverages and willing to show up Saturday at 1 P.M. to participate in a typing experiment. One evening after designing the experiment he sits down and analyzes his experiment. It looks like the typical formula for an experiment with one IV. The systematic variation ($V_B$) in this experiment will be the effect of alcohol.

$$V_T = V_B + V_W$$

At noon on Saturday, Harry is busily working to get the typewriters set up when another student comes in and asks Harry what he plans to do. After listening to Harry's experimental plans, the other student notices that 10 typewriters are brand X (electric), and 10 typewriters are brand Y (manual). He then comments that the different kinds of typewriters might influence the number of correct words per minute a person can type. He suggests Harry control this secondary variable. Harry agrees, so he decides to divide the typewriters equally by brand between the alcohol and non-alcohol groups, thereby equating the effects of typewriter differences. The other student says, "That's a fine idea, but why don't you revamp your study to include the brand of typewriter as an independent variable? This could be done with little trouble, and you would not only find out the effects of alcohol, but also quantify the effects of typewriter differences." Harry takes the advice and changes the design of his experiment. Harry's design before and after his decision to make typewriter brand an IV is shown in Table 4–2.

**TABLE 4–2**
*Conversion of a two-group design into a four-group design*

| | Before | | | | After | |
|---|---|---|---|---|---|---|
| | *Group A* (*no alcohol*) | *Group B* (*alcohol*) | | | *Group A* (*no alcohol*) | *Group B* (*alcohol*) |
| Typewriter Brand Y / Brand X | | | $\bar{X}_X$ | | 5 subjects $\bar{X}_{a_1}$ | 5 subjects $\bar{X}_{b_1}$ |
| | 10 subjects | 10 subjects | $\bar{X}_Y$ | | 5 subjects $\bar{X}_{a_2}$ | 5 subjects $\bar{X}_{b_2}$ |
| | $\bar{X}_a$ | $\bar{X}_b$ | | | $\bar{X}_A$ | $\bar{X}_B$ |

Originally, Harry would have obtained two means, $\bar{X}_a$ and $\bar{X}_b$. The means would represent the difference between subjects having alcohol and those not. If he had made sure each group had an equal number of typewriters of each brand, he would not be able to tell what effect the difference in typewriters made. In his after design he is carrying out the experiment exactly as before, except that he is keeping track of which typewriter is given to each subject. He then can calculate a mean for each of the five subjects who are experiencing the same alcohol and typewriter condition. To determine the effects of alcohol he can still contrast the mean of group A ($\bar{X}_A$) with the mean of group B ($\bar{X}_B$). To determine the difference caused by typewriter brand, the mean of the ten subjects using each typewriter could be compared ($\bar{X}_X$ versus $\bar{X}_Y$). Just by dividing his original 10-subject groups into groups of 5, Harry is able to calculate the influence of a secondary variable.

With a secondary variable now a second IV, the variation formula reads

$$V_T = V_A + V_B + V_W$$

Total variation in typing speed equals the influence ($V_A$) of alcohol plus the influence of the typewriter, plus the influence of all other secondary variables. In Harry's first design, the difference due to the typewriter brands would have been lumped in $V_W$ with all the other secondary variables.

Making a secondary variable an IV serves two functions. First, it decreases the size of $V_W$; and second, it adds more to our scientific knowledge than the other two control procedures do. It tells us how much of the DV fluctuation is caused by the secondary variable that is controlled. It should be apparent that making a secondary variable an IV is preferable to eliminating it or holding it constant.

### Randomization

Let us return to the example of demonstrating the effectiveness of an abstract method of teaching math. In that situation IQ was felt to be an influential secondary variable, so it was controlled by equating the control and experimental groups with respect to IQ. In this way, the effect of IQ was held constant. What would we have done if IQ scores were not available? How could we have controlled for this important secondary variable? *Randomization* is a procedure for controlling secondary variables by equating the control and experimental groups when no data are available for matching the groups on the particular variable. If the IQs were not available, the groups could have been equated on IQ by putting all the subjects' names in a hat, mixing them up, drawing them out one by one, and assigning every odd draw to group A and every even draw to group B. With this procedure each subject would have equal chance of being assigned to either of the groups. One of the theoretical principles underlying the concept of randomization states that if subjects are randomly assigned to two or more groups, there is a high probability that all groups will be equated in terms of any secondary variable or variables that all the subjects have in common. As an example, suppose we were going to randomly divide 900 people, 50 percent of whom were females, into 10 different groups. Each group would probably end up being equated in terms of the ratio of men and women. Using randomization, the same 900 people made up of 300 caucasians, 300 blacks, and 300

Indians would end up equally proportioned in the 10 groups. Each of the 10 groups would most probably consist of 30 caucasians, 30 blacks, and 30 Indians (each having 50 percent women).

Randomization, then, is a procedure for equating groups with respect to secondary variables. It does not guarantee that all groups are equal, but groups in which subjects were assigned randomly have a greater probability of being equated than groups in which subjects were not assigned randomly. Another theoretical principle of randomization is "The more subjects randomly assigned to groups, the higher the probability that the groups will be equated." In the previous example, 900 people were randomly assigned to 10 groups. There is a much greater probability that the 10 groups will be equated in this situation than in a situation in which only 30 people were to be divided into 10 groups.

Although eliminating a variable, holding it constant, or making it an IV are preferred methods of controlling a known secondary variable, randomization, with its equating effects through random assignment of subjects to groups, is considered to be the overall best tool for controlling many sources of secondary variation at one time. Randomization can equate groups for all secondary variables at the same time, including those not apparent even to the investigator while the investigation is in progress.

If we were to rank-order the control procedures covered so far in terms of effectiveness in controlling secondary variables, the order would be as follows: If you know of any secondary variable that may have a large effect on the DV, first try to make it an IV. If that is not feasible, eliminate it from the experiment. If that is not feasible, hold it constant. After applying the first three control procedures where possible, randomize the assignment of subjects to the groups involved in the experiment.

### Statistical Control

The preceding four types of control to reduce variability caused by secondary variables are generally classified as *experimental* control procedures. An alternative approach to reducing within variation involves the use of a *statistical* control procedure. With this approach, no attempt is made to limit the influence of secondary variables; the procedure involves measuring one or more concomitant secondary variables (covariants) in addition to recording the DV. These concomitant secondary variables are potential sources of within variation that have not been controlled in the experiment. Through an analysis of covariance, the DV can be statistically adjusted to remove the effects of the uncontrolled sources of variation due to the concomitant secondary variables. Analysis of covariance is simply a statistical procedure involving the combined application of correlational analysis and analysis of variance. Changes in concomitant secondary variables are correlated with changes in the DV. The amount of variation in the DV ($V_T$) is then adjusted to remove the possible amount of variation in DV due to the variation in the concomitant secondary variable(s).

A better understanding of statistical control may come with an illustration of the use of the analysis of covariance in a situation involving one concomitant secondary variable. Suppose you wanted to compare two methods of teaching math to third-grade students in a school district made up of only two rural grade schools, each in a different town 50 miles apart. It would be impractical to randomly assign students from the towns to one or the other grade school.[10] It is also probable that the two third-grade classes would not be equated in terms of intelligence, an important secondary variable. If differences in learning ability or similar characteristics exist between the two third-grade classes prior to the administration of the two teaching methods, these secondary variables would bias the evaluation. Using statistical control, intelligence could be controlled by making it a concomitant variable. An intelligence test could be given to each student, and any difference in the DV between the two classes could be correlated with any difference in IQ. The DV would then be readjusted to take into consideration the effect of IQ differences on the DV.

Numerically, the use of statistical control goes like this: For class A, the mean IQ is 100 and the mean of the math exam (the DV) is 80; for class B, the mean IQ is 90 and the mean of the math exam (the DV) is 60. The statistically adjusted mean for class A is $9/10 \times 80 = 72$. Using the math exam scores to compare the effectiveness of the two teaching methods, class A averaged 80, while class B averaged 60. The average IQ for class B was only 9/10 that of class A. The mean of class A is readjusted ($9/10 \times 80 = 72$).

|  | Class A | Class B |
|---|---|---|
| Mean IQ | 100 | 90 |
| Mean score on math exam (DV) | 80 | 60 |

Statistically adjusted mean of class A:
$$\frac{90}{100} \times 80 = 72$$

The comparison of 72 and 60 is a measure of the difference actually due to the teaching methods, rather than a comparison of 80 and 60.[11]

10. There is another alternative. We could try each technique in both classrooms by randomly dividing the students in each class into two different groups, then applying each method to one of the groups.

11. The way the adjustment was calculated here is not statistically correct. It is actually much more complicated, but the principle is basically the same as shown. This example is simply to give the reader a general idea of how it is done.

The exact statistical manipulations required to do this will be covered in a later chapter; here it is sufficient for the student to realize only that statistical control is possible and is one of the procedures for controlling within variation. It differs from the other four control procedures in that $V_W$ is not reduced by actually manipulating secondary variables, but by statistically adjusting for them.

There are two types of situations in which a statistical control procedure may have to be employed. One is when subjects cannot be matched or assigned at random to the different experimental groups (field experiments in psychology, sociology, and education are frequently faced with this situation). The other is when groups in an ongoing experiment are found to differ with respect to some secondary variable not taken into consideration prior to the start of the investigation. As an illustration, an experiment may be carried out to determine the effects of alcohol on ability to recall previously learned lists of nonsense syllables. Initially, subjects are randomly assigned to one of two groups, and each group is required to memorize the same list of nonsense syllables. If the two groups require different amounts of training to be able to recite all 20 syllables with no errors, it is possible that differences in learning abilities between the two groups exist. The investigator may feel that the amount of time it takes to learn the list will influence the ability to recall the list later. He then makes the amount of time it took to learn the list a covariate (concomitant secondary variable) and employs an analysis of covariance to control the experimentally uncontrolled secondary variable. Analysis of covariance, then, allows the experimenter to control secondary variables whose influence may not appear until after the experiment has begun.

## SOURCES OF SECONDARY VARIATION

After defining secondary variation and alternative ways of controlling it, the next step is to identify the general sources from which it may appear. To present these sources adequately, the concept of *validity* needs to be introduced. Validity is an attribute possessed by all evaluation measures which relates to the ability that measure has to make a prediction regarding some event. Aptitude tests are good examples. A psychologist may administer a test of mental ability in order to better counsel a student on the vocation he selects. The better the test can predict which vocation would be best for those taking it, the more valid the test. Measures must have a certain degree of relevance to the point of interest being studied. The measure of a boy's quickness would be a more valid measure of his ability at sports than a measure of his degree of skin pigmentation.

Scientific investigations also involve validity. When carrying out a research project, the investigator is attempting to isolate and identify some relationships, usually between an IV and a DV. The more effective an investigation is in identifying a true relationship, the more valid the investigation. To increase validity, the psychologist carefully controls secondary variables. The more secondary variation that slips unnoticed into an investigation situation, the greater the possibility that the IV was not responsible for DV changes. Secondary variation may influence the situation to such an extent that an incorrect conclusion is drawn, or the investigator, realizing the results obtained would be erroneous, discontinues the investigation. In both cases the investigation is said to be invalid.

Experimenters generally divide validity problems into two categories, *internal* validity and *external* validity. Internal validity is concerned with making certain that the IV manipulated was responsible for the variation in DV so that a correct causal relationship can be stated. External validity is concerned with generality. An investigator is not usually satisfied to demonstrate the IV influence on the particular subjects used in his investigation; he also wants to be able to state that this IV will affect similar subjects in similar situations. External validity is therefore important to the investigator in generalizing the results obtained to other situations and persons.

### Internal Validity

Nine major sources of secondary variation can produce internal invalidity in an investigation: proactive history, retroactive history, maturation, testing, statistical regression, experimental mortality, interaction effects, instrumentation, and experimenter bias. The first seven may be controlled by selecting the appropriate experimental design. The ability of different experimental designs to control for these seven different sources of secondary variation is one of the many reasons the use of experimental designs is considered such a basic issue in experimentation. The last two are only controlled for by the diligence of the experimenter as the investigation progresses.

**Proactive history.**    Proactive history refers to those learned and inherent differences subjects bring with them into the investigation. Sex, height, weight, color, attitude, personality, motor ability, and mental ability are all examples of variables on which subjects may differ. If the control and experimental groups differ on some variable, the difference in the DV measure between the two groups may be partly due to that unaccounted-for secondary variable. The validity of the investigation is then reduced. As an example, suppose you built two canoes that differed in design. To determine which is the best for running rapids in a river, you select two sixth-grade girls to paddle one and two sixth-grade boys to paddle the other. Both paddle down the same stretch of river. The boys and their canoe complete the course in half the time the girls and their canoe did. Should it be concluded that one canoe was better than the other? Obviously not, for the subjects differed in terms of some proactive history variables (sex, size, motor ability, etc.) that could easily have influenced the DV measure. This would not be considered a valid investigation.

Proactive history is possibly the most important potential source of invalidity for two reasons. First, it represents more secondary variables than any of the other eight sources. More possibilities for within variance can show up here than in any other source. Second, it is relevant for all investigations, whereas others may be relevant only in certain investigations. For example, testing would be of concern only in research where the subjects are given pretests. All nine sources of invalidity are not equally influential in each situation. To illustrate, sex differences may be an important secondary variable in an investigation analyzing women's lib, whereas it is relatively unimportant in studies dealing with intellectual potential. The most common way of controlling for proactive history is randomization, although constancy and elimination are also frequently used.

**Retroactive history.** Retroactive history refers to those changes in events and influences encountered in the course of the experiment or between a first and second testing time. As an example, if one were studying college students' political attitudes and two weeks into the study three campus radicals were unaccountably killed by police, obviously the subjects' attitudes would undergo some change and possibly render the original study internally invalid. Of the five previously mentioned control procedures, constancy and elimination are those generally used to control retroactive history. Certain experimental designs are also effective in controlling this source of invalidity. Retroactive history is especially liable to be encountered in a study using a lengthy time interval.

**Maturation.** Maturation, commonly defined as systematic changes in the organism over a length of time primarily due to a biological and/or psychological growth or change, is mostly influential in lengthy studies, much like retroactive history. Let us take a look at a commonly employed, though invalid, situation (invalid because no control was used to compensate for the maturation factor). A five-year-old child is chosen and pretested for motor coordination control in manipulating blocks. A tutor then instructs him in various exercises according to a new, scientifically based method. After one year he is again tested and it is found that his score has improved. It is obvious that in this particular case changes caused by experience and maturation were not adequately controlled. Could the child have progressed to a similar degree if he had not been enrolled in the tutor's class? Without a control procedure, maturation may be as valid a reason for the changes as the new method. None of the control procedures covered are usually used to guard against this source of invalidity; maturation effects are generally controlled for by experimental designs that include a control group. Effects due to maturation will then show up in both groups, so that change between groups will not be due to maturation.

**Testing.**   Psychologists often administer pretests to subjects before the IV is applied in an attempt to carry out a before and after comparison. In some cases, however, the pretest may cause the subjects to score differently in the posttest than they would have if no pretest had been given. When an individual is administered an intelligence test or a similar test the second time, it is well known that there is a high probability his second score will be higher than the initial score. In such a situation testing may be a source of internal invalidity and influence the DV measure when the test is administered the second time around. Though the second scores may be higher, it is improbable that subjects increased in IQ significantly over the period of time. Therefore, when the same or similar test is administered a second time without controls, the higher scores must be attributable or partly attributable to the repeated testing.

Pretests may also "sensitize" the subjects to the IV being given. Suppose you were carrying out an investigation to determine how attitudes toward violence change due to violent movies. Prior to having subjects watch a violent movie, you have them fill out a questionnaire dealing with attitudes on violence. This pretest may strongly bias what the subjects selectively attend to in the movie; any changes found in the before and after attitudes would not be a correct representation of the effect of the movie alone. Testing scores of invalidity are generally controlled for by using an experimental design that includes a non-pretested control group. The Solomon four-group design, to be covered in Chapter Eight, is a popular design because of its ability to control for testing effects.

**Statistical regression.**   In carrying out an investigation, the experimenter needs to consider yet another important characteristic of testing. A fundamental law of statistics is that in repeated testing both extremely high and extremely low numbers in the range of numbers will tend to be pulled toward a mean as the testing is repeated. Figure 4–2 represents a frequency distribu-

**FIGURE 4–2**

Frequency distribution of IQ test scores from a pretest measure

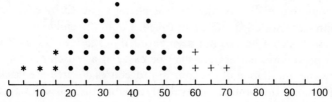

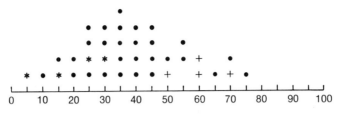

**FIGURE 4–3**

Posttest frequency distribution of IQ test scores demonstrating statistical regression

tion of scores on a particular IQ test. Each dot represents a subject's score; * represents the lowest scores; and + represents the highest scores. If a retest were given immediately following the first, the distribution could change to the one shown in Figure 4–3. The retest scores of those subjects receiving the lowest and highest scores on the first test would be closer to the mean, although the ability of the subjects had not been modified by any external variables. In other words, subjects scoring high or low on a test will tend to score closer to a mean on a successive test. This tendency of migration of scores toward the mean is termed *statistical regression*.

Psychological researchers often deal with extreme cases for investigation. One frequent situation is the selection of subjects because of their extreme scores on some psychological test. An IV is then commonly administered in an effort to influence this extreme score. School districts many times isolate gifted and poor students with the intention of improving learning capabilities with the use of a new teaching method. At the end of the study, a common finding is that the poorer students, after much testing, improved their grades by several points, whereas the gifted children tended to level off and come down slightly in their scores with respect to the main body of the children. To control for this tendency, the investigator could divide the extreme groups into their own comparison groups, control and experimental, and observe resulting differences between them. The method would then be the only contributing change.

**Experimental mortality.** Loss of subject by death, accident, or simple discontinued performance during experimentation obviously can and will affect comparisons between groups. The loss of subjects may invalidate one's whole experiment. Where analysis of results is still possible, it becomes more difficult than usual because of statistical adjustments which have to be made.

**Interaction effects.** Many investigations comparing two different elements or conditions will be limited in the sensitivity and validity of the method, depending on the order of testing. This order of testing or position in the sequence of effects is important when considering the interaction of those elements or conditions with one another. If an effect is experienced relating to the order of testing (e.g., going from drug A to drug B as opposed to going from drug B to drug A), variability of the results is greatly increased. Knowing there is a possible chemical reaction between two drugs, how would one examine the effects of the two drugs, A and B, in a single subject and control for possible interaction effects? A commonly employed procedure is the use of counterbalance design, in which subject 1 receives first drug A, then drug B, and then drug A. Reactions to the drugs are observed after each administration of the drug. Subject 2 is administered drug B, then drug A, and again drug B. Sequence of the drugs is thereby controlled, for a more accurate picture of the exact effects of each drug is obtained. Often interaction effects may be found when using a factorial design. Statistical calculations and certain experimental designs may be used for controlling for interaction. It should be apparent that interaction effects are not potential sources of invalidity if the investigation involves only one IV.

**Instrumentation.**   In the use of vast and varied amounts of equipment, one may readily observe slight physical changes and impairments that are accrued from day to day use. Not only does wear on equipment impair measurement, but the initial quality and calibration of the instrument is a measure that also affects results. A micrometer, for example, will measure distances much more precisely than a 12-inch ruler.

In measurement of social research studies, the instrument is the observer or interviewer. A natural change will occur as his skill in noting pertinent and more complete information is increased. For example, an observation is made of children in a second-grade class and the number of their interpersonal interactions is noted. As the observers spend more time with the children, their skill in noting interactions will naturally increase, as will the validity of their observations. As the situation and techniques become more familiar, the ease and accuracy of the observations also increase. Instrumentation need not be complicated equipment; it can also be the interview or questioning manner used by the interviewer. Instrumentation can also refer to the questions on the test as well as to the pencil and paper used by the subject. Changes in instrumentation may be a source of invalidity, especially if the experimenter acts as a recorder of "observed" data. Instrumentation is a function of the experimenter, not of the design used, and therefore cannot be controlled for by using a specific type of design.

**Experimenter bias.**   More recently, concern has grown over the total effect of experimenter bias on an experimental situation. Rosenthal [1966] demonstrated that the experimenter's expectations of an outcome may significantly influence gathered data. Many times a teacher will be "tipped off" by a colleague or informed by a highly popular IQ test that a student in question is "dumb" and unable to learn as fast as the class. Then, true to the teacher's expectations, the child "follows" the recognized characteristics of the "dumb." Actually, recent studies have found that teacher expectations preclude and dictate his actions toward the student. These actions in turn elicit the "expected" reaction from the student and the student is thereby classified and labeled. Such is the case in many an experimental setting. It is well known that though it may be unconscious and unintended, the expectations of an investigator may appreciably affect the collected data.

To control for this bias effect, a *double blind* control situation is often employed. In a double blind control procedure, the experimenter is not familiar with which subjects experience the intended IV and which do not. Thus, neither subject nor experimenter expectation can enter into the data outcome. In drug studies the double blind procedure is done through the use of coded but otherwise unidentified drugs and by the use of placebos (harmless materials labeled as real drugs).

As we have previously mentioned, both experimenter bias and instrumentation are functions of the experimenter and not of any specific experimental design he may use. The experimenter must control for these sources of internal invalidity by physically holding them constant.

### External Validity

We must be concerned not only with internal validity relating to the experiment but also with external validity. By *external* validity we mean how valid the results are when placed outside the experimental setting. Can we generalize from the experiment to real-life situations? The experimenter is interested in relating his findings with laboratory rat experiments not just to other rats, but to people in everyday situations as well.

It is important to realize that the more widely applicable the findings, the greater the importance of the finding. Mendel in his experiment provided us with the insight into the genetic development of the sweet pea. If his findings had ended there, it is doubtful he would hold the position he does in science. His findings, however, had a wide range of application—to plants, animals, and the human species.

In examining our ability to have external validity, we must realize that there are sources of secondary variation which may influence the ability of the experimenter to generalize his findings. These secondary variations, therefore, are of great concern to the experimenter. Four of the common ones are the Hawthorne effect, pretesting, selection bias, and multiple treatment interaction effect.

**The Hawthorne effect.** The Hawthorne effect is basically the effect that experimentation has on subjects due to their awareness of being specially treated. The discovery of this effect was made at the Hawthorne plant of the Western

Electric Company. Experimenters selected a group of workers and introduced certain changes in their working conditions (e.g., decrease in lighting, work hours, etc.). Regardless of the changes implemented, production increased. They concluded that the changes in production were due to the special treatment, because when similar IVs were used at other plants where the workers did not feel themselves to be participants in a study, work production did not change. The best way to control for this effect is to whenever possible limit the knowledge of the subjects about their special treatment.

**Pretesting.**   Pretesting is common in psychological research. Pretesting effects are similar to those of the Hawthorne effect, and in fact may be considered a subset of it. Pretesting may cause numerous reactions including defensiveness; hardening of the subject's already held commitments, opinions, or performance; reductions in attention; or even the tendency of the subject to overreaction toward change in an effort to please the experimenter. An example of this would be predisposition of the subject being heightened in one particular direction due to questions the experimenter asks so that it later affects the subject's reactions in the experiment.

To control for pretesting effects, the experimenter should find a measure that does not call attention to the fact that the subject is being assessed. If this is found too burdensome or impossible, the pretest should be dropped completely.

**Selection bias.**   Selection bias is another problem for external validity. If a study is to be used to prove the necessity of teaching social values in schools, it would be important to find a school district that would be a good cross section of those to whom the need seemed applicable. If only lower socioeconomic area schools were chosen and the study was to apply to middle- or upper-class schools as well, we obviously would suffer from external invalidity. To prevent this, all that is really essential is a randomization of the subjects involved to make sure that they cover all pertinent variables.

**The multiple treatment interaction effect.**   The final area needing control is that of the multiple treatment interaction effect. Here our problem is that when more than one IV has been given a subject, the first IV's effect may still be affecting the subject and therefore our results will be unclear. One example is drug residue. By administering a particular drug to a subject we measure a DV, then an hour or so later we administer another drug, again measuring the DV. The question arises, however, whether the second measurement was solely a result of the second drug, included the residue of the first combined with the second, showed no effect, or was even due to some pretesting effect carried over from the first experience. This effect is important in psychopharmacological studies and also in learning experiments in which some learning "residue" remains. Certain experimental designs can be used to detect this (e.g., counterbalance designs), but if you feel interaction might occur, the use of different subjects is one means of control.

## SUMMARY

Variance is a major concern of psychologists, for it represents the influence of different variables included in the situation on the DV being investigated. In any natural situation the total variation ($V_T$) is said to be equal to the influence of the relevant variables ($V_W$), none of which can be numerically isolated. In carrying out an experiment the investigator divides the subjects into at least two groups. In this way $V_T$ may be divided into two parts—the difference in the DV between the groups ($V_B$) and the difference in the DV within a group ($V_W$). By carrying out such a procedure the investigator may determine how much a particular IV is responsible for causing changes in the DV, although other variables are present in the situation.

Variation is divided into two main categories: variation due to the effects of the IV (systematic variation, $V_B$), and variation due to all other variables that differentially influence the situation ($V_W$, or secondary variation). Within variation was also divided into secondary variable fluctuations in the situation that are potentially controllable and small fluctuations due to chance which, practically speaking, cannot be removed.

The main objective of any scientific investigation is systematically to employ the five control techniques upon which all experimental designs are based in an effort to decrease the possibility that any differences in DV measures between groups are due to some secondary variable(s) instead of the IV. The five control techniques available to an investigator are elimination, constancy, randomization, making a secondary variable a second IV, and statistical control.

A distinction was made between internal and external validity. Internal validity refers to how well secondary variables have been controlled in the experiment, so that any difference noted between the experimental and control groups can honestly be attributed to the IV. External validity refers to how far the results of the particular experimental situation may be generalized to other situations. Although an investigation may be internally valid when it is not externally valid, the reverse is not possible.

There are nine main sources from which internal invalidity due to secondary variable effects may arise: proactive history, retroactive history, maturation, testing, statistical regression, experimental morality, interaction effects, instrumentation, and experimenter bias. All nine may not be relevant in all experimental situations. They are, however, the main points an investigator should check to ensure that his investigation will yield valid results. There are four common sources of external invalidity: pretesting, the Hawthorne effect, selection bias, and the multiple treatment interaction effect.

# 5

## Nondesign
## Experimental Procedures

*By looking over the Contents, the reader can see that much of the text will be spent on learning different types of designs. However, an investigator must take into account a number of things when planning an investigation that do not depend on the design employed. The objective of this chapter is to familiarize the reader with some of these nondesign issues.*

One of the most important aspects in carrying out a psychological investigation is the selection of an appropriate design. An experimental design for an investigator is analogous to the house plans for a general contractor. The design indicates the basic structure and format upon which the whole experimental operation is based. An investigator may choose from literally hundreds of different designs, each having certain advantages over the others. Chapter Eight presents some of the more common designs used by psychologists.

An aspect of experimentation that is usually discussed briefly in most texts is the nondesign issues with which an investigator must deal. These include how to select subjects for an experiment, how to select and measure the IVs and DVs, and how to carry out a pilot study. One of the reasons little attention is paid to the nondesign aspect is because it has become almost second nature to the person writing a text. Because he has carried out nondesign procedures so often (and they are less exciting than other parts of experimentation), he forgets to warn the novice investigator about them. Yet, they are essential to any investigation. House plans are not enough to build a house. One must know how to nail, cut lumber, and do all the other tasks involved in building. The purpose of this chapter is to present the student with some of the things other than the experimental design that he must consider to perform an acceptable research project.

## SELECTION OF SUBJECTS

The selection of subjects is important for two reasons. First, the subjects an investigator chooses for his experiment determine to a large extent how far he can generalize his results. An investigator is seldom interested in determining the effect an IV has on the particular subjects used in the investigation. He usually wants to make a general statement about some larger population. John Watson carried out research to understand emotion in all infants, not just a few. In order to generalize the results of an investigation to organisms other than those actually being treated, the investigator needs to choose his subjects in such a manner that they represent some larger group. Random selection is one of the best means of choosing subjects so that the investigator may generalize the results he obtains to a whole population. For example, if an investigator finds that his subjects worked harder for social praise than for monetary reward and he has randomly selected his subjects from the total population of girls at Brigham Young University, he may state in his conclusion that "Girls attending Brigham Young University work harder for social praise than for monetary reward." The investigator could generalize his findings to all students at Brigham Young University (and not just girls) if he had randomly selected his subjects from all BYU students. If the investigator has randomly selected his subjects from all the people in the world, he can make the statement that "People of all ages all over the world work harder for social praise than for monetary reward." In each of these instances the investigator would carry out his investigation exactly the same way. The only difference would be the population from which he randomly selected his subjects, and that would determine how far he could generalize the results he obtained. The reader should keep in mind the fact that if one is really randomly selecting his subjects, all members of the population should have the same chance of being selected. One of the most common mistakes made by novice investigators is that they forget what population their sample subjects represent.

Recently, a student in an experimental psychology class wanted to find out how people of college age felt about premarital sexual relations. As his class project he randomly selected 200 students from the student body of 25,000 at Brigham Young University. Each was sent a questionnaire that included two questions:

1. Do you believe in persons' engaging in sexual intercourse before marriage? (Yes/No)
2. In which of the following yearly income categories do your parents fall?
    $3,000–$6,000
    $6,000–$12,000
    $12,000–$30,000
    above $30,000

The student's purpose was to determine whether people of different economic levels had different attitudes about premarital relationships. He found from his results that approximately 70 percent of each of the four income categories did not believe in premarital sex. He concluded, "Most American people of university age do not differ on this point."

But he did not consider two main points. First, Brigham Young University is a religion-backed institution of higher learning, and therefore the attitudes, especially sexual or political, of the students may not adequately represent the views of all students across the country. Students attending Brigham Young University are more conservative on sexual issues than the average students because of their religious background. Second, his subjects were selected only from college students. Not all young people of college age (including those not attending college) had the same opportunity to be chosen to receive a questionnaire. The student carrying out the survey should not have generalized his results to all college-age people in the United States, only to students at Brigham Young University.

How do you go about randomly selecting subjects? First, define what population you want to make statements about. Second, give each member of that population an equal chance of being selected as a subject. This can be accomplished by assigning each member a number, putting all the numbers in a container, and drawing out the numbers until you have enough subjects to carry out the investigation. After the subjects have been randomly selected to participate in this project, they are than randomly assigned to the different groups in the investigation. Random selection of subjects for the experiment is used to allow the investigator to generalize his results to more than just the subjects used. Random assignment of the subjects to different groups in the investigation helps ensure equality of the groups so that any difference in the DVs between the groups is due to the IV and not some secondary variable.

The second reason choosing subjects is important in an investigation is because the type of subject an investigator uses may determine what type of investigation he can carry out. Rats, pigeons, human infants, children, adults, rabbits, and monkeys all have different characteristics. An investigator may capitalize on these differences to help him study different psychological problems. To illustrate this point, let us look at a situation I encountered several years ago.

In 1963, an article by H. S. Terrace was published that presented data suggesting an organism could learn without making mistakes. This discovery is one of the most significant in the area of learning in the last fifty years because it has been a commonly accepted idea that man must make mistakes in order to know what is wrong, so he may then know what is correct. To demonstrate that errors were not necessary in learning, Terrace trained a pigeon to peck at a translucent plastic disc referred to as a key when it was illuminated red, and not to peck at the same key when it was green. By the time the experiment was completed, the pigeon would peck at the red key for food and stand quietly when the key was green, waiting for the red to come back on. He learned to do this even though he never had pecked the green key to find out he would not get a reward for doing so. Later, other psychologists [Moore and Goldiamond, 1963; Sidman and Stoddard, 1967] demonstrated children could learn to do things without making mistakes and without being told what not to do. This line of research became especially interesting when it was noted that animals and children who learn without making mistakes are not as frustrated or aggressive as those who learn by making mistakes.

As research continued on "errorless learning," the question was raised whether man or animal could really learn without making mistakes. After all, in all the experiments carried out, the subjects were either adult animals or children at least four years old. It was certain that all had made mistakes before coming into the experiment. It was suggested that the only reason the children and the pigeons could be conditioned to continually respond to one color and not another without mistakes was because they had made mistakes previously in their lives.

Since this issue stirred my curiosity, I wanted to devise an experiment that would shed some light on it. One possibility would have been to use younger children and younger pigeons. If they could be conditioned error- lessly, it would add support to the position that errorless learning does not depend on prior mistakes. There was a better alternative, however, and that was to condition a newborn subject. If a newborn organism could be con- ditioned errorlessly, it would give strong credence to the position that errorless learning is not a function of prior mistakes.[1] The problem in carrying out such an investigation is that newborn pigeons and newborn human infants have not developed enough at birth to perform a color discrimination task. In my undergraduate training, I had taken a course in comparative psychology that dealt with species differences. I recalled that some animals such as guinea pigs and chicks are mobile and conditionable at birth. Using this information, I was able to select a subject which, because of one of its unique abilities, made it suitable for the problem. I employed chicks in my investi- gation and found that they could be conditioned to peck at the red key and not at the green key without ever hitting green. From this experiment came information that supported the conclusion that learning a task without mis- takes is possible when the subject has made few if any mistakes previously in his life.

Certain types of investigations can be carried out better on some species than on others. After selecting a problem to analyze, the investigator should

---

1. It would not definitely prove that prior mistakes are not necessary. For example, we know children can be conditioned in the womb before they are born. We would certainly have a strong case, however, that errorless learning is not a function of prior mistakes.

carefully consider his choice of subjects, which may determine to a large extent how he may go about analyzing the problem. Some of the more common research subjects available are listed below along with some of the unique characteristics an investigator may wish to consider.

### Common Research Subjects

**Rats.** The rat, the most common laboratory animal in psychological research, has many attributes that make it one of the best choices for a research project. It is small, inexpensive, and easily housed. It is also relatively resistant to disease and infection so that it can be deprived of food and water with less chance of getting sick than most animals. Rats are used in experiments dealing with heredity, perception, physiology, learning, and sensory processes. They are fairly easy to condition, slower than pigeons or guinea pigs in visual discrimination problems, but less flighty. They have an excellent olfactory system and can easily be conditioned to distinguish between different odors. One of the biggest advantages of using rats is that there are literally thousands of previous studies with which to compare data. Much is already known about the rat that may aid the student in carrying out a good investigation. By reviewing the literature, the student can find out such things as what type of response would be best to use as a DV, how to measure the response, how to present different types of stimuli to the rat, and what type of reinforcers can be used on the rat. Male rats give more consistent data in certain types of experiments than female rats because of the female's four-day estrous cycle. Information on the rat may be found in Michael [1963] and Barnett [1963].

**Pigeons.** Pigeons are also very good laboratory animals. They are small, inexpensive, and easy to care for and maintain. They do better on visual tasks than rats, but generally do worse on auditory and olfactory tasks. There is less difference in the behavior of male and female than is true for rats. Pigeons generally learn faster than rats, but are more easily distracted. Like the rat, much work has been done on the pigeon, so a student may review the literature to get ideas on what types of DVs and experimental conditions are appropriate. Information on the pigeon may be found in Reese [1971] and Ferster and Skinner [1957].

**Other nonhuman species.** Although rats and pigeons are the most common nonhuman subjects used in psychological research, many other species can be used that have unique characteristics making them more suitable for certain types of research. Monkeys are good experimental subjects, especially because of their higher intellectual capacity. They are frequently used in experiments on problem-solving, concept formation, delayed response and language development. Chicks and guinea pigs may be used in developmental studies because they are mobile at birth. They are easy to house and are just as good as pigeons in visual discrimination tasks. Chickens are easier to work with than pigeons or guinea pigs, for they do not startle as easily, and they do not have to be deprived down to 80 percent of their normal body weight. They are easily conditioned when deprived of food for only twenty-four hours. This makes them an especially fine laboratory animal for undergraduate psychology course work. Many times students will "accidentally" put someone else's pigeon back on free feed, after which it requires about five days of deprivation to get the pigeon back to 80 percent of its normal weight so it will work. This can severely hamper the progress of any class experiment.

Rabbits are excellent subjects for drug studies because they have unusually large blood veins in their ears. Drugs may be easily injected into these veins, and blood may be easily extracted for analysis. Goldfish are becoming popular as experimental subjects. They are easy to keep and inexpensive to buy. They can be conditioned with shock to make visual discriminations within one or two hours using swimming from one end of the chamber to the other as the response.

**Humans.**   Humans are the most common type of experimental subject used by students for class projects. As subjects, they have several advantages over nonhumans. They are easy to obtain and do not have to be housed or fed. Many experiments that take very little time may be carried out on them. They may simply be asked to answer questionnaires. They can be worked on in groups because they can respond to verbal instructions. Generally one must experiment on one animal at a time, and in most cases each animal requires several weeks of training. Verbal reports can be used as DVs with human subjects, and they can also be used in a greater variety of analytical situations.

There are also disadvantages to using humans. Some types of investigations cannot ethically be carried out using humans as subjects (e.g., brain lesion work, certain shock situations). The past history of the subjects is not as easily controlled as with nonhumans. Human subjects frequently invalidate investigations by trying to "outguess" the investigator. Humans may change their behavior more drastically when they know they are subjects in an investigation.

There has been growing concern in recent years about the ethical responsibility and obligations of investigators toward the use of human subjects. The issues of deception, invasion of personal privacy, and personal welfare have recently received much attention [Ruebhausen and Brim, 1966; Kelman, 1967; Seeman, 1969; Walfensberger, 1967; Conrad, 1967; Lovell, 1967; Sasson and Nelson, 1969; June, 1971]. Students should be particularly careful in ensuring that experimental practices are ethical.

In some situations the psychologist has no choice as to which subjects will be involved in his investigation. This is especially true in applied settings, where the psychologist is asked to solve a particular problem. How can I increase the product output of my employees? What effect does a mistake during learning have on mentally retarded children? Why is little Johnny so destructive? In applied situations such as these, the psychologist is asked to deal with a particular subject or type of subject. When an investigator finds himself in this position, his first step is to make note of all the subjects' attributes that could have a bearing on the problem he has to solve. These could include sex, age, mental capacity, physical abilities, union membership, ethnic origin, and socioeconomic background. If, for example, the psychologist wants to increase the output of factory employees, he may find out whether or not they are union members. Unions generally have a strong say in what kind of incentive programs may be implemented and if the working conditions of the worker may be changed. Whether the workers are unionized or not may restrict the procedures the industrial psychologist can use to stimulate production. Identifying the attributes of the subjects is especially important when the investigator has no choice of subject, because they may determine to a large extent how the problem he is confronted with can be solved.

### Use of Nonhuman Species

Two questions frequently asked by undergraduate psychology majors are "Why are animals used in psychological investigations?" and "Do the behavioral principles found with animals hold true for, or can they be generalized to, humans?" These are important questions—ones to which a student should have answers before starting his graduate training. In answering these questions, let us take the second one first: "Can you generalize behavior principles found with animals to man?" One of the cardinal rules of behavioral research is *generality is the rule rather than the exception.* Past experience has taught behavioral scientists that what holds true for one behavior generally holds true for other behaviors. The controlling factors of behavior for one species are generally the controlling factors of behavior for other types of animals.[2] The processes of conditioning, extinction, and spontaneous recovery, for example, are essentially the same for most species. The means by which an organism develops phobias and fears are basically the same for rats, dogs, and humans. When Pavlov identified the principles of classical conditioning using a dog salivating to a tone, he and most of the other behav-

2. It is obviously not true that what is true for one species is always true for others. Breland and Breland bring this out in their article "The Misbehavior of Organisms" [1963].

ioral investigators of the day saw no difficulty in generalizing those behavioral principles to humans. The behavioral principles identified by B. F. Skinner using rats and pigeons as subjects have been found to have wide interspecies generality. The factors that he found to influence key pecking and bar pressing in the laboratory have also been shown to influence a wide variety of human behaviors (e.g., crying, attention, cooperation, concept formation, talking, showing affection) in everyday situations.

What is learned in terms of animal behavior can usually be generalized to humans. However, the reverse is not as true. Man obviously has greater mental capabilities than lower species and has developed many sophisticated behaviors (e.g., his elaborate language) not found in his mental subordinates. Most of the basic principles involved in learning behavior are the same for humans and nonhumans.

Why are animals used in psychological research? The most common reply is "Because you can do things to animals that you cannot do to humans." Although true, this statement is not the major reason. Psychologists employ rats, pigeons, and the like in research mainly because they allow the investigator better control of secondary variables. In Chapter Four, sources of secondary variation were listed that could make an investigator draw incorrect conclusions about the effect of an IV on some DV. The differences in the proactive history of human subjects can often invalidate an investigation. An investigator can easily control for this by using naive animals who are much more homogeneous in terms of past experience. Retroactive history is also a more likely source of invalidity when humans are used. People's moods shift more from day to day. Some may have been up late the night before an experiment; some may have attitude changes during the course of an experiment because of problems in their personal lives. Animals are seldom bothered by changes going on outside the experimental contingencies. Generally, their attention is wholly directed toward what is involved in the experiment.

Animal investigations are not as susceptible to invalidity due to testing. Animals do not see themselves as being in or out of an experiment, and therefore their actions are more "natural" than is the case for humans in many types of experiments. Experimental mortality is higher with human subjects. They are not as dependable.[3] With animals, the investigator knows they are available when he needs them. Because proactive history, retroactive history, testing, and experimental mortality are responsible for 85 percent of the sources of invalidity, it is no wonder that behavioral researchers employ animals as subjects so often. The investigator has a much greater chance of

---

3. Keep this point in mind especially if you have decided to use college students as subjects. Always request more subjects than you actually need, for approximately 30 percent will not show up if they are to participate in the project outside class time.

determining what effect an IV actually has on behavior and a much smaller chance that his investigation has been infiltrated by confounding secondary variables.

How many subjects should be used in an investigation? This is one of the most frequent questions asked of an instructor in research courses. With the skill of a politician, he generally says, "Well, that depends." Though students find this an unsatisfactory answer, it is the truth, for some experiments can be carried out on two or three subjects while others require several hundred. The variables that determine how many subjects you need include how many groups are involved in the investigation, how much control of secondary variables one has, and how large an effect the IVs will have. For example, fewer subjects are necessary if one has more control of secondary variables and if the IV effects are strong.

Not being familiar with all the ramifications of investigatory analysis, the student may still feel shortchanged with the preceding answer and want some figure with which to start. One answer to this could be to use 5 to 15 subjects in each group involved in an experiment. If only two groups are involved, one should lean toward having 15 in each group, whereas 5 subjects would be more appropriate if six or eight groups were involved. One of the best ways of determining how many subjects are needed is to review the literature and note how many subjects were used in similar projects.

## SELECTION OF THE DEPENDENT VARIABLE

After an investigator chooses some problem to analyze and decides upon the IV, he then must choose some variable on which to measure the IV's effect. In psychological investigations, this variable, the dependent variable (DV), is generally a measure of behavior. There are two aspects an investigator must take into consideration when selecting a DV: (1) what type of behavior will serve as the DV, and (2) how that behavior will be measured.

### Types of Dependent Variables

There are literally hundreds of different types of behaviors an investigator can use in his investigation. Included among his choices are physiological behavioral measures such as EEG recordings, galvanic skin response, and respiration; overt behavioral motor actions such as rats running through a maze, pigeons pecking a key, children answering written math questions, housewives choosing grocery products, biting, bedwetting, hitting, hugging, walking, and sleeping; and verbal reports such as opinions, attitudes, feelings, and observations. Which should an investigator select? That depends on the nature of the problem and the IV being used.

### Dependent Variable Measures

If someone were to ask, "How do you quantify a behavior?" the reply would probably be, "Measure the number of times it occurs." An experimental psychologist may measure how many times the pigeon pecks the key or the number of correct turns a rat makes while traversing the maze. The applied psychologist may measure the number of times his patient loses his temper, while the industrial psychologist may measure the number of tasks the worker completes. In all these situations, the psychologist may measure the number of tasks the worker completes. And in all these situations the psychologist has measured the DV in terms of frequency of occurrence. Although frequency is the most common way of measuring DVs, it certainly is not the only way. Behavior can be measured in terms other than frequency, a possibility that most novice investigators fail to consider when planning an investigation. There are many measures of behavior. Five of the most common are frequency, latency, response duration, amplitude, and choice selection. To give the reader a better idea of how each of these may be employed, situations in which they have previously been used are presented along with an explanation of what they involve.

**Frequency.** There are two reasons for the popularity of frequency as a unit of measure. First, it is one of the easiest ways of recording data. Response duration and latencies, for example, involve the use of timers and require the investigator to keep an eye on time as well as the behavior. Second, most of our everyday behaviors are measured in terms of frequency: how many compliments we get, how many answers we get right on a test, how many customers we wait on, how much money we have, how many friends call us, and so on.

Frequency is a well-used measure in basic research. It is especially useful in research involving memory and retention. Murdock [1962], for example, was interested in determining whether the ability of a person to recall individual items from a list was a function of the position of the item on the list. Murdock presented a list of English words, one at a time, to a subject. After the presentation of the complete list, the subject was asked to recall as many of the words on the list as he could. Murdock also varied the number of words in the list to see what effect the number of words given had on recall. Figure 5–1 shows the results of his study. He found that the words at the ends of the lists were recalled most frequently, while the words in the middle of the list were recalled least often.

Frequency is also an important dimension in applied psychological investigations. Sulzbacker and Houser [1968] devised and implemented a psychological investigation designed to decrease the frequency of an often encountered but seldom discussed classroom behavior emitted by youngsters.

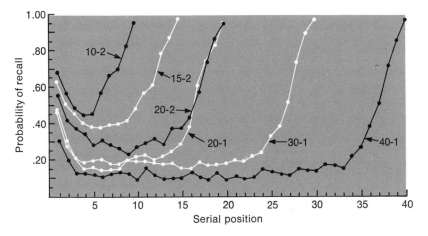

**FIGURE 5–1**

Probability of recall in free recall as a function of serial position of items in the original list

(Adapted from Murdock, 1962, Figure 2. Copyright 1962 by the American Psychological Association. Reprinted by permission.)

The behavior in question was the use of the "naughty finger" (raised fist with middle finger extended), and any reference to it or comments made by class members about it. The investigation was divided into three parts, as shown in Figure 5–2. First, the frequency of the undesired behavior in a class of fourteen educable mentally retarded children was recorded for ten days. In the second phase, the students were told they would all be given a special ten minute recess at the end of the day. However, anytime the teacher saw or heard about the naughty finger, one minute would be subtracted from the recess time. After seventeen days of this procedure, a third phase was instituted in which the class was informed that the special recess and the group contingency were no longer in effect. As can be seen in the figure, the rate of the undesirable behavior was drastically reduced when the contingency of losing recess time was in effect. Note that the undesired behavior returned when the contingency was removed.[4]

**Latency.** There are many instances of behavioral analysis in which the investigator is concerned with how long it takes for a behavior to be emitted. This is called *response latency*. How long it takes the child to solve the prob-

---

4. This type of experimental design, commonly called an ABA design, is a very good design. The first and third stage are integral parts of the investigation and are included to check whether the IV (loss of recess time due to bad behavior) was actually the cause of the change in behavior. Chapter Twelve covers this type of design in detail.

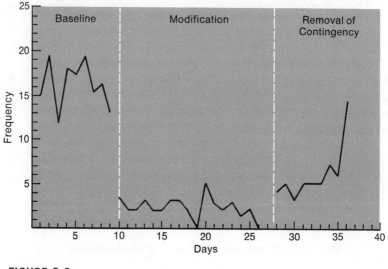

**FIGURE 5–2**

Frequency of occurrence of the undesired behavior under three contingency conditions

(Adapted from Sulzbacher & Houser, 1966, Figure 1. Reprinted by permission.)

lem, how quickly the drunk reacts when driving a car, how long it takes for the rat to traverse the maze are all behavioral measures involving latency. Employers are interested not only in whether an employee can perform a task, such as typing, but also in how long it takes. Latency is also a factor in determining a person's IQ, for some of the behaviors evaluated in intelligence tests involve determining how long it takes for the person to complete certain tasks. In recent years, latency of responding has taken on increased significance in research on emotion and motivation. It is even used as an indicator of fear and anxiety.

**Response duration.** If an investigator records the length of time in which a subject responds, the measure is called *response duration*. Measures of response duration include the time it takes for the effects of a drug to wear off, how long a subject persists at a particular task, how long the infant cries, and how long the student does his homework. Response duration is often used as one indicator of the mental development of a person. The attention span of mentally retarded children, for example, is much shorter than that of the average child, and many times they emit a behavior over and over again.

Response duration can also be used as a measure of anxiety level. The use of shock in psychological investigations generally raises the anxiety level of the subjects. In escape conditioning of rats, the subjects may have to learn to push a lever down several times in succession to turn off the shock. This is a somewhat difficult behavior to develop, for the rat will often hold the bar down rather than let it back up so it can be depressed again. The duration of holding the bar down in shock investigations is generally much longer than when the rat is taught to depress the lever many times to get food or water.

Although response duration is used as a DV in basic research, it is more frequently the DV in applied settings. Often people are guilty of emitting behaviors that are especially annoying to others because they persist for so long. A good example of this was Mary, an attractive sophomore at a western university who became the subject of an investigation. Mary was having difficulty keeping friends and getting dates because she talked so much. Although most young people find it hard to initiate conversation on a date, Mary had just the opposite problem. Being a bright young girl and an avid reader, she could expound for hours on such exciting topics as the high tariff on prune juice. Unfortunately, her dates and roommates did not enjoy her extended conversations. Space does not allow a complete presentation of what was involved in this investigation. Suffice it to say that the objective was to decrease the length of time she talked when around others. The procedure involved having her keep a written record of how often and how long she talked in her apartment, and having her intentionally decrease the length of her statements. At the end of two months, she was talking only one-tenth as long as before the investigation was instigated. At last report her dating life and relationships with roommates were much better.

**Amplitude.** Any measure of response strength that can vary along some dimension of intensity is termed *amplitude of response*. Response amplitude may be measured in a number of ways, depending on the response involved. The amount of force a subject uses in pressing a lever could be an amplitude measure. Response manipulanda may be purchased which indicate how much force is being applied to depress them. A handy little device frequently used in basic research involving shock is a bite bar. The intensity with which the rat bites the bar may be recorded and used as a DV.

In physiological research amplitude is often used as a measure of response strength. Brain wave activity may fluctuate in terms of cycles per second or height of the wave. The galvanic skin response (GSR) commonly used in lie detector tests is an amplitude measure of emotional responsiveness. Depth of breathing is an amplitude measure. The effects of a drug may be measured in terms of how deep a stage of anesthesia it develops, or in terms of the amount of constituents in the blood that change after its administration. The severity of epilepsy and rigidity of a patient in a catatonic state are also measures of response amplitude a clinical psychologist may encounter.

Measures of response amplitude are often employed in survey research. Subjects are frequently asked to respond in terms of some scale from one to seven on how effective they feel a product is or how intense a stimulus seems to be. Clinical psychologists are working with response amplitude in treating phobias when attempting to reduce fear and anxiety in their patients. Parents deal with response amplitude when they want their child to talk "quieter." Even quality of comments is a measure of response amplitude. An investigation may involve modifying the verbal behavior of juvenile delinquents to use less crude words in their vocabulary.

**Choice selection.** Subject preference is also a way of measuring the effects of some IV. The TV viewer is constantly reminded of this type of research. The housewife samples three brands of coffee and is asked which one she prefers. One toothpaste is chosen over another, one car is selected more than another. Making choices is an integral part of everyone's daily routine, and is therefore a behavioral measure that concerns most psychologists.

Choice is a response measure frequently used in psychological testing. Intelligence tests include sections in which the child is given four or five articles and asked to choose the one that does not belong (e.g., shoe, stocking, glove, bowl). Aptitude tests include sections in which the person chooses one situation over another (e.g., which would you rather do, work on a car or hammer nails). Subject responses on psychological tests are often used as DVs, especially in educational research. The effectiveness of different methods of teaching may be evaluated in terms of how the students respond on an achievement test.

The use of choice as a response measure is more common in field research than it is in laboratory investigations. When an investigator has a choice as to the kind of response measure he may employ in an investigation, frequency and amplitude are generally preferred because they allow a wider range of statistical tools to be used. Choice as a response measure is one of the more common DVs used in undergraduate course projects.

### Ways to Select a Dependent Variable

How does one decide on a particular DV? It depends. In some situations the problem selected by the investigator automatically sets the DV to be used. If the investigator is concerned with getting rid of bedwetting in junior high school subjects, the problem defines the behavior to be employed as the DV. Generally the DV is automatically set in psychological investigations carried out to solve the practical problems that confront clinical, educational, school, and industrial psychologists. In applied situations the psychologist is frequently restricted in terms of the subjects he will use and the DV to be studied in his investigation. In such cases, he does not have to worry about selecting the DV; he is concerned only with objectively defining the behavior so it can be measured.

When carrying out basic research, the investigator is not restricted in terms of the DV he may choose or the subjects he may use. This is an important advantage the research psychologist has over the applied psychologist. Because the research psychologist is not restricted, he has greater latitude in how he may approach a problem. He may choose the optimum type of subject and DV for analyzing a particular psychological principle. People often have difficulty in understanding why psychologists employ pigeons in their research rather than humans and why they use key pecking (a seemingly irrelevant behavior) as a DV measure. The reason psychologists use behaviors such as key pecking and bar pressing is quite simple—they are easy to quantify. The more exactly a DV can be measured, the easier it is to detect the influence of an IV. It is more difficult to measure other behaviors such as head scratching, yawning, head turning, vocalization, and love.

Will relationships found between an IV and bar pressing or key pecking hold true for other behaviors and other species? This is an important concern for most novice psychologists. Students are often worried about whether psychological principles found when studying key pecking and bar pressing hold true for (or can be generalized to) human behaviors, or even other behaviors of the same species. The rule about subject generality mentioned earlier is also true for DVs. What is true for one behavior is more often than not true for another. The novice usually has difficulty in accepting this idea, and as a result sets up an investigation involving a more practical type of behavior as a DV rather than selecting a DV that is easy to measure and quantify.

One of the best ways for the student to go about selecting a DV is to review the literature. He should go to *Psychological Abstracts*, look up previous investigations dealing with a similar problem, and see what was used as a DV. This will save a great deal of work in the long run and help him design a better investigation.

## SELECTION OF THE INDEPENDENT VARIABLE

Once an area of investigation has been decided upon, the psychologist must select an appropriate IV to represent the issue of concern. Suppose one wishes to study the effects of family love on a child's academic achievement in grade school. What variable would be selected to represent family love in the investigation—hugs and kisses from the parents, verbal praise by parents and siblings, smiles? What variable should be selected as the IV in a study aimed at determining the effect of punishment on a child's self-concept—spankings, verbal reproof, electric shock?

Selecting an IV that truly represents the interests of the psychological investigator is one of the major problems he may face. Other scientific disciplines do not have such a difficult time in selecting an IV. In biochemistry, for example, the scientist may be interested in studying the effects of acidity on enzyme action. Now, the terms "acid" and "enzyme" are fairly easy to define objectively, so the investigator has little difficulty in selecting as an IV a physical compound that most would agree represents the concept acid. He simply applies the selected IV, notes its effect, and concludes acidity has such and such an effect. The psychologist, on the other hand, has a much more difficult time of it because the terms he deals with are much more subjective. The variables that concern the social scientist are much more intangible than those dealt with in the physical sciences. Psychological terms such as love, motivation, emotion, anxiety, and self-concept cannot be quantified as easily as physical terms such as light, heat, acidity, and color. The inability of man to operationally define psychological terms was the main stumbling block when psychology was trying to become a science. A scientific approach required that psychological terms be defined in terms of things that were observable and recordable. If one is interested in studying an issue such as emotion, he should review the literature to find what operational measures have been accepted to represent it.

Even after an acceptable measure of a term has been chosen as an IV for some particular investigation, one must not forget that different quantitative and qualitative values are possible. How much IV, what type of IV, how long should it be given are all questions the investigator may have to answer. If, for example, a drug is the IV, too little may have no effect, while too much may have a terminal effect. In the first chapter, Sid employed a drug called apomorphone in his investigation. Small doses of apomorhone elicit compulsive gnawing behavior in subjects, yet in large doses it is commonly used in hospitals to induce vomiting. If Sid had not reviewed the literature and become aware of the characteristics of the IV he had chosen, he could have been unpleasantly surprised by the reactions of his subjects. An investigator should be sure to review the literature of his IV before initiating experimental procedures. An operational definition includes defining a selected variable in terms of both quality and quantity.

## ELIMINATION AND CONSTANCY
## AS NONDESIGN CONTROL TECHNIQUES

The reader will be shown in later chapters how experimental designs can be set up to make use of four control techniques for secondary variables—randomization, constancy, making a second IV, and statistical control. Secondary variables, however, may be controlled by means other than experimental designs. There are nondesign procedures that may help control for the effects of secondary variables in an investigation. These nondesign procedures include elimination and constancy.

After an investigator defines his IV, DV, and potential secondary variables, the next step involves setting up an experimental situation in which the secondary variables are controlled as much as possible. One of the best ways to make sure a secondary variable is not responsible for the difference between the control and experimental groups is to eliminate that variable completely from the experimental situation. Suppose, for example, that you were evaluating the ability of children to put certain puzzles together. If parents are present in such situations, it is not uncommon for the child to take cues from the parent. The child becomes aware of small changes in the parent's behavior (an unintended subtle frown when the child picks up the wrong piece) and solves the problem by cueing on the parent rather than attending to cues in the puzzle. In such cases, the parent is an important secondary variable. The investigator could easily control for this secondary variable by not allowing the parent in the room with the child while he is engaged in the experiment.

This secondary variable of cueing off people in the situation is also something to watch out for when animals are used as subjects. In Europe during the 1800s there was a horse (called Hans the Wonder Horse) that seemed to have extrasensory perception. Hans was used in an act in which he supposedly read a person's mind. The act involved having someone in the audience come forward and think of a number between one and ten. Hans, using his hoof, would then count off the number. Initially, many felt the trainer was somehow cueing the horse, but it was found that Hans could do it even if his trainer was not there. Later, it was shown that Hans could only do it if he could see the person, and not when the person was shielded from view. It was found that somehow the horse was able to sense the small behavioral changes a person would make whenever he had counted off the right number. Sensing these subtle changes, the horse would then stop.

Like randomization, elimination can easily be used to control more than one secondary variable in an investigation. By eliminating secondary variables, the investigator increases the possibility of showing his IV has an effect. Every secondary variable causes some fluctuation, though minor in many cases, between the DV measures of different subjects. The more secondary variables eliminated, the less non-IV variability between subjects. This allows the variability between subjects due to the IV to become more apparent. Elimination, then, is an important control procedure that can and should be used in every experimental situation.

Constancy is another control technique that can be applied irrespective of the design. Although it is true that constancy may be incorporated into a design (e.g., matching and blocking designs) to control for secondary variables, it may also be applied no matter what design is used. An experimenter may feel temperature variation might influence the behavior of his rat subjects in the experiment, so he makes sure the temperature is held constant. An investigator may give verbal instructions to his subjects; differences in the way the instructions are given may cause variations in subject's results. To cope with this problem, the experimenter may type out the instructions and read them off a card so that instructions are held constant in terms of what is said. If the investigator is worried about behavior mannerisms (e.g., voice inflection) unconsciously given with the instructions, the instructions may be presented by means of a tape recorder to hold them constant.

In some situations, a secondary variable may be held constant indirectly. There are times when the investigator may not be able to hold a particular variable constant, but can mask its influence by presenting another variable that overrides the first. For example, animals being run in test chambers are usually sensitive to small fluctuations in sound. Sounds from a person walking past the test chamber, a relay buzzing on a piece of equipment, a bell sounding in the adjoining hall, or a rat squeaking in a nearby chamber may disrupt the subject. To override the effects of these uncontrollable variables, a white noise (a rasping sound held at a constant intensity) is continuously presented inside the chamber at a high enough intensity so that the fluctuation in the other sounds cannot be heard. In this way, the secondary variable of extraneous noise is held constant. This procedure is called *masking* and is frequently applied in psychological research.

## EXPERIMENTER BIAS

One of the biggest sources of internal invalidity in a psychological investigation is experimenter bias. While conducting an investigation, a researcher may unknowingly confound the results of his project by not dealing with his subjects uniformly. An investigator may ask questions in a different manner to the control group than to the experimental group. If his experiment involves observing the subjects' reactions, he may have certain expectancies as to how they should act and read into their behavior things that are not really there. If, for example, the investigator has been told the drug he gave a subject will cause him to become more aggressive, neutral statements made by the subject while injected may be interpreted as being aggressive and obnoxious in nature.

There are ways an investigator may go about reducing the possibility of experimenter bias. If a drug or capsule of some sort is to be given to the subjects, a double blind technique may be used. In a double blind situation, neither the person giving the capsule nor the subject receiving it knows whether the person is in the experimental or control group, and each is unaware whether the subject received a placebo or the real IV. This decreases the possibility of experimenter bias or subject expectancy invalidating the results. If surveys are being taken, interviews given, or observations of subjects' behavior being recorded by some experimenter's helper, the helpers should not be made aware of the objective of the investigation if such knowledge could cause their behavior to bias the results. Experimenter bias is an especially potent source of invalidity in class projects because the novice experimenter becomes overly intent on supporting his hypothesis rather than on keeping an open mind to any results he may obtain.

## PILOT STUDIES

One of the best ways for the novice researcher to develop a firm experimental investigation is to first run a pilot study. A pilot study is one in which the investigator carries out what could be called a mini-experiment in which the IV is administered to a subject or two for only a short time. The experimenters use this practice run to try different levels of the IV or check out any of a dozen other things he may be unsure of. This dry run can give him a basic feel as to what will happen and may make him aware of important secondary variables he might have overlooked. One of the most common statements made by students after completing their projects starts out: "If I were to do it over, I would . . ." That sentence is most often completed by mentioning a particularly poor aspect of the investigation that would have been identified if a pilot study had been run.

## INSTRUMENTATION

In psychology's attempt at becoming a more exact science, greater emphasis has been placed on the use of more objective means of applying the IV and monitoring the DV. The internal validity of almost every type of psychological investigation can be increased by using mechanical and electronic instruments. The application of the IV can be done more exactly and consistently by decreasing fluctuations in amount of the IV given, the latency of its administration, and the duration of administration. Error variance in an investigation is reduced by the use of some instrument to measure the DV more uniformly. The types of behavioral research equipment available to the investigator are so numerous that a systematic coverage of them would require a book by itself. There are literally dozens of different ways electronically and mechanically to apply IVs including slide projectors, tape recorders, light sources, and mechanized syringes. Every type of DV measure (frequency, latency, etc.) can be monitored by devices such as counters, timers, polygraphs, and printout counters. In reviewing the literature, the investigator generally pays close attention to how the IV and DV were measured in related investigations.

## SUMMARY

There are a number of experimental issues an investigator must deal with that are not related to the design. Choosing the right subjects is important because the type of subject chosen often determines what type of investigation may be performed. Second, the way subjects are chosen determines how far the results of the investigation may be generalized. Different species are more suitable for certain types of experiments. The similarities and differences an investigator may consider when setting up his investigation are presented, along with two arguments for the use of nonhuman species by psychologists.

Five measures of DVs are frequency, latency, duration, amplitude, and choice. Each of these five is used in psychological investigations. DVs that are easy to quantify and adequately represent the issue under investigation should be selected. The investigator may find the best DV measure of his interest by reviewing the literature.

Selecting an appropriate operationally defined IV is more difficult for psychology than other sciences because psychological terms are more subjective in nature. The psychology investigator must then be more careful to make sure the IV he uses is operationally defined and therefore reproduceable.

Two secondary variable control techniques may be applied irrespective of the design used. These are elimination and constancy. The experimenter should be careful not to bias his results because of what he does. A pilot study should be carried out to give the investigator experience and to help him select appropriate IVs and DVs. Wherever possible, an experiment should be instrumentated to increase its validity.

# 6

# Methods
# of Data Collection

*In many areas of research, standard ways of collecting data have been agreed upon. Not being familiar with these, the novice investigator frequently is unaware of the accepted procedures and employs a less acceptable type of data. This chapter presents several methods of data collection commonly used in psychology. Note that the first three sections of the chapter emphasize how to go about collecting data, while the section on psychological tests emphasizes what kinds of tests are available and how to use them correctly.*

There are literally hundreds of different ways of collecting data. Some are objective, others are subjective; some are quite reliable and valid, others are less so. Once the investigator has selected his DV, he then decides on an acceptable way of measuring it. For example, how does one go about determining how well a child can hear? This may sound simple; just increase the volume of sound until the child says he can hear it. How do you carry out an interview? Just ask questions. Unfortunately, it is not as simple as it sounds.

The search for more objective, valid, and generalizable data has stimulated researchers to systematize their data-collection procedures. Over the years, standard DV measures have been agreed upon in particular research areas as being more acceptable than others.

Our objective here is to present some of the more standardized data-collection procedures used in psychological research. This is not an all-inclusive presentation, for each special research area has its own standards to some extent, and there are hundreds of special research areas. The data-collection procedures presented here, however, are some of the more general and well-known ones. Almost every psychologist during his training or professional practice will come in contact with them. There are two main reasons for including a discussion of data-collection procedures in this text. First, in case the reader decides to carry out investigations of his own which require these methods, the presentation may help him select an appropriate procedure. Second, even if the reader never carries out such investigations, he should still be aware of the proper procedures for doing so because the results from such investigatory procedures are used by all professionals in psychology. When reading a psychology text or journal, a person may come across a statement such as "the method of limits was used. . ." with no explanation of what the method of limits is. The author gives no explanation because the method of limits is a common data-collection procedure, and he assumes that his readers would have learned the main types of data-collection procedures as undergraduates.

## THRESHOLD MEASUREMENT

### Use of Threshold Techniques

The measurement of psychophysical thresholds has been one of the prime research concerns since the formation of psychology as a separate discipline. The analysis of man's sensory thresholds was psychology's first step toward an evaluative measure of man in an attempt to identify the internal physiological and mental processes he employs in dealing with his surroundings. One needs a means of interacting with the brain if an understanding of brain mechanisms is to be accomplished. The only known means of input is through the sense systems, and the only means the brain has of expressing its functions is through muscular and glandular reactions. Many investigators have carried out threshold investigations simply to determine a subject's range and sensitivity to various stimuli. Questions such as what sounds can man hear, to what wave lengths are people sensitive, and so on, have been and are continually being researched in psychology by means of threshold investigations.

In many instances a person's threshold is used as a DV to determine the effects certain IVs have. What effect do alcohol or other drugs have on man's ability to sense change? Is a person more or less sensitive to stimuli when he is angry or embarrassed? Can one "sharpen" his senses through training? Investigations seeking answers to these types of questions require the investigator to be familiar with the standard means of collecting threshold data.

### Types of Thresholds

Psychological investigations involving thresholds may be divided into two groups—*absolute* threshold investigations and *difference* threshold investigations. Absolute threshold investigations entail determining the least amount of energy that some particular sense system or systems require before that stimulus is detected. What is the lowest intensity of sound you can hear, how bright must a light be before you can see it, and how much pressure must be exerted on some part of your body before you "feel" something are all questions that are dealt with by absolute threshold investigations.

The ability of an organism to sense a change in the magnitude of some stimulus is what a difference threshold investigation determines. Suppose two lights were simultaneously presented to a subject. How much brighter would one have to be than the other before the subject could perceive a difference in brightness between the two? If a man is holding a 250-ounce weight in one hand and a 253-ounce weight in the other, can he sense that the weights are not the same? What if he had a 5-ounce weight in one hand and an 8-ounce weight in the other? These types of questions could be answered with difference threshold investigations. Difference thresholds are the minimum amount of change in stimulus magnitude some particular sense system or systems require before a change can be detected.

Past difference threshold investigations have shown that the difference threshold tends to be a constant fraction of the stimulus magnitude. To illustrate, let us look at whether a person can tell the difference between a 5-ounce weight and an 8-ounce weight. Previous investigations have found that the fraction a weight must change in magnitude for one to sense a change is 1/53. That means a person can detect the full difference between a 53-ounce weight and a 54-ounce weight, yet cannot distinguish between a 153-ounce weight and a 154-ounce weight. We would rightfully conclude, then, that a person could tell the difference between a 5- and an 8-ounce weight, but not between a 250- and a 253-ounce weight. Difference threshold investigations have shown that different sense systems have different fractions (meaning differences in sensitivity). Table 6–1 presents the fraction constants for several sense modalities. In difference threshold investigations, the minimum amount of stimulus change required to detect a change is referred to as a *jnd* (just noticeable difference). The *jnd* is commonly used for scaling the steps of sensation corresponding to increases in stimulus magnitude.

**TABLE 6–1**
*Fraction constants for difference thresholds
of four senses*

| Sense | Fraction constant |
|---|---|
| Vision | 1/100 |
| Hearing | 1/3 |
| Smell | 1/4 |
| Pressure | 1/5 |

### Calculation of Thresholds

Determining a person's absolute threshold for a stimulus (e.g., a tone) might initially seem rather simple and straightforward. If asked to perform such a task, you would probably begin increasing the volume of the tone after telling the subject to speak out when he first hears it. You would then want to define the absolute threshold of this person as that value to which he responded. It is not quite that simple, however, for if you repeated your procedure a second time, you would find he did not respond to exactly the same tone value as being the minimum he could hear. Past threshold investigations have taught researchers that a threshold is not a fixed and invariant level. Actually, one's threshold for stimuli fluctuates from one second to the next. This fact has required researchers to agree on what should be defined as threshold. The agreement reached was that threshold should be defined as that physical stimulus value at which 50 percent of the time a subject reported he could detect it and 50 percent of the time he reported he could not. This meant the stimulus should be presented many times over a range of values with each subject responding many times. The threshold would then be statistically determined by averaging the responses made. Figure 6–1 shows what a graph of the results of such an investigation might be like. The curve in Figure 6–1 is called a psychophysical function because it shows the relationship between a psychological variable (perception of a stimulus) and a physical variable (intensity of a stimulus).

The procedure for determining difference thresholds is basically the same as for determining absolute thresholds. There is no one single intensity

**FIGURE 6–1**

Illustration of a psychophysical curve. Plotted on the ordinate is the percentage of times a person answered yes when asked if he detected the presence of a stimulus. In this case the threshold would be defined physically as unit 8.

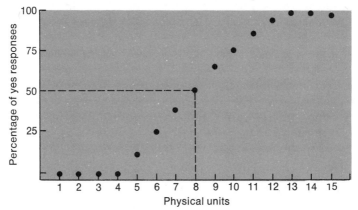

value or jnd value that represents the "true" threshold of a person for some stimulus. Both types of thresholds are statistically determined. When calculating either an absolute or difference threshold, the investigator needs to present each physical level of the stimulus several times to be able to calculate the threshold value.

### Stimulus Presentation

Two methods are commonly used to present stimuli in threshold investigations—the *method of limits* and the *method of constant stimuli*. Both involve presenting the subject(s) with a large number of stimulus values, with each value being presented several times. The main differences between the two are determining how and in what order the stimulus values are to be presented.

The method of limits is sequential; stimuli are presented according to their magnitude. The investigator begins by presenting the stimulus at an intensity he knows is well above the threshold of the subject. (The experimenter could also start out below threshold and go up.) After the subject's response is noted, a second stimulus of lower intensity is presented. This continues with successive presentations of the stimulus at lower intensity values as long as the subject continues to detect the stimulus. After the subject says he cannot detect the stimulus for a certain number of presentations (defined by the investigator), the descending series is terminated, and an ascending series is begun. Starting with a stimulus value well below threshold, the experimenter continues increasing the intensity of the stimulus by predetermined increments until the subject responds positively for several presentations. Several ascending and descending stimulus presentation series are carried out until a threshold estimate can be made. Figure 6–2 illustrates how the data sheet for an investigation using the method of limits looks.

Notice that the responses of the subject determine to an extent which stimulus values will be presented when the method of limits is used. The cue for terminating the ongoing sequence is when the subject changes his response. This also gives the experimenter an idea of the volume with which to start the next sequence. Such is not the case when the method of constant stimuli is employed. With this method, the investigator determines before any tests are run which stimulus values will be presented, and in what order. The stimulus values are not presented in order of ascending or descending intensity values; instead, they may fluctuate greatly from one presentation to the next. Figure 6–3 illustrates how the values may be presented. Fifty to one hundred trials may be used with the method of constant stimuli. Each square indicates the stimulus intensity applied, while the letters indicate subject responses.

As might be expected, each method has its advantages and disadvantages.

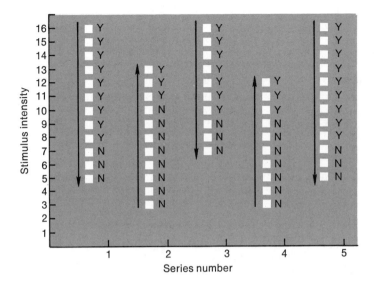

**FIGURE 6–2**

Sample data sheet for the method of limits. Each box represents the presentation of a certain stimulus intensity. The letters indicate whether or not the subject could detect the stimulus (Y = Yes, N = No). The arrows indicate whether the sequential presentation of stimulus values went from high to low, or from low to high intensity.

**FIGURE 6–3**

Sample data sheet for the method of constant stimuli. Each box represents the presentation of a certain stimulus intensity. The letters indicate whether or not the subject could detect the stimulus (Y = Yes, N = No).

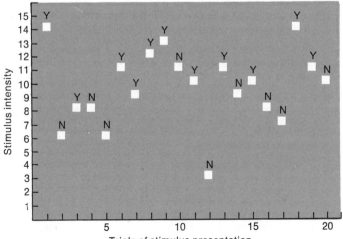

The method of limits does not require any previous knowledge of threshold values. The investigator can simply continue up or down the series, letting the responses of the subjects determine the range of stimulus intensity values. With the method of constant stimuli, the investigator needs much more prior knowledge of the possible threshold values of the sense modality he is working with because he must set the values and their range prior to testing the subjects. The predetermined increments selected by the investigator using constant stimuli procedures may be too great or too small. Because the method of limits may employ a sliding scale rather than just discrete changes in stimulus intensity, this method can easily provide a much more accurate threshold measure.

With the method of limits, however, the investigator must be more concerned with the possibility of the subjects' giving incorrect replies. Because the intensity of the stimulus is systematically increased or decreased in sequence, the subject may *anticipate* the next response. For example, it is more common for Yes responses to be given at lower intensities when using a descending series than when an ascending series is being given. These false positives and false negatives, as they are called, may be controlled for to some extent by the random injection of blanks (no stimulus given) throughout the presentations.

The method of limits is considered a more flexible procedure than the method of constant stimuli because the values of the stimulus do not have to be predetermined. In many instances this allows the investigation to be carried out in less time, for certain levels of stimulus would not have to be presented once it was noted that the threshold was not close to those values.

In some situations the successive presentation of several stimulus values at one time may interrupt the ongoing behaviors of the organism.[1] The method of constant stimuli allows the investigator more easily to introduce only one stimulus value at a time over longer periods of time. This makes it an especially effective procedure in analyzing stimulus-response generalization gradients [Guttman Kalish, 1956].

Can the method of limits and the method of constant stimuli be used on nonhuman subjects? Yes, they certainly can. The responses used in the illustrations so far have been verbal, but animals can be conditioned to make a response (e.g., press a bar, peck a key, squeal) if a stimulus is present or absent. Blough (1966) surveys a number of responses that can be used for animal threshold experiments.

Yes-no responding is not the only type of response human subjects can

---

1. In some cases the investigator may want to measure the threshold while the subject is involved in some task. The method of constant stimuli usually works better in such cases. Also, certain types of subjects (e.g., mentally retarded children, animals) may be easily distracted and lose their power of concentration when long periods of time are used to present stimuli sequentially.

make. A second type of indicator response is called the *forced choice* response. The subject responds in such a way that he actually selects a stimulus value from among several choices. One trial may consist of four successive intervals in which the stimulus was applied in only one of the four. The subject not only has to detect the stimulus, but also identify which of the four choices it occurred in. The forced choice method is commonly used in eye chart tests in which a dot is missing in one of four choices and the person has to identify which of the choices has only three dots (see diagram below). The size of the stimulus is then varied to determine visual distance threshold.[2]

## SCALING TECHNIQUES

Threshold measurement investigations involve comparing judgmental responses of subjects to physical scales such as intensity and brightness. There are situations, however, in which the investigation requires the subjects to compare stimuli along dimensions that are more qualitative than quantitative. Scaling techniques have been devised to measure such relationships. "Rank these makes of cars according to prestige"; "Rate how happy you feel on a scale from one to seven"; "Who will make the best president?"—questions such as these require the person responding to make a value judgment. People's preferences, attitudes, and beliefs are common DVs in psychological investigations. They usually present a problem to the novice investigator because he is not sure how he should deal with responses that involve comparing value judgments. Three of the several scaling techniques frequently employed in research are presented here: paired comparison, rank-order scaling, and ratio scaling.

### Paired Comparison Scaling

Which of the contestants is most beautiful? Which film did you enjoy most? In which situation are you most fearful? All these questions can be answered by randomly presenting pairs of stimuli to the subject and asking

2. A more in-depth coverage of threshold measurement techniques can be found in the following texts: Underwood [1960, Chapter Five]; Dember [1963, Chapter Two]; March [1973, Chapter Two]; and Kling and Riggs [1971, Chapters Two and Three].

him to select one or the other according to some attribute. Suppose a psychologist was interested in determining how prestigious people felt different occupations were. He might select seven occupations (milkman, store clerk, gas station attendant, plumber, carpenter, truckdriver, bricklayer), present them two at a time, and ask the subject to indicate which of each pair presented is most prestigious. Each alternative is paired with every other alternative. The pairings are not presented in sequence as shown below, but randomly. With seven stimuli, there are twenty-one pairings:

milkman–store clerk
milkman–gas station attendant
milkman–plumber
milkman–carpenter
milkman–truck driver
milkman–bricklayer
store clerk–gas station attendant
store clerk–plumber
store clerk–carpenter
store clerk–truck driver
store clerk–bricklayer
gas station attendant–plumber
gas station attendant–carpenter
gas station attendant–truck driver
gas station attendant–bricklayer
plumber–carpenter
plumber–truck driver
plumber–bricklayer
carpenter–truck driver
carpenter–bricklayer
truck driver–bricklayer

The investigator then records the number of times each alternative is chosen. Figure 6–4 shows how the data may look.

The result of a paired comparison procedure is a ranking of alternatives. Why might a psychologist want such a ranking? First, he might simply want to find out how a society might rank certain stimuli on some attribute. This would be considered simply a fact-finding or descriptive type of investigation. In such cases the investigator would present his findings as in Figure 6–4. The objective is not to analyze cause-effect relationships, only to report comparative findings. Second, two groups of subjects could be compared according to how they ranked the alternatives. How does ranking by children of different socioeconomic levels correlate with the rankings of their parents? This could give psychologists an idea as to whether attitudes are changing from one generation to the next. The statistical test employed to analyze

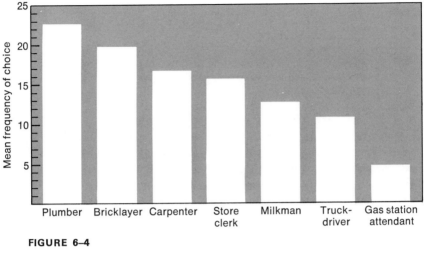

**FIGURE 6–4**
Paired comparison results

such data is called the coefficient of consistence K. An example of such an analysis may be found in Ferguson [1973, pp. 228–231]. Third, the rankings may be used to determine the effectiveness of some IV. The government is now trying to influence more high school graduates to enroll in trade schools. To achieve this, several vocational films have been produced to influence the potential graduate's attitude about certain vocations. The effectiveness of these films can be determined by showing them to one group and not another and then comparing the group rankings to see if they differ significantly. The paired comparison scaling technique, then, can be used to obtain three kinds of information: description of facts, analysis of trends, and cause-effect relationships.

### Rank-Order Scaling

A second procedure for measuring stimuli according to some judgmental dimension is called the rank-order procedure. As might be expected from its name, its objective is the same as that of a paired comparison procedure. Both give an investigator a means of ranking stimuli on some dimension, but the way of obtaining the ranking differs. In the rank-order procedure a subject is presented with all the alternative stimuli at one time and asked to rank them from high to low or low to high according to some attribute. I once asked students in an introductory psychology class to rank five teaching procedures. They were given the following instructions:

At the end of the course you will be given a final exam. The exam will be the only means by which you will be graded. Rank the following class procedures in terms of which you would prefer to be employed in this class for preparing you for the final exam. Rank them with 1 as your first choice.

    A.  Lecture three times a week
    B.  One lecture and two question-answer periods during the week
    C.  Lecture twice a week with one no-count exam given each week
    D.  No formal lectures; instructor just comes and answers questions
    E.  No class held at all

The results tabulated for ten students are presented in Table 6–2. A graph similar to Figure 6–4 could also be drawn with the data in Table 6–2. The results of such an investigation are usually statistically analyzed using a rank correlational method called the coefficient of concordance. An illustration of the statistical computations required to calculate the coefficient of concordance may be found in Ferguson [1973, pp. 225–227].

**TABLE 6–2**
*Illustrative data from rank-ordering of teaching procedures*

| Subject Number | | | | | |
|---|---|---|---|---|---|
| | $A$ | $B$ | $C$ | $D$ | $E$ |
| 1 | 3 | 2 | 1 | 4 | 5 |
| 2 | 5 | 1 | 3 | 2 | 4 |
| 3 | 2 | 3 | 1 | 4 | 5 |
| 4 | 1 | 2 | 3 | 4 | 5 |
| 5 | 3 | 1 | 2 | 5 | 4 |
| 6 | 5 | 3 | 4 | 2 | 1 |
| 7 | 1 | 2 | 3 | 4 | 5 |
| 8 | 3 | 4 | 5 | 2 | 1 |
| 9 | 1 | 2 | 3 | 4 | 5 |
| 10 | 4 | 3 | 5 | 1 | 2 |
| $X = 28$ | | 23 | 30 | 32 | 37 |
| Overall rank 2 | | 1 | 3 | 4 | 5 |

Both paired comparison and rank-order procedures give the investigator a means of analyzing judgmental responses. These rankings do not indicate how much the subject prefers or judges one stimulus above the other; it simply puts them in order. Paired comparison scaling is generally more time-consuming than rank-order, but the results are considered somewhat more reliable. Young children especially do better with paired comparisons where only two stimuli must be evaluated at a time.

### Ratio Scaling

The psychologist's interest in scaling is not restricted to rank-ordering. In some situations the investigator wants not only to rank stimuli one above the other, but also to determine some sort of distance measurement between them. He may want to know which of two sounds is louder, and how much louder the one is. Individuals can do more than make rank judgments; often they can assign magnitudes to their sensations and feelings. If two light stimuli, A and B, are presented to a subject, he may judge A to be twice as intense as B. Being able to obtain magnitude relationships is considered better than obtaining just ordinal relationships as is the case in the scaling methods previously covered. Ratio scales can give ordinal and magnitude information at the same time.

Two common ratio scale procedures are called *magnitude estimation* and *ratio production*. In ratio production, the subject is given a stimulus and asked to locate it on some attribute (e.g., goodness–badness, valuable–worthless, bright–dark) in comparison to other stimuli. A subject may be presented with a light of a certain intensity as a standard and then be required to select, from among several lights, one which is some fraction (usually half) of the standard light's intensity. Magnitude estimation is commonly used in grading essays; the papers are evaluated and given some score on their merits rather than just being ranked according to which is better. The scores on the essays may then be compared on some quantitative numerical relationship. With magnitude estimation, only one stimulus is presented at a time and the subject is asked to locate it on some attribute. The estimation is made with no reference to a second stimulus: the subject is asked to make an absolute judgment regarding the magnitude of the stimulus, rather than a relative judgment as in ratio production.

The objective of ratio scaling is to get a more quantitative scale than is possible with paired comparison or rank-order scales. Ratio scaling is especially interesting in psychology when investigators compare the physical measures of stimuli to the judgmental measures that subjects give those stimuli. The goal of many psychologists is to be able to assign quantitative numbers to sensations and perceptions, then relate these numbers to the quantitative numbers indicating the physical intensity of the stimuli.[3]

## INTERVIEWS

The interview method of data collection involves a face-to-face situation in which the investigator (or one of his associates) extracts verbal responses from subjects by asking questions. It may be employed in both experimental and EPF investigations. There are three main purposes for employing interviews. First, the interview can be used as a probing device to identify variables

---

3. A more in-depth coverage of scaling techniques may be found in the following texts: Underwood [1966, Chapter Six—good coverage with many examples], Dember [1963, Chapter Three], and Kling and Riggs [1971, Chapter Three].

and relationships of which an investigator may have no prior knowledge. Someone who has committed murder may be interviewed in an attempt to identify the psychological conditions under which that action occurred, or a psychologist may ask a child how he feels to get an idea of what is wrong. From comments of the child he may determine which variables he should deal with to solve the child's behavioral problems. Second, it may be used as an information-gathering device in its own right for research purposes. Questions may have been selectively chosen to shed some light on a particular hypothesis or assumption. The responses of the subjects, for example, could be used as a measure of hostility or preference indicating personal bias. Third, it can be used as a checking system in conjunction with other research procedures. It is not uncommon for an investigator to obtain unexpected results from his subjects. Rather than completely redesigning the experiment, the investigator may add an interview step with his subjects, asking why they did certain things or were they aware of certain things going on which they should not have been aware of.

### Structured and Unstructured Interviews

Interviews may be grossly divided into two categories—*structured* and *unstructured*. In a structured interview, the questions, their sequence, and their wording are fixed. This type of interview is generally carried out for the second of the three purposes—as a data-gathering device in its own right. Its function is to provide a psychometric measurement similar to an aptitude test on an attitude scale. A particular sequence of questions is asked dealing with an issue of interest to the investigator. The questions are arranged in such a manner that the responses will indicate the subject's position or ranking on some psychological dimension such as emotion, attention, apathy, or interest. Opinion polls are good examples of situations in which structured interviews are required.

The unstructured interview is generally used as a probing device. It is best illustrated by client-centered approaches used in the more applied clinical and counseling psychology situations. Although the interview is defined as being unstructured, the interviewer generally has some specific objectives in mind as he proceeds through the sessions. The questions, their sequence, and their wording are determined by the investigator, however, as the interview progresses. The additional flexibility allows the interviewer to let the responses of the subject being interviewed determine to a large extent the direction the interview may take. But the questions are asked in a manner intended to lead the respondent toward giving information related to the objectives of the investigation. Although the unstructured interview allows the investigator a great deal of latitude, preplanning of the basic interview format is still essential. Unstandardized interviews are considered the optimal approach to data collection in situations in which the type of information sought is difficult for the subjects to express or is psychologically distressing. The flexibility of this type of data-collection procedure allows the investigator to modify the structure of the interview in progress.

### Selection of Questions

Most structured interviews include three types of information: face sheet (identification) information, census-type or sociological information, and problem information [Parten, 1950, pp. 162–176]. Identification information refers to information, such as subject number, that identifies the subject being interviewed. In cases where different sequences of questions or different questions are used, identification information would also include which form was administered. Census information such as sex, age, education, income, and religious affiliation is also generally collected at the onset of the interview. The investigation usually involves measuring the correlation between this census information and the responses to the problem questions that are the main concern of the investigator. The questions concerning why the interview is being carried out make up what is called the problem information.

Structured interviews may be divided into two groups according to the types of problem questions employed—*fixed-alternative* or *open-end* items. With fixed-alternative items the subjects are asked to respond by selecting one of several choices supplied. An example of a fixed-alternative item is this:

> Are you in favor of the President of the United States having unlimited powers in matters of international conflicts or war? (Yes/No)

Fixed-alternative interview questions have several advantages. They are more uniform in terms of measurement, have greater reliability, and are easier to score and compare. They are, however, more restrictive and may not provide a response the subject considers most appropriate. This problem may be dealt with in two ways. First, one of the choices given is "other." This allows the subject an alternative response that he feels appropriate. Second, the subject may be allowed to make his response in terms of a continuum—for example:

> Rate TV as an entertainment activity on a scale from 1 to 7 in which 1 represents very poor and 7 represents excellent.

Open-end interviews add an important dimension to data-collection procedures by putting a minimum of restraint on the subjects' answers. In many instances, this allows the investigator to get a better picture of the respondents' actual beliefs and attitudes. It also has a somewhat relaxing effect on the respondents by allowing them to put answers in their own words. A combination of fixed-alternative and open-end items is commonly used in educational research because such a format generally provides both more objectivity and more depth than is possible with either type alone.[4]

## PSYCHOLOGICAL TESTS

Since one's abilities and mental capacity are potentials for behavior and are not directly observable, they are assessed indirectly with psychological tests. The idea of psychological tests is certainly not new to the reader; in fact, almost everyone has taken such tests at some point in life.

In the three previous sections we emphasized how stimuli were presented and how the response was measured when scaling, threshold, or interview methods are employed. This section emphasizes what types of measures can be obtained. The scores may be analyzed using the same analytical tools available when other similar types of measures are involved. The important question an investigator contemplating the use of psychological tests needs to answer is, "Does the test measure what I want it to measure?" Psychological tests can measure such things as achievement, aptitude, and personality traits.

### Types

**Achievement tests.**   The most common type of psychological test given is the achievement test. Achievement tests are designed to measure what a person has actually learned, not what he is capable of learning (aptitude tests). Achievement tests may be divided into two categories—*standardized* and *unstandardized*. Standardized achievement tests are those that have been designed for and tested on a large number of subjects. In this way the scores on the achievement test can be interpreted in terms of how a particular subject rates according to the populace in general. Many standardized achievement tests are available to the investigator. Some are designed to measure knowledge of specific facts, whereas others attempt to measure the student's conceptual understanding and mastery of basic principles pertaining to the subject matter. Standardized achievement tests generally consist of a battery of tests. The California Achievement Test (CAT), for example, contains tests in reading, language, and mathematics. The Sequential Tests of Educational Progress (STEP) include tests on essay writing, listening comprehension, reading comprehension, writing, science, mathematics, and social

4. A more in-depth coverage of how to conduct interviews may be found in Kerlinger [1973, Chapter Twenty-Eight provides an excellent and easy-to-understand coverage] and Kornhauser and Sheatsley [1959].

studies. The CAT takes only an hour and a half to administer; the STEP requires nine hours.

Unstandardized achievement tests are those that have not been given to a national sample. The tests given in college and other school classes at the end of the term are good examples of unstandardized achievement tests.

When selecting an achievement test for his research project, the investigator should first decide on what areas of achievement he wants to measure. Most investigations are designed to analyze only one area of achievement, so an investigator may select only one of the many test subsections in a battery. Achievement test batteries such as the CAT and the STEP were designed more for diagnostic reasons (e.g., to determine whether a student is behind in certain areas) than for research. Although unstandardized achievement tests are frequently used in research, standardized tests are generally considered better.

**Aptitude tests.**    Whereas achievement tests are used to determine what a person knows now, aptitude tests are designed to predict how a person will do in the future. Aptitude tests, then, are used to determine one's potential abilities. How is it possible to determine one's future abilities? Because the person has not performed future actions yet, the aptitude test, like the achievement test, must be based on past actions and performance. The questions in an aptitude test are actually samples of the person's past achievements. Since a person's ability to perform some future task depends to a large extent on his present abilities, aptitude tests measure present abilities. A person's aptitude is usually measured by combining a number of different achievement measures.

Tests are available to measure all types of aptitudes, including artistic, musical, mechanical, physical, foreign language, and mathematical. Aptitude tests that measure a wide range of abilities related to success in different occupations are also available. These are especially helpful in vocational counseling. The basic principle behind aptitude tests is the comparison of people's profiles (their scores on different categories of the test) with those of people who have previously been found to be successful. The General Aptitude Test Battery (GATB) measures a person's abilities in ten areas including verbal aptitude, numerical aptitude, motor speed, and clerical perception.

**Personality tests.**    There are a number of different types of personality tests that include personality inventories and projective tests. An inventory obtains information about personality by asking questions or requiring the person to respond to statements. Due to the fact that the questions employed in the inventory are direct, the subject can often guess the areas the investigator is attempting to measure. Personality inventories available to the investigator include the Minnesota Multiphasic Personality Inventory (MMPI) and the

Objective Analytical Test Battery. These inventories are considered more appropriate for research because the objectives of the questions are not as easy to detect.

Projective personality tests were developed based on the idea that one's personality is projected into his perceptions. The Rorschach Test, the Thermatic Apperception Test (TAT), and the House-Tree-Person Test fit into this category. The advantage of projective tests over inventories is that the subject does not know what is expected of him. It is less likely that he can falsify his responses, though it is still possible. By forcing the person to use his own imagination in responding to ink blots and pictures, or drawing particular objects, some psychologists believe they are forcing the subject to reveal the unconscious factors that make up his personality.

To illustrate the use of a projective test, let's look at the Rorschach. Ten ink blots in different shades of grey, black, or some other color are used. The subject is asked to describe what he "perceives" the ink blot to be. The scoring of the Rorschach is complex and difficult; examiners must undergo in-depth training to score the test properly. Different aspects of the subject's responses are interpreted to reveal different personality characteristics. The validity of this test, like other personality tests, varies to some extent according to the examiner.

### Uses

There are two main uses of psychological tests in research. First, they may be used to assign subjects to groups. An investigator may be interested in trying a special training technique on underachievers, intellectually gifted children, or people with certain personality disorders. In order to obtain subjects, psychological tests need to be administered. Aptitude and personality tests are most frequently used for this purpose. Second, psychological tests can be used as DVs in investigations. Educational psychologists are constantly determining the effects of variables by means of psychological tests. What effect does social praise have on achievement? Do children learn better in groups? Can older people learn languages as easily as children? Questions such as these are investigated using psychological tests. As previously mentioned, achievement tests are the most common type of psychological test used in research as a DV measure. Though aptitude and personality tests may be used as DVs, they are more often used for subject selection.

There are three main purposes for psychological tests: prediction, diagnosis, and research. As might be expected, aptitude tests are more commonly used for predicting abilities than as a research tool. Personality tests are primarily concerned with diagnosis. They are designed to uncover the characteristics a person has.

When asked to carry out a class experiment, most undergraduates think first of dealing with a topic concerning people's abilities, aptitudes, or personality dimensions. To carry out such projects, the investigator has to be able to select and administer the appropriate psychological test. This is not a simple matter, for it requires the investigator to have a good understanding of the tests, plus special training in how to administer them and evaluate the results. Because the undergraduate investigator does not usually have these skills, he should avoid psychological tests in class projects unless there is someone available who can select and administer them for him. The use of psychological tests is a sensitive issue in psychology at the present time, because most people do not understand what they are and how they can be misused. Even some practicing psychologists are guilty of inappropriately using psychological tests. In the next sections of this chapter we shall consider how psychological tests are devised and how easy it is to use them incorrectly.

### Development

Psychological tests are frequently treated as if they were exact measures. These tests are designed to measure the mental abilities and processes of man, abilities and processes that are unobservable in their own right and therefore are only indirectly measured and inferred from related observable responses. A child's mathematical ability, for example, is determined according to how many mathematical problems he can solve. A college student's achievement in class is often defined according to the score he obtains on the final exam.

Sometimes, however, his score on the final exam does not reflect his achievement. He may know the material, but be unable to interpret the questions; or the questions may not represent a valid measure of what is supposed to be measured. For example, a final exam consisting of algebra problems would not enable a professor to get a valid measure of what a student knows about abnormal psychology. Once the instructor for a social psychology course apparently rummaged through his test files and inadvertently selected a final exam designed for a course in personality. The mistake was not brought to his attention until the final exam period by students taking the exam. Much to his embarrassment, they were excused from taking a final exam because the only test available at that time would not have been a valid measure of what was discussed in the class.

How do psychologists go about developing valid psychological tests? This is a difficult problem and one that investigators should understand. There is no magic formula for selecting items for a test. The main ingredients for selection seem to be deductive reasoning plus large helpings of trial and error. Let us take a look at how the first successful intelligence test (a type of aptitude test) was developed.

In the early 1900s, the Paris school system was facing an important problem: How could it differentiate students needing special instruction from those who should go into the regular school system? What was needed was some measure of academic limitations and potential. In 1904, a commission whose members included Alfred Binet was formed to design methods for distinguishing between bright, average, and dull children. One of the reasons Binet was chosen was because he had been actively involved in such projects for many years. He had his formal training as a lawyer, and also had become a playwright. His interest in intelligence stimulated him to pursue a doctoral degree in psychology and to open the first psychology laboratory of the Sorbonne.

Binet's first attempts at devising an intelligence test included the analysis of handwriting and palm reading. Although these two approaches were unsuccessful, he continued testing as many factors as he could think of that might reflect intelligence. Using trial and error, he discarded methods that did not work, and kept those that seemed to have possibilities. One of his problems in finding a measure of intelligence was the fact that the term had never really been defined. His job, then, also included defining intelligence. Binet never directly stated what his intelligence test was to measure, but he felt it needed to include three factors:

1. Direction—the ability to set up a goal and work toward it
2. Adaptation—the ability to adapt oneself to the problem
3. Self-evaluation—the ability to evaluate one's own performance

The approach they finally came up with was to present various items and types of problems for the child to solve. The tasks in the test included (at the easiest levels) naming parts of the body and having the child select and hand objects to the examiner. Older children were asked such questions as which number was not in its correct position: 12, 9, 6, 3, 15. A more difficult task included verbally presenting seven digits (e.g., 8, 4, 5, 7, 2, 9, 1) and asking the examinees to repeat, in order, as many as they could. How were specific items determined to be representative of certain age abilities? Simple. If all children of age five, for example, could answer it, it was tested on six-year-olds, then seven-year-olds, and so on. Eventually a test was developed that consisted of items for each age level from three through fifteen years.

How was a person's intelligence determined? After administering the test to a large sample of the population, norms were determined for the various physical ages. Binet proposed the term *mental age* (MA). A person's mental age was to be worth a certain number of months' credit of MA. The total MA score obtained by the person was then compared to the mean score obtained by people of the exact same chronological age (CA). If a six-year-old child has been tested and found to have a MA of 6, this information is plugged into the formula:

$$\frac{MA}{CA} \times 100 = 10 \qquad \frac{6}{6} \times 100 = 100$$

A six-year-old with an IQ of 100 on the Binet test is said to be of average intelligence because he knows as much as the average six-year-old.

## Misuse

Unfortunately, most psychological investigators are not psychometricians (experts on psychological tests). The results of investigations using such tests are often overgeneralized because the investigator is not as familiar with the test as he should be. One should keep in mind the fact that the results of psychological tests are open to interpretation. They are not hard physical facts. Rather, they are responses from which internal processes and abilities are inferred. Too often the results of such tests are used as "proof" of the presence of mental abilities or personality characteristics. The code of ethics urges psychologists to behave in a reasonable manner when interpreting test data. Some psychologists, however, act as if the results of such tests are completely valid and beyond question. An example of this problem was reported by Jeffry [1964] concerning the issue of whether a psychologist may be considered an expert witness in criminal cases involving insanity:

Psychologist A testified that she had administered the following tests to Kent: the Wechsler Memory Scale, the Bender-Gestalt, the Rorschach, the Thematic Apperception Test, the House-Tree-Person Test, and the Szondi Test. From this evidence she diagnosed the defendant as schizophrenic, chronic undifferentiated type, characterized by abnormal thoughts, difficulty with emotional control, deficient in common-sense judgement, and lacking in close relationships with other people. She considered these as indicative of psychosis and that the crimes of housebreaking, robbery, and rape, of which the defendant was accused, were products of the mental disease. The cross examination of the psychologist went as follows:

    Q. What did the House-Tree-Person Test reveal?

    A. The major finding was a feeling of withdrawal, running away from reality, feelings of rejection by women.

    Q. And the results of the Szondi?

    A. This showed a passive, depressed person who withdrew from the world of reality, with an inability to relate to others.

    Q. Wasn't the Szondi Test made up around 1900, or the early 1900 period? And wasn't it made up of a number of pictures of Europeans who were acutely psychotic?

    A. Yes, that is true.

    Q. And this tells you something about his personality?

    A. Yes, you can tell something about the person from his responses to the photos.

    Q. And the House-Tree-Person Test—you handed the defendant, Kent, a pencil and a blank piece of paper, is that right, Doctor?

    A. That is correct.

    Q. And you asked him to draw a house?

    A. Yes.

    Q. And what did this tell you about Kent?

A. The absence of a door, and the bars on the windows, indicated he saw the house as a jail, not a home. Also, you will notice it is a side view of the house; he was making it inaccessible.

Q. Isn't it normal to draw a side view of a house? You didn't ask him to draw a front view, did you?

A. No.

Q. And those bars on the window—could they have been Venetian blinds and not bars? Who called them bars, you or Kent?

A. I did.

Q. Did you ask him what they were?

A. No.

Q. What else did the drawing reveal about Kent?

A. The line in front of the house runs from left to right. This indicates a need for security.

Q. This line indicates insecurity! Could it also indicate the contour of the landscape, like a lawn or something?

A. This is not the interpretation I gave it.

Q. And the chimney—what does it indicate?

A. You will notice the chimney is dark. This indicates disturbed sexual feelings. The smoke indicates inner daydreaming.

Q. Did I understand you correctly? Did you say dark chimneys indicate disturbed sex feelings?

A. Yes.

Q. You then asked Kent to draw a tree. Why?

A. We have discovered that a person often expresses feelings about himself that are on a subconscious level when he draws a tree.

Q. And what does this drawing indicate about Kent's personality?

A. The defendant said it was a sequoia, 1500 years old, and that it was diseased. This indicates a feeling of self-depreciation. Also, the tree has no leaves and it leans to the left. This indicates a lack of contact with the outside world—the absence of leaves.

Q. Don't trees lose their leaves in winter, Doctor? If you look out the window now, in Washington, do you see leaves on the trees? Perhaps the defendant was drawing a picture of a tree without leaves, as they appear in the winter.

A. The important thing is, however, why did the defendant select this particular tree. He was stripped of leaves, of emotions.

Q. You then asked him to draw a person?

A. Yes.

Q. And he drew this picture of a male?

A. Yes.

Q. And what does this drawing indicate about Kent?

A. The man appears to be running. This indicates anxiety, agitation. He is running, you will notice, to the left. This indicates running away from the environment. If he had been running to the right this would indicate entering the environment.

Q. How about the hands?

A. The sharp fingers may indicate hostility.

Q. Anything else?

A. The head and the body appear to be separated by a dark collar, and the neck is long. This indicates a split between intellect and emotion.

The dark hair, dark tie, dark shoes, and the dark buckle indicate anxiety about sexual problems.

Q. You then asked Kent to draw a person of the opposite sex. What did this picture indicate?

A. The dark piercing eyes indicated a feeling of rejection by women, hostility toward women.

Q. Are you familiar with the occasion upon which a Veteran's Administration psychologist gave this House-Tree-Person Test to 50 psychotics, and then gave 50 normal subjects the same test, and then a group of psychologists rated them?

A. No, I am not familiar with that research.

Psychologist B testified that he administered the Wechsler-Bellevue, the Graham Kendall, the Rorschach, and the Symonds Picture Story Tests. He also testified that he had diagnosed the defendant as schizophrenic, undifferentiated type, and that mental illness had produced the alleged crimes. The cross examination went as follows:

Q. Did you administer the Szondi Test, Doctor?

A. No, I don't happen to think much of it. The test assumes a schizophrenic looks a certain way, and we have evidence this isn't so.

Q. What responses did you receive from Kent on the Rorschach, the ink-blot test?

A. Wolf, butterfly, vagina, pelvis, bats, buttocks, etc.

Q. And from this you concluded the defendant was schizophrenic?

A. Yes, that and other things.

Q. You gave him the Wechsler Adult Scale?

A. Yes.

Q. On the word-information part of the test, the word "temperature" appears. What question did you ask the defendant?

A. At what temperature does water boil?

Q. You gave him a zero. Why?

A. Because he answered 190° and that is the wrong answer. The right answer is 212°F.

Q. What question did you ask about the Iliad?

A. I am not sure; I believe I asked him to identify the Iliad or who wrote the Iliad.

Q. And he answered "Aristotle?"

A. Yes.

Q. And you scored him zero?

A. That's correct.

Q. Now you asked the defendant to define blood vessels, did you not?

A. Yes.

Q. And his answer was capillaries and veins. You scored him zero. Why? Aren't capillaries and veins blood vessels?

A. I don't know. The norms don't consider the answer acceptable.

A third psychologist testified he saw the subject once at jail or the receiving home for an hour and a half; that he administered the Rorschach and started the Human Figure Drawing Test. The testing was interrupted when the defendant's father was announced, and Kent became very upset, highly emotional.

He diagnosed the defendant as schizophrenic, undifferentiated type. He thought productivity existed; that is, the schizophrenia produced the housebreakings, robberies, and rapes. The test showed severe thinking disturbance, an inability to control impulses, and disturbed sexual feelings. His cross examination went as follows:

Q. Why did you see the defendant, Kent?
A. Because of a call from Mr. Arens.
Q. Are you a member of the Washington School of Psychiatry?
A. No.
Q. The defendant made one drawing for you, right, Doctor?
A. Yes that is right.
Q. After the announced arrival of his father?
A. Yes.
Q. Do you use the House-Tree-Person Test?
A. Never.
Q. Does it have validity?
A. Yes.
Q. You do use the Szondi?
A. Five or six times.
Q. When did you stop using it?
A. At the fifth administration, about nine years ago.
Q. What does this drawing that Kent made for another psychologist indicate to you?
A. The transparency of the picture—that is, seeing through the figure to something beneath—suggests pathology.
Q. Do you usually use an extensive battery of tests before reaching a diagnosis?
A. Yes.
Q. Do you usually arrive at the diagnosis on the basis of one Rorschach administered twice within an hour?
A. Frequently.
Q. What else in the drawing is significant psychologically?
A. The irregularity or sketchiness of the lines may suggest tension and anxiety. The attention paid to details—to the belt-bow-tie, and pockets—indicate a little-boy-like quality about the defendant.
Q. Is it significant that the figure is running to the left, and not to the right?
A. To some people, yes. I don't place any significance on it.[5]

Notice how the psychologists called as expert witnesses contradicted each other by claiming the results of the tests to be exact and above interpretation. An investigator should be especially careful when using psychological tests as DVs, particularly when personality tests are used. Most psychologists agree that achievement tests are usually more valid than aptitude tests, which are also more valid than personality tests. When conducting an investigation involving the use of a psychological test, the investigator should take special care to select the appropriate test. Because the validity of most aptitude and personality tests can be influenced by who administers them, a psychometrician should be used to give the tests.

5. From Jeffry [1964, pp. 838–843]. Copyright 1964 by the American Psychological Association. Reprinted by permission.

## APPLICATION
## OF DATA-COLLECTION METHODS

How are data-collection procedures employed? Psychologists emphasize the use of data-collection procedures for identifying cause and effect relationships so much that their other uses are often overlooked. Psychological tests, scaling methods, and threshold techniques have several important uses, four of which are presented here:

1. Descriptive research
2. Subject selection
3. Prediction
4. As DV measures

**Descriptive research.** What is the range of human hearing? Which athletic event is most popular in the United States? How many schoolchildren are hard of hearing? Research conducted to answer such questions is termed *descriptive* because its objective is to gather information that "describes" or reports the frequency of occurrence of some event. No cause-effect relationship is sought in such projects, simply the presentation of information. Descriptive research is common in our society and includes political polls, attitude surveys, and marketing surveys. Almost every descriptive research investigation that deals with psychologically related factors involves the use of one of the data-collection methods presented in this chapter. Generally, descriptive research investigations are not considered appropriate as undergraduate class projects because they do not involve much in the way of data analysis.

**Subject selection.** Psychological tests, interviews, scaling methods, and threshold measurement techniques are frequently used by investigators to select subjects for research projects. What effect does high anxiety have on the ability to learn of mentally retarded, normal, and gifted children? Before an investigator can apply some anxiety-provoking IV to mentally retarded, normal, and gifted subjects, he must have some means of identifying subjects who would fit in these categories. Psychological investigations frequently involve determining the differential effects of some IV on psychotic versus neurotic subjects, tone deaf versus normal hearing children, introvertive versus extrovertive subjects, and high achievers versus low achievers. The data-collection procedures previously discussed are used in such projects for selecting subjects to serve in the different groups. This use of data-collection techniques for subject selection purposes is often overlooked in texts dealing with methods of data collection.

**Prediction.** Data-collection procedures such as aptitude tests are often given in an effort to predict future behavior. Vocational aptitude tests are employed by counseling psychologists to help predict at which type of work a person could succeed. Scholastic aptitude tests are given to most students applying for admission to universities in an effort to predict their chances of success. The predictive aspect of data-collection procedures is used more by applied psychologists in dealing with patients than as a research tool.

**Dependent variable measures.** Most psychological investigations involve the use of the data-collection procedures presented here as DV measures. The effects of different IVs may be determined by comparing the subject's responses with these methods. All psychological subfields including physiological, social, perceptual, learning, and clinical psychology employ these methods of data collection as DV measures. As previously mentioned, these methods all require the subject to make some sort of evaluative judgment. Whether attempting to identify an absolute threshold or applying a personality test, the investigator is indirectly trying to identify certain non-observable capacities or mental abilities. In such situations, the psychologist needs to pay special attention to the issue of whether the data-collection method he employs will give a valid measurement.

## SUMMARY

Several data-collection methods are commonly used in psychological research. These include threshold measurement techniques, scaling techniques, interviews, and psychological tests. Threshold measures are employed to determine both absolute and differential thresholds, and attempt to establish a "psychophysical function" (the relationship between a psychological variable such as perception and a physical variable such as intensity of a stimulus). Two procedures are frequently used to determine thresholds—the method of limits and the method of constant stimuli.

Scaling techniques are employed to compare subjects' behavior on a more qualitative than quantitative basis (e.g., better than, more prestigious). Three scaling techniques are paired comparison, rank-ordering, and ratio scaling. Ratio scaling includes magnitude estimation and ratio production.

Interview methods of data collection require the user to set up his questions and interview in certain ways. Structured or unstructured interviews with fixed or open-end items can be used. Three types of information are gathered in each—identification, sociological, and problem information.

Several types of psychological tests were discussed, including achievement, aptitude, and personality tests. Achievement tests can be employed to determine what a person actually knows or can do. Aptitude tests are designed to measure potential ability. Personality tests are designed to measure personality characteristics and attributes. How well a psychological test validly measures what it reports to measure varies from one test to another. Generally speaking, achievement tests are more valid than aptitude tests, which are more valid than personality tests.

There are four main uses of the data-collection methods presented here: for descriptive research, subject selection, and prediction, and as DV measures.

# 7

# Nonexperimental
# Designs

*As mentioned in Chapter Three, not all psychological investigations are experimental. Although experimental designs are of central importance in psychology, there are nonexperimental designs a psychologist may also use in his work, and the reader should be familiar with them. It would be unfortunate if the reader thought that experimentation was the only avenue of investigation the psychologist could choose. Pay special attention to the correlation section, for it tells how an investigator may try to determine the degree of relationship between variables rather than a cause-effect relationship.*

Scientific investigation is almost always thought of as a process of finding lawful relationships between variables or parameters that one finds in nature. Because these relationships are often obscured by being too complicated or too numerous, the experimental method was devised to simplify and clarify systematically one variable's relationship to another. The experimental method involves direct experimenter manipulation of situations to create parameters and variables that can logically be related only in certain ways. Such active manipulation of what scientists call independent variables has proved to be a powerful tool in science. Although many psychologists carry on basic research to clarify some theoretical principle of psychology, most psychologists are involved in solving practical everyday problems. Should couples have children early or late in their married life? Can children live normal lives after being raised in a closet for years by disturbed parents? What causes people to commit suicide or murder? All these are practical problems for which society turns to psychologists for answers.

Unfortunately, however, psychologists are often asked questions that either should not, or cannot, be investigated by experimental manipulation. It would be unethical, for instance, for a psychologist to manipulate a situation to create all the parameters and variables he believes would produce a murder and then wait to see if a murder occurs. Some experiments are physically impossible to carry out. One requiring an earthquake to study the effects of stress in an emergency situation would be impossible (as well as unethical) for a psychologist to arrange. Another kind of impossible experiment would be one in which a psychologist would have to travel back in time to change a variable here and there so that the present situation could be more readily clarified.

It is possible to carry out a scientific investigation without manipulating an IV. Relationships can be found between events without such manipulation. Ex post facto investigations allow an investigator to gather information without manipulating an IV. These investigations are just as sound as experimental investigations, but less powerful in terms of identifying causal relationships. The objective of nonexperimental designs is to provide an appropriate way of analyzing problems not amenable to experimental investigation.

Nonexperimental designs can be divided into four categories:

1. Quasi-experimental designs
2. Correlational designs
3. Contrast designs
4. Case study designs

## QUASI-EXPERIMENTAL DESIGNS

An EPF quasi-experiment is carried out exactly like a true experiment, except for two important variations. First, the investigator does not have the ability to assign subjects randomly to either the control or experimental groups. Rather than actively arranging an experimental situation consisting of a control and an experimental group, the investigator searches for a group of subjects that has been exposed to the particular IV he is interested in, and a second group, similar to the first in other relevant respects, that has not experienced the IV. Being unable to select subjects randomly greatly increases the possibility that secondary variables may contaminate the investigation. Suppose, for example, you wanted to see if giving elementary school children grades increases achievement. Using a quasi-experimental approach, you find two classes, one in which grades are given and one in which grades are not given. You then compare the two classes on an achievement test given to both at the end of their last year. Because you did not randomly select your subjects and set up your groups, the differences could be due to IQ, socioeconomic level, home training practices, and many other important secondary variables.

Second, the investigator cannot apply the IV whenever and to whomever he wishes. This also decreases his ability to draw a valid causal relationship. With these two variations restricting the control of secondary variables in quasi-experimental approaches, the investigator must rely more heavily on the control technique of constancy and exert more effort in trying to match his groups on important secondary variables. The more able he is in matching his groups on relevant secondary variables, the closer a quasi-experimental approach comes to being as good as a true experiment in identifying cause and effect relationships.

A good example of an EPF quasi-experiment was carried out in 1961 by Jo Taylor Auld. For years a controversy had been brewing over whether students within a class should be grouped according to ability and worked with by the teacher in this manner, or whether the teacher should work with the whole class as one unit. Auld's study set out to determine whether grouping or nongrouping was more effective. She searched around until she found two schools, one that grouped its students and one that did not, which were identical in terms of relevant secondary variables. Two elementary schools in South Carolina were used in the study. The neighborhoods served by the two schools were alike in terms of housing, community facilities, churches, and so on. The numbers and experience of the teachers from both schools were approximately the same. The classroom, library, and recreational facilities of the two schools were similar. Being in the same school district, the schools operated under the same policies and followed the same testing procedures.

In terms of socioeconomic status, the families were much alike for the two schools, although more fathers associated with the nongrouped school were engaged in professional occupations and slightly more mothers with children in the grouped school were employed outside the home. The median IQ of the children in the grouped school (school A) was 107; the median for the nongrouped school (school B) was 110. Fifth-grade students at school A had been divided into three intraclass groups, high, average, and low, after their first grade. They had been worked with in these groups for grades two through five. Auld then obtained the first-grade records of the fifth-grade students at school B and categorized those students into three groups, high, average, and low, in the same manner that they would have been grouped for instructional purposes if they had been enrolled in school A.

Auld thus established equivalent groups in the two schools and compared the two classes on the results of the Metropolitan Achievement Test given to all students of both schools at the end of their fifth-grade year. The results she obtained from the study were that (1) there were no statistically significant differences in performance of the students in schools A and B who were in the high and average categories; and (2) students in the low category from the ungrouped school (school B) achieved significantly higher than the low group students from school A.

Notice that the purpose of the EPF quasi-experiment is the same as that of a true experiment—to isolate a cause-effect relationship. The initial steps involved in an EPF quasi-experiment are essentially the same as those employed with experimental designs. First, a problem must be identified and a hypothesis spelled out in detailed and specific terms. The IV and DV are defined, and relevant secondary variables are identified. Random assignment of subjects to groups is not possible with EPF quasi-experiments and is therefore a handicap in control of secondary variables. The investigators are not able to apply the IV to whomever they please in this situation, and that also increases the possibility that the study may be internally invalid. The investigator is limited as well because he must rely on past records whose thoroughness and accuracy are unknown and because he had no control over the measuring of the DV. The statistical tests involved in analyzing the data are the same as those used to deal with data in true experiments.[1] The investigator cannot have as much confidence in drawing conclusions with EPF quasi-experimental designs because some of the assumptions (e.g., randomization) underlying the statistical tests have been violated, and the investigator had less control over secondary variables. With the exception of randomization, all the control techniques available for large $N$ experimental designs are also available to the EPF quasi-experiment, including statistical control. It is even possible to perform an analysis of covariance on the data of such investigations, as long as a covariate measure is available.[2]

EPF quasi-experimental investigations do have some advantages over experimental investigations. It is possible to seek answers to certain kinds of questions about past or unethical situations that could not be dealt with using experimental designs. Time can be saved by dealing with records that have been kept over the years rather than starting fresh. School, educational, social, and industrial psychologists may especially benefit from using EPF quasi-experimental investigations because schools, businesses, and government agencies generally secure and preserve records over many years.

1. No statistical example is given here because the statistical procedure is carried out exactly as in a true experiment. If the reader wishes an example to follow in calculating his data, he should turn to the chapter that presents the type of design used (e.g., two-group, one-way ANOVAR, etc.) and follow the steps shown there.

2. The statistical analyses used on quasi-experimental designs are discussed more specifically in the experimental design chapters to follow because they are employed in exactly the same manner in both experimental and quasi-experimental situations.

## CORRELATIONAL DESIGNS

Psychologists are constantly confronted with situations in which they are required to determine whether two or more variables are related in any way. Is the success of a person in later life related to the type of family training he received as a child? Is cigarette smoking related to lung cancer? Are there any particular behaviors a person contemplating suicide emits prior to committing the act that might warn us of his impending plan? In such cases the psychologist takes measures of each of the variables in question and correlates their presence or absence in given situations. These types of investigations are called correlational studies and they include all research projects in which an attempt is made to discover or clarify relationships using correlational statistical methods. Experimental research compares different groups of subjects in which an IV is either present or absent; correlational studies usually compare members of a single group in which the variables under scrutiny are present in varying degrees.

The basic design of correlational research is quite simple, involving nothing more than the collecting of two or more scores on the same group of subjects and computing a correlation coefficient from those scores. The objective of a correlational statistic is to index the degree of covariation that can exist between two variables. It may be seen by observation that when variable $X$ increases, variable $Y$ generally increases also and some measure is needed to index the relationship that might exist between $X$ and $Y$. By manipulating the data it can be shown, and proved mathematically, that the sum of the cross products between variable $X$ and $Y$, $XY$, becomes larger when the variables are compared in order of magnitude than when they are not. For example, if $X = (3, 2, 1)$ and $Y = (2, 1, 0)$, then $\Sigma XY = 6 + 2 + 0 = 8$. Now, if the order of magnitude is changed, $X = (3, 2, 1)$ and $Y = (1, 2, 0)$, then $\Sigma XY = 3 + 4 + 0 = 7$; or, if $X = (3, 2, 1)$ and $Y = (0, 2, 1)$, $\Sigma XY = 0 + 4 + 1 = 5$. This example shows that $\Sigma XY$ increases with the increase in covariation between $X$ and $Y$, reaching a maximum when $X$ and $Y$ are in corresponding order. Using this mathematical relationship, researchers have devised statistical methods for determining how closely the variations in one variable are related to variations in a second variable. To illustrate how this is done, let us take a look at a situation that arose several years ago.

Is the amount of time a student studies related to the scores he receives on a class exam? A psychology major enrolled in a senior seminar was not sure a strong relationship existed between these two variables and asked if she might carry out an investigation. Such an investigation would require the investigator to have control over the materials to be studied for the class, so it was not carried out until the next semester, when ten students enrolled in another senior seminar. At the beginning of the class the students were told that the material to be covered in the class was not available in text form and could not be purchased. Copies of the material would be available, however, in the reserve section of the library and could be checked out and used only in the reserve room of the library. They were told to do all the studying for the class in that room, and they were to sign in and out of the room so that a measure of the amount of studying they did could be kept. The amount of time each student studied during the semester was recorded in number of hours and the total number of points earned on the four fifty-point exams given during the term was also recorded. Table 7–1 shows the results of the investigation.

**TABLE 7–1**
*Results of study time investigation*

| Subject number | Number of hours studying (X) | Total number of term points earned (Y) |
|:---:|:---:|:---:|
| 1 | 88 | 18 |
| 2 | 60 | 16 |
| 3 | 76 | 21 |
| 4 | 68 | 18 |
| 5 | 56 | 12 |
| 6 | 180 | 36 |
| 7 | 76 | 12 |
| 8 | 104 | 16 |
| 9 | 140 | 47 |
| 10 | 192 | 32 |

A number of statistical methods are available for determining a correlation. The best-known correlational measure is the Pearson *r* correlation, which was chosen to analyze the data obtained here. The exact steps involved in calculating the correlation are presented so that the reader may follow them exactly if he is interested in carrying out a correlational analysis.

The formula for calculating a Pearson *r* correlation is

$$r = \frac{N\Sigma XY - (\Sigma X)(\Sigma Y)}{\sqrt{[N\Sigma X^2 - (\Sigma X)^2][N\Sigma Y^2 - (\Sigma Y)^2]}}$$

The next step is to calculate all the numbers ($N$, $XY$, $X$, and so on) required in the formula. This is done in Table 7–2. With these figures calculated, one simply plugs them into the formula to come up with the correlation coefficient.

**TABLE 7–2**
Calculation of a Pearson r correlation

| Subject number | $X$ | $X^2$ | $Y$ | $Y^2$ | $XY$ |
|---|---|---|---|---|---|
| 1 | 88 | 7,744 | 18 | 324 | 1,584 |
| 2 | 60 | 3,600 | 16 | 256 | 960 |
| 3 | 76 | 5,776 | 21 | 441 | 1,596 |
| 4 | 68 | 4,624 | 18 | 324 | 1,224 |
| 5 | 56 | 3,136 | 12 | 144 | 672 |
| 6 | 180 | 32,400 | 36 | 1,296 | 6,480 |
| 7 | 76 | 5,776 | 12 | 144 | 912 |
| 8 | 104 | 10,816 | 16 | 256 | 1,664 |
| 9 | 140 | 19,600 | 47 | 2,209 | 6,580 |
| 10 | 192 | 36,864 | 32 | 1,024 | 6,144 |

$N = 10 \quad \Sigma X = 1,040 \quad \Sigma X^2 = 130,336 \quad \Sigma Y = 228 \quad \Sigma Y^2 = 6,418 \quad \Sigma XY = 27,816$

$$r = \frac{(10)(27,816) - (1,040)(228)}{\sqrt{[10(130,336) - (1,040)^2][10(6,418) - (228)^2]}}$$

$$r = \frac{278,160 - 237,120}{\sqrt{(1,303,360 - 1,081,600)(64,180 - 51,984)}}$$

$$r = \frac{41,040}{\sqrt{(221,760)(12,196)}}$$

$$r = .79$$

The size of a Pearson $r$ correlation coefficient that a person may obtain from his data ranges from $+1$ through 0 to $-1$. The two important aspects of the correlation coefficient are its numerical size and its sign value. The larger the number, the stronger the relationship between the two variables. A correlation of 1.0 indicates a perfect relationship between the variables. A perfect relationship means one can exactly predict the numerical value of $X$, for example, if he knows what $Y$ is. A zero correlation means one cannot predict what $X$ is if $Y$ is known. The sign value indicates whether the relationship found is *directly* or *inversely* related. Figure 7–1 gives an example of both an inverse and a direct relationship that has a numerical value of 1.0. If we had obtained a $-1.0$ from our data (as shown in A), it would mean that the person studying the fewest hours would score highest on the exams, the second least studier would do second best, and so on right on down the line for the rest of the students.

A direct correlation of $+1.0$ (represented by B) would again mean that there was a perfect correlation between studying and exam scores, but in

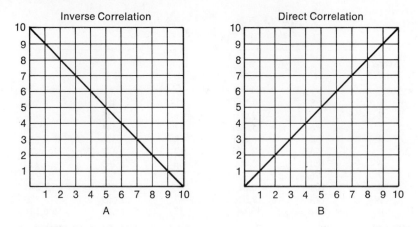

**FIGURE 7–1**
An inverse and a direct relationship

this case it would show the person studying the most would do best on the exam, and so on down the list of subjects. The +.79 obtained indicates that study time is highly correlated with achievement on exams, but not perfectly so. It tells us that if we knew how much a particular student studied in relation to his classmates, we could predict pretty closely how he will do in the course in comparison with the other students.

Correlational studies can and have been used to investigate almost the entire range of problems of psychological interest. Matheson, Bruce, and Beauchamp [1970] give a brief illustration of the range of correlational studies by listing several investigations in various areas of interest. They list correlational studies used to show that there are fewer erotic inscriptions (graffiti) in women's rest rooms than in men's (the difference was less in the Philippines than in the United States); that crackdowns on speeding did not result in any significant decrease in the number of traffic fatalities; and that scare promotional ads for seat belts had less effect than an ad featuring a professional race driver appealing to masculinity. Another area of interest that has been studied using the correlational method is the relationship between Down's Syndrome (Mongolism) and the age of the mother giving birth to the retarded child. It has been known for some time that the risk of having a Mongoloid child varies greatly with the age of the mother. The chance of a mother between the ages of fifteen and twenty-four having a Mongoloid child is only one in 1,500 births, but for a woman older than forty-five, the risk is one in 35 births [Robinson & Robinson, 1970]. Collmann and Stroller [1962] investigated the rates of Mongolism in Melbourne, Australia, for many years and found an exponential relationship between age and rate of Down's Syndrome. The correlation between the two variables was almost perfect.

It should be noted that although the correlational method points out a relationship between two variables, it does not specify the cause of the relationship. Is age of the mother the "cause" of Mongoloid births? Later studies have shown that Down's Syndrome is the result of a chromosome abnormality—in fact, two abnormalities. In younger women it is usually a hereditary abnormal chromosome, but with older women the abnormality is usually the result of a failure of meiosis, and the condition is not hereditary. Is, then, the "cause" of the abnormality the age of the woman? Stroller and Collmann [1965] did a later study and found a correlation of .81 for the incidence of Mongoloids per 100,000 live births and those of infective hepatitis per million cases. They then postulated that the virus-human interaction could well be the basis of the genetic abnormality. Recent data indicate that this may not yet be the full answer; first-born children of older mothers do not have the same chance of being retarded by Down's Syndrome as do later siblings. The studies of Mongolism and mother age offer an excellent example of what a correlational study can and cannot do. The method readily shows if a relationship exists between variables and the strength and direction of the relationship, but it does not show the cause of the relationship.

Although correlation does not technically show that one variable causes the occurrence of another, that psychologists often treat correlation as if it does. With human subjects, for example, past records have been analyzed, and have shown a high correlation between certain people being dead and the presence of arsenic in their gastrointestinal tract. Although law enforcement agencies have not carried out experiments to show a cause and effect relationship, most conclude such is the case. In the past, correlational studies showing a high relationship between cigarette smoking and lung cancer have been used to indicate cigarette smoking causes cancer.

On the other hand, there are many instances in which high correlations are found between variables, yet psychologists would not conclude causal relationships. There is, for example, a very high correlation between foot size and academic achievement. If a person would take into consideration people of all ages (from birth to adulthood) and calculate the correlation coefficient between foot size and achievement, a high correlation would be obtained. No cause relationship could be drawn, however. When is it permissible to draw conclusions about a cause-effect relationship using correlation? Generally speaking, a correlational study is not considered sufficient for drawing causal inferences. If, however, there are other types of supportive data that agree with the correlational findings, then correlational results are more acceptable when making such suggestions. Studies that correlate smoking with the incidence of lung cancer in humans are more accepted as showing cause-effect relationships because experiments on nonhuman species support such conclusions. Correlational investigations are not generally considered a proper type of investigation if one is seeking to find causes, unless the problem is not amenable to experimental manipulation. In such cases it may be permissible to use correlation to imply causation.

Correlational analysis finds application in four main types of research. First, it is employed in dealing with causality problems when experimental methods are inappropriate. Second, it may be used in a descriptive and predictive capacity. For example, personality traits and sociological characteristics associated with suicide cannot be studied with the experimental approach. After a person commits suicide, the researcher can only look at the historical records of the person's life, ex post facto. An example is offered by a study of suicide performed by Sainsbury and Barraclough [1968]. They found that the suicide rates in 1959 of foreign born U.S. citizens correlated .87 with the suicide rates in their country of birth. You could predict, given the suicide rates of their native lands, which of two immigrants was more likely to commit suicide. (Austrian immigrants, for example, were more likely to commit suicide than a person from Mexico.)

A third application of correlation is to control for secondary variables by means of the statistical control method. The analysis of covariance suggested earlier as a statistical control technique for removing the influence of some unwanted variable from the data is nothing more than a statistical formula made up by combining the principle of analysis of variance ($V_B/V_W$) with correlational principles ($\Sigma XY$). This has been a useful tool for research, mainly because it allows the investigator to adjust for secondary variables after an experiment is completed.[3]

The fourth application of correlation relates to the issues of reliability and validity. The correlational method is an excellent way to check on how close judges are in their ratings, one with another. For example, the coefficient gives a measure of how much alike two different judges rated or ranked some variable in an experimental situation. Such data can add to the internal validity of an investigation. This is an especially important concept in field research, where the DV is often measured by some observer rather than by a mechanical recorder in a laboratory. Suppose you wanted to study the effects of reinforcement on cooperative play. The DV would be cooperative play, a somewhat subjective term. A more objective, and reliable, measure of cooperative play could be obtained by first operationally defining what the term meant (e.g., playing in a game involving more than two children), and then having three or more observers, rather than one, record the DV. Later,

---

3. The way in which correlation is used, combined with the analysis of variance to statistically control secondary variables, is treated in detail in Chapter Ten.

the observers' records would be analyzed to see how well their judgments of cooperative play correlated.

## CONTRAST DESIGNS

Like correlational designs, the contrast, or comparative, design, as it is sometimes called, may be a substitute for experimentation. It is used primarily in the analysis of historical data, the number of cases of which are too small to permit meaningful statistical manipulation. The contrast design is often required in the comparative analysis of national units, which of course are few in number, or when comparing regions, cities, and other subnational units. Warwick and Osherson [1973] illustrate the method with a contrast study of suicide reported by Durkheim. One of Durkheim's central findings was that Protestants have higher suicide rates than do Catholics. The variable he used to explain the finding was the difference in the tenets and traditions of the two religions. Durkheim noticed, however, that in every country from which he investigated the data, Catholics constituted a minority group. Could it be, he asked, that the difference in suicide rates was due to minority status rather than to religion? To answer this question, Durkheim expanded his study to include regions such as Austria and Bavaria, where Catholics are a majority. In such regions he noted some diminution of the religious differences between Catholics and Protestants, but the Catholic rates were still lower. Durkheim was then able to conclude that the lower suicide rate of Catholics as compared to Protestants was not solely a matter of minority status. Durkheim used no statistical methods, yet he was able to approximate their use by means of a systematic contrast between one group and another.

The task of any investigator is to reduce the number of conditions that can influence the DV, isolate one condition from another, and make precise the role of each condition. Contrasting one group with another is necessary to accomplish this when the groups are small and statistical analysis is inappropriate. In sociology and developmental psychology, the effects of family size can be determined by contrasting the behavior and development of children from small families with those from large ones. Such studies have isolated differences from dependency behavior in nursery school to adult alcoholism rates. For example, children from small families have a higher activity level and seem to be more poised and self-confident with adults than do children from large families [Johnson & Medinnus, 1969].

The contrast design finds particular application in anthropologically oriented psychological studies. Much can be learned about the origins and development of human behavior by comparing one society with another, for differing social and physical environments often produce radical differences in acceptable behavior from one society to another. Of more telling interest, perhaps, are not the differences but the similarities that can be found between divergent and isolated groups. These differences and similarities make excellent contrast studies. For example, in some societies brides are not courted, they are bought. Is marriage in these societies more a matter of economics and less one of love than in societies where brides are courted? To test the proposition that a bride price (the price a man pays for his bride) is economic, an observer might undertake to see if the society he is studying perceives the transaction in the same way an economic transaction is perceived in our own society. Walter Goldschmidt [1973] set out to do exactly that with the Sebei, a Southern Nilotic people who live in Uganda. Among the Sebei, kinship is reckoned by male descent and clan relationships are of great psychological importance. One of their basic beliefs is that immortality is dependent upon having descendants. It is understandable, therefore, that the essence of Sebei marriage is the husband's concern with procreation. Goldschmidt studied the amount of bride price negotiated by 79 men between 1910 and 1960 and found the price paid was consistent with economic trends. The lowest price paid over the fifty-year period was $33, while the highest price was $420. Cattle were always exchanged and varied from 1 to 17.

Polygamy was a common practice among the Sebei, second and third wives being highly prized, which made single women of marriageable age rare. The Sebei believed, therefore, that second wives were very expensive. Goldschmidt found this was not the case. The first wife was usually more expensive than the second, and the third wife was the most expensive of all. However, the groom's parents usually help pay for the first wife, whereas the husband is on his own for the second. By the time he can afford a third, he is generally better off economically. All this paints a rather bleak picture for Uganda Valentine makers. The fact that the Sebei bride price is susceptible to economic analysis tells much about the Sebei. However much sentiment or emotion may enter into a Sebei man's desire to marry, he must at the same time face the economic realities of Sebei society and make his choice in an economic context.

## CASE STUDY DESIGNS

Whereas the correlational design may be used to investigate the relationship between variables with large groups and the contrast design allows investigation of small groups, what of the individual case? The study of individual cases has always been an important undertaking for numerous specialists, ranging from journalists and biographers, policemen and judges, to social workers and psychoanalysts. Professional journals serving clinical and other applied psychologists abound in case reports of individuals being treated for some form of mental illness or, at least, maladaptive behavior. All these reports are essentially like the case study design.

**Deviant case analysis.** Case studies do not manipulate an IV and look for change, but simply observe conditions as they unfold, whether in real time or ex post facto. An important subdivision of the case study is the deviant case analysis. This analysis attempts to take instances that are exceptions to the general trend and to locate IVs that set the instance off from the general. The investigator takes two groups or individuals that differ in outcome and attempts to locate diffences in conditions between them. One group, or individual is comprised of the deviant cases and the other by the majority of cases expressing the general finding. The method of deviant case analysis can be thought of as "reading backward" to approximate the experimental situation. In the experimental method, the IV is varied between experimental and control groups to produce different outcomes. In the deviant case analysis, the starting point is the difference already found and the investigator's task is to read backward to deduce the condition that produced the difference [Warwick & Osherson, 1973].

**Isolated clinical case analysis.** This is another important subdivision that is nothing more than an investigation of individual units with respect to some analytical problem. The method has been predominant in psychoanalysis. Freud's study of little Hans is well known, as are many other case studies. Freud's theories of human psychic response were formulated through the accumulation of many case studies of individuals. Many of the problems an analyst faces are unique or are found in a very small population. An excellent example is Wixen's [1973] study of the special problems of the children of the very rich. Wixen found that many children of the very rich suffer from lack of role image and goals, and a lack of normal social and psychological development that Wixen calls "dysgradia." Wixen's study of Brewer offers an interesting example of the case study.

> Brewer's grandfather, by working hard and investing wisely, amassed a respectable fortune in an automobile franchise and TV interests. His son, Brewer's father, had inherited the total and married a girl from a well-known family after she had become pregnant with Brewer. There was not much love in the marriage. After Brewer's birth, she was completely frigid towards Brewer's father and drank heavily. After being found in bed with one of the servants, she was divorced by Brewer's father and he was awarded custody of Brewer. The father seemed to genuinely be fond of Brewer, but left his upbringing completely to servants, especially to Elsie, a large, warm black woman of around fifty. Her entire life revolved around her ward, with whom she played out many of her own fantasies.
> Brewer did well in school, his grades were good, he was popular and did well

in sports. All this changed when he got into college. He was sent off with a large party and was given $1,000 a month allowance plus having his tuition paid along with the upkeep of his Porsche. Brewer was involved in accident after accident until he became an insurance risk. He was failing his classes, smoked a lot of marijuana, drank heavily, and began putting on weight. He contracted gonorrhea twice and had to pay for a girl's abortion. He could not handle his money and even with $1,000 a month would many times finish out a month living on bread and grape jelly. Brewer's father would become angry, write out a new budget, which Brewer would dutifully resolve to keep, and then continue in his ways. He finally dropped out of school and returned home. He was offered a job at his father's business. The first day he arrived two hours late, made a pass at a married personnel clerk and engaged in behavior termed "clearly self-destructive." In therapy, Brewer wept, "I don't know what got into me! I just wasn't thinking. I didn't want to embarrass Dad—or did I?"[4]

Wixen worked with Brewer for two and a half years and solved some of his basic neurotic problems generated by his deep distrust of all women and his conflict with his father. Brewer still lacked goals or any reasonable purpose in life. There was never any real need for him to work. He had all the money he would ever need to live on. From this experience, Wixen learned more about the special problems of the very rich and how to treat their problems.

The case study lends itself to naturalistic studies. Animals generally learn through repetition, often requiring many trials before a behavior becomes an established part of the repertoire. Exceptions are rare, and when observed, they offer a good example of the usefulness of the case study. Recently, a green heron at the Miami Seaquarium was observed to possess a complicated set of apparently self-learned behaviors. The heron had learned that by placing a bread pellet, sold for a nickel a handful at vending machines to visitors desiring to feed the fish, into the water, fish would be drawn to the spot and the heron had an easy meal. Robert F. Sisson, a photographer from the National Geographic, was called in to take pictures and record what he saw (Figure 7–2). Mr. Sisson states:

> . . . I am barely set with my camera when the heron picks up a dry pellet from the island and carries it in his bill down to the edge of the water. As he comes closer, his walk takes on the slow stealthy-sneaky manner typical of most herons. Reaching the channel, he pauses and seems to survey the water for the best fishing spot. Then slowly his neck stretches out and out, as if made of elastic, and ever so gently he drops the bait in the water.
>
> Now the fisherman in him really takes over. Hunkering down between two rocks he stays as still as a statue; his eyes never leave the pellet as it bobs in the water. [Sisson, 1974, pp. 144–145]

As the fish come to the bait, the heron strikes and seldom misses.

4. Paraphrase of case study from *Children of the Rich*, by Burton N. Wixen. © 1973 by Burton N. Wixen. Used by permission of Crown Publishers, Inc., New York.

**FIGURE 7–2**

A heron fishing with bait at the Miami Seaquarium (*clockwise from upper left corner*): heron taking a piece of bread to the stream; heron crouching in the rocks after dropping the bread in the water; fish coming up to the surface to eat the bread; heron lunging for the catch; heron holding his catch

(All photos copyright National Geographic Society.)

At least two other herons (the mother and a brother) at the same sea-quarium have apparently learned much of the same behavior, and one wonders if the heron's fishing behavior might be passed on to future genera-tions. Sisson continues:

> One afternoon I found my heron intently watching a school of fish. He was the picture of despair. He would feint with his bill, but they were just out of range. I threw a pellet on the ground just to his left. He turned, looked at the pellet, looked at the fish, then picked up the bait. He carefully placed it in the water just short of the fish. In their rush for the food, they inadvertently pushed it and themselves shoreward toward him. Like lightning, he struck. After gulping down his catch, he retrieved the bait, which had drifted downstream, and placed it once again within his range. (p. 146)[5]

It is interesting to contemplate how psychologists would have reacted to this phenomenon if it had been observed in the wild. Would we have con-cluded it was another example of instinctual behavior?

The case study can be a very valuable tool in research, for a single instance can lead to new knowledge. There are many situations that can happen only once or on rare occasions. Penfield showed that stimulation of the exposed brain could evoke fine details of memory in patients during open brain surgery [Halacy, 1970]. The rarity of surgery of this kind combined with a surgeon with the interests of Penfield necessitates studies involving only one or two persons. In such situations, the case study becomes a valuable method of organizing and analyzing knowledge.

## ADVANTAGES AND DISADVANTAGES
## OF NONEXPERIMENTAL DESIGNS

The major advantage of quasi-experimental investigations is that they may be applied in situations that do not lend themselves to experimental analysis. Even in situations where experimentation is possible, quasi-experi-ments may be run because they may be carried out in a relatively brief time. The investigator may simply analyze existing records rather than take the time, years in many cases, required to carry out a more powerful experimental analysis. Less money is usually required to carry out a quasi-experiment. Experimental situations do not have to be set up, hiring of people to carry out the procedures is not necessary, and so on.

The major limitation of quasi-experimentation is that it cannot provide safeguards as effective as those available with a true experimental design. The four major reasons for this fact include inability to assign subjects ran-domly to the control and experimental groups; less control over secondary variables during the course of the experiment; no direct manipulation of an

---

5. This and the above quote from Sisson [1974]. Copyright National Geographic Society. Reprinted by permission.

IV possible; no control over the recording of the DV. Lack of control over the recording of the DV is important because it may not be accurately recorded, and the recorder may have been biased in his recording (e.g., scores of certain students recorded higher than actually occurred because they "would fail anyway").

The correlational method has several advantages over other approaches. It provides information concerning the degree of relationship between variables that cannot be obtained by any other analytical approach. This is particularly important in the social sciences, where few things have an all-or-none effect. A correlational approach permits a number of variables to be simultaneously measured and correlated, whereas experimental approaches are geared mainly toward dealing with one or two variables at a time. Multiple correlational studies are especially pertinent in personality research. Correlational analysis may be employed as a control technique, and as a check for reliability and validity. It may also be used where experimentation is physically or ethically impractical. Experimental methods often introduce a high level of artificality into behavioral research situations. In contrast, correlational analysis usually permits the studying of behavior with less disruptions in the analytical setting.

The major disadvantage of correlational investigations is that they are not as effective in determining cause-effect relations as more experimentally oriented investigations. They do not provide the amount of situational control normally encountered with experiments. It is important for the reader to remember that correlational studies are not just a means of seeking cause-effect relationships. They should not be thought of just as a less powerful type of investigation for identifying cause, but as the most effective means of determining degrees of relationship between variables.

Contrast investigation has little advantage over other approaches except that it can be applied in situations not conducive to experimental, quasi-experimental, or correlational analysis. It is generally not acceptable for independent class projects in undergraduate psychology courses because it requires the investigator to devote a lot of time to developing experience in analyzing such situations. Because neither statistical nor manipulatory procedures are available to the investigator, as is the case in large $N$ and small $N$ investigations, the researcher must rely more on his inductive reasoning ability. This requires greater experience and background, yet does not ensure as powerful a means of drawing cause-effect conclusions as is true with the experimental designs.

The case study is essentially descriptive or exploratory in nature and is in the same predicament as the contrast method because help through statistical or manipulatory procedures is not available. In some cases, however, it is the only option open for obtaining information, and a basic principle of research is that some information is better than none. The case study is usually more effective in isolating relationships than a contrast design, however, because there are not as many secondary variables involved in a situation with only one person as there are when more people are involved. One case study approach is similar to the small $N$ approach in that it is based on verification and generalization by means of interinvestigatory affirmation. Unfortunately, a case study approach is often erroneously equated with a small $N$ approach in terms of power in determining cause-effect relationships, mainly due to a lack of understanding of the principles and procedures underlying small $n$ research. A small $N$ experiment provides tools for establishing baseline IV manipulation, monitoring the control of secondary variables, and obtaining a reliable cumulative record analysis not possible with the case study. Small $N$ designs (discussed in Chapter Twelve) are extremely powerful in determining cause-effect relationships, even better than large $N$ analysis in some situations, whereas case study is severely limited and must be used with caution if conclusions about causes are to be drawn.

## SUMMARY

Chapter Seven presents the four main categories of EPF designs. The first is the quasi-experimental design, which is carried out exactly like an experiment except for two differences: subjects are not randomly assigned to groups; and an IV is not directly manipulated. Two or more groups that are found to vary on the IV in question are compared. The quasi-experimental design relies heavily on the control technique of constancy. Correlational designs are a second type of EPF analytical approach. They differ from all other types of investigations (both EPF and experimental) in that they are designed not to determine cause and effect relationships between variables but to determine the degree of relationship between variables. Correlational analysis finds application in four general types of research: (1) in dealing with causality issues when experimental methods cannot be used, (2) in descriptive and predictive capacities, (3) as a statistical means of controlling secondary variables, and (4) in determining the reliability and internal validity of measures.

Contrast EPF designs are primarily used in the analysis of historical data that has too few measures to permit a meaningful statistical manipulation. They find particular application in anthropologically oriented psychological studies. The case study method does not involve the manipulation of an IV, but is an observational approach to analyzing ongoing or past situations. The three principal subdivisions of the case study method are deviant case analysis, isolated case analysis, and naturalistic observation.

The major advantage of EPF investigations is that they can be applied in situations where experimentation cannot be used because of ethical considerations, physical restrictions, or the prior occurrence of the event.

# 8

# *Experimental Designs*

*Chapter Three divided research investigations into two groups—experimental and ex post facto. The objective of this chapter is to give the reader a comparative overview of sixteen designs from which he may choose when carrying out an experiment. Sixteen designs may seem like an overwhelming number at this point, but they are elaborated on in the following three chapters. The most important concepts presented in this chapter are the two factors upon which all experimental designs are based, and how the investigator may combine aspects of these two factors to come up with the sixteen designs. Also presented here is the difference between exploratory and analytical designs. The last section of the chapter describes in detail three of the sixteen designs. Not all the sixteen designs presented are good; some poor designs are included because they are commonly used.*

## WHAT ARE EXPERIMENTAL DESIGNS?

Chapter Four dealt with variance, where it comes from, and basic ways of controlling it. The main objective of this chapter is to provide the student with the procedures required for applying those control techniques. This comes under the heading of experimental designs.

The term *experimental design* has two different though interrelated meanings. In a general sense, experimental design represents the six basic activities required for carrying out an experiment. All the procedures involved in an experimental investigation, from formulating a hypothesis to drawing conclusions, are considered by many researchers to be the experimental design of an investigation. A second definition of experimental design is more restrictive. In this sense, it is a procedure for assigning subjects to experimental conditions and selecting an appropriate statistical analytical procedure. The second definition is emphasized here, for it is the most common. When someone asks which experimental design you employed, he is generally expecting a reply such as a randomized two-group design or $2 \times 3$ factorial design rather than a discourse on all the steps you carried out in your experiment. Procedures that would be classified as part of an experimental design in the general sense, such as selecting appropriate IVs and DVs, deciding how many sessions to run and which equipment to use, were covered in Chapter Five.

When carrying out an experiment, an investigator wants to maximize the effect of systematic variance. Next, secondary sources of variance must be controlled for. Third, error variance should be minimized. The first and third objectives are for the most part dealt with by procedures other than assigning subjects to groups. For example, maximizing the effect of an IV may be done by increasing the magnitude of the IV, while error variance may be reduced by increasing the accuracy of measuring the DV. These two objectives and procedures for accomplishing them are mostly done by means other than the selection of the experimental design.

The major function of experimental designs is to meet the second objective—that of controlling for secondary variation. Experimental situations vary with respect to the ability of different sources of secondary variation to have an effect on any IV under investigation. Not all nine sources of internal invalidity influence each experimental situation to the same extent. For instance, subject sensitization due to pretesting may strongly influence some experiments and not be even potentially relevant in others. Different experimental situations are challenged by various combinations of relevant secondary variables. To help them cope more effectively with the large number of alternative sources of secondary variation that could invalidate an investigation, experimenters have developed designs that employ various combinations of the five basic secondary variation control procedures. Each of these experimental designs has its advantages and disadvantages. A particular design may provide the optimal control of secondary variation in one situation, and be hopelessly inadequate in others. It may allow cause-effect relationships to be drawn in some situations, yet not allow adequate inferences in others.

All experimental designs can be categorized by the type of control procedure employed and the number of groups involved. The type of control procedure employed is important in determining how reliable and valid the conclusions drawn from the experiment are, and may be used to restrict the opportunity of secondary variables to bias the results. The number of groups involved in an experiment is important not only for determining which control procedures may be employed in an experiment, but also for determining what types of research problems an investigation may answer.

### Control Procedures

Of the large number of designs from which an investigator may choose when carrying out an experiment, some are relatively basic, whereas others are more specifically designed for a particular type of research problem. In the next three chapters the reader will be introduced to sixteen experimental designs with which the undergraduate psychology student should be familiar.[1] Experimental designs to be covered may be categorized functionally according to the types of control procedures involved. Table 8–1 shows the five control procedures and the types of designs that employ each one. Experimental designs are generally labeled according to the type of control procedure involved. For example, an experimental design that employs randomization is called a randomized two-group design, randomized three-group design, and so on. A particular experimental design may employ more than one control procedure. In such cases, the name of the design is made up of a composite of the control procedure labels. A three-group design employing randomization and blocking would be called a randomized, blocked three-group design. Generally speaking, then, the name of the design is composed of the type of control procedure involved, plus the number of groups in the investigation. Some designs, however, have picked up second names due to their frequent use in particular situations and certain academic areas. Time series and Solomon four-group designs are good examples. The Solomon four-group design is actually a special type of 2 × 2 factorial design. It is used so extensively in educational research to check for the effects of pretesting that it is presented here as a specific design. In social research circles it is considered one of the finest designs available.

Notice that there is a dash following the control technique of elimination in Table 8–1. Elimination as a control procedure is not restricted to any

**TABLE 8–1**
Control procedures and designs

| Control procedure | Design |
| --- | --- |
| Randomization | Randomized |
| Constancy | Blocked, matched |
| Second IV | Factorial |
| Statistical control | Covariant |
| Elimination | — |

Note: Elimination is used irrespective of the type of design.

---

1. The student should have a basic understanding of the similarities and differences of these designs. Only the major similarities and differences are described in this text. More extensive coverage can be found in Winer [1963] and Kirk [1970].

particular experimental design. It is a nonexperimental design control procedure for eliminating secondary sources of variation that the experimenter
carries out irrespective of the design employed. An investigator may want to
eliminate variation due to sex differences, so he selects either all males or all
females. An experiment may be carried out on a nonwindy day if the influence of the wind is not desired. In either case, the investigator removes the
unwanted secondary variable, regardless of which design he uses.

One other control procedure may also be employed irrespective of the
experimental design used, and that is constancy. An investigator may feel
temperature will influence the DV so he holds room temperature constant,
no matter what design he decides to employ. However, secondary variables
can be held constant by using certain designs. Matching or blocking may be
added to a design in an effort to hold some variable constant.[2] An investigator may employ different races of people as subjects. In order to hold the
race variable constant, he will make sure each group has equal proportions
of each race. He has not eliminated the race variable, only equated the
groups on that variable. (The use of elimination and constancy as control
procedures not related to experimental design was covered in Chapter Five.)

### Number of Groups

A second factor to be considered in classifying experimental designs is
the number of groups involved. Experiments may be carried out using one,
two, three, up to an infinite number of groups. The number of groups
employed will to an extent determine what kind of control procedure an
investigator might use. Table 8–2 classifies experimental designs according
to type of control procedure and number of groups. Dashes within columns
indicate that a particular control technique is not applicable to the group
with which it is correlated. For instance, there is no such thing as a randomized one-group design.[3]

One-group designs are not considered a good experimental approach
for determining the effect of IVs. As has been emphasized in previous
chapters, experimentation involves manipulation, comparison, and evaluation. Manipulation entails applying an IV and noting its effect on the subjects' behavior. The manipulated subjects' behavior is then compared to
the behavior of subjects who have not experienced the IV. An evaluation of

---

2. *Matching* is the term used when individual comparisons with two groups are
employed, *blocking* is the term used when more than two groups are involved. The basic
principle of making the comparison groups more homogeneous is the same for matching or
blocking.

3. Actually, it would be possible to select randomly one group of subjects from a
population of subjects without having to divide randomly the chosen subjects into two
or more groups. However, this is not a very practical situation.

**TABLE 8-2**

Experimental designs by control procedure and number of groups

| Control procedure | One-group | Two-group | One-way ANOVAR | Factorial |
|---|---|---|---|---|
| Randomization | — | Randomized two-group design | Randomized three-group design | Randomized factorial |
| Constancy | Pretest-posttest one-group design | Matched two-group design | Blocked three-group design | Blocked factorial |
| Second IV | — | — | — | Any factorial |
| Statistical control | — | Analysis of covariance, two-group design | Analysis of covariance, three-group design | Analysis of covariance, factorial |

the influence of the IV on behavior is then carried out, based primarily on the comparison data.

Unfortunately, one-group experimental investigations do not generally allow comparison, for there is no second group with which a comparison can be made. Therefore, although manipulation is involved in one-group investigations, the lack of comparative data decreases the possibility that any valid conclusions will result. The investigator has no way of knowing how much the IV influenced the behavior, for he has no measure of the behavior without the IV. He has not been able to divide $V_T$ into $V_B$ and $V_W$. Measures of the DV for the subjects in a one-group comparison indicate only that the scores varied. The investigator cannot isolate the influence of the IV from that of any other variables present in the situation.

One-group experimental investigations can, however, be carried out in such a way as to allow comparison. To illustrate this point, let us first look at how an experimental situation would be dealt with using two groups. Suppose you wanted to carry out a two-group experiment to determine whether taking an introductory psychology course increases students' knowledge about psychology, a question asked by many psychology majors who survive such courses. You could select a number of subjects, divide them into two groups, have one take the course, and then give both groups a test on psychological terms and principles. The two groups would give you a measure of the DV (knowledge of psychology) with and without the IV (taking an introductory psychology course). The effect of the IV could then be isolated as the difference between the two.

A one-group design could also be used as an alternative approach to answering the same question about introductory psychology by using a pretest-posttest one-group procedure. Subjects could be selected and given a test (pretest) made up of psychological terms and principles. This would give the investigator a measure of what the students know about psychology without the influence of the IV. After taking an introductory course, all subjects would then be given a posttest. Next, all the subjects' scores on the posttest minus the pretest could be used as a measure of the influence of the IV.

One factor about one-group designs is emphasized by Table 8–2. Only one of the four control procedures possible with experimental designs is available for one-group investigations. Random assignment to IV and non-IV groups is not possible, for there is only one group. No secondary variables may be controlled by making them a second IV, for each IV would require a separate group.[4] Statistical control is also not available due to lack of comparative measures. The technique of constancy is a viable control procedure with one-group designs where more than one measure is taken for each subject, as is the case with time series and pretest-posttest one-group designs.

By setting up an experimental design involving two groups, the investigator has arranged conditions so that $V_T$ may be divided into $V_B$ and $V_W$, thereby allowing the effect of the IV to be isolated. He also automatically increases the number of control techniques he may use. It becomes possible to equate the effects of potentially confounding secondary variables by randomly assigning subjects to either the control or the experimental group. He may control other secondary variables by matching or balancing the groups on these variables.[5] A second group also makes statistical control possible.

By adding a third group and employing a one-way ANOVAR design, the investigator does not increase the number of control procedures available for use, but he does add an important dimension. Two major questions in research are "Does the IV have an effect?" and "How much of an effect does the IV have?" Analogous to these two questions are two types of experiments: *exploratory* and *analytical* experiments. Exploratory experiments generally involve only two groups, one to be a control and the second to receive the IV. This type of experiment answers the question, "Does the IV have an effect?" It does not answer the question of what levels of IV are required to get different amounts of change in the DV. The answer to the second question requires many groups, each receiving a different level of IV. These are analytical experiments. When an investigator ventures into an uncultivated area of research, the first question he seeks to answer is "Does the IV have an effect?" To answer this an exploratory investigation is launched. Later, if that question has been answered in the affirmative, the

4. It is possible to study more than one variable with one group using a small $N$ design and analysis by means of repeated measures. An excellent investigatory approach is based on different assumptions than those in the large $N$ statistical approach (see Chapter Twelve).

5. *Balancing* involves making sure each group has the same amount of a particular variable in each group, for example, making sure each group has the same number of males and females. The terms *matching* and *blocking* indicate designs using balancing.

researcher carries out an analytical (also called *parametric*) investigation to determine how much effect different values of the IV have.

Good examples of exploratory and analytical investigations are found in historical experimentations in the medical field. Before the 1840s operations were extremely painful ordeals in which the surgeon worked in great haste to shorten his patient's agony. Amputations, for example, were carried out in a few seconds. In the early 1840s, William Morton, a medical student at Harvard, started carrying out surgery on cats, dogs, and rats. After administering ether to some of them, he noted that those who received ether prior to surgery felt no pain during the operation, whereas those who did not suffered greatly. From these exploratory investigations, Morton concluded that ether could alleviate pain.

Having seen a demonstration by Morton, a venturesome doctor, Horace Wells, attempted to demonstrate the use of this anesthetic. During an exhibition at a large eastern hospital, the demonstration failed. Unfortunately, the patient woke too soon, screaming in pain. Although Morton's exploratory experiment had demonstrated ether was effective, it was not known what dosages were most effective or how long the drug would last. Parametric investigations were then carried out to answer the question "How much effect does ether have at different dosage levels?"

One-way ANOVAR experimental designs add a new dimension to experimentation by allowing more than one comparison to be carried out in one experiment. One-way ANOVAR designs are multigroup designs in which more than two levels of *one* variable are compared in one experiment. Although two-group experiments are generally used in exploratory investigations, one-way ANOVAR designs, like factorial designs, are generally used in analytical investigations.

One-group, two-group, and one-way analysis designs are alike in that all of them allow investigators to manipulate one IV. A factorial design is a multigroup design that allows the variation of two or more variables in an experimental setting. Factorial designs are especially important for psychological research because behavior is a function of many variables impinging on man simultaneously. In many instances factors simultaneously influencing behavior interact to produce results that do not occur when only one factor is free to vary. What a person will do in an emergency, for example, is determined both by the emotional state he or she is in and who else is in that situation. How a married woman will respond to various emergencies (e.g., fire, earthquake, physical harm) depends not only on the type of emergency, but also on whether her husband, children, and/or parents are present at the time. An investigation of how she would react in these situations could lead to misleading conclusions if the variable of "who is present" was held constant. Factorial designs allow investigations to be carried out to analyze the interaction effects of variables concurrently influencing an organism.

Table 8–2 indicates another advantage of factorial designs: they make more control procedures available than two-group or one-way analysis designs. Not only can factorial designs use randomization, constancy, and statistical control, they can also allow a secondary variable to be converted into a second IV. The effects of this second IV can then be quantitatively extracted from $V_T$. The formula for a factorial design would be[6]

$$V_T = V_{B_1} + V_{B_2} + V_W$$

The symbol $V_{B_2}$ represents the isolation of the effects of the secondary variable that was transformed into the second IV.

The decision, then, of how many groups an investigation will have is an important step because the number of groups to some degree limits what the investigator may do and the types of information that may be obtained. The reader should not conclude that an experimental investigation consisting of many groups is inherently better than one having only two groups. Although a factorial design with its added groups provides a larger selection of control procedures than a two-group design, it may not be any more functional for certain situations. In fact, it may be detrimental because of the increased number of subjects and preparations necessary.

## TYPES OF EXPERIMENTAL DESIGNS

By combining the experimental dimensions of number of groups and control procedures plus a little imagination, one can come up with numerous experimental designs. Table 8–3 presents sixteen experimental designs, symbolically diagrams them out, and indicates which control procedures they employ. The sixteen listed are not the only ones possible, but are those commonly used in behavioral research.

In Table 8–3 the symbolic representation $O$ represents the measurement of some DV, the $X$ stands for the application of an IV; and $R$ stands for randomization. A $Y$ represents some measure of a covariate. Each row of symbols represents one group. To illustrate, take the following symbols:

| A | B |
|---|---|
| $R \; X \; O$ | $R \; Y \; X \; O$ |
| $R \quad\;\; O$ | $R \; Y \quad\; O$ |

---

6. Technically speaking, the formula should read $V_T = V_{B_1} + V_{B_2} + V_I + V_W$. The term $V_I$ stands for interaction effects. $V_I$ will be presented later to prevent confusion at this point.

**TABLE 8–3**
Sixteen experimental designs

| Type of design | Symbolic representation | Randomization | Constancy | Second IV | Statistical control | Elimination |
|---|---|---|---|---|---|---|
| *ONE-GROUP DESIGNS* | | | | | | |
| 1. One-group posttest only | $X\ O$ | | | | | |
| 2. One-group pretest-posttest | $O_1\ X\ O_2$ | | + | | | |
| 3. Time series | $O_1\ O_2\ O_3\ X\ O_4\ O_5\ O_6$ | | + | | | |
| *TWO-GROUP DESIGNS* | | | | | | |
| 4. Posttest control group | $X\ O$ / $O$ | | | | | |
| 5. Randomized posttest only control group | $R\ X\ O$ / $R\ \ \ O$ | + | | | | |
| 6. Randomized matched posttest only control group | $RM\ X\ O$ / $RM\ \ \ O$ | + | + | | | |
| 7. Pretest-Posttest control group | $O\ X\ O$ / $O\ \ \ O$ | | + | | | |
| 8. Randomized pretest-posttest control group | $R\ O\ X\ O$ / $R\ O\ \ \ O$ | + | + | | | |
| 9. Randomized pretest-posttest control group, analysis of covariance | $R\ O\ Y\ X\ O$ / $R\ O\ Y\ \ \ O$ | + | + | | + | |

## ONE-WAY ANOVAR DESIGNS

10. Randomized ANOVAR

$R\ X_1\ O$
$R\ X_2\ O$
$R\ X_3\ O$

11. Randomized blocked ANOVAR

$RB\ X_1\ O$
$RB\ X_2\ O$
$RB\ X_3\ O$

12. Randomized analysis of covariance

$R\ Y\ X_1\ O$
$R\ Y\ X_2\ O$
$R\ Y\ X_3\ O$

## FACTORIAL DESIGNS

13. Randomized factorial

| | | IV 1 Levels | |
|---|---|---|---|
| | 1 | 2 | 3 |
| A | $X_{A_1}$ | $X_{A_2}$ | $X_{A_3}$ |
| B | $X_{B_1}$ | $X_{B_2}$ | $X_{B_3}$ |

IV 2 Levels

14. Solomon four-group

$R\ O\ X\ O$
$R\ O\quad O$
$R\quad X\ O$
$R\quad\quad O$

**TABLE 8–3 (Continued)**

| Type of design | Symbolic representation | Randomization | Constancy | Second IV | Statistical control | Elimination |
|---|---|---|---|---|---|---|
| 15. Randomized blocked factorial | (see diagram below) | + | + | + | | |
| 16. Randomized analysis of covariance factorial | (see diagram below) | + | | + | + | |

Symbolic representation for 15:

Levels

| | | 1 | 2 | 3 | 1 | 2 | 3 |
|---|---|---|---|---|---|---|---|
| IV 1: | | | | | | | |
| IV 2: | | $A$ | $A$ | $A$ | $B$ | $B$ | $B$ |

|  | | | | | | | |
|---|---|---|---|---|---|---|---|
| Blocks | 1 | $X_{A_{11}}$ | $X_{A_{21}}$ | $X_{A_{31}}$ | $X_{B_{11}}$ | $X_{B_{21}}$ | $X_{B_{31}}$ |
| | 2 | $X_{A_{12}}$ | $X_{A_{22}}$ | $X_{A_{32}}$ | $X_{B_{12}}$ | $X_{B_{22}}$ | $X_{B_{32}}$ |
| | 3 | $X_{A_{13}}$ | $X_{A_{23}}$ | $X_{A_{33}}$ | $X_{B_{13}}$ | $X_{B_{23}}$ | $X_{B_{33}}$ |

Symbolic representation for 16:

IV 1

Levels

| IV 2 Levels | | 1 | 2 | 3 |
|---|---|---|---|---|
| | $A$ | $YX_{A_1}$ | $YX_{A_2}$ | $YX_{A_3}$ |
| | $B$ | $YX_{B_1}$ | $YX_{B_2}$ | $YX_{B_3}$ |

178

Column A states that there are two groups ($R \, X \, O$ and $R \, O$); both have been randomly selected ($R$); one receives the IV ($X$) and the second does not. Column B is identical to A except for the inclusion of a measure of some covariate ($Y$). Two randomly selected groups are involved with one receiving the IV. The covariate measure $Y$ could represent the IQ level of each group of subjects.[7] If the groups did differ on IQ, the investigator could statistically adjust the differences in the group $O$s to remove that portion of the difference between the group DV measures due to group IQ differences.

Notice in Table 8–3 that all designs involving more than two groups are diagramed with boxes rather than symbolized by $R$s, $X$s, and $Y$s. There are two reasons for this. First, the use of boxes makes the representation less cumbersome and gives the reader a more graphic illustration of what is involved. The symbolic representation of the randomized factorial design (13) shown in Table 8–3 would be

$$R \; X_{A_1} \; O$$
$$R \; X_{A_2} \; O$$
$$R \; X_{A_3} \; O$$
$$R \; X_{B_1} \; O$$
$$R \; X_{B_2} \; O$$
$$R \; X_{B_3} \; O$$

The box diagram makes it easier to see that two variables, one with two levels and one with three, are involved. The second reason for not using $R$s and so on, is that it is generally assumed for studies involving three or more groups that each subject is randomly assigned to a group, and a DV measure $O$ is taken. Few investigators would go to the expense of carrying out a multigroup investigation without employing the control technique of randomization. The $X$ in the box indicates which IV condition that group experiences. The subscripts tell which level of each variable a group receives.

## ONE-GROUP DESIGNS

So far, the intent of this chapter has been to give the student an overview of all the designs to be covered and how they compare in terms of the control procedures involved. The remainder of this chapter and the three that follow

---

7. A covariate is any other variable on which groups in an investigation differ other than the IV. Suppose you were going to carry out a two-group experiment to see which of two types of puzzles is easiest to solve. Each of the groups would be given one of the two types of puzzles. The groups would then "vary" on only one variable, the type of puzzle they tried to solve. If the two groups also varied in terms of IQ (i.e., one group's IQ was higher than the other), then IQ would be a covariate.

are devoted to an elaboration of each experimental design, its basic points, advantages, and disadvantages. An example of each is included so that the student may see how it is statistically analyzed.

### One-Group Posttest Design (X O)

The city council of a town consisting of 30,000 people decided to set up a drug crisis center. Both youths and adults were encouraged to come to the center to obtain help with drug problems. Information regarding the effects of different drugs could be obtained at the center, and a group of people was available to provide social support for anyone desiring to deal with his drug problem. After the center had been operating for one year, the director of the program was requested to send information to the city council to demonstrate the program's effectiveness. In compliance with the request, the director sent the following letter:

*Dear Sirs:*

The drug center has been in operation in this town for more than a year now. At the end of the first year the staff of the center has carried out thoughtful discussions in an attempt to thoroughly and objectively appraise the effectiveness of the program. Empirical data was collected regarding the results of the program, as shown below:

| Type of patient | Number treated | Number cured |
|---|---|---|
| Marijuana smokers | 158 | 96 |
| LSD users | 256 | 149 |
| Glue sniffers | 463 | 298 |
| Opium addicts | 23 | 10 |
| Morphine users | 18 | 6 |
| Alcoholics | 563 | 84 |

From this data it is obvious that the drug center has been effective in our area. We are looking forward to your continued support of this project. Do not hesitate to call on us for any further information.

Yours truly,

Alfred Schwartz
Director
Drug Crisis Center

The preceding is an example of a one-group posttest design. In actuality this type of design is a forerunner of other present-day designs. It is commonly called a *preexperimental design* or a *pseudo-experimental design*, for it is not generally considered to be a good experimental approach because a formal comparison is not performed. For a scientific investigation to be a true experiment, at least one comparison must be carried out. Generally, data from the one group experiencing the IV is compared to the data from a second group that did not experience the IV.[8] Note that in the drug center problem, there was no control group to allow for a comparison. Although empirical observations are reported, the one-group posttest design has little power; that is, it provides little control with respect to ensuring that the IV and not some other secondary variable was the effective ingredient. Actually, the data presented could have been obtained without a drug center, for no information is presented showing how many cures would occur without a drug program available. It is possible that many people would have "cured" themselves without the center. The point to be made is not that the drug center had no effect, but that without carrying out some type of comparison between a group having the program and one not having the program, little can be demonstrated about any cause-effect relationship. The type of investigation carried out here was not, technically speaking, a true experiment. It might be better classified as an information investigation, for the data do provide descriptive information about what happened.

One-group posttest designs do not adequately control for any of the internal sources of invalidity. Let us look at how this particular design copes or does not cope with potential sources of invalidity. Proactive history has not been controlled for in any way, so the data obtained may be a function of a previous experience rather than the IV. Only certain people may have come to the center for help, and these people may have decided to change whether the center was there or not. Some of the change may have been due to time. It has been found, for example, that as glue sniffers, usually grade school children, get older they move toward more potent drugs. This could explain the reason for some of the decrease in glue sniffing. Some may have gone on to marijuana and other drugs. Testing does not apply, to one-group posttest designs. No pretest was given; therefore, it could not possibly influence the results. Regression is not applicable either, there being no comparison with which to evaluate regression. There are no means for controlling retroactive history or mortality, both of which are usually involved in one-group situations. Maturation may not be a relevant source of variability if the length of time involved is relatively short. The longer it takes to carry out the study (week, months, years), the greater the possibility that maturational effects are present. Only one IV was applied, so interaction would not be a relevant factor. As mentioned previously, neither instrumentation nor experimenter bias is controlled by a particular design. Both sources of inter-

---

8. Not all cases require a second group. Some experimental designs use one group for both control and experimental conditions. This is perfectly acceptable and allows a formal comparison to be made. The time series and ABA designs are examples of this procedure; more will be said of these designs in Chapter Twelve.

nal invalidity may fluctuate in an experimental situation irrespective of the design used, only the experimenter can make sure these are controlled.

It may seem puzzling that one-group posttest designs are included in this chapter on experimental designs. One reason for including them is that they are often used in social research [Campbell & Stanley, 1966] for drawing causal inferences, even though this is an incorrect use. Second, case studies that are in essence one-group posttest designs are frequently carried out in psychology. From therapeutic situations and the results obtained, cause-effect relationships are often inferred regarding therapeutic procedures and concurrent behavioral changes. The therapist may unwittingly conclude that he caused the change for the better when in fact the improvement was a result of something else.

The one-case study situation is not restricted to psychology. The same problems are encountered in other areas, such as applied medicine. A doctor may prescribe a certain drug to combat the flu or some other virus. If the patient gets better, it is sometimes concluded the drug was responsible, when the flu may just have run its course. The incorrect conclusions that may be drawn in therapeutic and medicinal situations are also analogous to an Indian doing a dance to bring rain. If it rains, the dance receives the credit. Although psychologists are most often restricted to the applied setting (one-case study situations), any conclusions drawn about the effectiveness of their techniques should come from experimental situations (either field or laboratory) rather than the actual case histories. Advances in field experimental procedures presently allow the clinical psychologist to carry out cause-effect analysis in most applied settings, even if only one subject is involved.[9]

### One-Group
### Pretest-Posttest Design (O X O)

The one-group pretest-posttest design is also considered to be a rather poor design, though somewhat better than the one-group posttest design. Suppose you want to try a new type of exercise plan on third-grade students to see if it increases their coordination. A pretest is given at the beginning of the year. The exercise plan is employed during the whole school year. A posttest may then be carried out to determine whether the scores on the pretest significantly differ from those on the posttest.

Initially this may seem like an adequate design, since a formal comparison can be carried out. The problem, however, involves inadequate control for internal and external validity. As can be seen, in Table 8–2, the one-group pretest-posttest design does little in the way of controlling secondary influ-

---

9. Chapter Twelve discusses procedures for carrying out cause-effect investigations in the applied setting.

ences on the IV. All the arguments for lack of control for internal invalidity presented for the one-group posttest only design are also true for this design, with the following exceptions: pretest influences, not applicable in the post-test situation, may influence scores on the posttest; and persons frequently do better when taking a test the second time due to the experience of taking it the first time.

Proactive history is more effectively controlled with the pretest-posttest condition. Both the pretest and the posttest should be influenced by the past history of the subject to the same degree, thereby equating the effects of this secondary source of variation. Mortality is also controlled for by the fact that a loss of subjects during the experiment could be checked by dropping the pretest scores of the subjects lost (this could bias the results).

In summary, though the one-group pretest-posttest design is better than the one-group posttest only design, neither is advocated. Neither design adequately controls for secondary variation. They may be appropriate if no other type of design is feasible, for some information is always better than none, but one must be careful in deducing cause-effect relationships with these designs. They are used all too frequently in situations in which more appropriate designs could be employed.

### Time-Series Design ($O_1$ $O_2$ X $O_3$ $O_4$)

Social research frequently involves analyzing the influence of a variable or variables over relatively long periods of time. Educators may be interested in determining the effects of a certain type of educational curriculum on grade-school children over several years. A case in point involves an experiment carried out by Wolf, Giles, and Hall [reported in Whaley & Malott, 1971, p. 282]. Wolf, Giles, and Hall selected culturally deprived children who had advanced only 0.6 years on the Scholastic Aptitude Test (SAT) administered by the public school over the past few years. The SAT scores were obtained previous to the administration of a modified educational program ($X$), and are represented by the symbols $O_1$ and $O_2$. All 16 fifth- and sixth-grade students involved in the study were at least 2.0 years below their grade level in reading achievement. The children were put on a token economy system in which they received trading stamps for completing class assignments and participating in academic endeavors. These trading stamps could be exchanged for opportunities to go on field trips including swimming, picnics, visits to the zoo, sporting events, and so on. During the first year the modified program was employed, the children typically gained 1.5 years on the scholastic aptitude test. The 1.5 would be $O_3$, with the next year's average $O_4$.

It is apparent that a time-series design is a better design than either of the aforementioned one-group designs. The repeated measure of the DV provides the investigator with information on the variability of the DV both before and after the IV is given. Like the other one-group designs, several sources of internal validity may not be controlled for, including retroactive history, instrumentation, and experimenter bias. Other variables may have simultaneously fluctuated to produce any effect noted in a time-series design making invalidity due to retroactive history a real possibility. In some time-series experiments, retroactive history may be a plausible alternative explanation, whereas in others it may not.[10]

Notice how the time-series design controls the remaining sources of internal invalidity. If maturation or testing is influencing the DV, the variations will show up between $O_1 - O_2$ and $O_3 - O_4$ as well as between $O_2$ and $O_3$. Regression effects are implausible in this design and would also show up between $O_1 - O_2$ and $O_3 - O_4$ if they were present. Due to the fact the same subjects are used throughout, proactive history is held constant. The effect of any subject lost during the experiment can be isolated from the other scores, and therefore mortality is controlled for.

The statistical analysis of time-series designs is somewhat complicated and will be covered in more detail after some of the more common designs and simpler statistical analyses have been discussed. Here it is sufficient to say that carrying out a $t$-test between $O_2$ and $O_3$ is not considered an appropriate statistical treatment of this design.

The time-series design is used by researchers whose interest lies in changes occurring over time. Many educators, developmental psychologists, political scientists, and sociologists are dependent upon a time-series, for their topic may not lend itself to two-group analysis. Generally, two-group designs are preferred over one-group designs. There are single-group designs, e.g., ABA designs, that are considered more effective than two-group designs, but these will be covered in Chapter Twelve.

## SUMMARY

An investigator has three main concerns when carrying out research: to maximize the effect of the IV, to control for secondary sources of variation, and to minimize error variance. The main responsibility of experimental designs is to control for secondary variation. Because the means for accomplishing this changes from one situation to another, alternative experimental designs have been constructed. Experimental designs are based on two dimensions—the type of control procedure involved and the number of groups

---

10. If some secondary variable fluctuated at the same time a variable was applied in a time-series design, the experimenter may not be as confident that any change occurring in the DV was actually due to the IV.

employed. Experimental designs are classified according to the control procedures being used and the number of groups required. More than one control procedure may be used in a particular experimental design. This allows greater control of secondary variable effects.

The number of groups employed in an investigation has two important effects on that investigation. First, it determines to some extent what control procedures may be employed. For example, controlling a secondary variable by making it a second IV cannot be done with only two groups; a factorial design is required. Second, the number of groups determines what types of experiments can be carried out. A distinction is made between analytical and exploratory investigations. Exploratory investigations consist of two groups, one group receives the IV and the other group does not, in an effort to determine whether the IV is effective. Analytical investigations require three or more groups and are carried out to analyze parametrically the effects of different levels of the IV.

Two-group designs may employ the control procedures of constancy, randomization, and analysis of covariance, and are restricted to exploratory investigations. One-way analysis of variance designs do not allow greater choice in control techniques over two-group designs, but they do give the added dimension of allowing the investigator the option of carrying out analytical investigations as well. Factorial designs allow both analytical and exploratory investigations to be carried out, plus adding an optional fourth control technique—making a secondary variable an IV. Alternative one-group designs are discussed. It is emphasized that most one-group designs are poor experimental designs and provide the investigator little or no control of secondary variables.

# 9

# Two-Group Designs

*This chapter discusses the cornerstone of psychological experiments—two-group designs. More two-group experiments are carried out than almost any other type of experiment. Six types of two-group designs are presented. The last, the analysis of covariance two-group design, is generally not covered in an undergraduate experimental psychology course, probably because the statistical manipulations involved frighten even most graduate students. Remember, however, that understanding the statistical analysis is not as important here as understanding when and where different designs should be used. Whether your instructor requires you to learn the formulas involved will depend on what level course you are in and whether you have had a prior course in statistics. By the time you finish your graduate training you will be expected to know them. The formulas and specific numerical examples on how to use them have been included here so that the student may carry out the statistical analysis whether he understands the statistics or not.*

## LOGICAL ANALYSIS
## OF TWO-GROUP DESIGNS

The mainstay of psychological experimentation is the situation in which the effects of an IV on some DV are determined using two groups. The investigator generally is interested in whether a particular variable will influence a particular behavior. To answer the question, only two groups are needed for carrying out the investigation: one to experience the IV and the second to act as a control. The control group should be as identical to the experimental group as possible so that any difference in behavior between the two groups can be attributed to the variable in question.

Most people assume that two-group comparisons have been the cornerstone of scientific inquiry for thousands of years. Although it is true that two-group comparisons have been carried out for centuries, they have come into their own only in the last eighty years or so. Prior to that time, systematic observation of ongoing behavior and comparative analysis[1] of past events were the rule in empirical investigations. Only the wealthy could afford to be scientists, and acceptance of a scientist's results was based primarily on his integrity and the social soundness of his previous statements. Because of the lack of statistical and manipulatory sophistication in experimentation, knowing what to look for, when to look, and how to report it concisely was considered more important than the ability to manipulate. Although manipulatory studies were carried out over the centuries, the importance of such research was not realized until the turn of the nineteenth century. Since that time, manipulatory and statistical procedures have continually been refined until both have become central figures in research circles.

The analytical foundation for two-group designs is based on the principle of variation presented in Chapter Four. With systematic natural observation, the investigation is based on the principle of causation due to temporal and spatial association. More simply, if some variable ($A$) was noted to change, any immediate change in some other variable ($B$) which was close to $A$ noted immediately was said to be "caused" by $A$.

Scientists began to realize that if they manipulated variable $A$ and a change in variable $B$ occurred, there was less chance that the fluctuation of $B$ was due to some other secondary variable. There are two main reasons for this assumption. First, if the investigator decides when $A$ is to be varied, there is less chance that some secondary variable may "just happen" to fluctuate at the same time and cause the variation in $B$. Second, an argument was commonly invoked which held in essence that variable $B$ was going to fluctuate anyway. By having the investigator apply the IV at will when he so desires, any change in $B$ following the application of $A$ increases the probability that any fluctuation in $B$ was due to $A$ rather than simply to random fluctuation. The idea that experimental manipulation was valuable initiated the rise of one-group experimental designs.

After experimental manipulation was accepted, the next important concept to gain credence was the idea of *control data*. It became apparent that an investigator could strengthen his demonstration of IV effects by showing that a second group of subjects not experiencing the IV responded differently from those receiving the IV. Adding a second group, then, gave the researcher

---

1. Comparative investigations are similar to what is presently called ex post facto analysis. One main distinction, however, between comparative investigations and present EPF research is that many statistical procedures developed in the last eight decades have enhanced confidence in EPF investigations.

a measure of the specific effects of the IV. This would show up as the difference in DV scores "between" the two groups, for ideally both groups are equated on all secondary variables.

The additional control group is important for another reason. With a second group, the investigator has the ability to identify the effect of the IV by dividing the total variation among scores into two categories, $V_B$ and $V_W$. The difference in the DV between the two groups ($V_B$) represents the amount of variation due to the IV, and the difference between the scores in a particular group ($V_W$) gives a measure of the amount of fluctuation in the DV between subjects due to uncontrolled secondary variables. This measure of within-group variation gives the investigator something with which to compare the difference between the two group scores. As mentioned in Chapter Four, the question in experimentation is not whether the DV measures of the control group differ from those of the experimental group. We expect they will not be exactly the same, even if the IV has no effect on one of the groups. The question is whether the difference between the two groups is significantly larger than the amount of random fluctuation usually found between scores in the given situation with no IV present. To calculate this, the difference in DV between the groups is divided by the difference between the scores within the groups. This ratio then tells how many more times the variation in DV between the groups was larger than chance fluctuation between scores.

Now, in a statistics course you are taught that it is possible for the DV measures of the IV group to be larger than the DV measures for the control group simply because of random fluctuation rather than because of any real influence of the IV. Therefore, a measure of $V_B/V_W$ could be larger than 1 when the IV had no effect. The probability of this happening, however, varies according to the size of the value obtained. (For example, the probability of $V_B/V_W$ equaling 1.25 by chance is higher than if the obtained $V_B/V_W$ ratio is 4.30.) The student does not need to calculate the probability of receiving a certain $V_B/V_W$ value due to chance; this has already been done for him in the $t$ and F tables. He simply takes the value obtained, looks it up on an appropriate $t$ or F table, and notes the probability.

In a two-group design situation, then, the investigator is interested in the following points:

1. Controlling secondary variables
2. Applying an IV to the experimental group while not giving it to the control group
3. Getting a measure of $V_B$ and $V_W$
4. Comparing $V_B$ to $V_W$ to determine the probability that the difference in scores between the two groups could be due to chance fluctuations

Six different types of two-group designs are covered in this chapter. All six involve these four points. Generally speaking, all carry out the last three points in exactly the same way. The differences center around the different way each carries out the first point—controlling secondary variables.[2] Each employs a different combination of the five control procedures presented earlier. The next six sections of the chapter present the types of two-group designs and examples of how each is carried out.

## TYPES OF TWO-GROUP DESIGNS

*Randomized Two-Group Design,*
*Posttest Only* $\begin{pmatrix} R & X & O \\ R & & O \end{pmatrix}$

The randomized, posttest only, two-group design is the most common two-group design, and possibly the easiest to understand. Let us take a hypothetical case in which the effects of household pain relievers such as aspirin or Bufferin are tested on the ability to memorize a list of words. First, we formulate the hypothesis that household pain relievers decrease the ability to learn previously learned lists of words. Second, we specify what the IV and DV will actually be. Four aspirin tablets will represent the category of household pain relievers, and the time it takes to memorize 15 nonsense syllables so that they can be repeated in order by a subject without making any mistakes is the DV representing the category of ability to remember. Third, we set about controlling secondary variables. We do not use the control procedure of making some secondary variable an IV because we have limited our investigation to a comparison between two groups. Isolating a secondary variable by making it an IV would require at least two more groups, so we skip this control possibility. We may then look for secondary variables that can be eliminated. We randomly select subjects from an introductory psychology class, eliminating any foreign students from the random selection because of possible language problems that would bias the results. Students afflicted with arthritis may also be excluded, for arthritis patients generally use large amounts of household pain relievers and thereby build up an unusually high tolerance for such drugs. Visual distractions (e.g., posters, pinups) may be removed from the room where the experiment is to be carried out. Next we look for secondary variables to hold constant. There may be sex differences,

---

2. Actually, two-group designs using statistical control (analysis of covariance) do differ from the others on point 3 also. This should not bother the reader to the extent that the similarities are not perceived.

so we make sure there are as many girls as boys in each group. Both groups are tested in the same large room at the same time. This will equate the effects of temperature, time of day, noise, and visual secondary variables. The same instructions are given to each group in the same manner. Next we look for any measurable covariates possible in the situation. IQ is a potential covariate, but unfortunately we do not have any measure of it, so statistical control is not possible. Finally, we randomize the assignment of subjects to the two groups. This should equate both groups on IQ and any other secondary variable not eliminated or held constant.

Our fourth major experimental step is the actual carrying out of the experiment and the application of the IV. Each subject in group B is given four aspirin tablets and subjects in group A are given none. Thirty minutes later both groups of 10 subjects are taken to a large classroom, where they are given the list of nonsense syllables to memorize. The time required for each subject to memorize the list to the point of being able verbally to repeat the list with no errors is recorded for each subject. The results obtained from the experiment are presented below. Each number represents the DV (number of seconds) for a particular subject.

| Group A | Group B |
|---------|---------|
| 178 | 191 |
| 175 | 202 |
| 187 | 183 |
| 170 | 196 |
| 175 | 195 |
| 173 | 193 |
| 163 | 207 |
| 171 | 198 |

The fifth major experimental step is the statistical analysis of the data. What empirical effect did the IV have on the DV? Is the effect significant? Did the IV cause the variation in the DV? Whenever an experiment involves two, and only two, groups, a statistical analysis called the $t$ test is carried out to determine if the IV did have an effect. A formula for determining $t$ for two randomized groups is

$$t = \frac{\bar{X}_a - \bar{X}_b}{\sqrt{\dfrac{SS_a + SS_b}{(n_a - 1) + (n_b - 1)}(1/n_a + 1/n_b)}}$$

Although this formula may seem somewhat awesome, it is actually rather easy to compute and understand. Remember that the numerator reflects the variation between groups and the denominator represents the variation within groups.

The first step is to compute the means for both groups. (The subscripts are added to indicate which group a particular statistic represents.) In the numerator $\bar{X}_a$ represents the mean of group A and $\bar{X}_b$ stands for the number of subjects in a particular group. Any use of large $N$ in this text will represent *all* the subjects in a particular experiment (in this example $N$ would equal 16). The Greek symbol $\Sigma$ (called sigma) will be employed to mean "the sum of" or "total." The mean for group A and group B can be calculated as follows:

$$\bar{X}_a = \frac{\Sigma X_a}{n_a} = \frac{178 + 175 + 187 + 170 + 175 + 173 + 163 + 171}{8}$$

$$= \frac{1,392}{8} = 174$$

$$\bar{X}_b = \frac{\Sigma X_b}{n_b} = \frac{191 + 202 + 183 + 196 + 195 + 193 + 207 + 198}{8}$$

$$= \frac{1,565}{8} = 195.625$$

After computing the means, the "sum of squares" is computed:

$$SS = \Sigma X^2 - \frac{(\Sigma X)^2}{n}$$

Group A

| Subject number | $X_a$ | $X_a^2$ |
|---|---|---|
| 1 | 178 | 31,684 |
| 2 | 175 | 30,625 |
| 3 | 187 | 34,969 |
| 4 | 170 | 28,900 |
| 5 | 175 | 30,625 |
| 6 | 173 | 29,929 |
| 7 | 163 | 26,569 |
| 8 | 171 | 29,241 |

$$n = 8 \quad \Sigma X_a = 1,392 \quad \Sigma X_a^2 = 242,542$$

$$\bar{X}_a = \frac{1,392}{8} = 174$$

$$SS_a = \Sigma X_a^2 - \frac{(\Sigma X_a)^2}{n}$$

$$= 242,542 - \frac{1,937,664}{8}$$

$$= 334$$

|  | Group B | |
| --- | --- | --- |
| *Subject number* | $X_b$ | $X_b^2$ |
| 1 | 191 | 36,481 |
| 2 | 202 | 40,804 |
| 3 | 183 | 33,489 |
| 4 | 196 | 38,416 |
| 5 | 195 | 38,025 |
| 6 | 193 | 37,249 |
| 7 | 207 | 42,849 |
| 8 | 198 | 39,204 |

$$n = 8 \quad \Sigma X_b = 1,565 \quad X_b^2 = 306,517$$

$$\bar{X}_b = \frac{1,565}{8} = 195.625$$

$$SS_b = \Sigma X_b^2 - \frac{(\Sigma X_b)^2}{n}$$

$$= 306,517 - \frac{2,449,225}{8}$$

$$= 363.88$$

We now have all the values required to compute the $t$. In summary, these values are

$$\bar{X}_a = 174 \qquad\qquad \bar{X}_b = 195.625$$

$$n_a = 8 \qquad\qquad n_b = 8$$

$$SS_a = 334 \qquad\qquad SS_b = 363.88$$

Plugging these values into the formula, $t$ is then computed.

$$t = \frac{195.625 - 174}{\sqrt{\frac{334 + 363.88}{(8-1)+(8-1)}\left(\frac{1}{8} + \frac{1}{8}\right)}} = \frac{21.625}{\sqrt{12.46}} = \frac{21.625}{3.53} = 6.13$$

Now that $t$ has been computed, a table of $t$ is found to determine the probability of obtaining a $t$ equal to 6.13 by chance. A $t$ table may be found in the Appendix. On the left-hand side of the table is a column labeled $df$.[3] In a randomized two-group design $df = N - 2$. The $df$, for example, equals 14 ($16 - 2$), so we run down the $df$ column to 14, then read across the row correlated with $df = 14$ until we come to a value just smaller than 6.13. In

---

3. The term $df$ stands for degrees of freedom. Degrees of freedom may be calculated differently for different types of experimental designs. If a student is unfamiliar with this term, it is suggested he turn to a text on statistics for a more thorough explanation.

this case, however, the largest number is 2.977. We now read up the column to the top where it says 0.01, which stands for the probability of 1 percent. Now if our *t* had equaled 2.977, the chart would tell us that the probability of getting $t = 2.977$ with 14 *df* by chance is 1 out of 100. Because the *t* obtained was larger than 2.977, this finding indicates that a difference between the two groups obtained in this experiment would occur by chance less than 1 time out of 100. Because a $p = .05$ is usually accepted as showing that the change was significant, we may in step 6 conclude that the aspirin did influence the time it took to learn.

| *Matched Two-Group Design* | $\begin{pmatrix} RM & X & O \\ RM & & O \end{pmatrix}$ |
|---|---|

Recall from Chapter Four that holding secondary variables constant was preferred over randomization for equating experimental groups on some particular variable. A matched two-group design is a modification of the totally randomized two-group design. With this design, both groups are matched in terms of some variable the experimenter feels would influence the DV. Suppose we want to carry out an experiment to determine whether words closely associated (e.g., bride, church, ring, white) are learned faster than words not so associated (e.g., tree, watch, hook, curtain, ruler). At the start of the project we believe that IQ will influence how well a person can retain words, so we match the two groups on IQ. We might have ten subjects available for the experiment with IQs as follows:

| *Subject number* | *IQ* |
|---|---|
| 1 | 120 |
| 2 | 120 |
| 3 | 110 |
| 4 | 110 |
| 5 | 100 |
| 6 | 100 |
| 7 | 100 |
| 8 | 100 |
| 9 | 90 |
| 10 | 90 |

In order to divide the ten subjects into two matched groups of five subjects each, we initially rank-order the subjects on the matching variable, in this case IQ. We then divide the ten subjects into five pairs by going down the list making 1 and 2 the first pair, 3 and 4 the second pair, and so on. We then randomly assign one of each pair to either group A or group B by flipping a coin and saying that the odd-numbered subject of the pair goes to group A if heads comes up or to group B if tails comes up. The coin would be flipped a total of five times, once for each pair. The random assignment of matched subjects to either group is done as a means of equating both groups on *all* secondary variables other than the one controlled for by matching. After matching and randomly assigning subjects, the composition of the two groups would be as shown in Table 9–1.

**TABLE 9–1**
*Matching subjects on IQ for a matched two-group design*

| Nonassociated Word Group | | Associated Word Group | |
| Subject number | IQ | Subject number | IQ |
|---|---|---|---|
| 2 | 120 | 1 | 120 |
| 3 | 110 | 4 | 110 |
| 6 | 100 | 5 | 100 |
| 7 | 100 | 8 | 100 |
| 10 | 90 | 9 | 90 |
| Total | 520 | Total | 520 |

After the groups have been made up, the IV (word lists) is applied. Each group is given five minutes to memorize their respective 20-word list. One week later the subjects are asked to recall as many words as they can from their list. The results are given in Table 9–2.

**TABLE 9–2**
*Raw scores for subjects in a matched two-group design*

| Nonassociated Word Group | | Associated Word Group | |
| Subject number | Retention score | Subject number | Retention score |
|---|---|---|---|
| 2 | 8 | 1 | 10 |
| 3 | 6 | 4 | 9 |
| 6 | 5 | 5 | 6 |
| 7 | 2 | 8 | 6 |
| 10 | 2 | 9 | 5 |

To carry out a statistical analysis of matched groups, the randomized *t* formula is somewhat modified.

$$t = \frac{(\bar{X}_a - \bar{X}_b)}{\sqrt{\dfrac{\Sigma D^2 - \dfrac{(\Sigma D)^2}{n}}{n(n-1)}}}$$

The symbols are basically the same for this calculation as for those used before. The only difference is the $D$ score, which is the difference between the recorded scores (DV scores) for each pair of subjects. To find $D$ in a pair of scores, subtract the first member of the pair from the second number member. In the example, subjects 2 and 1 scored 8 and 10, respectively. $D$ would therefore be $D = 8 - 10$, which equals $(-2)$. The presence of the negative sign actually makes little difference in the final score, since our next step is to square that value. The only preference for using that particular order in subtraction is for consistency. Completion of the $D$ calculation is shown below. The nonassociated word group is $X_a$, the associated word group $X_b$.

| Subject number | $X_a$ | Subject number | $X_b$ | $D$ | $D^2$ |
|---|---|---|---|---|---|
| 2 | 8 | 1 | 10 | $-2$ | 4 |
| 3 | 6 | 4 | 9 | $-3$ | 9 |
| 6 | 5 | 5 | 6 | $-1$ | 1 |
| 7 | 2 | 8 | 6 | $-4$ | 16 |
| 10 | 2 | 9 | 5 | $-3$ | 9 |

$n = 5$  $\Sigma X_a = 23$  $n = 5$  $\Sigma X_b = 36$  $\Sigma D = (-13)$  $\Sigma D^2 = 39$

$(\Sigma D)^2 = (-13)^2 = 169$

$\bar{X}_a = \frac{23}{5} = 4.6$  $\bar{X}_b = \frac{36}{5} = 7.2$

Recall that $n$ is the number of subjects in a group, not the total number of subjects in the entire experiment. The latter is noted as $N$. The numerator is the difference between the two DV means of the two groups, $\bar{X}_a$ and $\bar{X}_b$. The calculated means of the two groups are, respectively, 4.6 and 7.2. Substitute all those values in the equation and the results are as follows:

$$t = \frac{7.2 - 4.6}{\sqrt{\dfrac{39 - \dfrac{(-13)^2}{5}}{5(5-1)}}} = 5.10$$

To compute the $df$ (degrees of freedom) for the matched $t$-test, calculate $df =$ number of pairs $- 1$. Note the difference from the equation from the randomized two-group design. Upon consulting the $t$-test table, with a $t$ of 5.10 and 4 degrees of freedom, we find that the $t$ is significant at the .01 level.[4] We may then conclude that the groups differ to a significant degree. Our original hypothesis is confirmed.

4. The same $t$ table is used for both matched and unmatched two-group designs.

Pretest-Posttest $\quad\begin{pmatrix} RO_1 & X & O_2 \\ RO_3 & & O_4 \end{pmatrix}$
Control Group Design

One of the most common experimental designs in human investigations is the pretest-posttest control group design. It is a popular design, for it not only neatly controls for seven of the nine sources of secondary variation, but also provides a measure of the DV for each group prior to the administration of the IV. This also allows the investigator to employ an analysis of covariance if the DV is originally different for the two groups, and provides a measure of effects due to retroactive history. The scores on the pretest and posttest for the control group would be almost identical, unless some unsuspected secondary variable influences the DV while the investigation is in progress. When this happens, $O_3$ will vary from $O_4$, giving a measure of the effect of the unnoticed secondary variable. Upon spotting this fluctuation, the investigator may statistically adjust for this effect on the DV score of the group experiencing the IV. The following example illustrates the use of a pretest and posttest control group design.

Paul Stevens received his bachelor's degree in business education with a minor in psychology. After graduation Paul became a manager of a large meat packing plant dealing mainly with chicken processing. He was going over the books one day in an effort to find ways of cutting processing costs when certain figures caught his eye. Chicken pluckers were paid $1.80 an hour, and the average number of chickens plucked per hour was twelve. He recalled from the behavior analysis course that he had taken that the type of reinforcement schedule employed was shown to influence productivity. Remembering his instructor mentioned that people would produce more on a fixed ratio schedule, Paul decided to carry out an experiment to test this statement. From the list of 120 chicken pluckers applying for jobs, he randomly assigned 10 to one of two 5-man groups. After the 10 new men had been working a whole week for $1.80 per hour, Paul calculated the number of chickens plucked by each man per eight-hour shift. The results of this calculation are shown below.

| Group A | | Group B | |
|---|---|---|---|
| *Worker number* | *Pretest score* | *Worker number* | *Pretest score* |
| 1 | 92 | 6 | 93 |
| 2 | 96 | 7 | 95 |
| 3 | 94 | 8 | 99 |
| 4 | 98 | 9 | 97 |
| 5 | 94 | 10 | 96 |

He then told group B workers that they would be paid 12¢ a chicken for each one plucked rather than $1.80 per hour. Group A workers remained on the hourly wage. After four weeks had passed, Paul calculated the number of chickens plucked per eight-hour shift by each worker for the past week. The results are shown below.

| Group A | | Group B | |
|---|---|---|---|
| *Worker number* | *Posttest score* | *Worker number* | *Posttest score* |
| 1 | 96 | 6 | 112 |
| 2 | 98 | 7 | 116 |
| 3 | 97 | 8 | 108 |
| 4 | 101 | 9 | 110 |
| 5 | 98 | 10 | 114 |

Actually there are a few ways to analyze this type of design statistically, though the most common is a *t*-test on gain scores.

The tables and equations below demonstrate how to line up your data. The procedure basically involves subtracting each worker's pretest score from his posttest score. The difference is called the *gain score*. Each gain score is then treated as a raw score for each subject, and a *t*-test is carried out using the same formula employed with the randomized two-group design.

| Group A | | | | Group B | | | |
|---|---|---|---|---|---|---|---|
| *Worker number* | *Pretest score* | *Posttest score* | *Gain score* | *Worker number* | *Pretest score* | *Posttest score* | *Gain score* |
| 1 | 92 | 96 | 4 | 6 | 93 | 112 | 19 |
| 2 | 96 | 98 | 2 | 7 | 95 | 116 | 21 |
| 3 | 94 | 97 | 3 | 8 | 99 | 108 | 9 |
| 4 | 98 | 101 | 3 | 9 | 97 | 110 | 13 |
| 5 | 94 | 98 | 4 | 10 | 96 | 114 | 18 |

| Group A | | | Group B | | |
|---|---|---|---|---|---|
| *Worker number* | *Gain score* $(X)$ | $X^2$ | *Worker number* | *Gain score* $(X)$ | $X^2$ |
| 1 | 4 | 16 | 6 | 19 | 361 |
| 2 | 2 | 4 | 7 | 21 | 441 |
| 3 | 3 | 9 | 8 | 9 | 81 |
| 4 | 3 | 9 | 9 | 13 | 169 |
| 5 | 4 | 16 | 10 | 18 | 324 |

$n = 5 \qquad \Sigma X_a = 16 \quad \Sigma X_b^2 = 54$

$\bar{X}_a = \dfrac{\Sigma X_a}{n} = \dfrac{16}{5} = 3.2$

$SS_a = \Sigma X_a^2 - \dfrac{(\Sigma X_a)^2}{n} = 54 - \dfrac{(16)^2}{5} = 2.8$

$n = 5 \qquad \Sigma X_b = 80 \quad \Sigma X_b^2 = 1{,}376$

$\bar{X}_b = \dfrac{\Sigma X_b}{n} = \dfrac{80}{5} = 16$

$SS_b = \Sigma X_b^2 - \dfrac{(\Sigma X_b)^2}{n}$

$= 1{,}376 - \dfrac{(80)^2}{5} = 96$

Next, the values are plugged into the $t$ formula. The rule is to put the largest mean first in the numerator so that the resultant number is always positive.

$$t = \frac{\bar{X}_b - \bar{X}_a}{\sqrt{\frac{SS_a + SS_b}{(n_a - 1) + (n_b - 1)}\left(\frac{1}{n_a} + \frac{1}{n_b}\right)}} = \frac{16 - 3.2}{\sqrt{\frac{.8 + 96}{4 + 4}\left(\frac{1}{5} + \frac{1}{5}\right)}} = \frac{12.8}{\sqrt{4.84}}$$

$$= 5.82$$

Turning to the $t$ table with $t$ equaling 5.82 and $df$ equaling 8, we find the change in pay schedule to have influenced output, for the probability of a $t$ this size occurring by chance is less than .01, or less than 1 in 100.

It is not an uncommon thing for students to carry out an *incorrect* statistical analysis on a pretest-posttest design. Students frequently compute two $t$s, one for the pretest-posttest difference obtained with the experimental group and one for the pretest-posttest difference in the control group. If the $t$ test for the experimental group is significant and the control group's $t$ is not, they then conclude that the IV had an effect. The *incorrect* procedure is shown below.

|  | | Group A | | |
| Worker number | Pretest score | Posttest score | Difference (D) | $D^2$ |
| --- | --- | --- | --- | --- |
| 1 | 92 | 96 | 4 | 16 |
| 2 | 96 | 94 | −2 | 4 |
| 3 | 94 | 97 | 3 | 9 |
| 4 | 98 | 95 | −3 | 9 |
| 5 | 94 | 98 | 4 | 16 |

$$n = 5 \qquad \Sigma X_a = 480 \qquad \Sigma X_b = 480 \qquad \Sigma D = 0 \qquad \Sigma D^2 = 54$$

$$\bar{X}_a = \frac{480}{5} \qquad \bar{X}_b = \frac{480}{5}$$

$$\bar{X}_a = 96 \qquad \bar{X}_b = 96$$

$$t = \frac{\bar{X}_b - \bar{X}_a}{\sqrt{\frac{\Sigma D^2 - \frac{(\Sigma D)^2}{n}}{n(n - 1)}}}$$

$$t = \frac{96 - 96}{\sqrt{\frac{54 - 0/N}{5(5 - 1)}}}$$

$$t = 0 \text{ (not significant)}$$

If the $t$ for the experimental group is significant and the $t$ for the control group is not, it is erroneously concluded that the IV had an effect.

| Worker number | Pretest score | Group B Posttest score | Difference (D) | $D^2$ |
|---|---|---|---|---|
| 6 | 93 | 112 | 19 | 361 |
| 7 | 95 | 116 | 21 | 441 |
| 8 | 99 | 108 | 9 | 81 |
| 9 | 97 | 110 | 13 | 169 |
| 10 | 96 | 114 | 18 | 324 |

$$n = 5 \quad \Sigma X_a = 480 \quad \Sigma X_b = 560 \quad \Sigma D = 80 \quad \Sigma D^2 = 1{,}376$$

$$\bar{X}_a = \frac{480}{5} \qquad \bar{X}_b = \frac{560}{5}$$

$$\bar{X}_a = 96 \qquad \bar{X}_b = 112$$

$$t = \frac{\bar{X}_b - \bar{X}_a}{\sqrt{\dfrac{\Sigma D^2 - \dfrac{(\Sigma D)^2}{n}}{n(n-1)}}}$$

$$t = \frac{112 - 96}{\sqrt{\dfrac{1{,}376 - \dfrac{6{,}400}{5}}{5(5-1)}}}$$

$$t = \frac{16}{\sqrt{4.8}} = \frac{16}{2.19} = 7.3$$

This analysis is incorrect because it may lead to significant *t*s when in fact there was no significance.

### Static Group Design $\left(\begin{matrix} X \, O_1 \\ O_2 \end{matrix}\right)$

The static group design is identical to the randomized two-group design with one important exception: subjects are not randomly assigned to groups. This one factor makes a large difference in Table 9–2 between the static group design and the randomized two-group design. The randomized two-group design is much preferred, for randomization allows one to control for secondary variables. The static group design is devoid of any of the five control procedures previously covered, and it therefore leaves any conclusion from the results open to misinterpretation regarding the influence of the IV. In some cases, however, the situation leaves one no alternative but to use the static group design. Here is an example.

Suppose that during wartime a new type of fighter plane is developed. The war office wants a study carried out to determine whether the new plane is more effective in dog fights than the one currently being used. It is not feasible to supply two present air squadrons with one-half new and one-half old planes, for special training is required of the pilots and each squadron has to have all planes alike for coordinated flying. The practical solution is to compare one whole squadron equipped with the new fighter.

The type of statistical analysis carried out on a static group comparison is the same as for randomized two groups. One must be careful, however, in using this analysis. In order to justify the use of the *t*-test in experiments involving the comparison between means, two assumptions are necessary: first, the populations from which the subjects come should be normalized, and second, the population variances should be homogeneous.[5] When a static group comparison is carried out, the possibility that these assumptions are not met is much greater than when a randomized group design is used. It is strongly suggested that students refrain from using this design whenever possible. It is not considered adequate, especially for theses or dissertation research.

*Nonrandomized* $\begin{pmatrix} O & X & O \\ O & & O \end{pmatrix}$
*Pretest-Posttest*
*Control Group Design*

The nonequivalent control group design is related to the randomized pretest-posttest design in the same way the static group design is related to the randomized two-group design. It is identical to the pretest-posttest control group design except that the groups have not been composed of randomly assigned subjects. Therefore, it is highly probable that the two groups have not been equated. As a result, the same type of statistical analysis difficulties encountered with the static group design hold also for the nonequivalent pretest-posttest design. Because the same statistical *t*-test is employed for the pretest-posttest control group design as for the randomized two-group design, the problem of meeting the underlying assumptions is again present. Although the nonequivalent control group design is inferior to the pretest-posttest control group design, it has an advantage over the static group design. The pretest-posttest design may show differences in the groups prior to the administration of the IV. The experimenter may then adjust for this by using an analysis of covariance.

*Analysis of Covariance*
*Two-Group Design*

So far all the two-group designs have used a manipulatory approach to decrease the influence of secondary variables. Analysis of covariance is a means for controlling secondary variables using a statistical rather than a

---

5. By *normalized* we mean results will be more accurate the more symmetrical the population distribution curve. If there are too many deviances from the general trend, it is only logical that their presence would tend to skew the obtained results. By *homogeneity* we mean the within-group variances obtained should resemble, in degree variation, the within-group variation of the experimental group data. A complete explanation is found in Hays [1963].

manipulatory approach. Differences among observations in an experiment may be due in part to differences that existed among the subjects prior to the experiment and that persisted through the experiment. It is possible to adjust the observations for the purpose of eliminating these initial differences, if there are measures of these differences available.

In Chapter Eight the idea was put forth that variability in measures could be adjusted using regression analysis procedures. If an investigator had the numerical values of two different variables ($X$ and $Y$) for each subject involved in his investigation, it is possible to determine how much of the fluctuation of either variable was related to changes in the other. If, for example, the IQ score ($Y$) and scores on a math exam ($X$) are known for each child in the class, it is possible to determine how much of the variation in the math scores of the class were related to differences in the students' IQ. As shown in the formula

$$V_T = V_{IQ} + V_O$$

the total variation in scores is equal to the variability due to IQ ($V_{IQ}$) plus variations due to all other factors ($V_O$).[6] By means of correlational procedures the amount of variability due to IQ could be numerically identified and removed.

In an ideal experimental situation the investigator has employed adequate control procedures so that both groups in a two-group design are equal in terms of all secondary variables potentially relevant in the experimental situation. Most investigations, however, are not ideal. In some instances a potent secondary variable may not be adequately equated in both groups although control procedures were employed. In other situations it may not be possible for the investigator to equate the groups on all important variables. In such cases the investigator combines correlational analysis procedures with the normal analysis of variance procedures. Here is an example.

Carol Davis, a creative grade-school teacher for twelve years, developed what she felt was a better method of teaching first-grade children to identify written words verbally. With the support of the school board and another first-grade teacher in a nearby grade school, Carol set up a two-group experimental design to compare her new method of teaching (method A) with a more common approach (method B). She was to be responsible for teaching words to the two different first-grade classes. With one class, group A, she used method A, and with the other, group B, she used method B. She and the other teacher traded classes each day at noon. After lunch each day Carol

---

6. Remember, the phrase *related* to IQ is used, for IQ may not actually be causing the variability. The variability may represent the influence of some other variable that concurrently influences both IQ and math behavior to the same degree.

would drive to the second school, while the other teacher would drive over and take Carol's class for the last half of the day.

At the end of the year, all the children of both classes were given a test to determine their ability to identify written words verbally. The results of this test are shown below.

| Group A (Method A) | | Group B (Method B) | |
| *Student number* | *Score* | *Student number* | *Score* |
| --- | --- | --- | --- |
| 1 | 11 | 1 | 2 |
| 2 | 11 | 2 | 7 |
| 3 | 7 | 3 | 5 |
| 4 | 8 | 4 | 7 |
| 5 | 7 | 5 | 6 |
| 6 | 12 | 6 | 14 |
| 7 | 14 | 7 | 7 |
| 8 | 5 | 8 | 5 |
| 9 | 5 | 9 | 1 |
| 10 | 9 | 10 | 5 |

It was Carol's intent to determine the between-group variance and the within-group variance, and then calculate the $t$ of the two to determine whether her new method was better. She then proceeded to do the following statistical analysis:

$$t = \frac{\bar{X}_a - \bar{X}_b}{\sqrt{\frac{SS_a + SS_b}{(n_a - 1) + (n_b - 1)}(1/n_a + 1/n_b)}}$$

Group A

| *Student number* | $X$ | $X^2$ |
| --- | --- | --- |
| 1 | 11 | 121 |
| 2 | 11 | 121 |
| 3 | 7 | 49 |
| 4 | 8 | 64 |
| 5 | 7 | 49 |
| 6 | 12 | 144 |
| 7 | 14 | 196 |
| 8 | 5 | 25 |
| 9 | 5 | 25 |
| 10 | 9 | 81 |

$n = 10 \qquad \Sigma X_a = 89 \qquad \Sigma X_a^2 = 875$

$\bar{X}_a = \frac{\Sigma X_a}{n} = \frac{89}{10} = 8.9$

$SS_a = \Sigma X_a^2 - \frac{(\Sigma X_a)^2}{n} = 875 - \frac{(89)^2}{10} = 82.9$

Group B

| Student number | X | $X^2$ |
|:---:|:---:|:---:|
| 1 | 2 | 4 |
| 2 | 7 | 49 |
| 3 | 5 | 25 |
| 4 | 7 | 49 |
| 5 | 6 | 36 |
| 6 | 14 | 196 |
| 7 | 7 | 49 |
| 8 | 5 | 25 |
| 9 | 1 | 1 |
| 10 | 5 | 25 |

$$n = 10 \qquad \Sigma X_b = 59 \qquad \Sigma X_b^2 = 459$$

$$\bar{X}_b = \frac{\Sigma X_b}{n} = \frac{59}{10} = 5.9$$

$$SS_b = \Sigma X_b^2 - \frac{(\Sigma X_b)^2}{n} = 459 - \frac{(59)^2}{10} = 110.9$$

$$t = \frac{8.9 - 5.9}{\sqrt{\frac{110.9 + 82.9}{(10 - 1) + (10 - 1)}\left(\frac{1}{10} + \frac{1}{10}\right)}}$$

$$t = \frac{3.0}{\sqrt{\frac{193.8}{18}\left(\frac{1}{5}\right)}}$$

$$t = \frac{3.0}{\sqrt{(10.8)(1/5)}}$$

$$t = \frac{3.0}{\sqrt{2.16}} = \frac{3.0}{1.47} = 2.04$$

In checking the files on the first graders, Carol noted that the IQ levels appeared to be different for the two classes. Realizing that IQ might be an important secondary variable, Carol then decided to carry out an analysis of covariance to adjust for any differences in the experimental results (scores on the word recognition test) related to differences in IQ.

In order to carry out an analysis of covariance between the two groups, the $t$ formula had to be modified as follows:[7]

$$t = \frac{(1 - r^2)(\bar{X}_a - \bar{X}_b)}{\sqrt{\frac{SS_a - SS_b}{(n_a - 1)(n_b - 1)}(1/n_a + 1/n_b)}}$$

7. The analysis of covariance formula is a simplification of the exact formula. It has been modified here to make it easier for the reader to see what is involved in using analysis of covariance. Although this formula may be used for learning the logic behind analysis of covariance, one should employ the analysis of covariance using the F-test for two groups when statistically analyzing data from a real experiment, thesis, or dissertation. This procedure is covered in the following chapter. If one is interested in employing the

Notice the numerator has the added value $(1 - r^2)$. You may recall from Chapter Eight that $r$ stands for correlation coefficient and can be used for determining the amount of variability in $X$ related to some correlated variable ($Y$). The argument was put forth that if two variables were correlated, the square of the correlation between the two ($r^2$) would indicate the percentage of variations in $X$ that could be related to $Y$. The value of $(1 - r^2)$ would then represent the percentage of variability of $X$ due to factors other than variable $Y$. In the two-group design, the objective was to equate the two groups on all secondary variables in the experimental setting so that the difference between the group means could be due only to the IV. In the present case, the groups were found to differ also on IQ, a secondary variable known to be an important determinant for academic achievement. The obtained variation between the means $(\bar{X}_a - \bar{X}_b)$ is then partially a function of IQ. The following formula shows that the total variation between the means $(V_B)$ is equal to variation due to the IV $(V_{IV})$ plus the variation related to IQ $(V_{IQ})$.

$$V_B = V_{IV} + V_{IQ}$$

The variation related to IQ must then be extracted from the obtained difference between the means. If $r^2$ equals the percentage of $V_B$ due to IQ, then $1 - r^2$ should equal the percentage of $V_B$ due to the IV. With this fact in mind, the obtained $(\bar{X}_a - \bar{X}_b)$ is adjusted to obtain the predicted difference between the means if IQ had been held constant for both groups.

To accomplish the adjustment of $(\bar{X}_a - \bar{X}_b)$ the following calculations need to be made:[8]

Group A

| Student number | $X$ | $Y$ | $XY$ | $X^2$ | $Y^2$ |
|---|---|---|---|---|---|
| 1 | 11 | 5 | 55 | 121 | 25 |
| 2 | 11 | 5 | 55 | 121 | 25 |
| 3 | 7 | 3 | 21 | 49 | 9 |
| 4 | 8 | 3 | 24 | 64 | 9 |
| 5 | 7 | 3 | 21 | 49 | 9 |
| 6 | 12 | 4 | 48 | 144 | 16 |
| 7 | 14 | 9 | 126 | 196 | 81 |
| 8 | 5 | 4 | 20 | 25 | 16 |
| 9 | 5 | 4 | 20 | 25 | 16 |
| 10 | 9 | 5 | 45 | 81 | 25 |
| $N_a = 10$ | $\Sigma X_a = 89$ | $\Sigma Y_a = 45$ | $\Sigma XY_a = 435$ | $\Sigma X_a^2 = 875$ | $\Sigma Y_a^2 = 231$ |

true formula for analysis of covariance using a $t$-test, it may be found in Keppel's *Design and Analysis: A Researcher's Handbook* [1973].

8. $Y$ in the calculations represents a measure of IQ. Low numbers have been used instead of actual IQ scores so that the calculations would be less cumbersome. The letter $X$ represents the score of each subject.

Group B

| Student number | X | Y | XY | X² | Y² |
|---|---|---|---|---|---|
| 1 | 2 | 4 | 8 | 4 | 16 |
| 2 | 7 | 3 | 21 | 49 | 9 |
| 3 | 5 | 4 | 20 | 25 | 16 |
| 4 | 7 | 3 | 21 | 49 | 9 |
| 5 | 6 | 5 | 30 | 36 | 25 |
| 6 | 14 | 6 | 84 | 196 | 36 |
| 7 | 7 | 5 | 35 | 49 | 25 |
| 8 | 5 | 3 | 15 | 25 | 9 |
| 9 | 1 | 3 | 3 | 1 | 9 |
| 10 | 5 | 3 | 15 | 25 | 9 |

$N_b = 10$   $\Sigma X_b = 59$   $\Sigma Y_b = 39$   $\Sigma X Y_b = 252$   $\Sigma X_b{}^2 = 459$   $\Sigma Y_b{}^2 = 163$

$$r = \frac{N\Sigma XY - (\Sigma X)(\Sigma Y)}{\sqrt{[N\Sigma X^2 - (\Sigma X)^2][N\Sigma Y^2 - (\Sigma Y)^2]}}$$

$$r = \frac{(20)(435 + 252) - (89 + 59)(45 + 39)}{\sqrt{[(20)(875 + 459) - (89 + 59)^2][(20)(231 + 163) - (45 + 39)^2]}}$$

$r = .66$

$r^2 = .44$

After calculating $r^2$, the numerical value is plugged into the formula as follows:

$$t = \frac{(1 - .44)(\bar{X}_a - \bar{X}_b)}{\sqrt{\frac{SS_a + SS_b}{(n_a - 1) + (n_b - 1)}(1/n_a + 1/n_b)}}$$

$$t = \frac{1.68}{1.46} = 1.15$$

Notice that the correlation between IQ and test scores is fairly high (.66). By removing the differences in scores related to IQ, an adjusted $t$ is obtained that is no longer significant. This result suggested that Carol's new teaching method was no better than the old method.

Two points should be emphasized. First, if the secondary variable is not highly correlated with the DV measures, then carrying out analysis of covariance adds nothing to the study, for it does not increase control of secondary variable effects in such situations. Second, if the covariate is highly correlated with the DV, then the experimental investigation has been enhanced and is better than carrying out the easier noncovariance analysis.

## ADVANTAGES AND DISADVANTAGES
## OF TWO-GROUP DESIGNS

As mentioned it is possible to reach valid conclusions in experimental situations that do not include a second group for control. Carrying out non-control one-group manipulating investigations is a step toward more valid investigations. Being able to determine when an IV would be applied does allow an investigator greater confidence in concluding that any succeeding change in the DV was a function of the IV. Adding a second group made two important contributions to scientific analysis. First, it greatly increased the internal validity of the investigation by allowing the investigator to employ more methods for controlling secondary variables. Second, it furnished the conditions necessary for a true comparison to be made. With the control group, the investigator has a measure of the DV without the influence of the IV. Not only does the control group allow the investigator to see if there is a difference due to the IV, it also provides data necessary for available statistical tests to determine the significance of any obtained group differences.

Two-group designs are generally considered to be excellent for carrying out exploratory investigations aimed at determining whether a particular variable has an effect. They may also be appropriately used to determine which of two alternative variables is better, as was the case with Carol Davis's attempt to compare two teaching approaches. One of the main advantages of two-group designs is simplicity. Later on, the designs covered will involve more groups and more complex statistical procedures. The two-group designs are easier to conduct and analyze statistically, yet provide all the factors necessary for a scientific analysis. Too often students assume that the more groups involved and the more complex the statistical analysis, the better the project. Remember, you do not need a baseball bat to kill a fly. A flyswatter will accomplish the job just as well, and possibly faster.

It is difficult to rank-order two-group designs according to which one is best, for each has its good and bad points, and certain ones are more suited to specific situations. The analysis of covariance two-group design has the ability to control secondary variables better than the other two-group designs because it allows the investigator to apply a statistical control procedure in addition to elimination, constancy, and randomization. It also allows the investigator to adjust for the influence of a secondary variable that cannot be controlled experimentally because randomization or constancy is not possible or the effects of the secondary variable were not apparent until after the investigation began. Disadvantages of two-group analysis of covariance designs are: (1) a more complex statistical analysis must be carried out; and (2) a covariate measure must be available.

Randomized, matched two-group designs are also considered good designs, for they employ two control procedures—randomization and constancy. They are similar to randomized analysis of covariance two-group designs in that they can be used to adjust for the effects of a particular secondary variable, besides using randomization to control for all other secondary variables. The advantages of the matched design over the covariance design are in terms of the statistical analysis required. The matched *t*-test is much simpler and faster to calculate than an analysis of covariance. The covariant design is more advantageous in terms of when the control procedure can be applied. Matching for a particular secondary variable must be carried out prior to the beginning of the investigation, whereas a secondary variable may be adjusted for after the experiment begins when an analysis of covariance is used. Analysis of covariance of two-group designs may be used where matching is not feasible, such as in the investigation comparing teaching procedures. It was not feasible to match the two first-grade classes by making some of the students change schools.

Pretest-posttest designs are generally preferred over posttest only designs mainly because the investigator obtains more information. Pretests may be used to ensure that both groups are equated in terms of the DV when the investigation begins. In some situations an investigator may administer a pretest before assigning subjects to either of the groups. In this way, the investigator may match the two groups on the DV to ensure that the groups are equated. Pretest-posttest two-group designs may "sensitize" the subjects to what is going on in the experiment, thereby biasing the scores they make on the posttest. In many situations, carrying out a pretest is either not practical or not functional for dealing with the problem being investigated. Randomized two-group designs are always preferred over nonrandomized designs, no matter whether they involve pretests, posttests only, matching, or analysis of covariance.

Two-group designs are generally preferred to one-way analysis of variance and factorial designs because they are relatively easy to set up and carry out, yet they are just as scientifically sound as the more complex designs. Though simplicity is the two-group design's greatest asset, it is also its main disadvantage. Due to its simple statistical analysis and its limitation to two groups, it does not allow more than one between-group comparison to be made. If the investigator desires to carry out a parametric study or compare more than two variables at one time, two-group designs are not suitable.


## SUMMARY

Although two-group experimental designs have been around for centuries, their importance in scientific investigations has come about only in the last few decades. The basic idea behind adding a second group to an investigation is to provide some measure of a DV from subjects not experiencing the IV. The effect of the IV will then show up as the difference between the DVs of the two groups. Six two-group designs were presented: (1) the randomized two-group design, (2) the matched two-group design, (3) the pretest-posttest control group design, (4) the static group design, (5) the nonrandomized pretest-posttest control group design, and (6) the analysis of covariance two-group design.

# 10

# Multigroup Designs with One Independent Variable

*Obviously, experiments can be carried out in which three or more groups are employed. These are called one-way ANOVAR experiments. This chapter shows how such experiments are set up and carried out. The first section gives a logical explanation of what is involved in the statistical analysis of one-way ANOVAR designs. The explanation relates very strongly to the discussion of variance given in Chapter Four. The concept of sums of squares is explained. Although the student could simply follow the numerical illustrations given and carry out a statistical analysis without really understanding sums of squares, the explanation is provided for those interested in a more thorough understanding of what is involved in the statistical analysis. As was true with the last chapter, step-by-step examples showing exactly how the statistical tests are conducted have been included so that the student does not need a course in statistics to carry them out. Remember, knowing how to perform the statistical test is only one step in the investigation. The student should concentrate on understanding when one-way ANOVAR designs are used, how they differ from other types of designs, and the advantages and disadvantages of the different ANOVAR designs.*

So far, the most complex types of experiments discussed have been those consisting of two groups, an experimental and a control. The objective of these two-group experiments is to determine whether some IV differentially influences the DV of the experimental and control groups. Although two-group designs are the most common in psychological research, they are somewhat restrictive. Events in nature do not always conveniently order themselves into two groups. Frequently, the investigator asks which of several alternative variables has the greater effect, or he wants to compare the effect of different values of the same variable. Which of five different types of teaching machines is most functional for a particular educational program? What dosage of a certain anesthetic is required for deep anesthesia? Obviously, the design necessary to answer these questions requires comparison of more than two groups. Such designs are called one-way ANOVAR designs.[1]

Suppose you are hired by a pharmaceutical company to find out which of three cough remedies is most effective. The zealous student may see no trouble at all in carrying out such an investigation. Diligently he starts through the six steps of experimental analysis involved in a laboratory experiment. Being rather perceptive, he realizes all the methods of control for secondary variables covered are just as applicable to experiments involving three or more groups as they are to two-group investigations. He eliminates as many of the secondary variables as possible, holds others constant for all three groups, and randomly assigns subjects to the groups in an effort to equate all remaining secondary variables. The different cold remedies are then administered, one to each group. The number of minutes each subject goes without coughing over the next hour is then recorded as the DV.

So far the student has done very well. The procedure for carrying out one-way ANOVAR designs is the same as for two-group designs. The means of selecting a hypothesis, determining which IV and DV to employ, controlling for secondary variables, and actually carrying out the procedure are basically identical. The distinguishing feature between the two types of investigations is in the type of statistical analysis used. How do you compare three or more groups? The student may unhesitantly suggest that three *t*-tests be carried out—one between the first and second groups, one between the second and third groups, and one between the first and third groups. This analytical approach is generally considered to be unacceptable, however, and the reason involves the probability of drawing an incorrect conclusion about the results.

Remember, a scientist is very cautious about making a statement that some IV did affect the DV. He is so cautious, in fact, that he will not make such a statement unless there is only a 5 percent chance or less that the fluctuation of the DV occurring in an experiment could have been due to chance. He wants to be at least 95 percent sure that the variation in the DV is due to the IV and not some other variable. An analogy might be betting on a horse race. The scientist would not bet on a horse unless the horse had a 95 percent chance of winning, or inversely, only a 5 percent chance of losing. Most people betting, however, would jump at the chance to bet on a horse if it had even a 60 percent chance of winning.[2] The scientist has a reputation to

---

1. ANOVAR stands for analysis of variance. Analysis of variance is commonly abbreviated as ANOVA to represent analysis of variance as a statistical test.

2. Most gambling establishments in Las Vegas work on less than a 53/47 split (53 percent probability that the casino will win, 47 percent probability that the customer will win), yet people flock there to accept these odds.

protect. Society looks to him for direction in terms of what is effective and what will work. His statements of cause-effect relationships are respected, for he does not make outlandish claims. With his precision comes confidence by the people in his conclusions. The scientist is cautious in claiming causes of a disease, cancer, mental retardation, and so forth, just as he is cautious in claiming cures for such conditions.

Although the 5 percent significance level was somewhat arbitrarily selected, scientists revere it and look with disdain on investigators who do not adhere to it. This is the reason the suggested *t*-test analysis would not be acceptable. The effect of increasing the number of *t*-tests in an investigation is a correlated increase in the probability that an incorrect conclusion will be drawn. With one *t*-test the probability is 5 percent for concluding a cause-effect relationship incorrectly. With two *t*-tests the probability rises to 10 percent. Three *t*-tests raise it to 15 percent, and so on. From this you may rightly conclude that the probability of stating an incorrect causal conclusion is equal to the number of *t*-tests carried out times the 5 percent significance level of acceptance. Because of this fact, researchers are reluctant to carry out more than one *t*-test in an experiment. To cope with the analytical needs of a multigroup comparison, a different statistical technique is employed, an analysis of variance called the F test.

The F test is a statistical technique employed to deal with the problem of significant differences encountered when more than two groups are involved. It may be used in multigroup situations to determine statistically whether the IVs are actually producing differences in the various group DVs.[3]

## LOGICAL ANALYSIS
## OF ONE-WAY ANOVAR DESIGNS
## USING AN F TEST

As previously mentioned, the six basic steps for carrying out two-group or more than two-group experiments are essentially the same. The only real difference between two-group and multigroup experiments is in the way the statistical analysis is carried out on the data. The main objective of this chapter, then, is to show the student how the statistical analysis can be carried out and to help the student understand the reasoning behind the statistical F test.

In Chapter Four it was stated that the objective of an experiment was to divide total variation into two parts, that which can be accounted for (due to

---

3. An F test may also be applied in investigations involving only two groups. The principle behind the F and *t*-tests is the same, and the *t*-test was a specially devised test for only two groups.

the IV) and that which cannot be accounted for (due to unknown secondary variables and chance variations). We also saw that all experimental investigations involve dividing the variance between groups $(V_B)$ by the variance within groups $(V_W)$. Statistically speaking, this is called an F test. It tells the investigator whether the variance due to the IV was relatively larger than the variance expected by chance fluctuation alone. We will now look at this variance idea more closely and see how it relates to the statistical analysis of two-group and ANOVAR designs.

Let us return to the ball-throwing example in Chapter Four. Suppose six children were asked to throw a ball as far as they could, with the results shown in Figure 10–1. As one would expect, the scores vary. The variation in scores would be due to the differential influence of both genetic and environmental factors. All the subjects were not equal in terms of height, strength, and so on. Also, environmental factors such as wind, wetness of ball, and exact weight of ball were not identical on each throw. If one were able magically to take all the genetic and environmental variables present in the situation and redistribute their effects equally among all the subjects, making them all the same height, strength, and so on, the distance each subject threw the ball would be exactly the same as shown in Figure 10–2. The result would be that each subject would throw the ball a distance equaling the mean of the original scores shown in Figure 10–1.

Now that all variables are equally distributed, suppose you took one variable (weight of the balls thrown) and intentionally redistributed it in such a way that each subject had to throw a ball of different weight. Figure 10–3 shows the results of such a situation. Each score is different again, with the difference of each score from the mean due to the varied weights of the balls. The cause of the differences in the throws could truthfully be said to be due to the weight of the balls, for the effects of all other variables were

**FIGURE 10–1**

Theoretical distance six children threw a ball

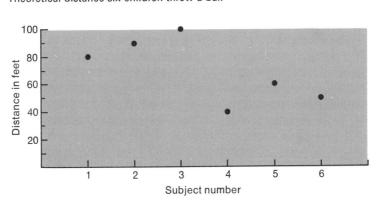

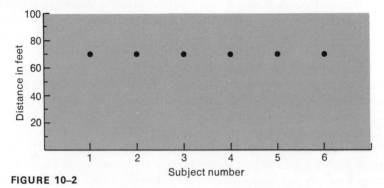

**FIGURE 10–2**

Theoretical distance six children equal in all respects threw a ball

equally distributed among the subjects. The vertical distance of each score from the mean would represent the differential influence of the ball's weight.

Suppose the six equated subjects were now divided into two groups, again with the weight of the ball being the only variable unequally distributed. Now, instead of six balls of different weights only two balls of unequal weight are thrown, one by group A and one by group B. With the results of Figure 10–4, it is not too difficult to conclude that the group B subjects threw the heavier ball. The mean for group A equaled 90 ($\bar{X}_A = 90$), while the mean for group B equaled 50 ($\bar{X}_B = 50$). The distance from each group mean to the grand mean of all the throws put together ($\bar{X}_G = 70$) would represent the influence of the ball's weight. It could be said that the weight is what caused the difference between the group means and the grand mean.

**FIGURE 10–3**

Theoretical distance six children equal in all respects threw a ball with the weight of the ball being different for each child

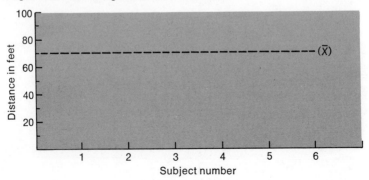

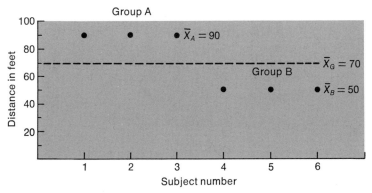

**FIGURE 10–4**

Theoretical distance six children threw a ball; all genetic and environmental factors were equal except the weight of the ball

Figure 10–4 shows the results of what could be an ideal experiment in which an investigator wanted to determine what effect a ball's weight would have on the distance children could throw. Ideally, he would select six subjects identical in age, weight, strength, and so on. He would divide them into three-subject groups (A and B). Group A would throw a 4-ounce ball, while group B would throw a 5-ounce ball.

Unfortunately, ideal subjects and situations are seldom found in research. We are stuck with the fact that all subjects are not equal and that environmental conditions are not exactly the same from one moment to the next. Being practical, an experimenter realizes all subjects in either group will not throw the ball the exact same distance as shown in Figure 10–4. The results shown in Figure 10–5 are more like what he would expect. Each subject

**FIGURE 10–5**

Theoretical distance six children threw a ball in a usual experimental situation

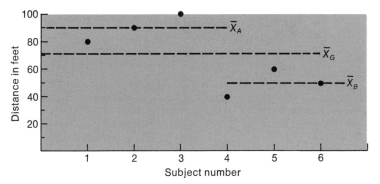

would throw the ball a different distance, though the mean distance for the group with the lightest ball would be farther than that for the group throwing the heavier ball.

Figure 10–5 diagrammatically represents the results of a typical experiment. An IV (weight of the ball) is systematically varied from one group to another. This causes scores to vary from the grand mean. A numerical measure of the effect of the IV is the difference of the group means from the grand mean. All the variation from the grand mean, however, is not due to the IV alone. The secondary variables (strength, size, etc.) and error fluctuations (e.g., inexact measurement of distance) are responsible for some. Figure 10–6 presents this point diagrammatically.[4]

The total distance any particular subject's score varies from the mean of all other scores $(\bar{X}_G)$ is equal to (1) the variation caused by the IV, and (2) the variation due to *all* the other unknown or unmeasured variables in the situation. A measure of the influence of the IV on any subject's score may be represented by the difference between the mean $(\bar{X}_g)$ of the group the subject was in, minus the grand mean $(\bar{X}_g - \bar{X}_G)$. A measure of the effects of all the unknown variables is found by subtracting the group mean from the subject's score $(X_{ig} - \bar{X}_g)$.[5] The total variation of any score can be divided as follows:

$$(X_{ig} - \bar{X}_G) = (X_{ig} - \bar{X}_g) + (\bar{X}_g - \bar{X}_G)$$

**FIGURE 10–6**

Diagrammatic representation of the reason any score differs from the mean

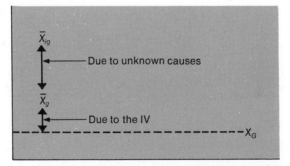

4. The symbol $X_{ig}$ is used through the text to represent *any* subject's score. The subletters ($i$ and $g$) stand for the $i$th subject of the $g$th group. If we were talking about the score of the second subject of group A, the score would be stated as $X_{2a}$.

5. Remember, all scores in a group should be exactly equal, as in Figure 10–4. The differences between the scores in a group is due to unknown variable influence. A measure of the effects of these unknown variables is obtained by subtracting $\bar{X}_g$ from these individual scores $(X_{ig})$.

The total amount any score ($X_{ig}$) varies from the grand mean is equal to the variation of the score from the group mean ($X_{ig} - \bar{X}_g$) *plus* the variation of the group mean from the grand mean ($\bar{X}_g - \bar{X}_G$). The total variation of any score from the other scores then can be divided into two additive parts: that caused by the IV ($\bar{X}_g - \bar{X}_G$), and that caused by all the unknown variables ($X_{ig} - \bar{X}_g$).

Simple algebra may be used to demonstrate the point that the total sums of squares of all scores in an experiment is composed of two additive parts, the within-group sum of squares ($X_{ig} - \bar{X}_g$) plus the between-group sum of squares ($\bar{X}_g - \bar{X}_G$). The difference between any score ($X_{ig}$) and the mean of all the scores in the study put together ($\bar{X}_G$, the grand mean) can be represented as

$$(X_{ig} - \bar{X}_G) = (X_{ig} - \bar{X}_g) + (\bar{X}_g - \bar{X}_G)$$

This identity states that the deviation of any particular score from the grand mean is comprised of two parts, a deviation of the individual score from the group mean ($X_{ig} - \bar{X}_G$), and the deviation of the group means from the total mean ($\bar{X}_g - \bar{X}_G$). To get back to sum of squares, the previous identity is summed and squared to read:

$$\Sigma(X_{ig} - \bar{X}_G)^2 = \Sigma(X_{ig} - \bar{X}_g)^2 + \overset{n}{\Sigma}(\bar{X}_g - \bar{X}_G)^2 + 2\Sigma(\bar{X}_g - \bar{X}_G)\Sigma(X_{ig} - \bar{X}_g)$$

This identity states that if you subtract each score from the grand mean, square the difference, and sum up those differences (in other words, calculate $SS_T$), the total will equal the difference of each score subtracted from the group mean squared and summed ($SS_w$) *plus* the summed squared difference of the grand mean subtracted from the group means ($SS_B$).[6]

The third portion of the right side of the equation will drop out, for it involves summing the difference between each score and its group mean ($X_{ig} - \bar{X}_g$), and this will always equal zero. What has just been demonstrated is the fact that the total sum of squares is equal to the within-group sum of squares plus the between-group sum of squares.

$$SS_T = SS_W + SS_B$$
$$\Sigma(X_{ig} - \bar{X}_G)^2 = \Sigma(X_{ig} - \bar{X}_g)^2 + \overset{n}{\Sigma}(\bar{X}_g - \bar{X}_G)^2$$

This point may be illustrated by plugging in raw scores obtained in Figure 10–6. The following calculations show how.

6. Remember that each score is composed of ($X_{ig} - \bar{X}_g$) plus ($X_g - \bar{X}_G$), so the second term on the right is actually the summation of the squared difference of the total mean subtracted from a group mean, for "every" score in the group. The "n" above the sigma sign is placed there to remind the reader to subtract the grand mean from the group mean for *every* score in each group.

Group A

| Subject number | $X_a$ | $\bar{X}_a$ | $(X_{ia} - \bar{X}_a)$ | $(X_{ia} - \bar{X}_a)^2$ |
|---|---|---|---|---|
| 1 | 100 | 90 | 10 | 100 |
| 2 | 80 | 90 | −10 | 100 |
| 3 | 90 | 90 | 0 | 0 |
| | $\Sigma X_a = 270$ | | | $\Sigma(X_{ia} - \bar{X}_a)^2 = 200$ |

Group B

| Subject number | $X_b$ | $\bar{X}_b$ | $X_{ib} - \bar{X}_b$ | $(X_{ib} - \bar{X}_b)^2$ |
|---|---|---|---|---|
| 4 | 50 | 50 | 0 | 0 |
| 5 | 40 | 50 | −10 | 100 |
| 6 | 60 | 50 | 10 | 100 |
| | $\Sigma X_b = 150$ | | | $\Sigma(X_{ib} - \bar{X}_b)^2 = 200$ |

$$\bar{X}_G = \frac{\Sigma X}{N} = \frac{100 + 80 + 90 + 50 + 40 + 60}{6} = 70$$

$$
\begin{aligned}
SS_T &= \Sigma(X_{ig} - \bar{X}_G)^2 \\
&= (100 - 70)^2 + (90 - 70)^2 + (80 - 70)^2 + (50 - 70)^2 \\
&\quad + (40 - 70)^2 + (60 - 70)^2 \\
&= 30^2 + 20^2 + 10^2 + 20^2 + 30^2 + 10^2 \\
&= 900 + 400 + 100 + 400 + 900 + 100 \\
&= 2,800
\end{aligned}
$$

$$
\begin{aligned}
SS_B &= \overset{n}{\Sigma}(\bar{X}_g - \bar{X}_G)^2 \\
&= (90 - 70)^2 + (90 - 70)^2 + (90 - 70)^2 + (50 - 70)^2 + (50 - 70)^2 \\
&\quad + (50 - 70)^2 \\
&= 400 + 400 + 400 + 400 + 400 + 400 \\
&= 2,400
\end{aligned}
$$

$$
\begin{aligned}
SS_W &= \Sigma(X_{ig} - \bar{X}_g)^2 \\
&= (100 - 90)^2 + (80 - 90)^2 + (90 - 90)^2 + (50 - 50)^2 \\
&\quad + (40 - 50)^2 + (60 - 50)^2 \\
&= 100 + 100 + 0 + 0 + 100 + 100 \\
&= 400
\end{aligned}
$$

Plugging the obtained values into the formula, we find:

$$
\begin{aligned}
SS_T &= SS_B + SS_W \\
&= 2,400 + 400 \\
&= 2,800
\end{aligned}
$$

What has just been mathematically demonstrated is the fact that the total variation of all scores from the overall mean in an experiment is composed of two additive parts: that due to the IV (represented by $SS_B$), and that due to all other unmeasured variables (represented by $SS_W$). This is a very important concept in experimentation, and one the student should understand thoroughly.

There is another procedure for calculating $SS_B$ and $SS_W$ which is much faster, for it does not involve the calculation of means and the subtraction of every score from the mean. Recall from Chapter Six the $SS$ calculated for the groups in the randomized two-group $t$-test analysis were equal to

$$SS_T = \Sigma X^2 - \frac{(\Sigma X)^2}{N}$$

This is simply another way of writing:

$$SS_T = \Sigma(X_{ig} - \bar{X}_G)^2$$

By employing the first of these two formulas, the total sums of squares could be calculated as follows:

| Subject number | $X$ | $X^2$ |
|---|---|---|
| 1 | 100 | 10,000 |
| 2 | 80 | 6,400 |
| 3 | 90 | 8,100 |
| 4 | 50 | 2,500 |
| 5 | 40 | 1,600 |
| 6 | 60 | 3,600 |
| $N = 6$ | $\Sigma X = 420$ | $\Sigma X^2 = 32,200$ |

$$SS_T = \Sigma X^2 - \frac{(\Sigma X)^2}{N}$$

$$= 32,200 - \frac{(420)^2}{6}$$

$$= 32,200 - \frac{176,400}{6}$$

$$= 32,200 - 29,400$$

$$= 2,800$$

$SS_W$ and $SS_B$ may be calculated with the following formulas:[7]

$$SS_B = \left[ \Sigma \frac{(\Sigma X_g)^2}{n} \right] - \left[ \frac{(\Sigma X)^2}{N} \right]$$

$$SS_W = [\Sigma X^2] - \left[ \Sigma \frac{(\Sigma X_g)^2}{n} \right]$$

7. The brackets are not essential and are provided only to help the student follow what is involved.

Here are the calculations:

| | Group A | | | Group B | |
|---|---|---|---|---|---|
| *Subject number* | $X_a$ | $X_a{}^2$ | *Subject number* | $X_b$ | $X_b{}^2$ |
| 1 | 100 | 10,000 | 4 | 50 | 2,500 |
| 2 | 80 | 6,400 | 5 | 40 | 1,600 |
| 3 | 90 | 8,100 | 6 | 60 | 3,600 |
| | $\Sigma X_a = 270$ | $\Sigma X_a{}^2 = 24,500$ | | $\Sigma X_b = 150$ | $\Sigma X_b{}^2 = 7,700$ |

$$SS_B = \left[\Sigma \frac{(\Sigma X_g)^2}{n}\right] - \left[\frac{(\Sigma X)^2}{N}\right]$$

$$= \left[\frac{(270)^2}{3} + \frac{(150)^2}{3}\right] - \left[\frac{(100 + 80 + 90 + 50 + 40 + 60)^2}{6}\right]$$

$$= \left[\frac{72,900}{3} + \frac{22,500}{3}\right] - \left[\frac{176,400}{6}\right]$$

$$= [24,300 + 7,500] - 29,400$$

$$= 31,800 - 29,400$$

$$= 2,400$$

$$SS_W = [\Sigma X^2] - \left[\Sigma \frac{(\Sigma X_g)^2}{n}\right]$$

$$= [10,000 + 6,400 + 8,100 + 2,500 + 1,600 + 3,600]$$
$$- \left[\frac{(270)^2}{3} + \frac{(150)^2}{3}\right]$$

$$= 32,200 - 31,800$$

$$= 400$$

Note that the $SS_T$, $SS_B$, and $SS_W$ obtained by each procedure is the same. The second method is much faster. The formulas used in the second procedure are called the *computational* or *raw score* formulas for calculating the sums of squares.

## TYPES OF ANOVAR DESIGNS

### Randomized One-Way ANOVAR Design

Now that the relationship between $SS_T$, $SS_B$, and $SS_W$ has been demonstrated, let us look at how this relationship is involved in the one-way analysis of variance. To illustrate, we will proceed with the cough remedies example. Table 10–1 shows the results of this hypothetical experiment.

Recall from Chapter Four that the analysis of variance in experimentation is carried out by calculating the between-groups variance, calculating

**TABLE 10–1**
*Raw data for a randomized three-group one-way ANOVAR design*

| Group A | | Group B | | Group C | |
|---|---|---|---|---|---|
| $X_a$ | $X_a{}^2$ | $X_b$ | $X_b{}^2$ | $X_c$ | $X_c{}^2$ |
| 4 | 16 | 12 | 144 | 1 | 1 |
| 5 | 25 | 8 | 64 | 3 | 9 |
| 4 | 16 | 10 | 100 | 4 | 16 |
| 3 | 9 | 5 | 25 | 6 | 36 |
| 6 | 36 | 7 | 49 | 8 | 64 |
| 10 | 100 | 9 | 81 | 5 | 25 |
| 1 | 1 | 14 | 196 | 3 | 9 |
| 8 | 64 | 9 | 81 | 2 | 4 |
| 5 | 25 | 4 | 16 | 2 | 4 |
| $\Sigma X_a = 46$ | $\Sigma X_a{}^2 = 292$ | $\Sigma X_b = 78$ | $\Sigma X_b{}^2 = 756$ | $\Sigma X_c = 34$ | $\Sigma X_c{}^2 = 168$ |

the within-groups variance, and then plugging the results into the ratio $V_B/V_W$. To do this, $V_B$ and $V_W$ are calculated using the following formulas:

$$V_B = \frac{SS_B}{df} \qquad V_W = \frac{SS_W}{df}$$

These formulas state that the between-group variance is equal to $SS_B$ divided by its degrees of freedom ($df$), while within-group variance is equal to $SS_W$ divided by its degrees of freedom.

What is *degrees of freedom*? The term refers to the number of values that are free to fluctuate after certain restrictions have been made on a particular set of data. Suppose five scores were to equal 30. To meet the criterion, we may pick any four scores whose sum would be less than 30. Once we have picked four, however, the fifth score is automatically determined. If we chose the numbers 6, 8, 3, and 7, the last score would have to be another 6. In any one group, then, the number of degrees of freedom will equal $n - 1$, the total number of scores in the group minus 1. If you had a total of three separate groups, the degrees of freedom for all the groups together would equal $N - 3$, for all scores in each group could fluctuate except the last one. Since there are three groups, a total of three scores should have no freedom to vary. They would automatically be set when all the other scores had been chosen.

Why employ degrees of freedom? Originally, variance was calculated using the formula:

$$V = \frac{SS}{N}$$

Variance was said to be equal to the sums of squares divided by the total number of scores involved. After this formula was originally devised and had been used for a while in statistical manipulations involving other formulas, it was noted that $V = (SS/N)$ did not adequately represent the variance of a group. This formula biased the variance measure in such a way that the variance calculated was consistently smaller than it should be. Remember, no formula devised by man is sacred. It has been devised to perform some function, and if it does not carry out that function as well as desired, it is then modified. In trying various modifications, researchers noted that a true variance estimate could be obtained if degrees of freedom was substituted in the denominator for the simpler term $N$.

From this brief discourse, it should be apparent that the variance formula was modified to read:

$$V = \frac{SS}{df}$$

The variance equals the sum of squares divided by the degrees of freedom. This formula is true for all three variance measures—$V_T$, $V_B$, and $V_W$.

**Calculation of $V_B$.**   The calculation of $V_B$ involves two major steps: calculation of $SS_B$ and the determination of the degrees of freedom for between-groups variance. The following material shows the data and calculations necessary for determining $SS_B$:

$$SS_B = \Sigma\frac{(\Sigma X_g)^2}{n} - \frac{(\Sigma X)^2}{N}$$

$$= \frac{46^2}{9} + \frac{78^2}{9} + \frac{34^2}{9} - \frac{(46 + 78 + 34)^2}{27}$$

$$= 1{,}039.55 - \frac{24{,}964}{27}$$

$$= 1{,}039.55 - 924.59$$

$$= 114.96$$

The sums of squares for between groups is calculated using the raw score formula. Keep in mind the fact that the $SS_B$ represents subtracting the grand mean from the group means for all scores ($\bar{X}_g - \bar{X}_G$). This represents the total amount that all the scores together varied from the grand mean because of IV influences.

With $SS_B$ calculated, the degrees of freedom are determined. The degrees of freedom for between groups is equal to the number of groups employed in the study *minus* 1. Notice the procedure for determining the between-groups degrees of freedom is consistent with that used in the $t$-test. In the present case $df$ equals $3 - 1$, or 2. Once $SS_B$ and $df_B$ are known, the calculation of $V_B$ is straightforward, using the following formula:

$$V_B = \frac{SS_B}{df_B}$$

$$= \frac{114.96}{2}$$

$$= 57.48$$

**Calculation of $V_W$.**    The calculation of $V_W$ entails the same steps involved in determining $V_B$. $SS_W$ is obtained, and the within-groups degrees of freedom are determined. Table 10–2 shows the data and calculations for determining $SS_W$.

**TABLE 10–2**
Raw data and the calculation of $SS_W$ for randomized three-group one-way ANOVAR design

| | Group A | | Group B | | Group C | |
| --- | --- | --- | --- | --- | --- | --- |
| $X_a$ | $X_a^2$ | $X_b$ | $X_b^2$ | $X_c$ | $X_c^2$ |
| 4 | 16 | 12 | 144 | 1 | 1 |
| 5 | 25 | 8 | 64 | 3 | 9 |
| 4 | 16 | 10 | 100 | 4 | 16 |
| 3 | 9 | 5 | 25 | 6 | 36 |
| 6 | 36 | 7 | 49 | 8 | 64 |
| 10 | 100 | 9 | 81 | 5 | 25 |
| 1 | 1 | 14 | 196 | 3 | 9 |
| 8 | 64 | 9 | 81 | 2 | 4 |
| 5 | 25 | 4 | 16 | 2 | 4 |
| $\Sigma X_a = 46$ | $\Sigma X_a^2 = 292$ | $\Sigma X_b = 78$ | $\Sigma X_b^2 = 756$ | $\Sigma X_c = 34$ | $\Sigma X_c^2 = 168$ |

$$SS_W = \Sigma X^2 - \Sigma \frac{(\Sigma X)^2}{n}$$

$$= [(292 + 756 + 168)] - \left[\frac{(46)^2}{9} + \frac{(78)^2}{9} + \frac{(34)^2}{9}\right]$$

$$= (1,216) - \left(\frac{2,116}{9} + \frac{6,084}{9} + \frac{1,156}{9}\right)$$

$$= 1,216 - 1,039.55$$

$$= 176.45$$

The sum of squares for within groups is calculated using *all* the individual scores obtained in the experiment. In this example, 27 scores are involved.

The within-groups degrees of freedom is defined as the total number of scores in the entire experiment *minus* the number of groups involved. In this case the $df_W$ equals $27 - 3$, or 24. The calculation of $V_W$ is then carried out as follows:

$$V_W = \frac{SS_W}{df_W}$$

$$= \frac{176.45}{24}$$

$$= 7.35$$

**Calculation of the F-ratio.**   With $V_B$ and $V_W$ calculated, the F ratio is then computed:

$$F = \frac{V_B}{V_W}$$

$$= \frac{57.48}{7.35}$$

$$= 7.82$$

In calculating the F ratio the investigator is asking, "How much larger is $V_B$ than $V_W$?" The F ratio will state how many "times" $V_B$ is larger than $V_W$. In the present example the obtained F ratio states $V_B$ is 7.82 times larger than $V_W$.

The next question the investigator needs to answer is, "Would an F equal to 7.82 occur by chance in conditions like this less than 5 percent of the time?" This question is answered by referring to an F table, where some statisticians have gone to the trouble of calculating what the F would be that would occur exactly 5 percent of the time. The F in the table is commonly called *critical* F. If the F obtained in the experiment is larger than the critical F, we know that the obtained F would occur by chance "less" than 5 percent of the time. It may then be concluded that the group DVs are significantly different.

Turning to the F table in the Appendix we find that it is different from a *t* table. The *t* table listed degrees of freedom only down the side, whereas the F table lists degrees of freedom both down the side and along the top. There is a very good statistical reason for the difference in the tables.[8] Suffice to say here that the size of any F depends both on $df_B$ and $df_W$. To read the F table, read across the top until you come to the number equal to $df_B$. Then read down the chart until you come to the number equal to $df_W$. The F shown in light type at that square is the critical F that would be obtained 5 percent of the time by chance.[9]

---

8. Explanations may be found in Hays [1973] and Kepple [1973].

9. The bold type indicates the F obtained 1 percent of the time by chance. This is included for some investigators who prefer to use a 1 percent significance level instead of a 5 percent significance level.

Notice that the critical F in this case equals 3.40. The F obtained in the experiment is larger than 3.40, so it may be concluded that the groups were significantly different in the experiment.

**Review of steps in the F test.** Now that the F test is completed, let us summarize the steps involved:

1. Calculate the between-groups sums of squares ($SS_B$).
2. Determine the between-groups degrees of freedom ($df_B$).
3. Compute the between-groups variance ($V_B$) by dividing $SS_B$ by the $df_B$.
4. Calculate the within-groups sums of squares ($SS_W$).
5. Determine the within-groups sums of squares ($df_W$).
6. Compute the within-groups variance ($V_W$) by dividing $SS_W$ by $df_W$.
7. Calculate the F ratio ($V_B/V_W$).
8. Compare the obtained F ratio to the critical F.

After calculating a few F tests, the student will realize the steps involved are not that difficult. Do not shy away from an F test because of the seemingly complex statistical manipulations involved. Remember, memorizing the statistical manipulations is not as important as understanding the rationale behind the F test. Though committing the formulas to memory would be helpful, most readers are not planning to be statisticians or experimental psychologists, instead, they will be educators, clinicians, counselors, and administrators. Like these professionals, you will have forgotten the specific formulas when you need them. What you should remember is when an F test would be appropriate. Then, when you need to perform such a test you can turn to your personal library of reference books, look up an example of an F test analysis in a text such as this, and carry it out in cookbook fashion.

The eight steps mentioned for carrying out an F test on a one-way analysis of variance are exactly the same for any experiment no matter how many groups are employed in the investigation. The procedure for carrying out an F test in a nine-group experiment would be just like that carried out in the cough remedies example. The calculations would be more cumbersome, however, due to the increased number of groups.

**Multiple group comparison tests.** It would be nice to say that the F test already presented here is all there is to a statistical analysis involving a one-way analysis of variance experimental design. Unfortunately, that is not so. There is one more statistical manipulation that needs to be covered—the statistical comparison of the groups within the experiment.

What does a *significant* F mean? If the F turns out to be significant, which means it is larger than critical F, the investigator now knows that the groups significantly differed in the amount of coughing (DV) after the three different cough remedies (IV) were administered. A significant F *does not* indicate which group coughed less or which group coughed most, all it tells the investigator is that the cough remedies did differ in their ability to influence coughing.

Now that it is apparent the remedies differed, the investigator must determine which was the most effective. To do this, a multiple-group comparison test is performed. There is a variety of multiple-group comparison tests available to the investigator. Because the reason for employing all the tests is basically the same, only one multiple-group comparison test will be presented here—the Scheffe test.[10]

With three groups there are three group comparisons that can be made: group A can be compared to group B, group A can be compared to group C, and group B can be compared to group C. There are three basic steps involved in carrying out a Scheffe test. First, a Scheffe F ($F_s$) is calculated, using the following formula:

$$F_s = \frac{(\bar{X}_a - \bar{X}_b)^2}{(V_W/n_a) + (V_W/n_b)}$$

Then the three comparisons are made:

| Comparison | Formula | | F |
|---|---|---|---|
| A, B | $F_s = \dfrac{(\bar{X}_a - \bar{X}_b)^2}{(V_W/n_a) + (V_W/n_b)}$ | $= \dfrac{(5.11 - 8.67)^2}{(7.35/9) + (7.35/9)}$ | $= 7.77$ |
| A, C | $F_s = \dfrac{(\bar{X}_a - \bar{X}_c)^2}{(V_W/n_a) + (V_W/n_c)}$ | $= \dfrac{(5.11 - 3.78)^2}{(7.35/9) + (7.35/9)}$ | $= 1.09$ |
| B, C | $F_s = \dfrac{(\bar{X}_b - \bar{X}_c)^2}{(V_W/n_b) + (V_W/n_c)}$ | $= \dfrac{(8.67 - 3.78)^2}{(7.35/9) + (7.35/9)}$ | $= 14.67$ |

The second step involves calculating F′ (F prime). F′ is a critical F that is adjusted to work with Scheffe's formula for determining $F_s$. F′ is calculated by multiplying the original critical F (obtained from the F table) by $df_B$. F′ in this case equals:

$$F \times df_B = F'$$
$$3.40 \times 2 \quad = 6.80$$

Third, the three $F_s$ are compared to F′. If an $F_s$ is larger than F′, then the two groups involved are said to be significantly different. In the present

---

10. A complete review of multiple-group comparison tests may be found in Ryan [1960] and Kirk [1969]. The Scheffe test was selected here not because it is necessarily the best, but because it may be the easiest for the reader to understand.

example group B is shown to significantly differ from groups A and C, while groups A and C do not differ significantly. The conclusion to be drawn from this investigation is that the cough remedy given to group B subjects was more effective than the other two remedies. After completing the multiple-group comparison test the investigator has completed his statistical analysis. He now knows the cough remedies differed in effectiveness *and* which one was most effective.

The F test and the $F_s$ test provide two different though closely related types of information. The F test indicates whether there is any significant difference between *any* of the groups in the experiment. If the F is not significant, the investigator stops there, for carrying out an $F_s$ test would have no value. If the F is significant, $F_s$ tests are performed to provide information as to the comparative effectiveness of the different levels of the IV.

### Randomized Blocked One-Way ANOVAR Design

With the randomized one-way ANOVAR design, the investigator relies solely on randomization to control the effect of secondary variables. It is possible to add a second control technique, constancy, by employing blocking. An investigator may be so strongly concerned about the potential influence of some particular secondary variable that he does not want to take the chance that randomization might not equate the groups for this variable. Instead, he ensures that all groups are equated on this variable by intentionally distributing the variable equally among the groups. Blocking one-way ANOVAR designs is a common practice, especially in educational and social investigations in which the investigator may be concerned with the secondary variables of age, sex, intelligence, race, or socioeconomic status and is restricted in the selection of his subjects (e.g., he may have to use the children in an already existing grade school class).

David Harris was interested in comparing three different instructional procedures at a regional Indian school. The student body consisted of Indian children who came from various tribal reservations in the western United States. Mr. Harris was interested in evaluating the educational progress of Indian students in a particular sixth-grade class. The class was to be divided into three subgroups for the year, with each subgroup experiencing a different instructional procedure. One group was taught math using teaching machines, the second group was taught math in a discussion group environment in which the logic of mathematical manipulations was emphasized rather than just exercises in calculations, and the third group was taught math in a regular individual desk classroom situation with the emphasis on written mathematical calculation exercises.

Realizing Indian tribes differ in terms of the training given the children,

Mr. Harris blocked his three groups of subjects according to tribal origin. The subjects were first divided up according to tribe:

| Tribe | Number of subjects |
|-------|--------------------|
| Ute | 12 |
| Blackfoot | 9 |
| Pueblo | 9 |
| Ouray | 12 |

Then the subjects from each tribe were randomly assigned to one of the three teaching groups in such a manner that each teaching group consisted of 4 Ute, 3 Blackfoot, 3 Pueblo, and 4 Ouray, as shown in Table 10–3. All three groups were equated on possible variation due to tribal background by blocking the subjects according to tribe prior to the randomization procedure. A strictly randomized one-way ANOVAR design would not have taken tribal background into consideration; it would be expected that random assignment alone would have automatically equated the groups.

**TABLE 10–3**
*Random assignment of subjects from each tribe to three groups differing in instructional procedure*

| | Group A (teaching machines) | Group B (discussion group) | Group C (written mathematical exercises) |
|-------|-------|-------|-------|
| Ute | 4 | 4 | 4 |
| Blackfoot | 3 | 3 | 3 |
| Pueblo | 3 | 3 | 3 |
| Ouray | 4 | 4 | 4 |

The statistical analysis of the randomized, blocked one-way ANOVAR design is exactly the same as that carried out for a randomized one-way ANOVAR design. Anyone wishing to see an illustration of the statistical calculation of the blocked ANOVAR design should refer to the calculations on page 223.

### One-Way Analysis of Covariance

Just as statistical control may be used with two-group designs, so may it be applied in one-way ANOVAR designs. The reasons for employing a covariance analysis with more than two groups are exactly the same for investigations involving two groups: the groups employed in the study differ on some important secondary variable at the beginning of the investigation and cannot be equated, or it becomes apparent as the investigation progresses that a secondary variable is differentially influencing the various groups.

**Statistical computations for analysis of covariance.** The principle behind the analysis of covariance for multigroup experiments is the same as that discussed for two-group situations in the last chapter; it differs on only one point. The sums of squares are adjusted in the analysis of covariance to remove the differences between the groups that are related to some covariate. In an analysis of covariance the $V_B/V_W$ ratio is still sought. The way the sums of squares are adjusted is shown in the following formula. The definitional formula for the sums of squares in an analysis of covariance is

$$SS_T = SS_B + SS_W$$

$$\left[ \overset{n}{\Sigma}(X_{ig} - \bar{X}_G)^2 - \frac{\overset{n}{\Sigma}[X_{ig} - \bar{X}_G)(X_{ig} - \bar{X}_G)]^2}{\overset{n}{\Sigma}(Y_{ig} - \bar{Y}_G)^2} \right]$$

$$= \left[ \overset{n}{\Sigma}(\bar{X}_g - \bar{X}_G)^2 - \frac{\overset{n}{\Sigma}[X_g - \bar{X}_G)(\bar{Y}_g - \bar{Y}_G)]^2}{\Sigma(Y_g - \bar{Y}_G)^2} \right]$$

$$+ \left[ \overset{n}{\Sigma}(X_{ig} - \bar{X}_g)^2 - \frac{\overset{n}{\Sigma}[X_{ig} - \bar{X}_g)(Y_{ig} - \bar{Y}_g)]^2}{\overset{n}{\Sigma}(Y_{ig} - Y_g)^2} \right]$$

Note that $SS_T$, $SS_B$, and $SS_W$ for analysis of covariance designs each have an additional component (indicated above by gray tint). The untinted parts of the formula are the same as in the illustration of a randomized one-way ANOVAR design. The tinted portions of the formula represent how one statistically removes the effect of some secondary variable. Note that these tinted portions are *subtracted* from the original $SS_T$, $SS_B$, and $SS_W$ components, thereby making them smaller because the effect of the secondary variable is removed. Though this formula may seem mindboggling, keep one fact in mind—it also seems mindboggling to most professional psychologists.[11] It is not really necessary at this time for the student to understand exactly what is involved in the mathematical derivation of this formula, since most graduate psychology programs include courses that delve into this more thoroughly. The student should, however, have a general understanding of how this formula deviates from the sums of squares formula given in the preceding section. The sums of squares formula for analysis of covariance

11. The $n$ above each $\Sigma$ is a reminder that calculations should be carried out for all the scores in the groups.

differs from the simpler analysis of variance sums of squares formula in that it includes a value being subtracted from each of the three parts of the formula. This subtracted value represents the amount of the variation between scores related to the $Y$ covariate on which the groups in the investigations were not equal. Once the sums of squares are adjusted, the remaining statistical steps are identical to those carried out with the simpler analysis of variance.

To illustrate the statistical procedures involved in a one-way analysis of covariance, let us take the following situation. Three groups of mentally retarded children having a mental age of 5 to 6 years were used to compare three teaching procedures on their effectiveness in helping mentally retarded children learn the alphabet. Group A children were taught the alphabet with no verbal aids, group B children were taught the alphabet using a rhyming jingle as an aid, group C children were taught the alphabet by pairing each letter with a word as they went along (e.g., *A* is for *apple*, *B* is for *bear*, *C* is for *cat*, and so on). The subjects were given the training for one week. The number of letters the children knew at the end of the week is shown below.

| Group A | Group B | Group C |
|---------|---------|---------|
| 19      | 22      | 14      |
| 8       | 17      | 15      |
| 14      | 16      | 10      |
| 11      | 18      | 12      |
| 16      | 12      | 10      |
| 13      | 19      | 16      |
| 12      | 15      | 11      |
| 15      | 23      | 17      |
| 10      | 21      | 20      |

After the experiment was over, the psychologist carrying out the investigation was talking to one of the children's parents, who mentioned her child already knew five letters of the alphabet prior to the initiation of the experiment. Realizing he had overlooked a very important secondary variable, the psychologist checked with all the parents to find out how many letters each child knew before the week of special training. His findings are presented below. The $Y$ columns indicate the number of letters each child knew before the training, and the $X$ columns represent the number of letters known after the special training. The covariate ($Y$) picked here was the number of letters each subject knew prior to the experiment. These scores could also be used as pretest scores, thereby converting this example into a pretest-posttest design. A better covariate for illustrating analysis of covariance would be IQ. Using the number of letters previously known, however, gives a smaller number to use in the statistical analysis.

| Group A | | Group B | | Group C | |
|---|---|---|---|---|---|
| Y | X | Y | X | Y | X |
| 5 | 19 | 8 | 22 | 0 | 14 |
| 3 | 8 | 9 | 17 | 3 | 15 |
| 1 | 14 | 4 | 16 | 5 | 10 |
| 3 | 11 | 2 | 18 | 2 | 12 |
| 6 | 16 | 7 | 12 | 4 | 10 |
| 4 | 13 | 6 | 19 | 5 | 16 |
| 4 | 12 | 5 | 15 | 3 | 11 |
| 2 | 15 | 7 | 23 | 6 | 17 |
| 5 | 10 | 4 | 21 | 3 | 20 |

From the data it was apparent that the groups differed in terms of the number of letters already known by the children. With this data the investigator then proceeded to carry out an analysis of covariance in an attempt to remove any differences in the DVs between the groups' final results due to preexperimental differences. Here are the statistical calculations carried out. The adjusted portions of the formulas and calculations are tinted gray to emphasize what new steps are required in an analysis of covariance as compared to the analysis of variance in a randomized one-way ANOVAR design.

| | Group A | | Group B | | Group C | |
|---|---|---|---|---|---|---|
| | Y | X | Y | X | Y | X |
| | 5 | 19 | 8 | 22 | 0 | 14 |
| | 3 | 8 | 9 | 17 | 3 | 15 |
| | 1 | 14 | 4 | 16 | 5 | 10 |
| | 3 | 11 | 2 | 18 | 2 | 12 |
| | 6 | 16 | 7 | 12 | 4 | 10 |
| | 4 | 13 | 6 | 19 | 5 | 16 |
| | 4 | 12 | 5 | 15 | 3 | 11 |
| | 2 | 15 | 7 | 23 | 6 | 17 |
| | 5 | 10 | 4 | 21 | 3 | 20 |
| $n$ | 9 | | 9 | | 9 | |
| $\Sigma Y, \Sigma X$ | 33 | 118 | 52 | 163 | 31 | 125 |
| $\bar{Y}_y, \bar{X}_g$ | 3.67 | 13.11 | 5.78 | 18.11 | 3.44 | 13.89 |
| $\Sigma Y_g{}^2, \Sigma X_g{}^2$ | 141 | 1,636 | 340 | 3,053 | 133 | 1,831 |
| $\Sigma XY$ | | 442 | | 947 | | 434 |
| $\dfrac{(\Sigma X_g)^2}{n}$ | | 1,547.11 | | 2,952.11 | | 1,736.11 |
| $\dfrac{(\Sigma Y_g)^2}{n}$ | | 121 | | 300.44 | | 106.78 |

$N = 27$

$\Sigma Y = 116$

$\bar{Y}_G = 4.30$

$\dfrac{(\Sigma Y)^2}{N} = 498.37$

$\Sigma Y^2 = 614$

$\Sigma \dfrac{(\Sigma Y_g)^2}{n} = 528.22$

$\Sigma X = 406$

$\dfrac{(\Sigma X)^2}{N} = 6,105.4$

$\Sigma X^2 = 6,535$

$\Sigma \dfrac{(\Sigma X_g)^2}{n} = 6,235.33$

$\Sigma XY = 1,823$

$\Sigma \dfrac{(\Sigma X)(\Sigma Y)}{n} = 1,805.01$

$\dfrac{\Sigma X \Sigma Y}{N} = 1,744.30$

---

$SS_T = \left[\Sigma X^2 - \dfrac{(\Sigma X)^2}{N}\right] - \left[\Sigma XY - \dfrac{\Sigma X \Sigma Y}{N}\right]$

$\quad = 6,520 - 6,105.04 - 1,823 - 1,744.30$

$\quad = 429.96 - 78.70$

$\quad = 336.66$

---

$SS_B = \left[\Sigma \dfrac{(\Sigma X_g)^2}{n} - \dfrac{(\Sigma X)^2}{N}\right] - \left[\Sigma \dfrac{(\Sigma X)(\Sigma Y)}{n} - \dfrac{\Sigma X \Sigma Y}{N}\right]$

$\quad = (6,235.33 - 6,105.04) - (1,805.01 - 1,744.30)$

$\quad = 130.29 - 60.71$

$\quad = 69.58$

---

$SS_W = \left[\Sigma X^2 - \Sigma \dfrac{(\Sigma X_g)^2}{n}\right] - \left[\Sigma XY - \Sigma \dfrac{\Sigma X \Sigma Y}{n}\right]$

$\quad = 6,520 - 6,235.33 - (1,823 - 1,805.01)$

$\quad = 299.67 - 17.99$

$\quad = 266.68$

---

$F = \dfrac{SS_B/df_B}{SS_W/df_W}$

$\quad = \dfrac{69.58/2}{266.68/23}$

$\quad = \dfrac{34.79}{11.59}$

$\quad = 3.00$

critical F $= 3.42$

---

The procedure for an analysis of covariance is quite similar to that for an analysis of variance, the main difference being that the sums of squares in an analysis of covariance must be adjusted. Note that the adjustment involves making the sums of squares smaller by subtracting a value representing some statistical relationship between the covariate ($Y$) and the final results ($X$). This statistical relationship represents the differences between the final result scores due to the difference between the children present when the investigation began. There is one other minor difference between an analysis of variance and an analysis of covariance. The degrees of freedom for within groups ($df_W$) in an analysis of covariance equals $N - k - 1$ rather than $N - k$, which is the case in an analysis of variance. The letter $k$ stands for the number of groups in the investigation.

Because the obtained F is smaller than the critical F, the conclusion drawn from this analysis is "The three training procedures do not significantly differ in terms of their ability to aid mentally retarded children in learning the alphabet."

**Steps in the analysis of covariance.** The steps for carrying out an analysis of covariance are these:

1. Partition the sums of squares into two parts, a within-groups component and a between-groups component, using the adjusted sums of squares formula.
2. Divide these sums of squares by their appropriate degrees of freedom (remember $df_W$ equals $N - k - 1$).
3. Calculate the F ratio.
4. Check the obtained F with the critical F.
5. If the F is significant, calculate the $F_s$ to determine which groups were significantly different.

Notice the steps for computing a one-way analysis of covariance are very similar to those for computing a one-way analysis of variance.

## ADVANTAGES AND DISADVANTAGES OF ONE-WAY ANOVAR DESIGNS

In comparison with two-group designs, one-way ANOVAR designs give the experimenter more latitude by allowing more than two groups to be compared at one time. Experimenters can carry out parametric investigations not possible with two-group designs. One-way ANOVAR designs do not provide more control techniques to use in checking secondary variables, all the secondary variable control techniques available for one-way ANOVAR designs are also applicable with two-group designs. Two-group designs are superior in that they generally involve fewer subjects and groups, making them easier to carry out and analyze statistically.

The randomized one-way analysis of covariance design allows more control of secondary variables than either the randomized or randomized blocked one-way ANOVAR designs. It is preferred in situations where subjects may not be randomly assigned to different groups (a common problem in educational and clinical settings), where preexperimental group differences on some important secondary variable become apparent only after the investigation is in progress (e.g., groups found to differ on IQ after an experiment is completed), and where groups differ on some important secondary variable as the experiment progresses (e.g., groups differ in the number of hours they study while in an experiment evaluating the effect of a varying number of term tests on learning material).

Blocked designs are preferred over nonblocked designs when the experimental situation may include variations in potentially important secondary variables apparent before the experiment begins. Blocking is commonly used in field investigations in which the experimenter must select his subjects from a heterogeneous group. Dimensions on which subjects are frequently blocked include sex, IQ, race, socioeconomic level, ethnic origin, and age.

## SUMMARY

One-way ANOVAR designs are parametric investigations that provide a means for comparisons involving more than two groups. The statistical analysis is based on the same concept as for two-group designs: the variance between groups is compared to the variance within groups ($V_B/V_W$) to determine whether the IV (theoretically the only factor causing differences in group scores) causes differences between the groups that are larger than differences between scores within groups. It was mathematically demonstrated that $SS_T = SS_B + SS_W$, an important concept for the reader's understanding of the rationale behind the more common statistical tests employed to determine cause-effect relationships.

The statistical analysis of one-way ANOVAR designs involves the calculation of an F ratio rather than a $t$. After a significant F is obtained a multigroup comparison test such as the Scheffe test must be carried out to determine which of the groups is/are significantly different. The statistical analysis of randomized and randomized blocked one-way ANOVAR designs is identical and similar to the analysis of covariance in one-way ANOVAR designs. The analysis of covariance was shown to vary in only one step—the sums of squares were adjusted statistically to remove the influence of some covariate.

In comparison with two-group designs, one-way ANOVAR designs increase the range of experimentation available to the investigator, but do not give the experimenter access to control techniques not also possible with two-group designs. A one-way ANOVAR design with analysis of covariance is generally preferred over a simpler one-way ANOVAR design, and randomization plus blocking is preferred over just randomization. An important point to remember however, is to *use the design most suitable for the particular situation.* Do not select a design simply because it includes more control techniques for secondary variables. If the situation does not include a variable that needs to be blocked or a variable that needs to be statistically controlled for, use a randomized one-way ANOVAR design. Always pick the simplest, most efficient design.

# 11

## Factorial
## Designs

*Factorial designs are the most complex of general experimental designs, and they complete the list of experimental designs from which an investigator may choose. Like two-group and one-way ANOVAR designs, factorial designs are classified as randomized, randomized blocked, and statistically controlled. By carefully comparing the procedures of one-way ANOVAR and factorial designs, the student will see that the statistical analyses are almost identical. The same F test is used to analyze statistically both one-way ANOVAR and factorial designs. The only difference is that more F tests are performed in factorial designs (one for every IV involved). Interaction, a concept previously not covered, is introduced as an important part of factorial designs. Factorial designs are considered by some to be too difficult for most students to handle and are frequently omitted in undergraduate experimental psychology courses. They are included here as the last major type of experimental design with which the student and professional should be familiar, and if they were left out, the reader would not receive the total picture of experimental designs. The student should realize that factorial designs are not much more difficult to understand than one-way ANOVAR designs, yet they add much greater versatility to any scientific investigation.*

Would college students learn more if they were not graded? Do examinations help the student learn? These two questions were the topic a group of psychology students chose to debate in a senior seminar presided over by the author several years ago. The issues were of such great concern that several students volunteered to help carry out an experiment on an introductory psychology class during the following term to answer those questions. Now, a number of different experimental situations could be devised to shed some light on these issues. After lengthy discussions on how to proceed, the following experimental plan was adopted. The class of approximately two hundred students would be divided up into four groups, with each group experiencing one of the following conditions:

I. Weekly exams that counted toward the student's grade
II. Weekly exams that did not count toward the student's grade
III. Monthly exams that counted toward the student's grade
IV. Monthly exams that did not count toward the student's grade

The investigation involved two IVs—frequency of exam and whether the students were graded or not. Each IV in the experiment had two levels. Diagrammatically, the investigation could be represented by Table 11–1. The results of the investigation are covered later in this chapter. For now, however, let us direct our attention to the design. What type of design is required to perform such an investigation? The reader should immediately rule out two-group and one-way ANOVAR designs, for they are employed in situations in which only one IV is involved.

**TABLE 11–1**
*A factorial design having two independent variables, each with two levels*

| | | iv 1 Frequency of Exam | |
| | | *Weekly* | *Monthly* |
|---|---|---|---|
| iv 2 Effect of Exam | *Graded* | Weekly exam, graded (Group I) | Monthly exam, graded (Group III) |
| | *Not Graded* | Weekly exam, not graded (Group II) | Monthly exam, not graded (Group IV) |

Up to now, all the designs have involved the manipulation of only one IV. But psychologists are not always interested in analyzing the influence of one variable at a time. A person's behavior is actually a function of the simultaneous influence of many variables or factors. Consequently, psychologists require experimental designs that allow the simultaneous manipulation of more than one IV at a time. These designs are called *factorial* designs. The term factorial design does not stand for one design, but rather for a group of designs. There are two-factor factorial designs, three-factor factorial designs, four-factor factorial designs, and so on.[1] The number in the factorial design stands for the number of IVs involved; a two factorial has two IVs;

1. More appropriately, they are called two factorial designs, three factorial designs, and so on, rather than redundantly speaking of two-factor factorial designs, and so on.

a three factorial has three IVs. Symbolically, factorial designs are referred to in the following way:

| Design | Symbolic representation |
|---|---|
| Two factorial | $A \times B$ |
| Three factorial | $A \times B \times C$ |
| Four factorial | $A \times B \times C \times D$ |
| $n$ factorial | $A \times B \times C \times D \cdots \times n$ |

Factorial designs vary on two dimensions: the number of IVs employed, and the number of levels for each IV applied. Suppose you were interested in determining how long it took for LSD to influence heart rate. You select room temperature and drug concentration as IVs, for you think that both variables may influence how long it takes for the drug to take effect. Your design may be diagrammed as shown in Table 11–2.[2]

**TABLE 11–2**

*A 3 × 2 factorial design*

|  | IV 1 Drug Dosage | | |
|---|---|---|---|
|  | $C_1$ (10 mg) | $C_2$ (20 mg) | $C_3$ (30 mg) |
| IV 2 Temperature — $R_1$ (72°) | $R_1C_1$ | $R_1C_2$ | $R_1C_3$ |
| $R_2$ (95°) | $R_2C_1$ | $R_2C_2$ | $R_2C_3$ |

You have selected an $A \times B$ design with three levels of drug and two levels of temperature. The design is also called a $3 \times 2$ factorial design.[3] This symbolic designation tells you that there are two IVs employed in the design; one having three levels and the other, two. If only two amounts of drug were used in the same experiment, the design would be classified as a

---

2. The letters $R$ and $C$ are used in the following tables to stand for column ($C$) and row ($R$). $C_1$ represents column 1, $R_1$ represents row 1, and so on. Each cell stands for a group. The $R_1C_1$ cell, for example, is the group of subjects that experience 10 milligrams of the drug in a room with a temperature of 72°.

3. The $\times$ stands for the word "by." A $3 \times 2$ factorial design is verbalized as "a 3 by 2 factorial design." The expression is analogous to calling a piece of wood measuring 2 inches by 4 inches a "2 by 4."

$2 \times 2$ and diagrammed as follows:

|  | $C_1$ | $C_2$ |
|---|---|---|
| $R_1$ | $R_1 C_1$ | $R_1 C_2$ |
| $R_2$ | $R_2 C_1$ | $R_2 C_2$ |

Each different cell in the diagram stands for a treatment. In the $3 \times 2$ factorial design, for example, the subjects selected for the $R_1 C_1$ treatment would be given 10 milligrams (mg) of LSD in a room whose temperature was 72°. The subjects experiencing the $R_2 C_1$ treatment would also receive 10 mg of LSD, but in a 95° room. A $3 \times 2$ design involves six different treatments; therefore, six different groups of subjects are required. Each treatment group could consist of only one subject, so as few as six subjects would be required. (It is preferable to have more than one subject per treatment, however.)[4] All treatment cells should have the same number of subjects. Equal numbers of subjects per treatment is not essential, but the statistical analysis is easier.

How many IVs and different levels of IVs can be employed in one factorial design? Theoretically, there is no limit; an experimenter may choose as many levels and IVs as he desires. Practically speaking, however, the experimenter is limited in terms of the statistical analysis to be carried out. Manually carrying out an analysis of larger factorial designs is a very time-consuming job. The computer is a welcome tool in this respect, for many more large factorial designs that an investigator would have avoided years ago are presently being carried out. This chapter will deal only with two and three factorial designs for two reasons. First, the highest percentage of factorial designs a student may encounter in the research literature are two and three factorial designs; and second, the experimental and statistical procedures of factorial designs with more than three factors are basically the same as those for two and three factor designs. A student capable of analyzing a three factorial design would also be capable of analyzing an eight factorial design, though the statistical analysis would be much more cumbersome.

There are three main reasons for employing factorial designs. First, they allow the investigator to control for a secondary variable by making it a second IV. This is the most desirable of all control techniques, for it not only controls for that variable, but it numerically tells you how much variation in the DV is due to that variable. Second, it allows the experimenter to study

---

4. With only one subject per group there is no within-group variation to represent error variance, so some other less preferable representative measurement must be used.

the effects of more than one variable at a time. This gives him a measure of the comparative effectiveness of the IVs, plus saving the time and money of two experiments. Third, factorial designs may be used to study interaction effects of IVs that are present at the same time. Interaction is an important concept in psychological research, although a somewhat difficult one to understand. It has not been discussed with prefactorial designs because it cannot occur unless two or more IVs are involved.

If the effect of an IV (let us call it *H*) on some DV is a function not only of its own value but also of the value of some other variable (*L*) in the situation, it is said that there is an interaction between the variables *H* and *L*. Suppose someone asked, "Does the wearing of lipstick increase the amorous advances a person receives from the opposite sex?" The answer would be, "That depends on whether the person wearing the lipstick was a guy or gal." In other words, the effect lipstick has on amorous behavior depends not only on its presence, but also on the sex of the person wearing it. If one wanted to carry out an experiment to determine whether lipstick and sex of the person influenced amorous affection, he could set up a factorial experiment like the one in Table 11–3. Four groups of subjects would be compared:

**TABLE 11–3**
*A 2 × 2 factorial design to illus-
trate interaction*

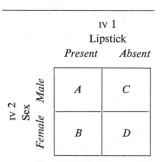

males wearing lipstick (*A*), males not wearing lipstick (*C*), females wearing lipstick (*B*), females not wearing lipstick (*D*).

Assuming some measure of amorous advances was obtained (e.g., number of kisses each group received from the opposite sex), three possible results could be obtained, as shown in Table 11–4. The first set of data (I) shows more amorous behavior for females than males, for there are differences between the first and second row. The presence or absence of lipstick in this case has no effect, for there is no difference between the two columns. Data in situation II indicate just the opposite: lipstick is important, while sex is not. The data for situation III show interaction. It is apparent from these data that amorous behavior depends both on whether a person wears

**TABLE 11–4**
*Three possible results of a 2 × 2 factorial design, with III showing interaction*

| | I Present | I Absent | | II Present | II Absent | | III Present | III Absent |
|---|---|---|---|---|---|---|---|---|
| *Male* | 7 | 7 | *Male* | 14 | 7 | *Male* | 7 | 14 |
| *Female* | 14 | 14 | *Female* | 14 | 7 | *Female* | 14 | 7 |

lipstick and on the sex of the person. In the first case you could predict that females get more kisses than males irrespective of whether lipstick is present or not. In the second case, the presence of lipstick gets more kisses than the absence of lipstick, irrespective of the sex of the person. In the third case, the effects of lipstick and sex interact. Lipstick and sex do not always have the same effect. The results from employing lipstick depend on whether the user is male or female. Whenever you have to answer the question, "Does IV $H$ have an effect?" by saying, "That depends on the value of $L$," there is interaction involved in the situation between the two variables. In the lipstick example, the effect of lipstick *depended* on whether the wearer was male or female.

Interaction is an effect on a DV that must be checked for whenever an investigation involves the manipulation of two or more variables. The statistical logic involved in determining its presence is hard for most undergraduates (and some graduates for that matter) to follow. The student should not feel anxious if he is unable to understand the mathematical logic behind its computation, for that will come later in graduate courses on experimental design.

## LOGICAL ANALYSIS OF FACTORIAL DESIGNS

As you might expect, the six steps in carrying out two-group and one-way ANOVAR investigations are also employed with investigations involving factorial designs. In summary, these steps are:

1. Formulation of a hypothesis
2. Selection of appropriate IVs and DV
3. Control for secondary variables
4. Manipulation of the IV and the DV
5. Analysis of variations in the DV
6. Drawing of conclusions regarding the relationship between the IVs and the DV.

Recall that one-way ANOVAR designs differ from two-group designs only in terms of variations in the procedures for carrying out the statistical calculations. Both types of designs could include the use of three control techniques—constancy, randomization, and statistical control. Factorial designs allow the experimenter to use those three techniques plus one more—making a secondary variable a second IV. One should not be misled by this statement and conclude that factorial designs are only used in situations in which the investigator wants to make some secondary variable an IV. Although this is one reason, most factorial designs are carried out simply because the investigator has two or more primary variables in which he is interested.

A second feature of factorial designs that distinguishes them from two-group and one-way ANOVAR designs relates to step 5 of carrying out an experiment—the statistical analysis of variations in the DV. With more IVs and groups involved, we could rightly predict that the statistical computation of factorial designs will be more complex. But if the reader is observant, he will soon realize the statistical analysis of factorial designs is strikingly similar to the analysis carried out on one-way ANOVAR designs. Little is new. Most of the calculations are simply more of what was done in one-way ANOVAR analysis: more sums of squares are calculated, and more F ratios are computed. For example, three sums of squares are calculated in a 2 × 2 factorial design compared to one in a one-way ANOVAR analysis (excluding any multigroup comparisons that might be necessary). In factorial designs at least three F ratios are calculated, in contrast to only one in a one-way ANOVAR analysis.[5]

The differences in one-way ANOVAR and factorial analysis in terms of sums of squares are shown with the following formulas:

$$\text{One-way ANOVAR:} \quad SS_T = SS_{\text{IV}} + SS_W$$

$$\text{Two factorial:} \quad SS_T = SS_{\text{IV1}} + SS_{\text{IV2}} + SS_I + SS_W$$

In one-way ANOVAR experiments the total sums of squares was divided into two parts—that related to the IV and that related to all other unknown variables.[6] In a two-factorial investigation, variations between the scores can be divided into four categories:

1. Variation due to IV 1
2. Variation due to IV 2

5. The number of Fs mentioned here does not include Scheffe's F calculations, which can vary a great deal depending on the number of groups.

6. One should keep in mind the fact that sums of squares represents variation between the scores due to variables present in the situation.

3. Variation due to any interactive effects between IV 1 and IV 2
4. Variation due to unknown secondary variables

Three of the sums of squares ($SS_{IV1}$, $SS_{IV2}$, $SS_I$) represent intended variations in the subjects' scores brought about by experimenter manipulation.
Numerically, they show up as differences between groups in the investigation.
The calculation of $SS_{IV2}$ and $SS_{IV1}$ is the same as for $SS_B$ in previous designs. $SS_I$ is a new concept and is calculated differently, as we shall see. $SS_W$
is calculated the same as in one-way ANOVAR designs. To illustrate how the
sums of squares are calculated, the sums of squares are computed for the
data shown in Table 11–5. Eight rats were divided into four groups, each

**TABLE 11–5**
A 2 × 2 factorial design with two raw scores in
each group

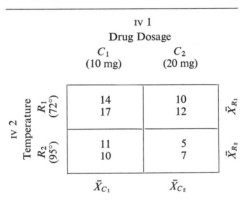

consisting of two subjects. The objective of the investigation was to determine
whether dosage level of the drug and temperature of the room influence the
time it takes for rats to become anesthetized. The two values in the four cells
represent the number of minutes it took for the subjects to lose consciousness. The formula for the variation in this situation would be

$$V_T = V_{dosage} + V_{temp} + V_{interaction} + V_W$$

**Calculation of sums of squares.**  The sums of squares of this formula are
calculated as shown below.

$$SS_T = \Sigma X^2 - \frac{(\Sigma X_G)^2}{N}$$

$$= (14^2 + 17^2 + 10^2 + 12^2 + 11^2 + 10^2 + 5^2 + 7^2)$$

$$- \frac{(14 + 17 + 10 + 12 + 11 + 10 + 5 + 7)^2}{8} = 99.5$$

$$SS_{IV1} = SS_C = \Sigma \frac{(\Sigma X_C)^2}{n} - \frac{(\Sigma X_G)^2}{N}$$

$$= \left[ \frac{(14 + 17 + 11 + 10)^2}{4} + \frac{(10 + 12 + 5 + 7)^2}{4} \right]$$

$$- \frac{(14 + 17 + 10 + 12 + 11 + 10 + 5 + 7)^2}{8} = 40.5$$

$$SS_{IV2} = SS_R = \Sigma \frac{(\Sigma X_R)^2}{n} - \frac{(\Sigma X_G)^2}{N}$$

$$= \left[ \frac{(14 + 17 + 10 + 12)^2}{4} + \frac{(11 + 10 + 5 + 7)^2}{4} \right]$$

$$- \frac{(14 + 17 + 10 + 12 + 11 + 10 + 5 + 7)^2}{8} = 50.0$$

$$SS_I = \Sigma \frac{(\Sigma X_{RC})^2}{n} + \frac{(\Sigma X_G)^2}{N} - \Sigma \frac{(\Sigma X_R)^2}{n} - \Sigma \frac{(\Sigma X_C)^2}{n}$$

$$= \left[ \frac{(14 + 17)^2}{2} + \frac{(12 + 10)^2}{2} + \frac{(11 + 10)^2}{2} + \frac{(5 + 7)^2}{2} \right]$$

$$+ \frac{(14 + 12 + 10 + 12 + 11 + 10 + 5 + 7)^2}{8}$$

$$- \left[ \frac{(14 + 17 + 11 + 10)^2}{4} + \frac{(10 + 12 + 5 + 7)^2}{4} \right]$$

$$- \left[ \frac{(14 + 17 + 10 + 12)^2}{4} + \frac{(11 + 10 + 5 + 7)^2}{4} \right] = 0$$

$$SS_W = \Sigma X^2 - \Sigma \frac{(\Sigma X_{RC})^2}{n}$$

$$= [(14^2 + 17^2 + 10^2 + 12^2 + 11^2 + 10^2 + 5^2 + 7^2)]$$

$$- \left[ \frac{(14 + 17)^2}{2} + \frac{(12 + 10)^2}{2} + \frac{(11 + 10)^2}{2} + \frac{(5 + 7)^2}{2} \right] = 9$$

A comparison of the way sums of squares were calculated on page 220 for one-way ANOVAR designs with the calculation of sums of squares in this example shows the similarity of the two procedures. $SS_T$ and $SS_W$ are calculated exactly the same way. The $SS_{IV1}$ and $SS_{IV2}$ are also calculated the same way as $SS_B$ in a one-way ANOVAR design, though it is not as apparent at first glance. $SS_{IV1}$ is calculated as if there is no other IV and as if there are only two groups involved in the investigation. The data are treated as if only two groups $(C_1, C_2)$ exist; group $C_1$ rats given 10 mg of drug and group $C_2$ rats given 20 mg. Temperature differences are ignored for the moment because the two $C$ groups are equated on this variable.

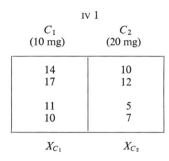

$$SS_C = \Sigma\frac{(\Sigma X_C)^2}{n} - \frac{(\Sigma X_G)^2}{N}$$

$$= \left[\frac{(14 + 17 + 11 + 10)^2}{4} + \frac{(10 + 12 + 5 + 7)^2}{4}\right]$$

$$- \frac{(14 + 17 + 11 + 10 + 10 + 12 + 5 + 7)^2}{8}$$

$$= 40.5$$

The sums of squares for the second IV is then calculated as if there were no IV 1, and as if only two groups are involved.

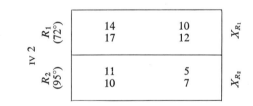

$$SS_R = \Sigma\frac{(\Sigma X_R)^2}{n} - \frac{(\Sigma X_G)^2}{N}$$

$$= \left[\frac{(14 + 17 + 10 + 12)^2}{4} + \frac{(11 + 10 + 5 + 7)^2}{4}\right]$$

$$- \frac{(14 + 17 + 10 + 12 + 11 + 10 + 5 + 7)^2}{8}$$

$$= 50$$

Notice that the formula for calculating the sums of squares for the rows and columns is identical to the formula for $SS_B$ except that $\Sigma\frac{(\Sigma X_C)^2}{n}$ or $\Sigma\frac{(\Sigma X_R)^2}{n}$ is substituted for the symbol $\Sigma\frac{(\Sigma X_B)^2}{n}$.

**Calculation of the F ratios.** With the sums of squares calculated, we turn to the computation of the F ratios. As previously mentioned, three F ratios are calculated with a two factorial design.

$$F = \frac{SS_R/df_R}{SS_W/df_W}$$

$$F = \frac{SS_C/df_C}{SS_W/df_W}$$

$$F = \frac{SS_I/df_I}{SS_W/df_W}$$

The first F listed would need to be calculated to determine whether temperature influenced the time it took for the drug to act. The second F would be used to determine whether dosage influenced the time it took for the drug to act. The third F is used to determine whether the time it took for the drug to act was influenced by the interaction of the two IVs. Table 11–6 summarizes the computation of the three Fs.[7]

**TABLE 11–6**
*Summary of the analysis of variance for a factorial design*

| Source of variability | Formula | Numerical value | Obtained F | Critical F |
|---|---|---|---|---|
| Dosage | $F = \frac{SS_C/df_C}{SS_W/df_W}$ | $\frac{40.5/1}{9/4}$ | 18 | 7.71 |
| Temperature | $F = \frac{SS_R/df_R}{SS_W/df_W}$ | $\frac{50/1}{9/4}$ | 22.22 | 7.71 |
| Interaction | $F = \frac{SS_I/df_I}{SS_W/df_W}$ | $\frac{0/1}{9/4}$ | 0 | 7.71 |

$df_C = $ (columns $- 1) = 2 - 1 = 1$
$df_R = $ (rows $- 1) = 2 - 1 = 1$
$df_I = $ (rows $- 1$)(columns $- 1) = (2 - 1)(2 - 1) = 1$
$df_W = N - $ (rows)(columns) $= 8 - (2)(2) = 4$

It is apparent that both dosage level and temperature significantly influence the time it takes for the drug to act, for both obtained Fs (18 and 22.22) are larger than the critical F (7.71) shown in the F table.

The steps involved in the statistical analysis of a two factorial design are as follows:

---

7. The reader should keep in mind the distinction between $F_s$ and Fs. $F_s$ represents Scheffe F, whereas Fs is simply the plural of F.

1. Calculate the sums of squares for:
   the columns $(SS_C)$
   the rows $(SS_R)$
   the interaction $(SS_I)$
   the within groups $(SS_W)$
2. Calculate their correlated degrees of freedom:
   $$df_C = C - 1$$
   $$df_R = R - 1$$
   $$df_I = (r - 1)(C - 1)$$
   $$df_W = N - (R)(C)$$
3. Divide the sums of squares by their appropriate degrees of freedom.
4. Calculate the F ratios.
5. Check the obtained F ratios with the critical Fs.
6. For each significant F, calculate the $F_S$ to determine which groups were significantly different.

At this point it would be wise for the reader to compare these steps to those for a one-way ANOVAR design in the preceding chapter. Notice that the steps are identical; the only difference is that more Fs must be calculated. The way they are calculated does not change. Even the use and calculation of $F_S$ is unchanged.

## RANDOMIZED FACTORIAL DESIGNS

As previously mentioned, one of the main reasons for employing factorial designs is to save time and money by analyzing two IVs in the same experiment. Such was the case in the experiment designed to determine the importance of grading and exam frequency in college classrooms. A second reason for using the factorial design is that there might be an interaction between the two variables. That is, it was felt grading might be most effective when more exams were given. The rationale for such an assumption was the idea that the amount of feedback students would receive from many exams might provide enough motivation to stimulate academic achievement without grades. Table 11–7 shows the results of the investigation. The numbers in the cells represent the raw scores of the subjects on the final exam.[8] The design employed in this investigation was a $2 \times 2$ factorial design. Since the statistical calculations involved are identical to the $2 \times 2$ (drug $\times$ tem-

---

8. Each group in the study actually had over thirty subjects. Nine were elected from each group in an effort to decrease the amount of statistical computation and make the example easier for the reader to follow. The results depict the actual results obtained in the investigation.

**TABLE 11–7**

*A 2 × 2 factorial design with exam frequency and grading conditions as IVs*

|  | IV 1 Frequency of Exam | |
|---|---|---|
|  | *Weekly* | *Monthly* |
| **Graded** | 54 | 46 |
|  | 47 | 43 |
|  | 44 | 44 |
|  | 48 | 41 |
|  | 50 | 50 |
|  | 45 | 47 |
|  | 51 | 45 |
|  | 49 | 45 |
|  | 53 | 44 |
| **Not graded** | 31 | 35 |
|  | 38 | 30 |
|  | 40 | 40 |
|  | 38 | 38 |
|  | 37 | 35 |
|  | 45 | 36 |
|  | 36 | 35 |
|  | 37 | 34 |
|  | 40 | 32 |

(IV 2 — Effect of exam)

perature) presented in the preceding section of this chapter, the statistical computation is carried out here with little explanation. The reader may answer any questions that arise by comparing the two examples and noting the previous explanations. Table 11–8 shows the statistical calculations involved.

**TABLE 11–8**

*Statistical calculations in a 2 × 2 factorial design*

| Group I (Weekly exam, graded) | | Group II (Weekly exam, not graded) | |
|---|---|---|---|
| $X$ | $X^2$ | $X$ | $X^2$ |
| 54 | 2,916 | 31 | 961 |
| 47 | 2,209 | 38 | 1,444 |
| 44 | 1,936 | 40 | 1,600 |
| 48 | 2,304 | 38 | 1,444 |
| 50 | 2,500 | 37 | 1,369 |
| 45 | 2,025 | 45 | 2,025 |
| 51 | 2,601 | 36 | 1,296 |
| 49 | 2,401 | 37 | 1,369 |
| 53 | 2,809 | 40 | 1,600 |
| $\Sigma X_\mathrm{I} = 441$ | $\Sigma X_\mathrm{I}^2 = 21{,}701$ | $\Sigma X_\mathrm{II} = 342$ | $\Sigma X_\mathrm{II}^2 = 13{,}108$ |

| Group III (Monthly exam, graded) | | Group IV (Monthly exam, not graded) | |
| --- | --- | --- | --- |
| $X$ | $X^2$ | $X$ | $X^2$ |
| 46 | 2,116 | 35 | 1,225 |
| 43 | 1,849 | 30 | 900 |
| 44 | 1,936 | 40 | 1,600 |
| 41 | 1,681 | 38 | 1,444 |
| 50 | 2,500 | 35 | 1,225 |
| 47 | 2,209 | 36 | 1,296 |
| 45 | 2,025 | 35 | 1,225 |
| 45 | 2,025 | 34 | 1,156 |
| 44 | 1,936 | 32 | 1,024 |
| $\Sigma X_{III} = 405$ | $\Sigma X_{III}{}^2 = 18,277$ | $\Sigma X_{IV} = 315$ | $\Sigma X_{IV}{}^2 = 11,095$ |

$$SS_C = \left[\Sigma\frac{(X_C)^2}{n}\right] - \frac{(\Sigma X_G)^2}{N}$$

$$= \left[\frac{(441 + 342)^2}{18} + \frac{(405) + 315)^2}{18}\right] - \frac{(441 + 342 + 405 + 315)^2}{36}$$

$$= (34,060.5 + 28,800) - 62,750.25$$

$$= 110.25$$

$$SS_R = \left[\Sigma\frac{(\Sigma X_R)^2}{n}\right] - \frac{(\Sigma X_G)^2}{N}$$

$$= \left[\frac{(441 + 405)^2}{18} + \frac{(342 + 315)^2}{18}\right] - \frac{(441 + 342 + 405 + 315)^2}{36}$$

$$= (39,762 + 23,980.5) - 62,750.25$$

$$= 992.25$$

$$SS_I = \left[\Sigma\frac{(\Sigma X_{RC})^2}{n}\right] + \left[\frac{(\Sigma X_G)^2}{N}\right] - \left[\Sigma\frac{(\Sigma X_C)^2}{n}\right] - \left[\Sigma\frac{(\Sigma X_R)^2}{n}\right]$$

$$= \left[\frac{(441)^2}{9} + \frac{(342)^2}{9} + \frac{(405)^2}{9} + \frac{(315)^2}{9}\right] + \left[\frac{(441 + 342 + 405 + 315)^2}{36}\right]$$

$$- \left[\frac{(441 + 342)^2}{18} + \frac{(405 + 315)^2}{18}\right] - \left[\frac{(441 + 405)^2}{18} + \frac{(342 + 315)^2}{18}\right]$$

$$= [21,609 + 12,996 + 18,225 + 11,025] + [62,750.25] - [62,860.5] - [63,742.5]$$

$$= 2.25$$

$$SS_W = \Sigma X^2 - \Sigma\frac{(\Sigma X_{RC})^2}{n}$$

$$= 64,181 - 63,855$$

$$= 326$$

$$df_C = (C - 1) = 2 - 1 = 1$$
$$df_R = (R - 1) = 2 - 1 = 1$$
$$df_I = (R - 1)(C - 1) = (2 - 1)(2 - 1) = 1$$
$$df_W = (N - RC) = 36 - (2)(2) = 32$$

$$F_C = \frac{SS_C/df_C}{SS_W/df_W} = \frac{110.25/1}{326/32} = \frac{110.25}{10.19} = 10.82 \qquad \text{critical } F = 4.15$$

$$F_R = \frac{SS_R/df_R}{SS_W/df_W} = \frac{992.25/1}{326/32} = \frac{992.25}{10.19} = 97.37 \qquad \text{critical } F = 4.15$$

$$F_I = \frac{SS_I/df_I}{SS_W/df_W} = \frac{2.25/1}{326/32} = \frac{2.25}{10.19} = .22 \qquad \text{critical } F = 4.15$$

It is apparent from the statistical analysis that both grading and frequency of exam are significant variables in the academic achievement of students. Because the F for interaction was insignificant, it may be concluded that (1) grading is better than not grading irrespective of whether exams are given weekly or monthly, and (2) weekly testing is better than monthly, no matter whether the exams count toward the grade or not.

Randomized factorial designs are favored by many professional psychologists concerned with educational, social, and industrial field experiments because of their ability to convert secondary variables into measurable IVs. Field situations frequently include important secondary variables that cannot be eliminated. The factorial design allows the investigator to determine not only the influence of an IV he brings into the situation but also the primary effect of some relevant secondary variable already present in the selected field situation.

As an example, the psychology department at a prominent university was interested in improving its introductory psychology course. It was decided to try three different teaching procedures and compare their effectiveness in terms of academic achievement and how well the students rated the procedure they experienced. The three procedures compared were three lectures a week procedure, go at your own pace discussion procedure, and no class, just a final exam procedure. This started out to be an investigation requiring a three-group one-way ANOVAR design. As the planning of the experiment progressed, several members of the department felt an important secondary variable already present in any classroom situation should be taken into strong consideration. That variable was student grade point average (GPA). It was felt by most of the faculty that students varying in GPA may differ in their responsiveness to the three procedures. For example, it was felt that the brighter student might function better in the nonclass situation, for he would not be held back by other students. It was also suggested that the less bright student might do better in the highly structured lecture situation.

After some discussion it was decided to get a measure of differences related to the brightness of the student by dividing the students involved in the experiment into groups according to their GPA. The students who enrolled in the introductory course were divided (without their knowledge) into three groups: group A, GPA .0–1.99; group B, GPA 2.00–2.99; group C, GPA 3.00–4.00. Table 11–9 shows the eventual design of the experiment.

**TABLE 11–9**
*A 3 × 3 factorial design*

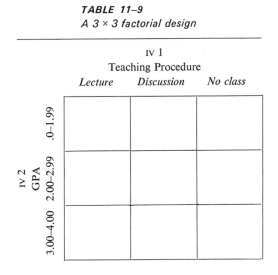

The result was a 3 × 3 factorial design. Notice that by blocking the subjects on their GPA and performing a statistical analysis of the differences in GPA levels, a one-way ANOVAR design can be converted into a factorial design.

The statistical analysis of this 3 × 3 factorial design is identical to a 2 × 2 design, except that the computation is a little more cumbersome due to the additional groups. An interesting aspect of the results was that the students who attended no class performed slightly better on the final exam than the students in the lecture group. Some students felt that this fact supported the idea that things learned while sleeping may inhibit active studying.

## RANDOMIZED BLOCKED FACTORIAL DESIGNS

Blocking may be carried out in an experiment to remove differences between groups that may be due to a secondary variable rather than an IV. Returning to the drug-temperature example of a factorial design, suppose the rats used as subjects came from three different strains. Now, it is known that different strains of rats differ in their sensitivity to various drugs. Rats from a certain strain could become anesthetized faster than rats from another strain, even though both strains are given the same drug with temperature and dosage held constant. The difference between the groups could then be due partially to strain differences in subjects from group to group. If different strains were involved in the situation, the wise investigator would equate the groups by blocking them on the variable (strain differences), as shown in Table 11–10. The dashed lines are included to show that each group is

**TABLE 11–10**
*A blocked 2 × 2 factorial design*

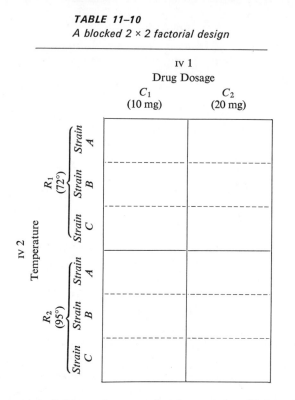

actually composed of three subgroups, but is treated as if the subgroups did not exist. By means of blocking, each major group has been equated on strain differences.

With blocking accomplished, the groups are equated on the variable of strain, and any differences between groups in the time it takes to become anesthetized cannot be attributed to strain. There is a good chance that randomization alone would automatically equate groups in an experiment on secondary variables such as this. However, one principle of randomization is that as a control technique it becomes more effective the larger the number of subjects in each group. That is, the probability that groups in an experiment are equated on all the secondary variables by randomization can be increased by increasing the number of subjects in the groups.

Generally speaking, as the number of groups in an experiment increases, the number of subjects per group decreases. This does not have to be so, but it is a common occurrence in social science investigations. Having 15 subjects in each group of a two-group design is not uncommon. The total number of subjects in the study would equal 30. It is generally not too difficult to find 30 subjects on which to carry out an investigation. Suppose however, you were carrying out a $3 \times 2$ factorial design. Now 90 subjects would be needed to have 15 per group. It should not be hard for the reader to conclude from these statements that the number of subjects used per group in a factorial design is much smaller than in two-group designs. In fact, two or three subjects per group is not uncommon in factorial designs, whereas the same number of subjects per group is not acceptable in a two-group design.

One other point should be clear: as the number of groups in an experiment increases, the investigator must rely more heavily on alternative procedures for controlling secondary variables. For this reason, the investigator should give more consideration to blocking secondary variables in factorial designs than he might in two-group designs.

## STATISTICAL CONTROL WITH FACTORIAL DESIGNS

One of the potential problems discussed while the teaching procedure experiment was being planned was the concern that subjects in the four groups might initially differ in terms of what they know about psychology. If the groups differed in knowledge of psychology before the experiment began, the difference on final exam scores could be at least partly due to prior knowledge rather than totally to the effects of grading and exam frequency. To check for this, a pretest was given at the beginning of the class. In the actual experiment the groups were found to be relatively identical in terms of prior knowledge. Of 140 multiple-choice questions, the average number of questions answered correctly for each group was 27, 29, 31, and 26. To illustrate the use of statistical control with factorial designs, the pretest scores will be modified to indicate a difference in the groups. The reader will then be able to compare the results of this example employing an analysis of covariance with the factorial analysis carried out on the randomized factorial design example given previously. The reader should compare the formulas and computations carefully so that the differences in statistical procedures are clearly understood. The data obtained with the $Y$ scores

**TABLE 11–11**
A 2 × 2 factorial design

| | | | | iv 1 Exam Frequency | | | |
| | | | | Weekly | | Monthly | |
| | | | Y | X | Y | X |
|---|---|---|---|---|---|---|---|
| | | *Graded* | 11 | 54 | 10 | 46 |
| | | | 14 | 47 | 13 | 43 |
| | | | 12 | 44 | 11 | 44 |
| | | | 10 | 48 | 9 | 41 |
| iv 2 | Effect of Exam | | 12 | 50 | 11 | 50 |
| | | | 13 | 45 | 12 | 47 |
| | | | 11 | 51 | 10 | 45 |
| | | | 14 | 49 | 13 | 45 |
| | | | 11 | 53 | 10 | 44 |
| | | | Y | X | Y | X |
| | | *Not graded* | 5 | 31 | 4 | 35 |
| | | | 7 | 38 | 6 | 30 |
| | | | 6 | 40 | 5 | 40 |
| | | | 5 | 38 | 4 | 38 |
| | | | 6 | 37 | 5 | 35 |
| | | | 7 | 45 | 6 | 36 |
| | | | 5 | 36 | 4 | 35 |
| | | | 7 | 37 | 6 | 34 |
| | | | 6 | 40 | 5 | 32 |

representing the student's scores on the pretest and the $X$ scores representing final exam scores are shown in Table 11–11. In this example both exam frequency and grading were significant variables, even after group differences in pretesting were adjusted for. The calculations follow:

| Group I (Weekly, graded) | | Group II (Weekly, not graded) | |
| X | $X^2$ | X | $X^2$ |
|---|---|---|---|
| 54 | 2,916 | 31 | 961 |
| 47 | 2,209 | 38 | 1,444 |
| 44 | 1,936 | 40 | 1,600 |
| 48 | 2,304 | 38 | 1,444 |
| 50 | 2,500 | 37 | 1,369 |
| 45 | 2,025 | 45 | 2,025 |
| 51 | 2,601 | 36 | 1,296 |
| 49 | 2,401 | 37 | 1,369 |
| 53 | 2,809 | 40 | 1,600 |

$\Sigma X_I = 441$    $\Sigma X_I^2 = 21,701$    $\Sigma X_{II} = 342$    $\Sigma X_{II}^2 = 13,108$

| Y | XY | Y | XY |
|---|---|---|---|
| 11 | 594 | 5 | 155 |
| 14 | 658 | 7 | 266 |
| 12 | 528 | 6 | 240 |
| 10 | 480 | 5 | 190 |
| 12 | 600 | 6 | 222 |
| 13 | 585 | 7 | 315 |
| 11 | 561 | 5 | 180 |
| 14 | 686 | 7 | 259 |
| 11 | 583 | 6 | 240 |

$\Sigma Y_I = 108$  $\Sigma XY_I = 5,275$    $\Sigma Y_{II} = 54$  $\Sigma XY_{II} = 2,067$

| Group III (Monthly, graded) | | Group IV (Monthly, not graded) | |
|---|---|---|---|
| X | $X^2$ | X | $X^2$ |
| 46 | 2,116 | 35 | 1,225 |
| 43 | 1,849 | 30 | 900 |
| 44 | 1,936 | 40 | 1,600 |
| 41 | 1,681 | 38 | 1,444 |
| 50 | 2,500 | 35 | 1,225 |
| 47 | 2,209 | 36 | 1,296 |
| 45 | 2,025 | 35 | 1,225 |
| 45 | 2,025 | 34 | 1,156 |
| 44 | 1,936 | 32 | 1,024 |

$\Sigma X =_{III} 405$  $\Sigma X_{III}^2 = 18,277$    $\Sigma X_{IV} = 315$  $\Sigma X_{IV}^2 = 11,095$

| Y | XY | Y | XY |
|---|---|---|---|
| 10 | 460 | 4 | 140 |
| 13 | 559 | 6 | 180 |
| 11 | 484 | 5 | 200 |
| 9 | 369 | 4 | 152 |
| 11 | 550 | 5 | 175 |
| 12 | 564 | 6 | 216 |
| 10 | 450 | 4 | 140 |
| 13 | 585 | 6 | 204 |
| 10 | 440 | 5 | 160 |

$\Sigma Y_{III} = 99$  $\Sigma XY_{III} = 4,461$    $\Sigma Y_{IV} = 45$  $\Sigma XY_{IV} = 1,567$

$$SS_C = \left[ \Sigma \frac{(\Sigma X_C)^2}{n} - \frac{(\Sigma X_G)^2}{N} \right] - \left[ \Sigma \frac{(\Sigma X_C)(\Sigma Y_C)}{n} - \frac{(\Sigma X_G)(\Sigma Y_G)}{N} \right]$$

$$= \frac{(441 + 342)^2}{18} + \frac{(405 + 315)^2}{18} - \frac{(441 + 342 + 405 + 315)^2}{36}$$

$$- \frac{(441 + 342)(108 + 54)}{18} + \frac{(405 + 315)(99 + 45)}{18}$$

$$- \frac{(441 + 342 + 405 + 315)(108 + 54 + 99 + 45)}{36}$$

$$= [34,060.5 + 28,800 - 62,750.25] - [7,047 + 5,760 - 12,775.5]$$

$$= 110.25 - 31.5$$

$$= 78.75$$

$$SS_R = \left[\Sigma \frac{(\Sigma X_R)^2}{n} - \frac{(\Sigma X_G)^2}{N}\right] - \left[\Sigma \frac{(\Sigma X_R)(\Sigma Y_R)}{n} - \frac{(\Sigma X_G)(\Sigma Y_G)}{N}\right]$$

$$= \left[\frac{(441 + 405)^2}{18} + \frac{(342 + 315)^2}{18} - \frac{(441 + 342 + 405 + 315)^2}{36}\right]$$

$$- \left[\frac{(441 + 405)(108 + 99)}{18} + \frac{(342 + 315)(54 + 45)}{18}\right.$$

$$\left. - \frac{(441 + 342 + 405 + 315)(108 + 54 + 99 + 45)}{36}\right]$$

$$= [39,762.0 + 23,980.5 - 62,750.25] - [9,729 + 3,613.5 - 12,775.5]$$

$$= 992.25 - 567.0$$

$$= 425.25$$

$$SS_I = \left[\Sigma \frac{(\Sigma X_{CR})^2}{n} + \frac{(\Sigma X_G)^2}{N} - \Sigma \frac{(\Sigma X_C)^2}{n} - \Sigma \frac{(\Sigma X_R)^2}{n}\right]$$

$$- \left[\Sigma \frac{(\Sigma X_{CR})(\Sigma Y_{CR})}{n} + \frac{(\Sigma X_G)(\Sigma Y_G)}{N} - \Sigma \frac{(\Sigma X_R)(\Sigma Y_R)}{n} - \Sigma \frac{(\Sigma X_C)(\Sigma Y_C)}{n}\right]$$

$$= \left\{\left[\frac{(441)^2}{9} + \frac{(342)^2}{9} + \frac{(405)^2}{9} + \frac{(315)^2}{9}\right] + \left[\frac{(441 + 342 + 405 + 315)^2}{36}\right]\right.$$

$$\left. - \left[\frac{(441 + 342)^2}{18} + \frac{(405 + 315)^2}{18}\right] - \left[\frac{(441 + 405)^2}{18} + \frac{(342 + 315)^2}{18}\right]\right\}$$

$$- \left\{\left[\frac{(441)(108)}{9} + \frac{(342)(54)}{9} + \frac{(405)(99)}{9} + \frac{(315)(45)}{9}\right]\right.$$

$$+ \left[\frac{(441 + 342 + 405 + 315)(108 + 54 + 99 + 45)}{36}\right]$$

$$- \left[\frac{(441 + 342)(108 + 54)}{18} + \frac{(405 + 315)(99 + 45)}{18}\right]$$

$$\left. - \left[\frac{(441 + 405)(108 + 99)}{18} + \frac{(342 + 315)(54 + 45)}{18}\right]\right\}$$

$$= [63,855 + 62,750.25 - 62,860.5 - 63,742.5]$$

$$- [13,374 + 12,775.5 - 12,807 - 13,342.5]$$

$$= 2.25 - 0$$

$$= 2.25$$

$$SS_W = \left[\Sigma X^2 - \Sigma \frac{(\Sigma X_{CR})^2}{n}\right] - \left[\Sigma XY_G - \Sigma \frac{(\Sigma X_{CR})(\Sigma Y_{CR})}{n}\right]$$

$$= (21,701 + 13,108 + 18,277 + 11,095) - \left[\frac{(441)^2}{9} + \frac{(342)^2}{9} + \frac{(405)^2}{9} + \frac{(315)^2}{9}\right]$$

$$- \left[(5,275 + 2,067 + 4,461 + 1,567)\right.$$

$$\left. - \frac{(441)(108)}{9} + \frac{(342)(54)}{9} + \frac{(405)(99)}{9} + \frac{(315)(45)}{9}\right]$$

$$= 326 + 4$$

$$= 330$$

$$df_R = R - 1 = 2 - 1 = 1$$

$$df_C = C - 1 = 2 - 1 = 1$$

$$df_I = (C - 1)(R - 1) = (2 - 1)(2 - 1) = 1$$

$$df_W = N - RC - 1 = 36 - (2)(2) - 1 = 31$$

$$F_C = \frac{SS_C/df_C}{SS_W/df_W} = \frac{78.75/1}{330/31} = \frac{78.75}{10.65} = 7.39 \qquad \text{critical } F = 4.16$$

$$F_R = \frac{SS_R/df_R}{SS_W/df_W} = \frac{425.25/1}{330/31} = \frac{425.25}{10.65} = 40.00 \qquad \text{critical } F = 4.16$$

$$F_I = \frac{SS_I/df_I}{SS_W/df_W} = -\frac{2.25}{330/31} = \frac{2.25}{10.65} = .21 \qquad \text{critical } F = 4.16$$

Statistical control, like blocking, is more important in factorial designs than in two-group designs for a couple of reasons. First, groups contain fewer subjects, making randomization less effective. Second, field situations in which factorial designs are used have more secondary variables to take into consideration than the more selective laboratory environment. Unexpected secondary variables frequently show themselves only after the investigation is underway. This problem is compounded in factorial designs, for the more IVs involved, the greater the possibility more secondary variables will interact with them. (For the sake of simplicity within group variance has been used as the denominator in this example when calculating the F-ratios. Sometimes the interaction variance is the proper term to use. See Keppel [1973, Chapter 16] for Details.)

## ADVANTAGES AND DISADVANTAGES OF FACTORIAL DESIGNS

Factorial designs have several advantages over less sophisticated designs. First, factorial designs provide an additional control procedure—making a secondary variable a second IV. This is an important addition, because it is the only technique that not only controls the secondary variable, but also tells how much of an effect it has in a situation. Second, factorial designs are the only designs that allow the investigator to study interaction effects.

Factorial designs may be used in certain situations to conserve time and energy. It may not be feasible to carry out more than one experiment at a time because of inadequate physical facilities, not enough subjects, or lack of time. This type of problem can be alleviated by using a factorial design and administering more than one IV at a time to each subject.

Factorial designs may be more practical in many field situations because of the large number of secondary variables present and because of limited time to work. An industrial psychologist may be brought into a corporation to determine the cause of certain manpower problems. Results are required in a short time. To accomplish his task, he may manipulate several variables concurrently to save time. A clinical psychologist may employ a factorial design because of limited time to determine the effects of certain IVs on a group of mentally retarded children.

The disadvantages of factorial designs center mainly around the increased complexity over two-group and one-way ANOVAR designs. They include taking more time than one single two-group experiment, requiring more subjects, and a more complicated and cumbersome statistical analysis. There are also many situations in which factorial designs are impractical and unnecessary. A teacher may want to know whether her students learn math better with a teaching machine than on their own. This question can be answered with a simpler two-group design. It should be remembered that an investigator should select the simplest design that will answer his particular question. Do not fit your interests to a design, let your design serve your interests.

## SUMMARY

Experimental designs that involve more then one IV are called factorial designs. Factorial designs are classified according to how many IVs are involved (two factorial, three factorial, and so on). They are also defined in terms of how many levels of each variable are employed (e.g., $2 \times 3$ factorial design). The procedure for carrying out a factorial experiment is the same as for a one-way ANOVAR experiment, except that more groups are used. The F test and multiple-group comparison tests are used in analyzing factorial designs the same way they are used in ANOVAR designs. The statistical analysis for factorial designs is carried out by treating each IV as if it were the only one employed. The multiple-group comparison tests are also calculated in the same way as with one-way ANOVAR designs.

Factorial designs have three main advantages over other types of designs: (1) they allow more than one IV to be studied at one time; (2) they allow the interactive effects of two or more IVs to be determined; and (3) they provide an additional control technique. The main disadvantage of factorial designs is the complex statistical calculations involved.

# 12

# Small N Designs

*Chapter Twelve shows how a scientifically sound experiment can be carried out using only one or two subjects. This concept may seem foreign to those who have a strong background in statistical analysis and have been taught that an investigation must include large numbers of subjects to be scientifically sound. This chapter presents an alternative approach to carrying out investigations that is not based on a statistical method of data analysis. Although it has been shown to be exceptionally effective in basic research, one of its strongest attractions is its effectiveness in applied settings. Small N designs provide teachers, case workers, counselors, and other practicing psychologists the opportunity to demonstrate scientifically the effectiveness of their approaches in field settings where they deal with only one or two problem subjects. Notice that small N designs involve the use of elimination and constancy as control techniques more than large N designs do.*

## ORIGIN OF SMALL *N* DESIGNS

The types of experimental designs covered up to now have been what are commonly termed large *N* group designs. The procedural format for all these designs centered around choosing a large number of subjects, dividing them into groups, and statistically comparing the behavior of one group with the behavior of another. The group design approach, however, does not meet all the needs of psychology. In many instances the psychologist is faced with situations in which large numbers of subjects are not available. The clinical psychologist, for example, is generally faced with a problem involving only one or two persons, and he is expected to carry out an investigation to solve that problem.

In the past he was unable experimentally to demonstrate the effectiveness of a certain therapy, or scientifically to isolate certain principles of behavior because he had no strong means of controlling for secondary variables. A person would come to him with a problem, he would apply a certain therapy over many sessions, the behavior would change, and the patient would leave. Feeling good about the results, the clinician would then present those results at a psychological convention, stating that the technique he employed was responsible for the "cure." He would then be attacked by experimental psychologists challenging the validity of his investigation. Their criticisms would include "You haven't controlled for proactive history," "You haven't controlled for retroactive history," "Where is your control group showing the person wouldn't have gotten better by himself," "How do you know it wasn't something else in the situation (your cute secretary, for example) that cured him rather than the therapy you used," "You don't have enough subjects to make a general statement that your therapy is effective." Realizing their points were well taken, the clinician would return to his situation somewhat dejected by the fact that he was unable to apply most of the experimental control procedures considered necessary by the scientific community to demonstrate cause and effect relationships. He would return to performing correlational and case study investigations in an effort to isolate cause-effect relationships, for no control procedures had been identified so that a scientific manipulatory investigation could be carried out on only one or two subjects. As is true in most cases, however, where there is a will there is a way; so it was only a matter of time (and creative effort) until methods were devised that would allow controlled experimental investigations to be performed using only a small number of subjects. Before covering the procedures employed in small $N$ investigations, let us briefly review how large $N$ experimental designs became accepted for psychological investigations. This will help the reader understand why large $N$ designs are used and why a small $N$ design procedure was necessary.

Recall that at the turn of the century, psychology (and other scientific disciplines, for that matter) was seeking to find better ways of determining cause and effect relationships. Prior to the early 1900s, the statistical tools so commonly used by psychologists today had not been perfected. Although experimental designs involving the comparison of one group to another had been employed since 1834 (in agricultural field research), psychology did not become strongly involved in group investigations until the early 1900s. Thorndike, McCall, and Chapman [1916], for example, carried out a four-group experiment on the effect of ventilation on mental work. Even at the time of this experiment, however, randomization as an effective control technique and the powerful statistical tests based on randomization (e.g., $t$-tests, F tests) had not been developed. It was not until the 1920s that randomization became generally accepted as a control technique in scientific circles. Prior to that time, elimination and constancy were the only techniques available for psychological investigation. With the acceptance of randomization as a control technique came statistical analytical procedures (e.g., the analysis of variance) based on random selection of subjects. These statistical tests were a major step forward, for they were a much more powerful means of empirically determining whether the differences in DV measures between groups were significant. They provided a measure of variation ($V_W$) representing how much variation occurs between experimental subjects exclusive of the influence of the IV. The investigator could now make a comparative analysis ($V_B/V_W$) and determine the probability that such variation could occur by chance.

The statistical tests also became the springboard from which other control techniques were launched. Adequate development of statistical procedures was a prerequisite for the implementation of two other control techniques, statistical control and making a secondary variable an IV.[1] Because three of the five procedures for controlling secondary variables are related to statistical procedures, it should not be surprising that scientific investigators turned their efforts to an elaboration and refinement of statistical procedures. And much to the chagrin of most undergraduate psychology majors struggling through statistics courses, that is exactly what happened. For the next fifty years, mathematicians and researchers from all scientific disciplines began directing a large portion of their time to investigating the application of statistical tools to research investigations. As with most scientific disciplines, statistics has become an integral part of the training program for psychology students.

One of the principles upon which these statistical tools are based is "The more subjects an investigator employs in his project, the more effective are the statistical tests." An in-depth explanation of this point is left to books on statistical methods [Hays, 1973; Keppel, 1973], but an important point the reader should remember there is that the more subjects he employs in his investigation when carrying out a large $N$ design, the greater the chance of obtaining a $V_B/V_W$ that is significant.[2] Because of this principle, researchers were admonished to employ large numbers of subjects in their projects.

Although the development of more effective large $N$ designs and their related statistical procedures had advantageous effects on psychological research, it also had some drawbacks. Due to their great success in identifying cause and effect relationships, large $N$ statistical designs captivated most social scientists to such a degree that they began to equate good experimental

---

1. Both statistical control and making a variable second IV require statistical calculations involving the analysis of a variance in order for them to be used as control techniques.

2. Actually there is a limit, for one can have too many subjects. This does not happen very often, however, and the problem is usually in the opposite direction. There is no hard and fast rule as to exactly how many subjects there should be in a research project, but 15 to 30 is generally an acceptable number. Having over 100 subjects is not uncommon.

research with large *N* designs. This was more serious for psychology than for most other social sciences because psychology was the study of individuals more than of groups of people. Psychologists often deal with only a few people at a time. What they also needed was a scientifically sound experimental procedure that could be employed on one or two persons at a time. Unfortunately, however, the wave of enthusiasm for statistical procedures steered most researchers away from even attempting to develop sound experimental procedures involving only a few subjects.

Fortunately for psychology, not all psychologists turned their efforts toward statistical procedures. Among those who did not was B. F. Skinner. Skinner felt that an effective experimental analysis of behavior based on the behavioral study of only a few subjects was possible. Since the control techniques of randomization, making a secondary variable an IV, and statistical control were closely tied to statistical manipulations, Skinner's approach was based on elimination and constancy. Almost singlehandedly (at least in comparison to the hundreds of investigators working on statistical refinements), Skinner laid the foundation for a small *N* experimental approach to analyzing behavior that most psychologists agree has been one of the two greatest achievements in research in the history of psychology. Although Skinner began his work on small *N* designs only a few years after statistical methods entered the research scene, it was to be many years before the discipline of psychology accepted this approach as scientifically adequate. It did not receive the immediate recognition and acceptance given to large *N* designs, due in part to the fact that Skinner's approach was based on two methods of control that had been employed for decades. With the popular appeal of the newly developed statistical tools, Skinner's emphasis seemed outmoded. Few psychologists realized that Skinner was developing an unusually sensitive analytical approach that involved the application of elimination and constancy in a unique way.

To give the reader a quick look at the basic difference between a large *N* and a small *N* approach, let us look at how each would deal with a particular situation. Suppose we landed a spaceship on Mars, found living beings, and wanted to learn something about them. If the astronauts were trained in large *N* experimental procedures, they might ask these beings if a few hundred of their kind could be made available for testing purposes. Some would serve as control subjects (receiving no IV); others would be given the IV. From such experiments, the astronauts would draw conclusions regarding the attributes of Martians.

If the astronauts were trained in small *N* procedures, their approach would be somewhat different. They would take only one or two Martians, constantly monitor their behavior, apply and remove different IVs, and then draw conclusions about the attributes of Martians. Now, although these two approaches differ, each is accepted as a scientifically sound method for analyzing situations. The assumptions upon which each is based are different, as we shall see later in this chapter.

## LOGICAL ANALYSIS OF SMALL *N* DESIGNS

As previously mentioned, small *N* designs are based on the control techniques of elimination and constancy. The way they are applied to control secondary variables when only a few subjects are involved is somewhat different than the way they are used in large *N* designs. In large *N* designs these two control techniques are usually applied before the subjects begin responding in the experimental situation; they are not built into the design of the experiment. Prior to the actual carrying out of the experiment some variables may be eliminated from the situation while others are held constant by ensuring that each group of subjects in the investigation has been equated on some important secondary variable. In small *N* designs, constancy and elimination are employed not only before, but also while the investigation is in progress. This is accomplished by taking repeated measurements from each subject and continually monitoring the DV while the experiment is in progress. Thus, the investigator may "sense" irregularities in the DV due to secondary variables. He then identifies them and eliminates or holds them constant.

Small *N* designs are generally divided into three main parts, as shown in Figure 12–1. When setting up the experiment, the investigator takes special care in selecting his DV. First, some behavior is selected and recorded repeatedly by the investigator to obtain a stable measure of the DV prior to the

**FIGURE 12–1**

Basic format for small *N* designs

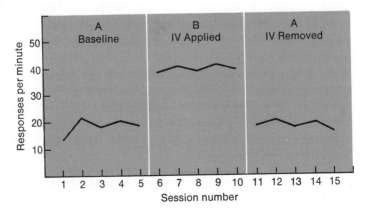

administration of the IV. This is commonly referred to as the *baseline*. A DV used with small $N$ designs should have the following characteristics:

1. It should be objectively measurable.
2. It should be easily emitted by the subjects.
3. The subject should be able to emit the behavior at length without fatigue.
4. It should be sensitive to changes that may occur in the situation.

The characteristics listed here are the ones a researcher expects of his DV in basic research settings where the experimenter may choose his DV. In many situations (like clinical settings) the psychologist has no choice in the behavior he has to deal with (such as a patient's bedwetting problems); the DV is already determined for him. In such cases, the psychologist determines the *best* way to measure the behavior confronting him. Chapter Five lists the types of measures he may choose from.

Frequently in these experiments there is no set number of experimental sessions defined as the baseline. The decision as to when the IV condition is to start generally is made while the experiment is in progress. The criterion for deciding when to apply the IV is the stability of performance by the subject. How is stability defined? Stability may be defined in various ways, depending on the DV measure being used. If, for example, the subjects are in an experiment involving error responses and correct responses, stability may be defined as the subject making a certain percentage of his responses as errors. If the experiment involves just getting a stable rate of responding, stability may be defined as 5 percent or less variability in responses per minute for four consecutive sessions. Stability, then, may be defined differently in various small $N$ experiments, depending on the type of response measure being used as the DV. By reviewing the literature of small $N$ designs employing the same type of DV, the investigator may find an appropriate way of defining stability in his experiment.[3] The criterion of stability should be set before the baseline is started.

After the criterion of stability is reached, the second part of the investigation is implemented. The IV is administered with all other aspects of the experimental situation remaining exactly the same as during the sessions in which the baseline was being established. How long does the IV condition last? The B condition, like the baseline, continues until the DV again stabilizes, with stability again being defined in terms similar to the baseline (e.g., 5 percent variability from one session to the next). The criterion of stability for condition B is also generally set prior to the start of the experiment.

---

3. Good sources are *The Journal of the Experimental Analysis of Behavior*, the *Journal of Applied Behavioral Analysis*, Murray Sidman's *Tactics of Scientific Research*, and Werner Honig's *Operant Behavior*.

Once the DV in condition B has stabilized, the IV is removed so that the subject is again experiencing the same situation presented during the baseline. Why is the second A condition carried out? Recall from Chapter Three that the ability of the investigator to apply the IV whenever and to whomever he desires is considered one of the investigator's most important tasks because that additional control of any situation greatly reduces the probability that some secondary variable was responsible for any concomitant change in a DV occurring when an IV enters the experimental situation. The ability of an investigator to demonstrate the DV changes when an IV is "removed" is just as poweful in indicating a cause-effect relationship as the demonstration that the administration of an IV influences the DV. The ability to apply and remove the IV, with the DV changing in some direction when the IV is given and returning to its original level when the IV is removed, is an even more powerful demonstration of a cause-effect relationship than simply applying or removing the IV and noting a change in the DV. The reverse condition (the second A condition) should be included when carrying out psychological research with a small *N* design where possible.

## ABA SMALL *N* DESIGNS

The ABA design is the major type of small *N* design. It involves establishing a baseline, applying an IV, and removing that IV (returning to the pre-IV condition). It may be employed whenever the effects of the IV can be removed. Such IVs include drugs, visual cues, praise, deprivation, emotion inducing stimuli, sounds, and almost any change in the environment.

Several years ago, two undergraduate students were conducting an experiment on pigeons for a class project. The purpose of the experiment was to determine the effects of a certain drug on behavior. They conditioned two pigeons to peck a small plastic key for food reinforcement. They were then going to inject the drug into the subjects during every other experimental session and compare the behavior of the pigeons when injected with the drug against their behavior when they were not influenced by the drug. After several days of running the experiment, the students complained that they were having trouble with the lights inside the pigeon test chamber. For some reason the chamber lights had been getting dimmer over the last four sessions and now were almost totally out. We located their electrical problem, but in looking over the data records, something caught my eye. Their records showed that the pigeons were pecking faster as the lights were getting dimmer. This was interesting, for generally pigeons roost when placed in a dark chamber.

After thinking the situation over for a while, I decided to carry out an investigation to see if light intensity did affect the behavior of pigeons. Eight pigeons were selected to serve as subjects in the experiment. Two of the pigeons were individually trained to peck a key on a fixed ratio schedule of 100 (that is, they were given grain every time they pecked the key 100 times), while two others were trained to peck the key on a variable interval schedule of reinforcement. The variable interval schedule is a little difficult to conceptualize for someone who is unfamiliar with the idea of schedules of reinforcement. Basically, it involves two things—a certain amount of time must pass, and the pigeon must peck the key after that time is up before it will be rewarded. The length of time that must pass varies from one time to the next so that the pigeon generally responds at a somewhat low and constant rate when on this schedule of reinforcement. Two pigeons were trained on a variable ratio (VR–100) schedule of reinforcement in which the birds were reinforced for pecking the key a certain number of times, but the exact number changed from one reinforcement to the next. This is the same schedule used by slot machines in Las Vegas. The customer must pull the lever a number of times to win, but the number he must pull varies from one win to the next.[4] The last two pigeons were trained to respond on a fixed interval schedule (FI). In a FI schedule, both a set amount of time must pass and the subject must respond after the time is up before he is reinforced. Figures 12–2 and 12–3 show the number of responses per hour (the DV) emitted by the subjects during the whole experiment.[5]

The pigeons who were reinforced on a fixed ratio schedule are labeled FR; those reinforced on a variable interval schedule are labeled VI; those reinforced on a variable ratio schedule are labeled VR, and those reinforced on a fixed interval schedule are labeled FI.

All the pigeons were run for 30 one-hour daily sessions during the first condition of the experiment. The last 10 of those sessions are shown in the figure and were used as the baseline in the experiment. At the start of condition B, the house and key light in the chamber were slowly reduced in intensity over the next few sessions until the pigeons were pecking the key in total darkness. The arrows indicate the first whole session each subject was run one whole session in total darkness, with no lights on in the chamber. Condition B lasted for a total of 20 sessions. The lights (house and key) were then turned on at full intensity at the beginning of session 51 and remained on for the last 10 sessions of the experiment. From the data shown in Figures 12–2

---

4. A VR schedule generally gets the subject to respond more per unit of time than any of the other schedules, and is obviously why it is used in casinos.

5. This example may be difficult to follow unless it is read over several times and the figure studied closely. This experiment was published in *The Journal of the Experimental Analysis of Behavior*, 1974, **24**, 14–21.

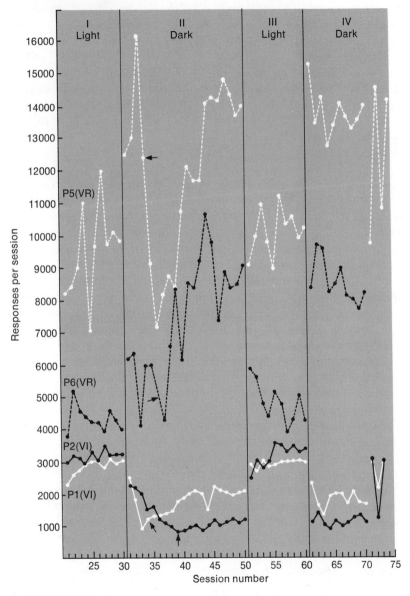

**FIGURE 12–2**

Total number of responses emitted per session for pigeons on a variable-interval (P1, P2) and a variable-ratio (P5, P6) schedule of reinforcement

(Adapted from Robinson & Shelley [1974], Figure 1. Reprinted by permission.)

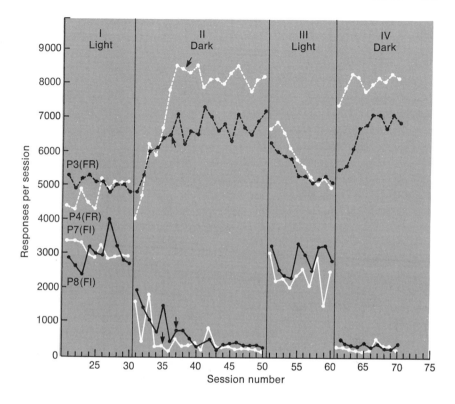

**FIGURE 12–3**

Total number of responses emitted per session for pigeons under the fixed-interval schedule of reinforcement (P7, P8) and under a fixed-ratio schedule (P3, P4).

(Adapted from Robinson & Shelley [1974], Figure 2. Reprinted by permission.)

and 12-3, it is apparent not only that light intensity influences key-pecking behavior, but also that its effect on rate of behavior differs depending on which schedule of reinforcement the subject is on.

At this point, the reader may be somewhat skeptical and argue that the results simply show that the presence or absence of light did influence the behavior of the subjects, but that no real conclusions can be drawn because the direction the behavior changed and the amount it changed was different for each bird. The reader might argue that the difference obtained might simply be due to the individual differences of the few subjects employed and that to draw such conclusions properly many more pigeons need to be run.

The arguments would be incorrect for reasons that relate to two of the principles upon which small $N$ designs are based. First, the possibility of a small $N$ design being internally invalid is less than that of a large $N$ design because there is much better control of the experimental situation and a more accurate measure of the DV. The better control comes from the fact that the investigator monitors his experiment much more closely than is the case in large $N$ experiments. He gets a continuous running measure of the DV during all phases of the experiment rather than just a one-shot measure. Because each subject is used as his own control (commonly called *intrasubject* control), many sources of internal invalidity are automatically controlled for. Those secondary variables that did happen to fluctuate during the experiment would show up as fluctuations in the DV. The investigator who is constantly monitoring his data would take note of the DV change, search for the cause, and remove it. He would also wait to apply his IV until after the baseline behavior had restabilized.

The second reason deals with the way of determining the generality of the findings. Although large $N$ experiments increase the generality of their findings by increasing the number of subjects employed in a particular investigation, small $N$ designs use a different means for determining whether the data are representative. This is called *interinvestigatory affirmation*. In small $N$ research the investigator is more dependent on previous research.[6] The small $N$ researcher checks the behavior against previous studies that have used the same DV. How did I know, for example, that the behavior emitted by the pigeons during the baseline was representative of the average pigeon's behavior on such a schedule of reinforcement? There have been literally thousands of sessions previously carried out on pigeons by researchers all over the country. Being familiar with the literature on pigeons' behavior under the control of different schedules of reinforcement, I simply compared the behavior of the present subjects to that of those published in the literature. The fact that the behavior of these subjects was representative of pigeons was affirmed by comparing their behavior to that of pigeons in other similar investigations.

A knowledge of previous investigations comparing the behavior of pigeons on different schedules of reinforcement also helped explain the apparent contradiction in behavior of my subjects—some increased their response rate while others decreased it. Notice which of the subjects' behavior increased and which decreased. The pigeons whose ability to obtain reinforcement depended on their rate of responding (fixed and variable ratio) increased their rates. This could indicate that the birds were attending more to their task because there were fewer distractions in the chamber when the lights were out, or it could indicate that pigeons are simply more active when the lights are out. A look at the behavior of the birds on interval schedules (both

---

6. Notice the phrase "more dependent" was used. Large $N$ investigations also employ interinvestigatory affirmation, but not as much.

fixed and variable) helps in deciding which of the two conclusions could be correct. Now if the pigeons on interval schedules were to attend more closely to the schedule of reinforcement they were on, their response rates should not increase, but actually decrease. In this way they would be more efficient— get the same number of reinforcers for less work. Since that is exactly what happened, the conclusion drawn was that pigeons attend to the schedule of reinforcement they are on better in total darkness than in lighted chambers. The differences in the behavior of the pigeons in the experiment were then explained in terms of the differential effects of schedules of reinforcement and light intensity rather than capricious differences in the subjects.

It should be apparent that an investigator must be more familiar with the literature if he is going to employ a small $N$ rather than a large $N$ experimental design. This dependency of small designs on past literature is one reason small $N$ research has taken longer to gain acceptance as an appropriate technique. A backlog of data had to be accumulated to substantiate the validity of the procedure. Although the development of statistical tools and the development of small $N$ design procedures were begun about the same time, small $N$ designs have gained general acceptance by most psychologists only in the last twenty years, whereas statistical designs have been accepted for the last fifty years. The great success of large $N$ designs was probably responsible for inhibiting the acceptance of small $N$ designs because so many researchers began to believe that the only means for determining whether the data of an experiment was generalizable to other subjects was by means of statistical analysis.

How well do small $N$ designs control for sources of internal invalidity? Proactive history is controlled for by the constant monitoring of the DV during condition B and by the procedure of reversing the conditions. If the secondary variable varied during condition B at some time other than the exact point at which the IV was presented, the investigator would detect it as a fluctuation in the DV during that phase of the experiment. Figure 12–4 gives such a situation. In session 10 some secondary variable changed and it showed up in the DV.[7] If a secondary variable happens to change at exactly the same time the IV is introduced (a very unlikely situation in the first place), it will be detected when the IV is removed and the DV does not return to the level obtained during the baseline. Maturation may also be checked for by the removal of the IV. Retroactive history effects will show up as fluctuations in the DV during the experiment, and sometimes by the inability of the DV

---

7. The data given in Figure 12–4 are fictious but do represent how the principle works. In a past class experiment using pigeons, the feeding mechanism jammed during the experiment and the response rate dropped. Noting the fluctuation in the DV, we searched for the cause of the change, found it, and corrected it. The DV then restabilized, and the experiment was continued.

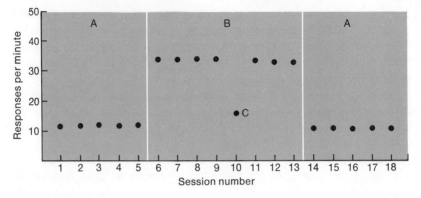

**FIGURE 12–4**

Illustration of some secondary variable fluctuation causing a notable change in the dependent variable, which is then fixed

to reverse in the second A condition. Statistical regression is controlled for by using the subjects as their own control and also by the second A condition of the experiment. Experimental mortality is controlled for by the close monitoring of the investigation by the investigator.

Because few subjects are normally used, the investigator may thoroughly check the circumstances under which that subject was lost and detect whether it was due to the IV or some secondary variable. Pretesting is controlled for by the use of each subject as its own control and the second A condition. If more than one IV is employed in the study, interaction may be checked for by adding additional B conditions, as shown in Figure 12–5. Any differ-

**FIGURE 12–5**

Illustration of a small *N* investigation involving more than one independent variable

| A | B₁<br>IV 1 Only | A | B₂<br>IV 2 Only | A | B₃<br>Both IVs Used | A |
|---|---|---|---|---|---|---|

ences in the effects of the IVs alone or together would show up by comparing the DV measures in $B_1$, $B_2$, and $B_3$. The A conditions interspersed between the Bs allow the investigator to check for any carryover effects from the experiencing of more than one IV. Although an ABA design does not totally control for instrumentation and experimenter bias, it comes closer to controlling for them than large *N* designs. Variation in DV due to instrumentation fluctuations, for example, will show up more easily because repeated measures are taken.

## OTHER TYPES OF SMALL *N* DESIGNS

The ABA experimental design is not the only type of small *N* design an investigator may use. There are a number of different acceptable ways of setting up a small *N* design, and although space does not permit an in-depth coverage here, a few types will be presented to give the reader a general idea of what is involved.[8]

### Staggered Baseline Designs

In some situations the investigator may wonder whether the behavior of the subjects will revert to the original level obtained in the baseline. There are variables (e.g., learning experiences) that may change the subject's behavior in such a way that his behavior cannot reverse. Suppose, for example, a subject is trying to solve certain types of problems and is consistently making mistakes. You measure the number of mistakes he makes each day for several days and find he makes about 35 mistakes out of 100 attempts each day. This serves as the baseline. Now you teach him a new approach to deal with the problems he is working on (this is the IV). The number of mistakes he makes now declines to 5 out of 100 for the next few days. You want to reverse back to the original baseline condition now, but you realize you cannot remove the knowledge you gave him. Can small *N* designs be used in such situations?

The answer is yes, and the procedure involves staggering when the IV condition is given to the different subjects. Figure 12–6 shows how this is done. The As represent a session in which the baseline is being established, while the Bs represent the application and presence of the IV. In the example given, the first B for each subject would represent the first session after which a subject had been taught a new approach. Staggering when the IV is applied decreases the probability that some secondary variable just happened to fluctuate at the same time the IV was administered and was actually responsi-

8. See Sidman, *Tactics of Scientific Research*. He does an excellent job of presenting both the rationale and the procedures involved in small *N* research.

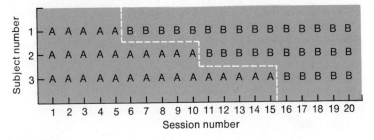

**FIGURE 12–6**

Diagrammatic representation of a staggered baseline design

ble for the change in the DV. A second type of staggered baseline design involves only one subject. In this design, the investigator monitors three (the exact number may vary) behaviors of one subject rather than one behavior of three subjects. The IV is then applied to each of the behaviors at a different session. This approach is often used in behavior therapy.

Although the staggered baseline design is cosidered a good small $N$ design and includes the two characteristics essential for a small $N$ design (a large number of DV measures being taken, and a baseline phase), it is not generally considered to be as powerful as the ABA design. The ability to apply and remove an IV in an experimental situation with a concomitant change in the DV is more effective in inferring cause-effect relationships.

### Analytic ABAB Design

Both small $N$ designs presented so far are what were previously termed exploratory experiments; that is, two conditions are compared, one with the IV and one without, to determine whether a certain IV had an effect. Analytical experiments are also possible with small $N$ designs. Suppose you want to determine the effect of different dosages of a particular drug that is a central nervous system depressant. Figure 12–7 shows how this type of design could be set up with some fictitious data included. First a baseline rate of behavior is established during five daily one-hour sessions in which the subject emits about 50 responses per minute on some task. Then the subject is given 2 mg of the drug for each of the following five sessions. During the third set of five sessions, the subject is run without being given any drug. The last fifteen sessions of the experiment involved five sessions with 4 mg of drug given, five no-drug sessions, and finally five drug sessions with 6 mg of drug given. The relative effectiveness of different drug levels could then be determined by comparing the behavior of the subject under different levels of the drug.

This procedure can also be used to carry out investigations involving

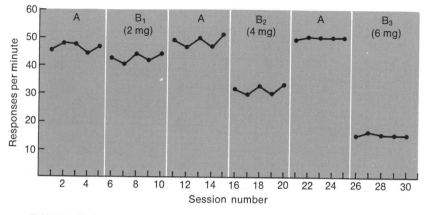

**FIGURE 12–7**

Diagrammatic representation of an analytical small *N* design

more than one IV that are called factorial experiments when large *N* designs are employed. Rather than administer different levels of one particular level, the investigator could substitute different IVs in the alternating B conditions.

### Concurrent Multiple Response Designs

Instead of investigating the effects of more than one variable using only one DV, a researcher may study the effects of two (or more) IVs on two different responses being emitted during the same experimental situation. In this situation two different responses are used to generate simultaneously two different baselines, each under the control of a separate set of maintaining contingencies. Suppose, for example, an investigator wants to determine whether extinction or punishment was a better means of eliminating behavior. Initially a rat could be placed in a chamber containing two levers. He would the be taught to respond on both bars to get reinforced; pressing either bar would get him food. After the bar-pressing behavior had stabilized for both bars, the investigator could set it up so that the rat would be shocked every time he pressed the left bar (punishment), and simply not get food any longer (extinction) when he pressed the bar on the right side. Later on, the original baseline conditions could be reinstated.[9]

Concurrent ABA designs can be employed to carry out both exploratory and analytical experiments. They also give the investigator an opportunity

9. Concurrent ABA designs should be avoided by the novice investigator because there are several aspects of these designs that can lead to incorrect conclusions (e.g., the contingencies programmed for one behavior may exert control over the second also). Effective use of concurrent designs requires sound knowledge of concurrent design techniques.

to study how the changing of conditions controlling one's behavior might influence other behaviors. Concurrent designs could be employed to deal with such practical questions as "How does decreasing the working hours of a person affect his work efficiency and his leisure activity?" A baseline for both work and leisure activity could be obtained for a couple of prison inmates, for example. The amount of work required could then be varied to determine how it affected their work output and the types of things they did in the exercise yard.

## COMPARISON OF SMALL *N* AND LARGE *N* DESIGNS

At this point, it might be well to bring out some important distinctions between large and small $N$ designs.

### Types of Control Techniques

Large $N$ designs may employ randomization, making a secondary variable an IV, and statistical control, whereas small $N$ designs do not. Small $N$ designs do use randomization as a means of subject selection, but not as a procedure for controlling secondary variables in the experiment. Although both large $N$ and small $N$ experiments employ elimination and constancy as control techniques, how they use them differs. In large $N$ designs secondary variables are eliminated or held constant at the beginning of the investigation. In small $N$ experiments, elimination and constancy are employed as the investigation is carried out, as well as at the beginning. If a secondary variable happened to vary during the baseline of a small $N$ experiment, the investigator would spot the effect on the DV, search for the responsible variable, remove it, and continue on with establishing the baseline. In such a case with a large $N$ design, the experiment would have to be scrapped or the investigator would need to obtain a covariate measure that would allow the effects of the fluctuating secondary variable to be removed. Notice that small $N$ designs allow the investigator to control for secondary variables after an experiment is in progress, even though statistical adjustment is not possible.

In small $N$ experiments the investigator not only tries to hold secondary variables constant but also increases his control of the experimental situation by getting a constant or continuous measure of the DV. This gives him a truer measure of the DV with less chance that the DV measure he deals with is simply a measure of some chance fluctuation, which could be the case if he took only one measure of the DV per subject. Large $N$ investigations control for chance fluctuations by using an increased number of subjects;

small $N$ designs control by using an increased number of responses per subject.

### Manipulation of the Dependent Variable

In large $N$ experiments the investigator sets up his experimental design, controls for all the secondary variables he can, applies an IV, and takes a one-shot measure of the DV. Little is done about the DV except simply taking a measure of it. With small $N$ designs the investigator can actually manipulate the DV by varying secondary variables. This procedure is carried out in an effort to develop a stable DV measure prior to the administration of the IV. Just as an auto mechanic may adjust variables such as the carburetor and the spark plugs to obtain a smooth-running engine before applying some chemical (an IV) to the gas to note its effect on engine performance, so may the psychologist change the value of certain secondary variables in an effort to smooth out and "tune up" measures of the DV before the IV is given. In this way the actual effects of the IV may become more apparent.

### Monitoring the Experimental Data

In large $N$ experiments little analyzing of the data is done until the investigation is over. In small $N$ designs, however, the experimenter continually monitors his data. This is done to watch for changes in secondary variables that may occur during the experiment, and also because the shifting from one condition to the next is usually determined by the behavior of the subjects.

### Data Analysis

Large $N$ experiments employ the use of some statistical calculations to determine the significance of the data. A $t$-test, F test, or something similar is performed in the fifth step of carrying out a large $N$ experiment. Frequently in small $N$ investigations no statistical test is used in evaluating the data. The data are simply presented in graphic form. Graphs such as Figure 12–1 which show an overall comparison of the subject's behavior from one session to another are often presented. Besides an overall graphical comparison, daily records such as those shown in Figure 12–8 are also included so that the reader can analyze more closely what the behavior (DV) of the subject was like from one moment to the next during a session. Figure 12–8, for example, consists of two daily session records, one recorded during the baseline when the house and key light were on (left record), and one taken when the pigeon was pecking in total darkness (right record).

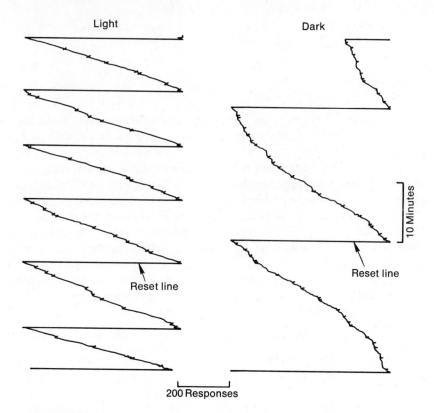

**FIGURE 12–8**

Cumulative records of a pigeon pecking in light and dark conditions on a variable interval schedule

(Adapted from Robinson & Shelley [1974], Figure 3. Reprinted by permission.)

To read these cumulative records correctly, one needs to understand how they are made. Figure 12–9 shows diagrammatically how a cumulative recorder operates. The paper is continuously being passed over roller A at a very slow speed (approximately 1 inch per five minutes). A pen rests on the paper and draws a vertical line on the record as long as no responses are made by the subject. When the subject does respond, the pen steps a fraction of an inch to the left. (It generally takes 500 steps for the pen to move all the way from the right to the left side of the paper.) When the pen reaches the left side, the recorder automatically resets the pen back to the right side so that it can continue to step each time a response is made. Two of the lines made by the recorder when the pen was reset are marked in Figure 12–8.

By looking at records such as these, the trained researcher can tell quite a bit about how the subject was reacting during the experiment. One of the more obvious things Figure 12–8 tells the investigator is that the subject made

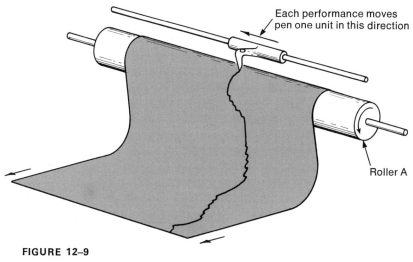

Each performance moves
pen one unit in this direction

Roller A

**FIGURE 12–9**
A cumulative recorder

over 3,000 responses during the light conditions (notice the recorder had to reset six times; $6 \times 500$ responses $= 3,000$), while the subject only responded about 1,200 times during the dark session.

The reader may wonder why so much attention has been given to explaining how to read records. The reason is that analyzing individual subjects' records is an important part of carrying out a small $N$ design. Just as a researcher who frequently uses statistical tests is able to use them to identify different interesting aspects of the data he is analyzing, so can the small $N$ researcher become proficient in analyzing cumulative records. By simply looking at cumulative records, well-trained investigators can tell such things as what schedule of reinforcement the subject was on, if some secondary variable changed during the session (in some cases the record can even identify the variable for him), if the subject was frustrated, if the subject was getting satiated, and if the equipment worked properly.

### Generality of Results

A topic closely related to data analysis is the issue of generality of results. How well do the results obtained in the investigation represent what would be obtained with other subjects? There is an important distinction between the way large $N$ investigations control for generality of the results and the way small $N$ experiments accomplish the same task. In large $N$ experiments the investigator may increase the generality of the results by increasing the number of subjects in the investigation. It is a well-known principle of data collection that the larger the sample chosen from the population to be subjects in an experiment, the closer will the obtained mean and variance measures of the sample be to the true mean and variance measures of the population. This statistical principle is so well known, in fact, that many scientists have come to believe that generality of results can only be obtained by statistical methods. This assumption is not correct, however, for the concepts of generality and statistical methods are not exactly synonymous. To help bring out the fallaciousness of such reasoning, let us look at a situation in which increasing the number of subjects does not increase the generality of the experiment results.

Suppose, for example, you carried out an experiment on ten rats to see if shocking a rat intermittently while he was carrying out a particular task would influence his behavior. The results you obtained showed all ten rats stopped working and hovered in the corner when shock was applied. Is this reaction characteristic of all rats? The question deals with intraspecies generality. Is it true that the more rats you use in your experiment, the greater the possibility that the results you obtain are true. Can you generalize for all members of the species called rat? What about interspecies generality? Does increasing the number of rats used in the study increase the possibility that the results also hold true for dogs, cats, and humans? Suppose you found from an investigation that a certain teaching procedure was effective for teaching math to young grade-school children. Could you increase the possibility that it could also be effective for mentally retarded children by running additional normal children in your study? Obviously not. The procedure of generalizing from one species to another or from one type of situation to another is carried out through inductive reasoning. The investigator uses his past experience and research to compare the similarities and differences of various species. From these similarities and differences, the investigator determines how generalizable his data are. Statistical methods can be employed to determine intraspecies generality because in such cases the investigator is comparing "quantitative" differences in variables—not the case when comparing one species with another or one situation with another. Small $N$ designs, then, determine generality of results by inductive reasoning rather than by inferential statistical methods, as is the case with large $N$ designs.[10]

## SMALL $N$ DESIGNS IN THE APPLIED SETTING

It was mentioned in Chapter One that present-day psychologists in the applied areas are required to be more familiar than practitioners of the past with ways of performing experimental research because advances in experi-

---

10. Sidman [1960] points out that many dimensions of intraspecies generality can be effectively handled in nonstatistical ways. In fact, he argues that increasing the number of subjects does not always increase the intraspecies generality of results.

mental techniques now make it possible for the applied psychologist to carry out a scientific experiment with only one or two subjects. The development of small $N$ designs is the major reason why applied psychologists now can and should perform such investigations. To illustrate how an ABA design may be applied to everyday problems, here is an experiment that was carried out several years ago.

Dave, a neighbor of mine, was the principal at a nearby school. At a social gathering one evening, he began expressing concern about a student, Mary, who for the past three years seemed to be withdrawing socially more and more from her classmates. He had referred her to the school psychologist three years ago because of her "poor socializing and reading ability," but she was not making progress. I suggested he might try some behavior modification therapy on her, but he said he did not think reinforcement therapy would be effective. In fact, he graciously stated he did not "believe such approaches were effective." He continued, "Although I don't believe it would work, I would certainly be willing to give it a try if I could find someone to do it." Humbly, I leaped into the breach. "I'll try it on one condition," I replied. "You must agree to let me carry out the investigation in such a manner that we may determine what it was that changed her behavior—assuming that it changes, of course." My purpose in making such an offer was simply to show him, if possible, that behavior modification therapy is an effective therapeutic approach, and one of the many alternatives available to the practicing psychologist. Not realizing that my condition meant reverting Mary to her original unsocial behavior once she was socializing, he accepted.

Mary was an attractive 15-year-old girl from a middle-class family enrolled in a class of educable retardates, homogeneous in terms of chronological age (14 to 16) and mental age (80 to 85). A portion of her teacher's report said, "Mary does not mix with any of her peers, just reads and does her work alone. . . . She has good art skills and shows a definite respect and friendliness to her art teacher. . . ." After reviewing the situation, I decided to work with Mary 30 minutes every school day during art period. First, a baseline was taken in which I sat in the back of the room and monitored Mary's behavior. Every 30 seconds I marked on a data sheet whether she was socializing (talking to other students, with other students, or even looking at other students) or not socializing (working alone at her desk or off somewhere by herself). These data were then converted into the percentage of the one-half hour session time she spent socializing and recorded on a chart, as shown in Figure 12–10.

After a week of getting a baseline, condition B was begun. Since Mary enjoyed social interaction with her art teacher, the IV was designated as attention from him. Every time Mary socialized with her classmates, I cued her teacher to go over to Mary, smile, and verbally interact with her for 15 seconds, and then move away. Teacher attention was thus used to reinforce

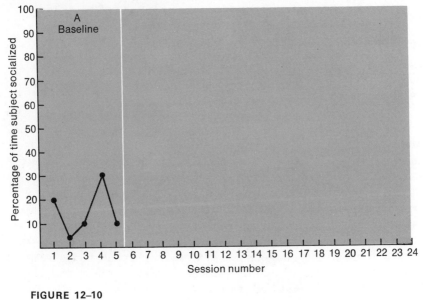

**FIGURE 12–10**
Baseline phase of Mary's therapy

Mary's peer socializing. Reinforcement was carried out for the next two weeks, and the percentage of time Mary socialized was again recorded on the chart (Figure 12–11).

By the end of the second week of reinforcement, Mary was spending 95 percent of her time socializing with her classmates. As one might expect, the principal was overjoyed at the dramatic change in Mary's behavior.[11] At this time, I suggested that Mary's antisocial behavior was probably the result of increased attention by her teachers. Dave said he did not agree, but did not really care, for she was no longer antisocial with her peers, and that was what he was concerned with. I told him we were now ready to see if the attention was in fact the determining factor by removing the attention for socializing and seeing if she would return to her antisocal ways. Amazed that I should even suggest such a thing, he said he was pleased with the results and that the investigation could terminate now. I then reminded him of his promise and told him not to worry. We would reimplement the attention later and bring her social behavior back up.

11. The change in Mary's behavior is actually not as astounding as it may seem. Prior to the start of the experiment, I checked with Mary's parents. They told me that she was not withdrawn at home. This information led me to conclude that Mary's abnormal sociability was not a deeply ingrained personality problem but a result of something specific at school. Since Mary was probably getting more than her share of attention from teachers when she acted antisocial, I hypothesized that the extra attention was actually causing her problem.

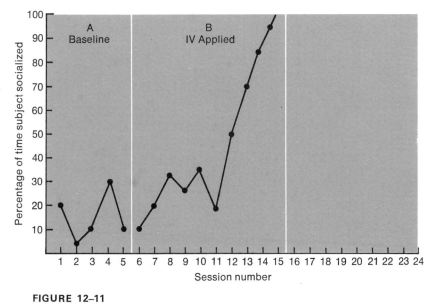

**FIGURE 12–11**

Mary's therapy through the baseline and independent variable administration phase

For the next three sessions Mary was no longer given teacher attention when she mingled with her classmates. In fact, she was given teacher attention for emitting antisocial behavior.[12] Notice in Figure 12–12 that the social behavior declines to the baseline level during the second A condition. The IV was reinstated in sessions 19 through 22, and the behavior again climbed to the final level obtained in the first B condition. At last report, one year following the investigation, Mary was doing fine and was no longer considered withdrawn.

Notice that only one subject was involved in this investigation, yet the conclusions drawn about teacher attention causing the withdrawal were substantiated in a scientifically acceptable way. The data obtained from this ABAB design leave little doubt that teacher attention was responsible for increasing Mary's social behavior. Prior to the development of an ABA small *N* approach, the applied psychologist's investigations involved only the second stage of what has been done here. He would simply apply his technique and note the behavior that resulted. No attempt was made to establish a baseline or to reverse the conditions, both of which are extremely

12. This technique is commonly used in ABA designs. Not only is the reinforcer removed from the desired behavior, but it is applied to antagonistic behaviors. This procedure is more effective in determining cause-effect relationships than simply returning to baseline conditions.

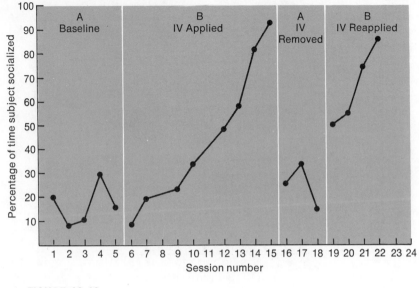

**FIGURE 12–12**

Mary's therapy through all conditions of the experiment

important in making this a scientifically acceptable investigation. The ABAB design is a welcome addition to the psychologist's arsenal of analytical procedures because it allows the research to be carried out in applied settings. In his normal, everyday routine, the practicing psychologist generally carries out only the AB portion of this design to help his patient. Whenever he desires to substantiate cause-effect relationships, he needs to add at least the reversal condition to his investigation. When doing research, the applied psychologist will add the second B condition, whereas the basic researcher will not. The second B condition is necessary in the applied setting because the patient wants his problem cured, not simply a demonstration that it *could* be cured.

## ADVANTAGES AND DISADVANTAGES
## OF SMALL *N* DESIGNS

Obviously, the biggest advantage of a small *N* design is the ability to carry out a scientifically sound investigation with only one or two subjects. This is more important to the psychologist than other social scientists because so much of his time is spent dealing with only one person. Small *N* designs allow the investigator to control the experimental situation more effectively by establishing a continuous measure of the DV throughout the experimental situation. There is also less chance that some secondary variation may change during the investigation without being noticed because the investigator constantly monitors his data. The investigator may in fact "tune up" the DV, thereby making it more sensitive to the possible effects of an IV. No statistical tests need be performed, a point considered an advantage by many who dislike carrying out statistical computations. Both exploratory and analytical investigations may be carried out with small $N$ designs, as well as investigations involving two or more IVs. Small $N$ designs allow the investigator to eliminate and hold constant secondary variables that do not show up until after the investigation is under way. ABA designs are generally preferred over the staggered baseline design because the ability to reverse the conditions is a much more effective experimental procedure than varying the point at which an IV is applied. Small $N$ intrasubject comparison controls for secondary variables better than intersubject comparisons, which is the case for large $N$ designs.

In terms of disadvantages, small $N$ designs are not appropriate for certain types of psychological research such as surveys or ex post facto situations. One must have the ability to control and manipulate an IV to be able to use a small $N$ design. The investigator needs to be more versed in related research literature than is generally required to carry out a large $N$ experiment. This is true partly because the investigator must rely more on inter-investigatory affirmation rather than on statistical analysis of his data. Three of the control techniques are not possible with small $N$ designs (this is not a very severe disadvantage because small $N$ designs use other means to accomplish the task). Small $N$ designs generally take months to complete, whereas many large $N$ designs can be carried out in one session. Small $N$ research requires expensive control equipment more often than do large $N$ designs.

## SUMMARY

Small $N$ experimental designs allow scientifically sound investigations to be carried out on only a few subjects. The analytical assumptions underlying small $N$ and large $N$ designs are somewhat different.

Historically, the development of experimental procedures for employing large $N$ and small $N$ designs started about the same time. Yet, because of the initial success of large $N$ designs and the support they received from the scientific community, small $N$ designs have only recently been acknowledged as a scientifically sound approach to determining cause effect relationships. The basic format of small $N$ designs involves using subjects as their own control in carrying out an experimental investigation. First a baseline is established to determine the value of the DV prior to the administration of an IV. Next, the IV is administered for several experimental sessions with the DV continually being monitored. The experimental conditions present during the baseline are then replicated by removing the IV for several sessions with the DV continually being monitored. The effect of the IV is determined by noting how the DV changed when the IV was applied and removed. Several different types of small $N$ designs were presented. These included the ABA design, the staggered baseline design, the analytical ABAB design, and the concurrent multiple response design.

Some of the more important distinctions between large $N$ and small $N$ designs were discussed. Although both large $N$ and small $N$ designs emphasize quantifiable data gathering and strong control of secondary variables in an investigation, the ways in which they accomplish these tasks differ. Large $N$ designs emphasize the use of randomization and statistical manipulations of data; small $N$ designs use elimination and constancy as control techniques and interinvestigator affirmation as a means of determining the significance of the data. Advantages and disadvantages of small $N$ designs were also discussed.

# 13

# Contemporary Experimental Psychology

*Most students have misconceptions about when and where different analytical approaches are actually used in psychology. The purpose of this chapter is to show the student that the various types of investigations presented in this text are employed by all subfields of psychology. It also attempts to show that any problem of psychological interest may be approached from several analytical directions. The student should keep in mind that the topics presented here are only a few of the many with which psychologists deal. This chapter may also provide ideas for class projects.*

Now that the reader is familiar with the basic analytical designs the psychologist has at his disposal, it might be well to look at how and where they have been used. One of the major problems faced by the novice investigator is determining what is an appropriate problem for analysis. Not being familiar with current research literature, the psychology student does not know whether or not (1) his research idea has already been done, (2) his idea is technically feasible, or (3) his idea is scientifically sound. The investigations presented in this chapter should give the reader help on these points by giving him some idea of what is currently being done.

Students often pigeonhole certain analytical approaches as being applicable to only certain subfields in psychology: clinical psychologists carry out only case study investigations; experimental designs cannot be used to study developmental aspects of psychology; a good researcher never uses anything but the experimental approach; and so on. All the analytical approaches previously presented in this text (two-group experiments, EPF studies, case studies, correlational methods) are employed throughout the subfields of psychology. Although certain areas may rely on some methods more than others, every analytical approach has made contributions to all subfields.

There are several points to look for in this chapter. First, notice how interrelated the different areas of research are. An investigation presented in the section on memory, for example, could also fit nicely in the section on brain dynamics. Information gleaned from one research project may have applications in many psychological dimensions. This is one reason why psychologists should be familiar with information obtained in the different areas. Second, notice the conditions under which an investigation is performed. In the past, most students have gone through their training programs concentrating on what "facts" about behavior are known and paying little attention to what types of investigations and subjects were employed in identifying those facts. Such facts as humans are innately aggressive, depth perception is innate, information in the brain is stored in RNA molecules, and man's personality is partly determined by heredity are all learned by the student in his classes. However, these facts are not universal truths. They are conclusions drawn from psychological investigations. The validity of these conclusions depends on a number of things including the type of investigation employed, how well secondary variables were controlled, and the subjects used. The practicing psychologist should not simply concentrate on what conclusions have been drawn in psychological research, but also be familiar with the circumstances under which they were obtained. As a psychologist, the reader will be considered an expert on facts of behavior; and as such, it is his responsibility to know under what conditions certain conclusions may be correct.

Third, notice how much psychology depends on nonhuman investigations to isolate behavioral relationships. Many applied psychologists have a condescending attitude toward animal research in psychology and fail to recognize how much of what is known about human behavior was concluded from nonhuman research investigations. Generality of principles from nonhumans to humans is more common than even many practicing psychologists realize. This point relates well to the issue presented in the previous paragraph. Psychologists should be aware of where the principles they expound come from.

The remainder of the chapter has been somewhat arbitrarily divided according to academic areas. Questions are posed to give the reader an idea of the types of questions contemporary research is designed to answer, and these are followed by summaries of investigations that have been carried out to find answers.

## DEVELOPMENTAL AND GENETIC RESEARCH

The question "How much of man's behavior is determined by his environment?" has been the stimulus for a major portion of psychological research over the years. There are two subfields in psychology whose prime concern is to determine what portion of behavior is a function of innate behavioral patterns of genetic predispositions. A substantial portion of the experimental research in these areas is carried out on nonhuman species because of the many drawbacks associated with using humans in such investigations. There are major ethical restrictions. Selective breeding for research purposes is unacceptable, as is manipulating a child's environment to any great extent. Also, longitudinal genetic studies on humans take generations to complete.

### Is IQ Genetically Determined?

As you might expect, nonexperimental correlational investigations are frequently employed when humans are used as subjects in developmental research. Two such investigations were carried out by Burks [1928] at Stanford University and Leahy [1935] at the University of Minnesota. The Burks study included 214 foster children put up for adoption before their first birthday and 105 control children living with their blood parents. Leahy's investigations involved a comparison of 194 control children. The IQ of the adopted and control children of both EPF field studies were compared to the IQ of the father and mother they were living with. The correlation coefficients obtained in the studies are presented in Table 13–1. Contrary to the

**TABLE  13–1**

*Correlation coefficients between foster and blood children and the parents they lived with*

|  | Mother's IQ | Father's IQ |
|---|---|---|
| *IQ of foster children* | | |
| Burk's study | .19 | .07 |
| Leahy's study | .24 | .19 |
| *IQ of blood children* | | |
| Burk's study | .46 | .45 |
| Leahy's study | .51 | .51 |

Sources: Burks [1928] and Leahy [1935].

expectations of the authors, the IQ correlations between adopted children and their foster parents were insignificant, whereas the correlations between children and their blood parents were significant. These results suggest that heredity is influential in determining IQ.

A controlled laboratory experiment carried out by R. C. Tryon in 1949 supported the conclusion drawn by Burks and Leahy. In a relatively simple but classic experiment, Tryon tested the ability of a large number of rats to traverse a rather complicated maze. He then attempted to develop a "bright" and a "dull" strain of rats. He selectively mated the male rats who ran the maze the fastest with the fastest females. The same was done with the slowest male and female rats. He continued to mate the fastest and slowest male rats with their respective female counterparts for seven consecutive generations. Figure 13–1 shows the results of the investigations. By the seventh generation there was little overlap in the scores of the bright and dull groups. Tryon continued to breed the rats selectively for eighteen generations, but the difference between the groups failed to widen any further than that noted in the seventh generation. Another interesting point was that the brightest of the new offspring were not brighter than the brightest of the original group of rats. Finally, when the descendents were tested twenty years later, the distinction between the bright and dull groups remained.

Tryon's work stimulated many behavioral scientists. With the help of

**FIGURE 13–1**

An experiment in selective breeding

(Adapted from Tryon [1949]. Used with permission of the National Society for the Study of Education.)

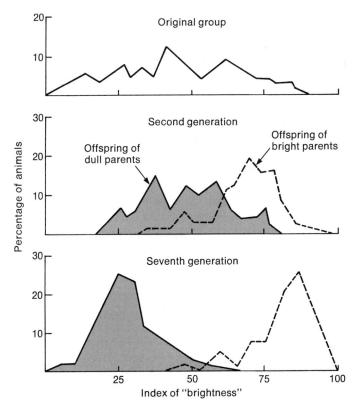

geneticists, over the years certain species have been inbred to develop specific strains that have little genetic variation. Many strains of rats and mice have been inbred to provide the investigator a selection of subjects with a choice of behavioral characteristics to analyze. Some strains of mice, for example, exhibit food-hoarding behavior to a much greater extent than other strains in identical environmental conditions. By crossbreeding such strains, psychologists can determine the amount of influence heredity has on certain behaviors.[1]

With this point in mind, Manosevitz [1970] set out to determine how much of the hoarding behavior of certain strains of mice could be due to heredity. Two strains of mice expressing a large difference in hoarding behavior were chosen as parental groups. To aid in distinguishing the two parental groups, the high hoarders used had pinkish-looking coats, and the low hoarders had black coats. The pink mice were then interbred, as were the black mice. At maturity, each offspring was given 30-minute tests in which the number of food pellets a mouse would bring to its home cage from a bin at the opposite end of the runway was recorded. The pink and black mice were then crossbred, and the hoarding scores of the offspring were found to be in the middle of the scores obtained by their parents. This result would be expected if the genes from each parent contributed an equal amount to the hoarding behavior. When the crossbreeds were mated back with the original parents, the hoarding scores went up for the backcrosses with the black-coated parents. The results indicated one-third to one-half of the hoarding behavior could be attributed to inherited factors.[2]

### What Effect Does Early Experience Have on Normal Development?

Although all the investigations in this section so far have indicated that genetic factors determine behavior, environmental determinants are not overlooked. A question commonly batted around by psychologists concerns the issue of the role of early experience on normal development. Levin, Chevalier, and Korchin [1956] conducted a laboratory experiment to shed some light on this issue. The purpose of the investigation was to determine whether painful or traumatic experiences in infancy cause emotional disor-

---

1. This summary of Tryon's investigation was originally reported in Rubinstein [1975], p. 502, published by The Dushkin Publishing Group, Inc., and used by permission. The book is composed of many abstracts of relevant research carried out in psychology. Students interested in a much broader coverage of current research than is presented here are referred to this publication.

2. Rubenstein [1975], p. 504. Used by permission of The Dushkin Publishing Group, Inc.

ders in adulthood. Rats were chosen as subjects for the experiment. They were divided into three groups. Infant rats of one group were given mild electric shocks at the same time each day for several consecutive days. A second group of rats was placed in the shock chamber on the same days and not shocked. A third group of rats was left in its home cages and not handled at all. The results of the experiment were quite surprising to the investigators, who were expecting the shocked rats to be the most emotionally disturbed (defined by greater defecation and cowering) of the three groups upon reaching adulthood.

Contrary to expectations, the behavior of the shocked rats was no different from that of the rats who were handled but not shocked. Even more surprising was the fact that the rats left in their home cages were the most emotionally disturbed. Surprised by the results, the experimenters replicated the experiment several times, and the results were always the same. In all instances it was the group receiving no extra handling that exhibited disturbed behavior. After going over and over the results, the authors came to a conclusion that agrees with the results of related investigations: some degree of stressful experience such as handling and shocking is necessary for an organism to successfully adjust to the environmental situations encountered in later life.[3]

This investigation illustrates an important point in psychological research. An investigator should not discard the results of his investigation simply because they do not fit his hypothetical expectations. Results may appear inconsistent, suggesting some uncontrolled secondary variable(s) came into play. The seasoned investigator will also look around for alternative explanations consistent with the results obtained. Often, investigations that disprove the hypothesis they were designed to test are more fruitful than those that support expectations.

### Does Environmental Stimulation Influence Brain Mechanisms?

What about the possibility of behavior influencing the brain? Psychologists are not only interested in determining how innate brain mechanisms may influence behavior, but also in how behavior may influence the central nervous system. One such experiment was reported by Rosenzweig, Bennett, and Diamond in 1972. From 12 different litters the authors selected a total of 36 rats that had just been weaned, and randomly divided them into three 12-subject groups. One group was then housed in standard laboratory cages with 3 rats to a cage. The second group of 12 rats was all housed together in

---

3. *Ibid.*, p. 509. Used by permission of The Dushkin Publishing Group, Inc.

a large cage containing many play objects. The third group of rats was individually housed in isolated cages where only food and water were available (this was considered an impoverished environment situation).

After a month in these conditions, all the subjects were sacrificed, and various measurements of their brains were made. Rats from the enriched environment were found to have a heavier and thicker cerebral cortex. Electronmicrograph enlargements of brain sections showed these same rats also had more connections between nerve cells in the brain. Another finding has important behavioral implications. All the rats used in the investigation had come from strains raised for several generations in the laboratory in metal cages with wire floors. None had ever been housed outdoors. When some of the laboratory-bred rats were placed in an outdoor 30-foot by 30-foot enclosure, many quickly began to make burrows. Rats kept for 30 days in this setting showed even greater brain development than the rats from the laboratory enriched situation. It was suggested from these results that the natural environment was even more enriched in stimulus and response alternatives than the laboratory enriched environment.[4]

All the experiments presented in this section were carried out on nonhuman subjects. What implications do they have for man? Was more learned about man from the correlational EPF field studies on IQ or the more controlled laboratory experiments on rats? The reader should by now have come to the conclusion that such a question may not be very relevant. In some ways it is like asking "Which is better, an apple or an orange?" Both procedures have their advantages and disadvantages. Second, the IVs and DVs under investigation were qualitatively different, making a direct comparison difficult. The results of an investigation in any research area adds another piece to the puzzle, and it is difficult to state which piece is more important. Frequently, the results of an investigation are considered of little importance, only to be found in later years to be extremely valuable. The key to how valuable the findings of some project are is generally more a function of how well secondary variables were controlled (thereby allowing more valid results) than a function of the type of subjects used.

## COMPARATIVE RESEARCH

The psychologist most often thinks of animal investigations in terms of how they aid in better understanding human behavior. There are other reasons, however, for carrying out investigations on animals. The investigator may simply be interested in the behavior of the animal per se. A number

4. *Ibid.*, pp. 511–512. Used by permission of The Dushkin Publishing Group, Inc.

of psychologists analyze the behavior of nonhuman species simply to gain a better understanding of the subject; no effort is made to relate findings in such studies to human behavior.

Animal investigations are also carried out for the sake of determining the possible use of animals to perform tasks most commonly carried out by either humans or machines. This is becoming an interesting avenue of investigation in contemporary psychology. For example, one of the uses to which man has employed animals is in warfare. Hundreds of years ago Hannibal came up with the creative idea of using elephants to fight the Romans. He carted these large mammals all the way from North Africa across the Alps and down through the Italian countryside. Although the elephants were effective beasts of burden, their main use for Hannibal was psychological. The intimidating effect such large and unusual creatures would have on the minds of the Romans was Hannibal's main objective, and a rather effective one, even though he lost.

Another significant contribution was the use of homing pigeons to carry messages during wartime. The messages were inserted into small cannisters with a diameter similar to that of a pen, and the cannisters were attached to the pigeons' legs. When set free, the pigeon, having an extraordinary homing sense, would fly hundreds of miles, when necessary, back to his roost. Pigeons are difficult to hit, especially with an infantryman's rifle, so they were quite valuable for getting information through enemy lines.

During World War II, the British used a simple but effective technique for keeping German submarines out of the English Channel. The Germans were intent on getting into the Channel to disrupt the supply route from England to the Allied forces fighting in France. However, every time they sent a submarine into the Channel, it was sunk. Not until after the war did they find out how the British knew of the presence of their subs. The British would occasionally send their submarines up the Channel and have them surface and throw garbage overboard. Seagulls, having learned that dinner was usually served by submarines, would fly along above the submerged crafts, waiting for them to surface and supply a meal. When sighting a flock of seagulls at sea, spotters on both sides of the Channel would check to see if an Allied sub was scheduled in the area at that time. If not, word was sent out that a German sub was in the area, and it was promptly sunk.

In all these examples, little in the way of complicated experimental manipulation was actually done with animals. Quite a bit of experimental training has, however, been involved in the conditioning of animals for certain tasks. For example, dogs have been trained to work both as guard dogs and medical supply carriers. One of the most unique and interesting projects in which experimental psychologists have become involved occurred during World War II. The Germans had developed the V-2 guided missile, whereas the Allies had no such weapon. A guidance mechanism needed to be developed. Two psychologists, Keller Breland and B. F. Skinner, heard of the problem and decided to try to develop a system by which pigeons could be trained to pilot the missile.[5] The objective was to train a number of Kamikaze pigeons (Figure 13–2). Figure 13–3 diagrammatically shows what was involved.

The pigeon was secured in a cylindrical jacket and placed in the missile in such a manner that he was facing a small monitor screen approximately 3 inches in diameter. The monitor was used just like a small television. A camera was positioned in the nose of the missile. Whatever the camera became focused on was projected on the monitor screen. In this way the pigeon could see whatever was positioned in front of the missile. Covering the monitor screen was a large piece of translucent plastic mounted on small sensing switches placed around its edges. This large circular plastic key served as the means by which the pigeon controlled the missile. Figure 13–4 illustrates what the key and sensing device looked like. If, for example, a ship came on the screen, the pigeon could direct the missile right on the ship by pecking the key at the place containing the image of the ship. In doing so the ship's image could be brought to the center of the crosshairs, which meant the missile was right on target as it sped toward the ship. The pigeons were trained to hone in only on ships and planes bearing the German insignia.

The pigeons could also be used to guide ground-to-ground missiles from, say, England to a particular target in some German town. The missile could be launched in such a manner that it would be projected without the pigeon's

**FIGURE 13–2**
Pigeon in a missile

5. Other psychologists later joined the project.

**FIGURE 13–3**
Pigeon scanning the monitor screen

assistance to the general vicinity of the town. As the aerial view came on the screen, the pigeon (previously conditioned with aerial photographs of the town) would peck at a particular building complex to which he had been trained to respond in the laboratory. In this manner, the pigeon could be trained to be a very sensitive control mechanism—an inexpensive and compact biological computer with very good discriminating capabilities that could not be jammed by the enemy.

**FIGURE 13–4**
Cross section of a missile with a pigeon in the harness

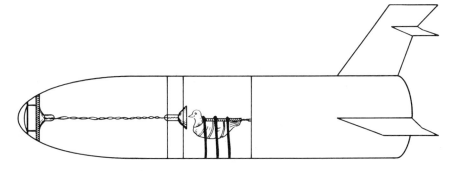

Unfortunately, the story of this project had an unhappy ending in 1943. Representatives from the Office of Scientific Research and Development were given a demonstration of the pigeons in action. Although the birds performed flawlessly, the committee still could not believe what they saw. As Skinner states:

> It was a perfect performance, but it had just the wrong effect. One can talk about phase lag in pursuit behavior and discuss mathematical predictions of hunting without reflecting too closely upon what is inside the black box. But the spectacle of a living pigeon carrying out its assignment, no matter how beautifully, simply reminded the committee of how utterly fantastic our proposal was. I will not say that the meeting was marked by unrestrained merriment, for the merriment was restrained. But it was there, and it was obvious that our case was lost.[6]

Although the committee members felt the project was preposterous, and had it halted, they classified it top secret, thereby not allowing any further work. It was not declassified until the late 1950s.

Many experimental psychologists are currently involved in federally funded projects dealing with the prospective use of animals and their unique abilities for both war and peaceful pursuits. Recently, a group of psychologists at Brigham Young University of which I was a member worked on the idea of using hawks in rescuing people lost in wilderness areas. A hawk has excellent visual acuity and can see a mouse move in a field a mile and a half away. We believed that a hawk could be trained to canvas in a few hours an area that would take days to be covered by men. A hawk could do the job faster, and more thoroughly. Upon spotting the stranded person, the hawk could be trained to land nearby and initiate an electronic pulse sent from the small transmitter he would wear by pulling the string on the transmitter with his talons. The rescue party could then simply follow the beeping to its source and pick up the person. Like the missile project, our investigation ran into problems. The State Fish and Game Board would not issue permits allowing us to keep our three hawks. They already had been trained to select a person out of a crowd after being shown a photograph of the person. After giving a number of reasons why the permits could not be issued (including the one that there are not very many hawks around nowadays), the director of the State Fish and Game Department said the committee felt that such a project was unrealistic.[7]

Research has also been carried out to investigate the potential use of

6. Skinner [1959], p. 426.12. Reprinted with permission of Prentice-Hall, Inc., Englewood Cliffs, New Jersey.

7. We checked with the president of the State Falconers Association, and he said that the hawk population of the state was actually increasing. I returned to the Fish and Game director and asked where he obtained his statistics on the decreasing hawk population. He said, "Well, as you drive down the highway, you hardly see a hawk anymore."

**FIGURE 13–5**

Pigeon working on an assembly line

(Courtesy Thom Verhave.)

animals in industrial situations. Thom Verhave (1966) was engaged by a large pharmaceutical company to investigate the possible use of animals to perform assembly-line tasks that are rather boring for humans. Pigeons were trained to inspect medical capsules moving down an assembly line. Unfortunately, space does not permit a more complete coverage of how this idea was implemented. Within one week, however, Verhave trained the pigeons to peck at a small disc when a bad capsule appeared, causing it to be ejected from the assembly line. Figure 13–5 shows a pigeon inspector at his post. The efficiency of the pigeon was 99 percent, while the efficiency of human inspectors was much lower. William Cummings [1966] employed a similar technique to train pigeons to pick out defective electronic components on an assembly line for a large electronics firm.

## BRAIN DYNAMICS

Like the other research areas presented, brain dynamics is a productive area of investigation in contemporary psychology. In the formative years of psychology many thought that the final answer concerning why man behaves the way he does would ultimately come from a physiological analysis of the brain. Most psychologists now agree that that was a somewhat naive hope, for it implied that there was a final and ultimate end to the quest for knowledge. This of course is not so. Knowledge is a continuum with no absolute end. Each investigation answers some questions about man, but also raises several more. Placed in its proper perspective as one of several important approaches to understanding behavior, physiological psychology has produced possibly more than its share of information. Several investigations will be presented here to give the reader an idea of the types of questions physiological psychologists are dealing with.

### Where Is Information Stored in the Brain?

There is a dominant-hemisphere hypothesis which states that certain learning and memory functions, such as language production, are located in only one cerebral hemisphere, the "dominant" one. The human brain has a right and a left half (hemisphere). These halves are connected mainly by a tract of nerve fibers called the corpus callosum. When the corpus callosum is severed, the separated halves of the brain continue to function. For some years, a group of researchers at the California Institute of Technology have been studying the behavioral and psychological effects of separating or splitting the brain in two. In the 1950s, this work was done on lower animals, but, more recently, interesting work has been performed on human epileptic patients. Severing the corpus callosum has been found to alleviate some otherwise hopeless behavioral problems (for example, severe, dangerous convulsive seizures). In general, all or a substantial part of the epileptic patients' symptoms disappear as a result of these operations, and they are able to resume normal living. What did the cerebral deconnection do to behavior? Studies attempting to answer this question have produced fascinating data, as exemplified by an EPF laboratory study conducted by Sperry and Gazzaniga [1968] on eleven serious epileptic patients who had to have their corpus callosums severed.[8]

The effects of separating the hemispheres are not obvious, and ordinary behavior appears to be unaffected. However, appropriate tests can demonstrate important changes, especially in vision. By controlling visual input in such a way that only one hemisphere receives information, the memory and information-processing capacities of each brain half can be investigated. This method is made possible by the fact that each half of the visual field of each eye is connected to only one hemisphere. Facing forward with the viewer, the right side of the visual field is received on the left side of each eyeball, which is connected to the left hemisphere. Similarly, the left side of

8. Rubenstein [1975], p. 573. Used by permission of The Dushkin Publishing Group, Inc.

the visual field is received on the right side of each eyeball, which is connected to the right hemisphere of the brain.

To control visual input, the subject is placed in front of two screens and is asked to fix his vision on a point midway between the screens. When he does this, visual information on the right screen reaches the left hemisphere only, while stimuli on the left reach the right hemisphere only.

Under these circumstances, right-handed disconnected subjects will respond normally to any object in their right visual field (or right hand): shown a pencil or handed a pencil in his right hand, a subject will say, "That is a pencil." But the same object, when presented to the left visual field (or left hand), will elicit different answers: the subject will say he saw only a flash of light with no details or that his left hand feels numb. What is happening here is that the subject's language-production capacities are located only in the left hemisphere. Consequently, when the subject answers a question verbally, only his left hemisphere is speaking—and the left hemisphere does not know what is happening in the left visual field or the left hand.

Does this mean the right hemisphere is "inferior" to the left? The right hemisphere does lack language-production capacities, but further tests showed that the right hemisphere can understand verbal instructions, and when objects are placed in the left hand, the right hemisphere can identify them by pointing with the left hand at pictures on the left screen. In other words, though the right hemisphere cannot verbally name or describe an object, it can identify the object by using gestures, or it can even draw with the left hand what it sees in the left visual field. Sperry [1968] also showed that if the word "key" appears in the left visual field and "case" in the right, the subject will say he does not know what he saw on the left, but he still can search with the left hand and find a key. But when he is asked what he holds in his left hand, the subject says it is a case of some sort.

These simple but dramatic demonstrations show that two independent, conscious brains are produced by cerebral disconnection, two brains that can no longer communicate with each other directly. As the cliche goes, the left hand does not know what the right hand is doing. Because only the left hemisphere can produce language, the right half is "speechless" but nevertheless functional and capable of understanding and intellectual performance. The left hand, controlled by the speechless right hemisphere, cannot write language either.

Normally, the brain halves can communicate with each other and exchange information originally detected only by one half. But with cerebral bisection, the hemispheres function independently. The fact that each independent half receives only part of the perceptual information is not a serious handicap for the former epileptic patients in their daily lives, where their behavior is indistinguishable from other people's. It is not a handicap because most of the time both hemispheres receive that same perceptual information anyway, and all verbalization is controlled by the "dominant" left hemisphere (in the case of right-handed people, who are in the majority). The dominant hemisphere is also slightly larger than the other one, and its dominance extends to the normal individual's handedness preferences. It is interesting that Sperry also notes that the right, nonspeaking hemisphere appears to be superior to the left (dominant) in understanding spatial and geometric relationships. For example, when duplicating a pattern of blocks, the right hemisphere (left hand) does it quickly and smoothly, while the left hemisphere (right hand) must go slowly, a step at a time.[9]

### What Influences Information Storage in the Brain?

One of the most popular methods for testing and measuring consolidation processes in the brain has been the use of electroconvulsive shock. In this method, an animal learns some simple response to a stimulus, and then a strong electrical current is passed through its brain. When the animal is placed in the same learning situation as before, will it be able to remember to make the same response? If there is a consolidation process, then the electroconvulsive shock may succeed in disrupting that process and make the animal forget what it learned. Some years ago, Duncan [1948] performed the first experiment of this kind, and his results tended to show that the shock could disrupt consolidation and "erase" what the animal had learned. Because there were interpretive problems with Duncan's early procedure, more recent investigators have sought ways to define more clearly what is involved and how long the supposed consolidation process must take before the animal has a "permanent," nonerasable memory. One experiment dealing with these issues was performed by Kopp, Bohdanecky and Jarvik [1966] and is described below.

Mice were assigned to one of three general conditions. All mice were placed in the brighter of two connected boxes. Under these circumstances, a mouse will soon approach the darker box and enter it. The animals in the experimental condition received a severe, punishing shock (not electroconvulsive) to their feet as they stepped through the opening. Ordinarily, this one experience is enough to make a mouse totally reluctant to ever step through into darkness again; thus this mouse has learned to avoid the dark box. Could it be made to forget what it learned?

After this one learning trial, the animals in the experimental group received electroconvulsive shock (ECS) at different intervals of time, one interval per mouse: 5, 20, 80, 320 seconds, one hour, or six hours after learning. One control group received the same learning trial (foot shock), but no subsequent ECS. A second control group received no punishing shock, but did receive ECS 10 seconds after stepping through.

All mice were given a retention test twenty-four hours after learning

9. *Ibid.*, pp. 573–574. Used by permission of The Dushkin Publishing Group, Inc.

by placing them again in the two-chamber box. The experimenter then recorded how much time passed before a mouse entered the darker box. As can be seen in Table 13–2, the mice in the main control group (no ECS) only rarely returned to the darkened box: they remembered to avoid it. For the experimental mice, the sooner they had received ECS after learning, the more likely they were to forget, and therefore step through sooner. The second control group, having received no punishment, quickly went to the darkened box in an average time of 5 seconds.

**TABLE 13–2**
*Results of experiment using electroconvulsive shock*

| Time interval ECS administered after learning | Typical retest time (in median seconds) |
|---|---|
| 5 seconds | 9.3 |
| 20 seconds | 27.8 |
| 80 seconds | 50.3 |
| 320 seconds | 82.8 |
| 1 hour | 127.7 |
| 6 hours | 195.0 |

Source: Kopp, Bohdanecky, and Jarvik [1966], p. 1548.
Copyright 1966 by the American Association for the Advancement of Science.

This study illustrates what is called consolidation. The sooner ECS occurs after the original learning experience, the more likely it is that the experience will be forgotten. Evidently memory processes are time-dependent. Other studies have shown that, after eight hours, administration of ECS will no longer affect long-term memory, and the animal will always avoid punishment just as non-ECS animals do.[10]

### How Is Information Stored in the Brain?

The issue concerning the exact form in which information is stored in the brain is one of the most enticing areas of investigation in psychology. Unfortunately, we cannot yet say that "this exact area of the brain holds this exact information in this specific form." We are still performing somewhat general research to identify general substances or sites in the brain that are involved in information storage. One hypothesis on information storage put forth by Holger Hydén proposes that RNA (ribonucleic acids) are the chemical containers of information. In an effort to throw some light on this idea, Hydén [1970] carried out a laboratory experiment on rats.

Like people, rats are usually right- or left-handed: when they use their paws in complex movements, they prefer to use one paw or the other. In one

10. *Ibid.*, pp. 577–578. Used by permission of The Dushkin Publishing Group, Inc.

experiment, right-handed rats were trained to use the left paw to retrieve food from far down a narrow glass tube. Training took place over a period of days, with each rat receiving two training sessions of 25 minutes each per day. After five or six days, the rat could readily retrieve the food from the glass, quickly and smoothly, with its initially "nonpreferred" left paw.

At this point, the rats were killed and their brains analyzed for chemical changes. It was found that there were increases in the amount of RNA per cell on the learning (right) side of the brain cortex surface that corresponds to the left hand. This increase was relative to the amount of RNA present in control rats whose brain cells were analyzed on the first or second day of training, before the response had been learned well. The increase was also relative to the same rats' cells on the other side of the brain, which had not received training.

In the second study, Hydén trained animals to walk up a wire placed at an angle of 45 degrees to the floor in order to obtain food. When the animals had learned to perform the task well, they were killed, and cells of the brain-stem vestibular nuclei were analyzed for the amount of RNA present. The vestibular nuclei are brain cells involved in gravity perception and balance, those abilities that had to be trained in the animals who learned to walk the wire. An increase in the amount of RNA in the cells of the vestibular nuclei occurred after training.[11]

As you may have guessed, a fair amount of research in physiological psychology is carried out on nonhuman species. Most of the research on humans is EPF in nature and employs correlational and case study analysis, as exemplified by the work of Penfield reported in this chapter in the section on memory. Ethics is obviously one reason for the small percentage of physiological experiments on humans, but it certainly is not the only reason. In an earlier chapter it was mentioned that nonhuman species are often used by psychologists even when humans are available because psychologists can have greater control of secondary variables, and generality between humans and nonhumans is the rule rather than the exception. The principle of generality is especially true in physiological investigations, as we know from the vast amount of comparative biological research that has been done in the areas of physiology, anatomy, biochemistry, medicine, and pharmacology.

## AGGRESSION—A SOCIAL RESEARCH ISSUE

One person's influence on another has always been an important research dimension in psychology. Although the psychologist is mostly concerned with determining characteristics of individuals (in contrast to sociol-

---

11. *Ibid.*, p. 579. Used by permission of The Dushkin Publishing Group, Inc.

ogists, for example, who are more interested in group dynamics), psychology as a discipline spends a good portion of its time analyzing the relationships between people.

The social situations in which a person finds himself are possibly the major variable or class of variables that determine what he is and how he acts. A subarea of psychology has evolved in which the prime interest is the study of individuals in their social context. This area is appropriately termed social psychology. The range of interests of social psychologists may be shown by listing some of the issues with which they deal: the generation gap, drug use in society, the population explosion, aggression, violence and bystander apathy, group structure and leadership, and coercive persuasion (brainwashing).

Research on one of these topics, aggression, is presented to give the reader an idea of what is currently going on in this area. There is a second purpose to this section, and that is to show that no one area of psychology stands by itself. It is difficult to make a neat separation of some psychological subarea from other areas of psychological study. Although a particular topic such as aggression may generally be considered to come under the heading of one particular subfield, many subfields are generally involved in researching the issue. Many facets of any issue must be analyzed before an adequate understanding is reached. The research to be presented here comes from social psychology, ethology, comparative psychology, physiological psychology, clinical psychology, and learning psychology.

A major contribution to the study of aggression has come about through ethology. The subject has been of particular interest to ethologists because aggression occurs frequently in nature and appears in almost every species, from the lowly insects to the highest limb of the phylogenetic tree primates. Using the method of systematic observation, ethologists have investigated the behavior of animals in field situations and proposed that aggressive behavior is largely instinctual in nature. This conclusion has been drawn because of the frequency of occurrence observed in natural settings and frequency in showing up from one species to another. For example, Alexander [1961] noted that aggressive hierarchies are found in some insects. Male crickets were observed to kick with their hind legs, butt with their heads, and bite with their mandibles. Encounters between males that rank next to each other on the dominance scale were usually more intense than encounters between highly dominant and highly submissive males. Van Lawick and Goodall [Hinde, 1968] systematically observed that chimpanzees become more aggressive when the food supply becomes exhausted. They also noted that on many occasions one animal threatens its grooming partner when the latter stops grooming.

An alternative approach for analyzing aggressiveness is exemplified in a physiologically oriented experiment performed by Smith, King, and Hoebel

[1970]. Rather than observe subjects in the field, they actively manipulated an IV in a laboratory experiment in an effort to identify brain mechanisms involved in killing. After selecting rats as their subjects, they divided their subjects into two groups: killers and nonkillers. Some rats seem to kill spontaneously while others do not. In a methodical and deliberate manner, the killer rat will approach the mouse and bite its victim in a particular place in the neck, severing the backbone. Killers were defined as any rat that killed his companion mouse in less than two minutes from the time they were put together.

Small cannular tubes were then implanted in the rats' brains, allowing chemicals to be administered directly to the hypothalamic region.[12] In the first of their experiments, carbachol (a chemical similar to the naturally occurring neurohumers in the brain that transmit information from one neuron to the next) was injected in half of the nonkillers, while the other half of nonkillers were given a salt solution injection. Carbachol elicited killing in all 12 of the nonkiller rats that received it, while none of the rats receiving the salt solution killed mice. The killing behavior pattern of the carbachol-injected rats was noted to be identical to those of killer rats, although they had never seen a killer rat in action prior to receiving the drug. Smith et al. carried out several related experiments and concluded:

1. There is an instinctual brain mechanism for killing that may be normally inactive.
2. The amount of acetylecholone (a chemical transmitter in the brain) a rat has is important in determining whether he kills.
3. The hypothalamus is the area of the brain in which this killing mechanism is housed.

Laboratory experiments dealing with aggression have also been carried out on humans. For example, Berkowitz and LePage [1967] performed an experiment to determine whether weapons "elicit" aggression in people.[13] One hundred male college students served as subjects; they were divided into six groups. Table 13–3 shows how the groups were treated. The numbers in the table indicate a particular group of subjects. Subjects were worked with one at a time.

When a subject arrived in the laboratory, he was informed that two men were required for the experiment and the that second man had not shown up. He was then asked to find someone else (actually a confederate) to serve

12. The hypothalamus is a small area of the brain that has known control centers for behaviors such as eating, drinking, and sexual activity.

13. This goes along with the current argument that if policemen did not carry guns, there would be less violence.

**TABLE 13–3**
*A 3 × 2 factorial design specifying six conditions of the experiment*

| Treatment by Confederate | Subjects Told That the Weapons Present: | | No Weapons Present |
| | *"Belong to confederate"* | *"Left by previous experimenter"* | |
| --- | --- | --- | --- |
| Angered | 1 | 2 | 3 |
| Not angered | 4 | 5 | 6 |

Source: McGuigan and Woods [1972], p. 253. Used with permission of Prentice-Hall, Inc., Englewood Cliffs, New Jersey.

as a substitute. The subject and confederate were asked to list ideas a publicity agent might use in order to improve a popular singer's record sales and public image. They were then told each would evaluate the other's ideas. After both had written their list, their papers were exchanged and the confederate was to evaluate the other person's first. The subject was hooked up to a shocker and told he would be given from one to ten mild shocks by the other subject depending on how good his list was considered to be. One shock meant the list was very good; ten shocks meant the list was very poor. Actually the confederate made no such evaluation, but half of the subjects in the experiment were given seven shocks (defined as angered in this situation), while the other half received only one shock (defined as not angered).

After a subject had been shocked, the confederate was supposedly hooked up to the shocker while the subject went to a room containing a button that supposedly allowed him to shock the confederate. The subject was then to read the confederate's list and shock him from one to ten times according to how good he felt the list was. When the experimenter brought the subject into the room containing the shock button and apparatus, there was also either a weapon (shotgun) present or not. If a weapon was present, the subject was told that it belonged to either the confederate or to someone else who had been using it in some other experiment and had accidentally left it behind. The number of shocks a subject administered to the confederate in each of the six groups served as the DV. Table 13–4 shows the mean number of shocks given by subjects of each group. The authors drew these conclusions:

1. Aggressive behavior is more likely to occur in situations where weapons are present than absent.
2. Someone angered is much more likely to act aggressively when weapons are present.
3. More attention should be paid to aggression-provoking stimuli in the environment.

**TABLE 13–4**
Mean number of shocks given in each condition

| Treatment by Confederate | Subjects Told That the Weapons Present: | | No Weapons Present |
|---|---|---|---|
| | *"Belong to confederate"* | *"Left by previous experimenter"* | |
| Angered | Condition 1 6.07 | Condition 2 5.67 | Condition 3 4.67 |
| Not angered | Condition 4 2.60 | Condition 5 2.20 | Condition 6 3.07 |

Source: McGuigan and Woods [1972], p. 255. Used with permission of Prentice-Hall, Inc., Englewood Cliffs, New Jersey.

The contrast method of investigation has also been employed in studying aggression. R. H. Seiden [1966] carried out an investigation on student suicide, aggression toward oneself. Using data collected on 23 University of California at Berkeley students who committed suicide during the ten-year period 1952 to 1961, he contrasted suicides with the entire student body population on certain variables, as shown in Table 13–5.

Some of the main conclusions of the study were these:

1. *Concern over studies*—In many cases acquaintances of the students made such judgments as he "pushed himself too hard," "worried over grades," "felt his grades were not as good as they should be," or described similar scholastic anxieties which, they felt, triggered the suicidal crisis. It is difficult to evaluate these inferences, since "worry over grades" is often seen by informants as a most likely explanation. In any event, if true, their exaggerated concern over studies contrasted vividly with generally excellent academic grades.

2. *Unusual physical complaints*—A number of the students complained of inability to eat or sleep. Others worried about possible deterioration, such as the student who feared that his "failing sight" might ruin a prospective medical career. A few pupils, however, presented physical complaints of a bizarre, semidelusional quality.

3. *Difficulties with interpersonal relationships*—Combined under this heading were two different types of conflicts, both reflecting problems in personal relationships. First were the students involved in stormy love affairs. Here the critical stresses were feelings of rejection that had been engendered by broken romances. Much more typical, however, was the essentially asocial, withdrawn student. These particular students were uniformly described as terribly shy, virtually friendless and alienated from all but the most minimal social interactions.

TABLE 13–5
Selected demographic characteristics of suicidal and nonsuicidal students at the University of California at Berkeley, 1952–1961

| Demographic characteristics | Suicidal students (*percentage*) | Total student body population (*percentage*) | Do groups differ significantly? |
|---|---|---|---|
| *Age* | | | |
| Under 25 | 39 | 70 | Yes |
| 25 and above | 61 | 30 | |
| *Class standing* | | | |
| Undergraduate | 52 | 72 | Yes |
| Graduate | 48 | 28 | |
| *Sex* | | | |
| Male | 74 | 67 | No |
| Female | 26 | 33 | |
| *Marital status* | | | |
| Married | 14 | 23 | No |
| Never married | 86 | 77 | |
| *Nationality* | | | |
| USA | 83 | 96 | Yes |
| Foreign | 17 | 4 | |
| *Major subject* | | | |
| Language and literature | 25 | 9 | Yes |
| All other majors | 75 | 91 | |
| *Grade-point average* | | | |
| Undergraduate | | | |
| Above mean | 91 | 50 | Yes |
| Below mean | 9 | 50 | |
| Graduate | | | |
| Above mean | 40 | 50 | No |
| Below mean | 60 | 50 | |
| *Mental-health service* | | | |
| Psychiatric patient | 34 | 10 | Yes |
| Nonpatient | 66 | 90 | |

Source: Seiden [1966], Table 1, p. 391. Copyright 1966 by the American Psychological Association. Reprinted by permission.

## MEMORY

The concept of memory has always been an exciting research topic in psychology because it is viewed as a study of higher mental processes that cannot be directly observed. The first major studies of memory were carried out by Hermann Ebbinghaus at about the time psychology as a separate discipline was born. Using himself as a subject, he studied such things as how many times it was necessary to repeat something before it was committed to memory. Ebbinghaus' work made such a great impact that it is estimated more experiments have been based on his research than on any other single source in the history of psychology. Some of the dimensions along which current research in memory is moving include: What influences the ability to remember? What causes forgetting? and, Is memory stored for years?

### What Influences
### the Ability to Remember?

One variable known to influence one's ability to remember is "meaningfulness." One investigation that analyzed the effects of meaningfulness of words was carried out by Cieutat, Stockwell, and Noble [1958]. One hundred and seventy college students were divided into four groups. Each student was shown ten pairs of words (e.g., apple-spoon, chair-coat). Later the first word of each pair (apple, chair) was presented one at a time and the subject was to respond by verbalizing the paired word. For one group (L-L), both the first and second word of each pair were of low meaningfulness (e.g., matrix, femur). For a second group (H-H), both words were much more meaningful (e.g., army, kitchen). A third group (L-H) learned a list in which the first word was low in meaning while the second word was high in meaning. The fourth group (H-L) was given high-meaning first words and low-meaning second words. The percentage of correct responses of the second word when shown the first were recorded for each trial (each presentation of the list). Figure 13–6 shows the results, indicating meaningfulness does influence the rate of learning.[14]

### What Causes Forgetting?

A number of theories attempt to explain why people forget things they have learned. One theory suggests that forgetting occurs because memories interfere with each other. In support of this idea, Jenkins and Dallenbach [1924] carried out an investigation using two college students as subjects. Both were given different lists to learn at various times and were asked to recall them under different conditions (e.g., after sleeping or after being awake so many hours). The subjects remembered far more words after being asleep than after an equivalent time of wakefulness. These results suggest that new memories formed from activities while a person is awake interfere with recall.

Skinner [1960] also carried out a long-term experiment that supported the interference theory of forgetting. After his pigeon-guided missile project was shelved, he retained several birds that had been trained during the war.

14. *Ibid.*, pp. 426–427. Used by permission of The Dushkin Publishing Group, Inc.

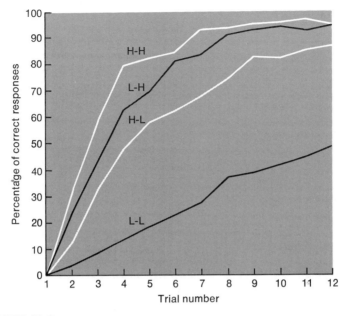

**FIGURE 13–6**

Results of a verbal learning experiment

(Adapted from Cieutat, Stockwell, & Noble [1958], Figure 1. Copyright 1958 by the American Psychological Association. Reprinted by permission.)

For seven years he kept them individually housed in their small home cages without any further training. At the end of seven years he put them back in the original training apparatus, and all the birds immediately began pecking at the precise feature they had been trained to peck.

### Is Memory Stored for Years?

A famous brain surgeon, Wilder Penfield, has analyzed the memory functions of the brain by electrically stimulating the cerebral cortex at different points. These operations can be carried out with local anesthetics with the subject totally conscious. He has found that stimulating certain areas causes past memories to be recalled. Commenting on two of his patients, he stated:

Occasionally during the course of a neurosurgical operation under local anesthesia, gentle electrical stimulation in the temporal area, right or left, has caused the conscious patient to be aware of some previous experience. The experience seems to be picked out at random from his own past. It comes back to him in great detail. . . . A woman heard an orchestra playing an air while the electrode was held in place. The music stopped when the electrode was removed. It came again when the electrode was reapplied. On request, she hummed the tune, while the electrode was held in place, accompanying the orchestra. It was a popular song. Over and over again, restimulation of the same spot produced the same song. The music seemed always to begin at the same place and to progress at the normally expected tempo. All efforts to mislead her failed. She believed that a gramaphone was being turned on in the operating room on each occasion, and she asserted her belief stoutly in a conversation some days after the operation.

A boy heard his mother talking to someone on the telephone when an electrode was applied to his right temporal cortex. When the stimulus was repeated without warning, he heard his mother again in the same conversation. When the stimulus was repeated after a lapse of time, he said, "My mother is telling my brother he has got his coat on backwards. I can just hear them." The surgeon then asked the boy whether he remembered this happening. "Oh yes," he said, "just before I came here."[15]

## PERSONALITY

Chapter Six described some evaluative measures that are generally considered to be the sole property of psychology. These include psychometric tests, personal interviews, projective tests, and personality rating scales. Because the objective of this field of psychology is to define the pool from which traits were drawn to make up the variety of human personalities, the objective of the personality psychologist is similar to that of the chemist of decades gone by who set out to identify the basic chemical elements (known now to be slightly over 100) from which the thousands of different physical materials are derived. The personality psychologist wants to identify the basic elements of man's personality and how they combine to make the uniqueness of individual differences. Unfortunately, psychologists are not as far along in identifying their basic elements as are the chemists. We are still in the formative stages, and there are many theories. The investigations presented here do not necessarily represent the most popular personality theories in psychology today; they have been chosen simply to give the reader an idea of what can be and is being done in this area.

### What Are the Origins of Personality?

One theory of personality attributes variations to genetic differences in physiology and anatomy. One of the well-known constitutional theories was formulated by William Sheldon in 1940. He claimed that personalities could be divided into three main categories: viscerotonic (good-natured and food-oriented people), somatotonic (aggressive and activity-oriented people), and cerebrotonic (sensitive and intellectual people). Constitutional theories such

15. Penfield [1959], p. 1721. Used by permission. Copyright 1959 by the American Association for the Advancement of Science.

as Sheldon's suggest that the differences between people that exist at birth will determine to a large degree their personality throughout life. Certain recent investigations in psychology have supported this position. Thomas, Chess, and Birch [1971] carried out an EPF correlational field study that attempted to identify consistent personality differences in very young infants over a period of years. Various measures were used, including interviews, systematic observation, and psychometric tests. They measured behaviors of 141 children, starting at two and three months of age.

Initially, the most important measures were ratings of the two-and three-month-old infants' behavior. Each baby was scored on a three-point scale (high, medium, and low) for such things as overall activity level, acceptance of new experiences, and adaptability to changes in the environment. All the data were analyzed and combined in terms of three "types" of infant temperament, which were called "easy," "slow to warm up," and "difficult." Of the children studied, 65 percent could be categorized as having one of the three types of temperament, and the other 35 percent displayed a mixture of traits. These differences were apparent at two months of age.

The behavior of many of the children was observed in the months and years following the original assessment. Later behavior cannot be attributed to any one set of factors, since temperamental and environmental factors (such as parental treatment) become inextricably intertwined. However, the researchers did note that "as a child grows, his temperament tends to remain constant in quality: if he wriggles while his diaper is being changed at two months, his high activity level is likely to be expressed at one year through eager eating and a tendency 'to climb into everything.' A five-year-old child who behaved quietly in infancy may dress slowly and be able to sit quietly and happily during long automobile rides."[16]

### What Are Some Dimensions
### That Differentiate Personalities?

Not all psychologists have taken the same approach as Sheldon. Raymond B. Cattell conducted a long-term research program to reduce all possible descriptions of personality to a finite and manageable number of dimensions. After reviewing over 18,000 words used to describe personality, he came up with 171 traits he felt represented the building blocks for all personalities. The 171 were condensed into a smaller number of what he termed "source traits." In 1965, Cattell published a book in which he reported an EPF correlational field study he had carried out.

Over a period of years psychological tests were devised and administered to thousands of people. All 171 of the dimensions of Cattell's personality

---

16. Rubenstein [1975], p. 251. Used by permission of The Dushkin Publishing Group, Inc.

sphere were represented in the tests. The scores on some of the tests turned out to be correlated; that is, a person who scored high on one also tended to score high on another. When test scores correlate in this manner, they can be viewed as measuring the same factors to some degree. What factor analysis does is describe the underlying factor or dimension responsible for correlations among tests. By using it, Cattell was able to reduce the 171 traits to 19 factors or source traits. Variations on these dimensions encompass and "explain" variations in performance on all 171 traits. Note that factor analysis did not throw out dimensions until only 19 were left; rather, all the dimensions were collapsed or combined into only 19. Those 19 source traits, in essence, contained the same meanings as the original personality sphere.

The words used to label the 19 source traits were to some extent arbitrary choices. The final list appears in Table 13–6, where traits with strange names are described enough to give you an idea of what the dimension involves. Unlike the 171 traits of the sphere, these 19 factors are relatively independent of each other. That is, scoring near one end of one dimension does not predict one's score on some other dimension.[17]

**TABLE 13–6**
*Personality dimensions as identified by Cattell using factor analysis*

| Factor | Polar ends of the dimension |
|--------|------------------------------|
| A | Cyclothymia (easygoing, frank, generous, warmhearted) vs. schizothymia (obstructive, indifferent, secretive, impassive) |
| B | Intelligence vs. unintelligence |
| C | Ego strength (mature, patient, stoic, unworried) vs. ego weakness (infantile, impatient, anxious, worrying) |
| D | Activity vs. inactivity |
| E | Domination vs. subordination (submissive) |
| F | Surgency (enthusiastic, talkative) vs. desurgency (silent, brooding) |
| G | Superego strength (conscientious, responsible, persevering) vs. superego weakness (unscrupulous, irresolute, undependable) |
| H | Parmia (carefree, brave) vs. threctia (careful, cowardly) |
| I | Premsia (sensitive, sentimental) vs. haria (insensitive, callous) |
| J | Coasthenia (self-oriented, independent) vs. zeppia (dependent, group-oriented) |
| K | Comention (cultured, elegant) vs. abcultion (crude, awkward, uncouth) |
| L | Protension (suspicious, wary) vs. security (trustful, gullible) |
| M | Autia (self-absorbed, abstract) vs. praxernia (earnest, practical, outward) |
| N | Shrewdness vs. naivete |
| O | Guilt proclivity (timid, depressed) vs. guilt rejection (self-confident) |
| Q(1) | Radicalism vs. conservatism |
| Q(2) | Self-sufficiency vs. group sufficiency (seeking social approval) |
| Q(3) | Controlled will vs. uncontrolled will (taking chances) |
| Q(4) | Id significance (frustrated, anxious) vs. id insignificance (relaxed, composed) |

Source: Cattel [1965]. Used by permission of Penguin Books.

17. *Ibid.*, pp. 256–257. Used by permission of The Dushkin Publishing Group, Inc.

Notice that both investigations on personality reported here were EPF studies. The analysis of personality as it is most frequently carried out in psychology does not lend itself well to experimental investigation. Many have argued that this is the main reason little headway has been made in this area of research. Another possible reason is the subjectivity of the terminology and variables being investigated. Kissler [1972] suggests that one of the main reasons a personality approach to analysis has been somewhat elusive is that the terms and variables dealt with need to be more operationally defined (the point is well taken for any psychological investigation).

## PERCEPTION

Perception is commonly defined as the process by which an organism interprets and catalogs incoming sensory information. Stimuli (light, heat, sound, movement, and so forth) are constantly bombarding the sensory receptors of all organisms. The process by which this stimulation takes on meaning and significance is the focal point of perceptual research, which is divided into two main areas: research investigating sensory systems of the body and how they deal with incoming stimuli, and research aimed at identifying the processes that convert this sensory information into perception. An eigthteenth-century Scottish philosopher, Thomas Reid, exemplified this distinction when he commented that the various receptor systems of the body "sensed" redness, roundness, and pleasant odor. The brain then transformed these sensations into the "perception" of a rose.

### To What Extent
### Are Perceptual Capacities Innate ?

Just as the psychologist is interested in distinguishing those aspects of learning that are innate and those that are developed through experience, so is the perception researcher interested in dichotomizing perception in the same way. But the dichotomy is not discovered through one investigation or even one line of research, it must be approached from a number of different routes, as exemplified by the previous section on aggression. One area of perceptual research that has sought answers to innate components of perception has to do with the question of whether depth and space perception are innate perceptual abilities.

Gibson and Walk [1960] carried out an EPF laboratory study with human infants to determine their ability to discriminate depth. Infants who were just beginning to crawl (six months to one year old) were placed in the center of the apparatus shown in Figure 13–7. Observations and measurements were made of where they crawled. Some infants consistently

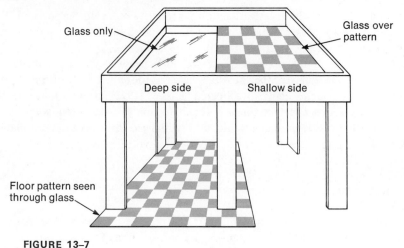

**FIGURE 13–7**
A visual cliff for depth perception investigations

avoided the "deep" side of the table, refusing to crawl across it even when their mothers called to them. When called from the "deep" side, some infants crawled in the opposite direction; others cried but still refused to cross the apparent chasm. The study indicates that most human infants can discriminate depth as soon as they can crawl. It does not prove that depth perception is innate in humans, however, because the infants already had a lot of visual experience.

How might an investigator change his experiment to decrease the possibility that subjects' resistance to stepping off a cliff was due to prior learning? The same problem was discussed in Chapter Five, where it was shown that a subject's ability to learn some task without making mistakes wasn't due to prior experience. The solution employed in that situation was to pick a type of subject that is mobile at birth. Walk and Gibson [1961] did the same thing. They used baby and adult chickens, goats, turtles, and rats. With some variation from species to species, the same general procedure was followed for all animal subjects. Each was placed on the center of the table, on the platform between the "deep" and "shallow" sides of the visual cliff. If the subject consistently avoided the deep side, it was considered capable of perceiving depth.

Some of the animals were reared from birth in darkness, while others had lived in light. All definitely tended to avoid the deep side of the cliff—both light-reared and dark-reared rats, infant goats, and chicks. There were some species differences: for example, turtles seemed to have less aversion to the apparent chasm than other animals. Taken together, the data strongly imply that depth perception is for the most part innate in many species.

### How Is the Perceptual Organization of Coordinated Movements Influenced?

One hypothesis states that feedback is necessary before stimulus-response relationships can be developed. The ability of a person to reach out and pick up a perceived object has been found to be dependent on simultaneous visual and kinesthetic feedback. Held and Hein [1968] carried out an experimental investigation to study such relationships.

Kittens were raised in total darkness from birth to an age of about ten weeks. From then on, they spent three hours a day, in pairs, using the gondola apparatus shown in Figure 13–8. The rest of the time they were kept in the dark. The experimental apparatus, as the illustration shows, allowed both kittens to have the same view of the cylinder, but permitted only one of

**FIGURE 13–8**

Kitty trolley for restricting motor movement

(From Held & Hein [1963]. Copyright 1963 by the American Psychological Association. Reprinted by permission.)

them—the "active" kitten—to push the gondola around. If visual experience alone was sufficient for visual-motor coordination, the experimenters reasoned, the "passive" kittens should do as well on coordination tests as their active partners. On the other hand, if both vision and feedback from self-produced movement are necessary, then the active kittens should perform better on the tests.

In the first test of visual-motor coordination, the experimenter held a kitten in his hands and moved the animal forward and down toward the edge of a table. A normal kitten extends its paws as it approaches the table edge, anticipating contact. In every pair of kittens in this experiment—they were tested after each three-hour session—the first kitten to respond normally was the active one.

When tested on the visual cliff, all the active kittens behaved normally, choosing the shallow side of the cliff every time they were tested. The passive kittens showed no indication that they could tell the two sides apart. These results confirm the importance of self-produced movement as well as visual experience for the development of coordinated behavior.[18]


## LEARNING PSYCHOLOGY

Research on learning covers one of the broadest spectrums of any research area: it includes educational instruction, concept learning, and physiological correlates of learning. Since several research examples on instructional research and some of the more common dimensions of learning have already been presented, two less publicized issues currently gaining much attention in psychology are discussed here. These issues deal with the questions "Is there such a thing as state-dependent learning?" and "Can one learn to control physiological processes?"


### Is There State-Dependent Learning?

Can a person know how to perform a task when under the influence of alcohol or some other drug, yet not know how to perform the same task when not drugged? Most people are familiar with the morning-after syndrome in which the suffering husband asks his wife whether he had a good time at last night's party. What student has not had the experience of learning text material thoroughly in his or her room, and yet not quite been able to retrieve that locked-in knowledge during a classroom examination. The phenomenon of learning some behavior in one condition, yet being unable to reproduce it in another is termed *state dependent learning*.

18. *Ibid.*, p. 397. Used by permission of The Dushkin Publishing Group, Inc.

Goodwin, Powell, Bremer, Hoine, and Stern [1969] carried out an investigation to determine whether some types of tasks are more state-dependent than others.

The subjects were 48 male medical students paid to participate in a training session (Day 1) and a testing session (Day 2) separated by 24 hours. They were randomly assigned to four groups of 12 subjects each. One group (SS) was sober on both the training day and also on the test day. (The letters S and A indicate whether the subjects were "sober" or "alcoholic," and the order of S and A indicate the day for the state.) A second group (AA) was intoxicated both days. A third group (AS) was intoxicated on Day 1 and sober on Day 2. And the fourth group (SA) was sober on the training day and intoxicated on the test day. Intoxicated subjects, depending on body weight, consumed between 8 and 10 ounces of 80-proof vodka, diluted in a soft drink, over a 1-hour period, after which testing began. All subjects drinking this amount showed outward signs of intoxication. (Concentrations of alcohol in the blood of these subjects, as determined by breath analyses, varied from 80 to 140 mg/ml, with a mean of 111 mg/100 ml.) Equivalent amounts of the soft drink were given to nondrinkers. The subjects knew in advance that they might receive alcohol but had no other knowledge of the experiment.

Tests were administered in the same order to all subjects over a 40-minute period. The tests, specified later, were designed to measure interference, recall, and recognition. To measure interference an avoidance task was used. The subject was randomly presented four different patterns of lights. Each pattern could be turned off by a different switch controlled by the subject's hands or feet. If the subject made an incorrect response, that is, chose the incorrect switch for the particular pattern on display, or failed to respond at all, he was presented with a noxious tone. The term "avoidance task" is thus used to indicate that the subject tried to *avoid* the unpleasant tone. The subjects worked at this avoidance task until they were able to produce a series of 20 correct responses. The total number of errors that they made was taken as the measure of performance. The task was identical on both the training and testing days, *except* that on the test day the correct switch for each pattern was changed from what it was on Day 1. Thus the subjects' performance on the task on Day 2 reflected *interference*; that is, the greater the number of errors on Day 2, the greater the amount of *interference* from the Day 1 experience.

Recall was measured by a verbal *rote learning task*. The subjects memorized four five-word "sentences" varying in meaningfulness. Meaningfulness was varied by using a normal sentence, an irregular sentence, a series of anagrams, and a list of unrelated words as the tasks to be learned by rote. On Day 2 the subjects were asked to recall the "sentences" that they had memorized on Day 1, and then a relearning session was conducted. Performance was measured as the number of errors made in recalling the sequence of words.

Recall was also measured by using a *word association test*. The test consisted of 10 words that had been previously shown to produce few associations for most people; such words are called *low association words*. The subjects were instructed to respond to each of the 10 words with the first word that came to mind. On Day 2 the stimulus words were repeated and the subjects were asked to recall the response that they had made on Day 1. (Words with low association values were used to cut down on the possible interference of a large number of associations and to relate more directly to the subject's ability to remember what it was he had associated on Day 1.) The performance measure was the number of mistakes made on the recall test on Day 2.

Memory recognition was measured by using a task involving pictures. The subjects were shown 20 pictures on Day 1, and on Day 2 they were asked to select these same pictures from a total of 40 pictures. Half of the pictures, showing mail-order catalogue models, were designated as "neutral," half were chosen from nudist magazines and were designated as "emotional."[19]

Table 13–7 shows the average number of errors for each group. The conclusions drawn were that simple recall and interference were most clearly influenced by state change, whereas picture recognition was relatively uninfluenced by state change.

**TABLE 13–7**
*Mean errors on memory tasks for the four groups*
*of either sober or intoxicated subjects*

| | NATURE OF TASK | | | | | |
|---|---|---|---|---|---|---|
| | Interference (avoidance task) | | Recall (rote-learning task) | | Recall (word association task) | Memory Recognition (picture task) | |
| GROUP | Day 1 | Day 2 | Day 1 | Day 2 | | *Neutral pictures* | *Emotional pictures* |
| AA | 8.28 | 9.12 | 16.96 | 16.45 | 2.50 | 5.08 | 3.67 |
| SS | 6.91 | 8.13 | 12.05 | 13.75 | 1.25 | 4.92 | 1.67 |
| AS | 8.99 | 7.15 | 20.56 | 24.55 | 4.58 | 5.00 | 4.25 |
| SA | 6.02 | 7.20 | 12.29 | 15.10 | 2.25 | 5.08 | 2.50 |

Note: The first letter in group designations refers to condition on Day 1; the second letter, condition on Day 2; A, Alcohol; S, no alcohol. No measure of Day 1 errors was possible for the word-association and picture-recognition tasks, due to the nature of the task.
Source: McGuigan and Woods [1972], Table 1, p. 204, © 1972. Reprinted by permission of Prentice-Hall, Inc.

### Can Control of Involuntary Physiological Processes Be Learned?

There has been much interest over the past few years regarding the ability of man to learn to control physiological processes. The layman has heard about such things as yoga and transcendental meditation. Psychological research labels this type of research *biofeedback*. The ability of man to regulate his own blood pressure, heart rate, skin temperature, and other internal

19. Goodwin et al. [1969], pp. 1358–1360. Copyright 1969 by the American Association for the Advancement of Science. Reprinted with permission from the author and the American Association for the Advancement of Science.

processes has been an issue for years in psychology, but only in the last few decades has it been experimentally demonstrated that the ability to control these processes can be learned. Budzynski, Stoyva, and Adler [1970] carried out a biofeedback investigation on fifteen adult volunteers. Three groups of subjects were instructed to relax as much as possible, particularly concentrating their efforts on their foreheads, as they sat in a dimly lit, quiet room with frontalis muscle tension being recorded on an electromyograph (EMG). The experimental group received feedback from their frontalis muscle in the form of a tone that rose in pitch as tension increased and fell in pitch as tension decreased. One control group received no such feedback, while a second control group received irrelevant feedback (a steady low tone). In this way, the relaxing effects of the direct muscle feedback could be compared with the depth of relaxation achieved by subjects who tried to relax without feedback.

In three sessions, the experimental group had lowered frontalis EMG levels 50 percent, compared with 24 percent for the no-feedback group, and a 28 percent rise for the irrelevant feedback subjects. The conclusion drawn from this study was that people can relax without any feedback but that the amount of relaxation can be greatly increased with the aid of tension feedback.[20]

## RESEARCH IN CLINICAL PSYCHOLOGY

Since psychology was launched as a separate discipline, it has sought to become an effective applied science. For many people, "applied clinical psychology" and "science" have been a contradiction in terms. "Science" means dealing with objective, empirical dimensions; "clinical psychology" means dealing with internal, nonphysical dimensions of personality. As a consequence, some of the psychodynamic approaches employed over the years are based on theoretical principles that have not been validated. This does not necessarily mean they are ineffective. Clinical psychologists have become more concerned with determining the effectiveness of alternative therapeutic approaches. Figure 13-9 shows the number of studies carried out over a fifty-four-year period aimed at determining the effectiveness of different therapies. Notice how concern with this topic has increased. In 1952 Eysenck surveyed the literature concerning the effectiveness of therapeutic approaches and noted that approximately 66 percent of nontreated people with psychological problems improve, whereas only 60 percent of patients treated with psychotherapy improve. As you might expect, this survey caused great concern, for it implied that psychotherapy may even be inhibiting

---

20. Rubenstein [1975], p. 611. Used by permission of The Dushkin Publishing Group, Inc.

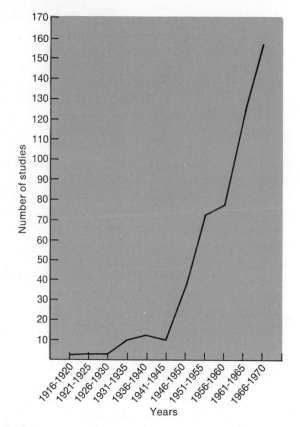

**FIGURE 13–9**

Distribution by five-year intervals of 501 outcome studies (excluding behavioral) published from 1916 through 1967

(Adapted from Bergin & Garfield, *Handbook of psychotherapy and behavior change.* Copyright © 1971 by John Wiley & Sons, Inc. Reprinted by permission of John Wiley & Sons, Inc.)

improvement to some extent. Eysenck's findings were published again in 1961, 1965, and 1966, with general acceptance by the clinical profession.[21]

The point to be made here is not that psychotherapy is ineffective, but that one of the major issues in contemporary clinical psychology is analyzing methods. This has included a push to a more objective therapeutic approach. Two investigations are presented here to give the reader an idea of how clinical psychologists are investigating this problem.

21. Bergin [1971] presents evidence to suggest Eysenck's data may be interpreted in a way that paints a somewhat brighter picture of the effectiveness of psychotherapy. He suggests psychotherapy has been "mildly" effective.

## Is a Particular Therapy Effective ?

One approach taken by clinical psychologists was to carry out more experiments designed to determine the effectiveness of particular therapies. In 1954 Butler and Haigh carried out an investigation on 41 adults to determine whether client-centered therapy was effective. All 41 subjects were tested first to determine how they felt themselves to be in fact and then to determine how they would like to be ideally. The test itself consisted of simple declarative sentences, such as "I am a hard worker," "I am really disturbed," "I am afraid of a full-fledged disagreement with another person," and so on. The subjects were required to sort these into nine piles ranging from "like me" to "unlike me" and "like ideal" to "unlike ideal."

The subjects were divided into two groups. The first group consisted of 25 clients who actually showed up for therapy. Before this group started therapy, there was relatively little correspondence between their actual and ideal self-concepts. Thus, the goal of client-centered therapy with these patients was to produce some significant relationship between the two self-concepts.

The second group of subjects consisted of 16 matched controls who were *not* clients for therapy. These were matched with the first group in terms of sex, age, socioeconomic status, and student-nonstudent status. While the first group was receiving therapy, this second control group went about their usual daily activities for an equivalent length of time. It was expected that a comparison of the test scores of the two groups would indicate whether any change resulted from the passage of time or from the experience with the test.

To determine whether motivation for counseling rather than counseling itself produces congruence between actual and ideal self-concepts, 15 of the original 25 from the therapy group underwent a sixty-day control period prior to counseling. Test scores over this sixty-day period should indicate whether test results of clients change as a result of motivation for therapy per se.

After the experimental group had been given treatment, all subjects again took the self-ideal tests. The first group, consisting of those who received therapy immediately and those who waited sixty days, showed a significant increase in congruence between the actual self and ideal self-concepts. The control group showed no significant increase. This beneficial change continued in follow-up tests six months to one year after the completion of therapy. The findings indicate that, as a consequence of client-centered therapy, a rise in clients' level of self-esteem and adjustment was brought about.[22]

22. Rubenstein [1975], pp. 332–333. Used by permission of The Dushkin Publishing Group, Inc.

## A Comparative Analysis
of Therapeutic Approaches

Several investigations have recently been carried out in an attempt to compare the effectiveness of different approaches. Gordon Paul [1966] conducted a nicely designed experiment comparing systematic desensitization (a therapy involving relaxation and the slow increasing of intensity of fear-provoking situations) with two other methods in the treatment of students with extreme fear of speaking in public. He enlisted the services of five experienced psychotherapists whose school affiliations ranged from Freud to Sullivan. Nine cases were allotted to each therapist, who was required to use three different methods—one for each three subjects. The methods were (1) the therapist's own customary insight therapy, (2) a stylized procedure involving suggestion and support called "attention-placebo" therapy, and (3) systematic desensitization, which the therapist had to be trained to administer. Each patient received five therapeutic sessions. The results (see Table 13–8) showed significantly superior effectiveness for systematic desensitization on a variety of measures. In terms of conventional clinical change, 86 percent of the patients treated by desensitization were much improved and 14 percent improved. This compares with 20 percent much improved and 27 percent improved for the insight group. In the attention-placebo group none were much improved, and 47 percent improved.

**TABLE 13–8**
Breakdown of cases in traditional "improvement" categories
from stress condition data

| Treatment Group | Number of Subjects | Unimproved (percentage) | "Improvement" Classification (percentage) | | |
|---|---|---|---|---|---|
| | | | *Slightly improved* | *Improved* | *Much improved* |
| Desensitization | 15 | — | — | 14 | 86 |
| Insight | 15 | 7 | 4 | 27 | 20 |
| Attention-Placebo | 15 | 20 | 33 | 47 | — |
| Treatment-Control | 29 | 55 | 28 | 17 | — |

Source: Paul [1966], Table 7, p. 37. Reprinted courtesy of Stanford University Press.

## SUMMARY

One objective of this chapter was to give the reader an idea of how the different investigatory approaches are being employed in contemporary psychology. Examples of two-group experimental designs, factorial designs, small $N$ designs, correlational studies, contrast studies, and case studies were presented from the various psychological research areas.

A second objective was to present research that is indicative of what is being done presently in psychology. The research described included work dealing with developmental, comparative, physiological, social learning, personality, perception, and applied psychology. The interrelatedness of these areas was emphasized.

# 14

# Communication
# in Psychology

*Almost every undergraduate psychology program in the country requires its students to learn how to write reports according to the rules of the American Psychological Association. The purpose of this chapter is to present the guidelines set down by the APA along with sample published reports. Also included is a section devoted to showing students how to look up journal articles in* Psychological Abstracts.

Conducting psychological investigations is not the only responsibility of a psychologist; the objective of research is not simply gratification for the investigator. It is the responsibility of any psychologist to communicate information that would be useful for the advancement of the discipline. The most common means of communication in scientific communities is the written report. After the investigator has designed his investigation, carried out the procedural steps, and analyzed his data, he still has one thing to do—write a report summarizing the investigation. This is generally considered an arduous task. The actual carrying out of the experimental routine is usually fascinating and the statistical analysis merely a necessary step; even the drawing of conclusions and inferences is a challenge. But to most, the drudgery of having to write up the findings is looked upon as an unrewarding, laborious task to be put off as long as possible. Most research psychologists have a drawer full of data from past projects that they cannot seem to find the time to report.

## ROLE OF THE REPORT

The obvious question raised by beginning research students is why are journal reports so dreadfully dull. As one student put it, "I barely got to sleep when I realized I was still on the introduction and I had only 10 more minutes before class," or "Why don't they ever say this in English?" Though scientific journal reports have yet to win Pulitzer prizes, their role in communication is important.

Why do reports in general seem to be so uninteresting to the student or uninformed general reader? Reports are exactly that—reports. They are reports of observations and collections of data culminating in conclusions and inferences drawn by the experimenter. All observations, relevant manipulation techniques, and apparatus require description in a particular scientific vocabulary so that the experimenter can communicate precisely what he means. Precision in definition is the crux of the question. Although a specific action or process can be defined by many different slang expressions and colloquialisms in everyday life, the scientist must seek exactness in universally accepted definitions understood by all in the same or similar situations. Therefore, the scientist must seek detail and exact meanings in order to transmit his intentions or method.

Take, for instance, the simple observation of a subject's behavior. In an everyday life situation, a common observation could be this: "Upon giving the medicine to the subject, he seemed to be worried and anxious until the negative thing was taken away." The statement is vague on several points. A researcher reading such a communication would wonder what was actually involved. What were the exact living conditions of the subject? Who was the subject? What was the dosage and the mode of application of the IV? and so on. If the statement was in a journal report, the reader would expect all important terms to be operationally defined.[1] What did the observer mean when he described the subject as being "worried" and "anxious"? If the subject was nonhuman, a rat, did he run about the confinement or chew his fingernails? Just what behaviors led the observer to think he was "anxious"?

The scientist would also inquire about the operational definition of the "negative thing" mentioned by the observer. The definition of a "negative thing" may be a punishment to the observer, whereas the researcher reading the report may define it personally as merely a noxious but not necessarily punishing stimulus. Because individuals have their own personal definitions of words, some kind of universal standard of definition is necessary. Since scientific writing is precise, using exactly defined words and phrases, it is not unusual for it to be termed "dull" and "uninteresting." Reports are written in a pure, unambiguous way, so no question about how the experiment was conducted or the definitions entailed is left unanswered.

---

1. An *operational definition* is one in which a term is defined by the operations used to measure them. For example, someone trying to operationally define a chocolate cake would describe the operations used to measure its properties: its color, texture, composition, and so on. Try to operationally define hunger. It could be operationally defined as so many hours of food deprivation.

## OBJECTIVES OF THE REPORT

Let us take a look at what makes writing the report a "chore." Need it cause anxiety and ulcers for both student and researcher?

We agree that communication is the most oft-used source of learning; it is the key to the transfer of knowledge from one individual to another. It is also the intrinsic component of report writing. The report is the transmission of one's efforts, observations, conclusions, and inferences to another, with the assurance that the same or similar results will be derived by others if the directions are followed as outlined by the original experimenter. Can you imagine the frustration of a second researcher if he decided to duplicate a particular study and found that his results indicated a large degree of insignificance when the original study resounded with significance and purported to be a valuable discovery? This frequently occurs because the initial report was vague and unclear on important points that need to be replicated exactly in order to obtain the reported results. One principle for the student to remember is that every relevant aspect, each important observation or manipulation of variables, should be noted and included in the report.

In effective communication, organization is clearly an important asset for the writer as well as the reader. The writer can rely on an effective organization of material to help ensure that his thoughts and data are communicated correctly. It acts as a guide to enable him to progress in a logical manner. Organization also helps the writer to be concise and stick to a planned pattern, and avoid the temptation to ramble or slip off on a tangent. Most of all, his own thinking is enhanced by efficient organization, and he is assured his point will be thoroughly discussed. To the reader, tight organization of the material is an advantage. The burden of "plowing through" is lessened considerably, and it is easier to understand the point the author is making.

Deeply entwined with organization are the following: clarity, accuracy, quality, and readability. These four points distinguish the good writeup from the mediocre. Readers assume the accuracy of the printed material they quote as "authority," and journals, being sources of authority, demand it. Of deeper consequence is the original purpose of scientific writing—the relaying of observations and data accrued in the study situation. When accuracy is sacrificed, the study (and the reason to do the study) is worth very little to the reader and in turn much less to the scientific world.

Accuracy, clarity, and conciseness are important attributes in any report. Accuracy is dulled by an inconsistent and unreadable text. The novice investigator usually finds it difficult to incorporate these attributes into his report. He is not alone, however; seldom is a report submitted to a journal for publication not returned to the author for editing.

How does one go about writing a well-organized, concise, accurate, clear report? There are few places a researcher can go to get help in making his report accurate, clear, and concise. These attributes generally depend on the literary abilities of the writer and improve with practice. There is, however, quite a bit of help available to aid the writer in organizing his report because psychologists have selected a particular format for acceptable reports. Actually, several different types of formats could have been used, but the American Psychological Association realized that it would ease the problems of both reading and writing reports if a standardized form was adoped. A large portion of this chapter is devoted to presenting the standardized aspects of report writing found in a well-written psychology report.

## ORGANIZATION OF THE REPORT

One aid to both reader and researcher is a formal written outline of intentions and conclusions. In scientific writing, certain organizational procedures and conventions have become fairly standardized. The finest and most accessible source is the *Publication Manual* of the American Psychological Association, commonly known as the "Webster's" of psychological report writing. It is a useful addition to the library of every psychology student or researcher.

The standard experimental writeup includes the following primary sections and subsections: title and title page, abstract, introduction, method (including subjects, apparatus, and procedure), results, discussion, and conclusions. In order to help the reader visualize what a published journal article looks like, an article written by Frank Logan and Douglas Spanier published in the *Journal of Comparative and Physiological Psychology* has been reproduced here in its entirety (Figure 14-1). The main sections and subsections are each described below. Examples, some of them from the Logan and Spanier article, are included.

### Title and Title Page

The title should be short but clearly indicative of the exact topic covered. It is generally known that the report is "a study of . . ." or "an investigation of . . ." so that type of introductory phrase should be avoided. The IV and the DV employed in the investigation should be stated in the title.

If desired, a title page may be included. The information, commonly centered on a separate page, should include the following: the name of the experiment, the researcher or those involved, and the date the report is submitted. Although optional for some journals, the title page is considered a handy source for identification and for that reason is required by many editors.

*Journal of Comparative and Physiological Psychology*
1970, Vol. 72, No. 1, 102–104

# RELATIVE EFFECT OF DELAY OF FOOD AND WATER REWARD[1]

FRANK A. LOGAN[2] AND DOUGLAS SPANIER[3]

*University of New Mexico*

Hungry or thirsty rats were given the appropriate reward after 1- or 30-sec. time of delay in a between-groups 2 × 2 design. In one experiment, delay was imposed in the goal box; in another experiment, delay was imposed in the straight alley just before the goal box. In both experiments, the thirsty rat ran somewhat slower at the short delay and somewhat faster at the long delay, producing significant interactions. Hence, delay of water reward was found to be relatively less detrimental than delay of food reward. This finding may be related to the degree to which incompatible responses are elicited by the different drive stimuli during the time of delay.

Among the most clearly established principles of learning is that the effectiveness of reward is reduced the longer the time it is delayed after a response. The detrimental effects of delay may be attenuated by minimizing incompatible responses during the time of delay (Harker, 1956) or by bridging the time of delay with chained behavior (Ferster, 1953). Nevertheless, organisms certainly prefer shorter to longer delays of reward (Logan, 1965).

In spite of the quite substantial body of literature concerning delayed reward, it appears that this research has been done exclusively using hungry organisms responding for food reward. While the principle is undoubtedly of wider generality than that, it is at least possible that the parameters of the gradient of delay of reinforcement depend importantly upon the nature of the motivating conditions. Perhaps there is no a priori basis for anticipating this possibility, but preliminary research in the related context of decision-making by rats strongly suggested that delay of water reward was not as detrimental as delay of food reward.

The present study was designed to test this possibility in a conventional instrumental-learning context. Specifically, hungry or thirsty rats were trained to run for food or water under conditions of immediate or delayed reward. Given reasonably comparable conditions of drive and incentive, the resulting performance should reveal whether delay of reward interacts with the nature of the motivating conditions.

## METHOD

### Subjects

The subjects were 76 male hooded rats bred in the colony maintained by the Department of Psychology at the University of New Mexico. They were about 100 days old at the beginning of the experiment and were housed in individual cages with water freely available for the hungry rats and food freely available for the thirsty rats. Twelve grams of laboratory chow daily were given the hungry rats, and 15-cc water were given the thirsty rats immediately after each experimental session.

### Apparatus

The apparatus was an 8-ft. straight runway with a solid black floor, black plastic sides, and clear plastic top. Its inside dimensions were 4 × 4 in. A 3 × 6 in. aluminum start box provided access to the runway when a spring-loaded aluminum door was released. At the goal end of the alley was a brass block containing two cups 1 in. in diameter and 1 in. deep. A goal door 2 ft. from the reward cups was operated manually. Reward of three 45-mg. Noyes pellets or .1-cc distilled water was delivered into the appropriate cup. Timing started when the rat broke a photobeam located 1 in. into the runway and terminated when the rat broke a photobeam inside the reward cup (Experiment 1) or a photobeam located 6 in. before the closed goal door (Experiment 2). The entire apparatus

[1] This research was supported by a grant to the first author by the National Science Foundation. The authors are indebted to William Candelaria and William Wither for assistance in running the subjects.
[2] Requests for reprints should be sent to Frank A. Logan, Department of Psychology, University of New Mexico, Albuquerque, New Mexico 87106.
[3] Now at Stanislaus State College.

---

**FIGURE 14–1**

Reproduction of a complete journal article

was housed in a sheet-metal enclosure with a blue plastic top providing ventilation and indirect lighting from below.

### Procedure

The rats were run six trials/day, rotated in squads of four to provide an intertrial interval of about 3 min. In Experiment 1, the goal door was open when the rat was released from the start box and was closed after it broke the photobeam inside the reward cup. Reward was then delivered automatically after the appropriate delay timed by a Hunter timer. In Experiment 2, the goal door was closed when the rat was released from the start box, and a second door located 2 ft. further back from the goal was closed to detain the rat in that section for the appropriate delay interval. The rat was then released to run to the goal where reward was delivered immediately upon breaking the photobeam in the reward cup. Training continued for a total of 312 trials (52 days) in both experiments.

### Design

Each experiment comprised a 2 × 2 factorial, animals being either hungry or thirsty and receiving the appropriate reward after either 1- or 30-sec. delay. The only difference was that this delay was imposed in the goal region with access to the empty reward cups in Experiment 1 and in a comparable 2-ft. section of the runway away from the reward cups in Experiment 2. Ten rats were randomly assigned to each of the four groups in Experiment 1 and 9 rats to each group in Experiment 2.

### Results

Terminal running speeds averaged over the last 10 days of the experiments are shown in the two panels of Figure 1. Both experiments showed a significant overall effect of delay (Experiment 1: $F = 25.3$, $df = 1/36$, $p < .01$; Experiment 2: $F = 542.5$, $df = 1/32$, $p < .01$). More importantly, however, both experiments also showed a significant interaction between delay and the nature of the motivating conditions (Experiment 1: $F = 7.2$, $df = 1/36$, $p < .02$; Experiment 2: $F = 9.6$, $df = 1/32$, $p < .01$). This interaction can not be attributed to unequal units of measurement or to gross differences in motivation, since the conditions employed were such that the thirsty rats ran somewhat slower under the 1-sec. delay and somewhat faster under the 30-sec. delay.

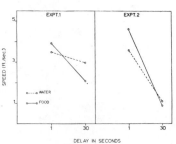

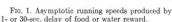

FIG. 1. Asymptotic running speeds produced by 1- or 30-sec. delay of food or water reward.

### Discussion

The principle of the gradient of delay of reinforcement applies when a thirsty animal is running for water much as it does when a hungry animal is running for food. But the parameters of those gradients are not the same. Specifically, delay of water reward is relatively less detrimental to performance than delay of food reward. This obtains whether the delay is imposed in the goal box or in the maze before the goal box.

A possible basis for this difference might be found in the nature of the fractional anticipatory goal responses appropriate to the two rewards. It is at least conceivable that food-anticipatory responses such as salivating are more frustrating than water-anticipatory responses such as lip-licking. However, the fact that organisms can survive longer without food than without water would provide little evolutionary justification for such a speculation.

A more probable account relates to the delay-engendered competing responses. While no objective records are available, it is reasonable that thirsty animals would maintain greater orientation toward the goal during a delay than hungry animals. This clearly appeared to be the case in the first experiment where the thirsty rats tended to lick longer at the dry water cup than the hungry rats licked at the empty food cup, and a similar though less conspicuous effect could have occurred in the

**FIGURE 14–1. Continued**

maze. This would suggest that there are different unlearned responses to the drive stimuli provided by hunger and thirst, an interpretation distantly related to the difference in these two drives with respect to alternation behavior (Petrinovich & Bolles, 1954). Insofar as competing responses occur during a delay and become anticipatory to interfere with the instrumental response, an inherent difference in the tendency to make such responses as between hunger and thirst would account for the differential effects of delay under these two sources of motivation.

REFERENCES

FERSTER, C. B. Sustained behavior under delayed reinforcement. *Journal of Experimental Psychology*, 1953. **45**, 218–224.

HARKER, G. S. Delay of reward and performance of an instrumental response. *Journal of Experimental Psychology*, 1956, **51**, 303–310.

LOGAN, F. A. Decision-making by rats: Delay versus amount of reward. *Journal of Comparative and Physiological Psychology*, 1965, **59**, 1–12.

PETRINOVICH, L., & BOLLES, R. Deprivation states and behavioral attributes. *Journal of Comparative and Physiological Psychology*. 1954, **47**, 450–453.

(Received August 30, 1969)

**FIGURE 14–1.  Continued**

*Sample*

# RELATIVE EFFECT OF DELAY
# OF FOOD AND WATER REWARD

Frank A. Logan

Douglas Spanier

August 1, 1969

## Abstract

Most psychological journals require the submission of an abstract with the manuscript. Often located at the beginning of the work, the abstract sometimes takes the place of the summary traditionally put at the end of the article. The abstract should be no more than 12 to 15 lines in length (approximately 100 to 120 words), and it should be written in complete sentences. A main heading is used to identify the abstract section in the typed manuscript, although it does not show up in the actual publication. The abstract is centered on a page by itself.

An abstract generally has four parts:

1. The objective of the investigation
2. A brief description of the experimental procedures
3. A statement of the results
4. The conclusions or implications of the findings

Only pertinent data are included and they should be stated in condensed form. Be sure to mention the number and kind of subjects used as well as the design and the significance level of the results. The results should be mentioned or at least the trend of the results should be included. The suggested length may follow this pattern: objective, one or two sentences; procedure, five or six sentences; results, one or two sentences; and conclusion, one sentence. The results and conclusion are sometimes combined into one sentence.

*Sample*

### Abstract

Hungry or thirsty rats were given the appropriate reward after 1- or 30-sec. time of delay in a between-groups 2 × 2 design. In one experiment, delay was imposed in the straight alley just before the goal box; in another experiment, delay was imposed in the goal box. In both experiments, the thirsty rat ran somewhat slower at the short delay and somewhat faster at the long delay, producing significant interactions. Hence, delay of water reward was found to be relatively less detrimental than delay of food reward. This finding may be related to the degree to which incompatible responses are elicited by the different drive stimuli during the time of delay.

### Introduction

The sole purpose of the introduction is to state the question asked of the experiment and the rationale behind the study. In other words, the theoretical propositions from which your hypothesis are drawn are stated in the introduction. The logic used, summarized relevant arguments, and supporting data are also included.

Two points need to be emphasized: (1) a statement of and background to the problem, and (2) a statement of the objective of the study. The statement of the objective is the formally stated hypothesis and should be written in terms of the IV and the DV. If needed, additional sentences are added to more exactly define the IV and DV.

A brief review of the literature is often advantageous, for it gives the reader a foundation for a more complete understanding of the issue. It also gives the writer a foundation on which to start the report. No heading is needed or recommended for this section. The introduction section starts on a separate page following the abstract.

*Sample*

Among the most clearly established principles of learning is that the effectiveness of reward is reduced the longer the time it is delayed after a response. The detrimental effects of delay may be attenuated by minimizing incompatible responses during the time of delay (Marker, 1956) or by bridging the time of delay with chained behavior (Ferster, 1953). Nevertheless, organisms certainly prefer shorter to longer delays of reward (Logan, 1965)....

The present study was designed to test this possibility in a conventional instrumental-learning context. Specifically, hungry or thirsty rats were trained to run for food or water under conditions of immediate or delayed reward. Given reasonably comparable conditions of drive and incentive, the resulting performance should reveal whether delay of reward interacts with the nature of the motivating conditions.

### Method

The method section is the body of the report. In this section the reader should be given the precise manner in which the experiment was conducted. Enough detail should be included to allow the replication of the experiment by the reader; remember, however, that too much detail obscures the facts.[2] Remember too that the functional value of each fact determines whether it should be mentioned in the writeup. Quality exceeds quantity in the final evaluation of any report. The test for any material should be the answer to these questions: "Was it used during the experiment?" and "Is this necessary for the reader to replicate the experiment?" Include in this section the following:

1. Subjects involved
2. Sampling procedures used
3. Control devices used
4. Design of the study
5. Techniques of measurement and observation
6. Logic of the data

In order to help clarify what is involved, the method section is frequently divided into three subsections, and in some cases four. The three subsections are subjects, apparatus, and procedure. In instances where the design of the experiment is rather complicated, a subsection called design is included.

**Subjects.** The first step of any recipe is to define and describe what is going to be used in the work. First define and describe the population and how it was sampled in detail. It is important to notice if any subjects were unused or taken out of "active service" (students who did not show up for appointments, rats that died), since a change in the population may lead to unrepresentative and inconsistent results due to the loss of randomness.

*Sample*
Subjects

The subjects were 76 male hooded rats bred in the colony maintained by the Department of Psychology at the University of New Mexico. They were about 100 days old at the beginning of the experiment and were housed in indi-

---

2. The problem most report writers have is usually the opposite: they fail to be thorough in their procedural explanation.

vidual cages with water freely available for the hungry rats and food freely available for the thirsty rats.

**Apparatus.** As the heading tells us, all relevant aspects of the devices and machinery, quizzes or questionnaires used should be included in the report. Remember, the reader may wish to repeat the study and to do so accurately he requires conditions similar to those originally experienced by the subjects of the experiment. When complicated machinery is used, a diagram is useful, though in some journals it is not required. Where standard types of apparatus are used, often you may see only the name of the apparatus. Note that any material or device used with which the subject came in contact is considered apparatus.

*Sample*
Apparatus

The apparatus was an 8-ft. straight runway with a solid black floor, black plastic sides and clear plastic top. Its inside dimensions were 4 × 4 in. A 3 × 6 in. aluminum start box provided access to the runway when a spring-loaded aluminum door was released. At the goal end of the alley was a brass block containing two cups 1 in. in diameter and 1 in. deep. A goal door 2 ft. from the reward cups was operated manually. Noyes pellets or .1-cc distilled water was delivered into the appropriate cup. Timing started when the rat broke a photobeam located 1 in. into the runway and terminated when the rat broke a photobeam inside the reward cup (Experiment 1) or a photobeam located 6 in. in before the closed goal door (Experiment 2).

**Procedure.** Detail, precision, and readability are the keys in discussing the collection of data. This is the "how" subsection; how the IV was manipulated, how the DV was recorded, and so on. Three basic criteria should be considered: design, steps for conducting the experiment, and how the measurement of the subjects' behavior was accomplished. Summarize instructions if you, the experimenter, gave them to the subjects; or, if the subjects were not human, describe the schedules of reinforcement used. Refer to the planning form described in Chapter One.

*Sample*
Procedure

The rats were run six trials/day, rotated in squads of four to provide an intertrial interval of about 3 min. In Experiment 1, the goal door was open when the rat was released from the start box and was closed after it broke the photobeam inside the reward cup. Reward was then delivered automatically after the appropriate delay timed by a Hunter timer. In Experiment 2, the goal door was closed when the rat was released from the start box, and a second door located 2 ft. further back from the goal was closed to detain the rat in that section for the appropriate delay interval. The rat was then released to run to the goal where reward was delivered immediately upon breaking the photobeam in the reward cup. Training continued for a total of 312 trials (52 days) in both experiments.

**Design.**   Type of design, the method of experimental versus control group comparison, is the essential part of this subsection. Specification of subjects or groups and the identification labels assist the reader in understanding further references to them later in the writeup: e.g., group $X$ = experimental group; group $Y$ = control group. Here, also, the variables mentioned in the hypothesis need to be operationally defined. Mention should be made of the IVs and the DVs as well as of the experimental control devices and techniques used.[3] This subsection, though helpful in some instances, can be absorbed by the preceding subsection and need not be separate.

Does a method section have to be divided into subsections? Not all the time. Remember, the purpose of subsections is to help clarify potentially complex material. Do not use subsections unnecessarily. For example, if the only materials used in the investigation were paper and pencils, a separate apparatus subsection would be unnecessary.

### Results

All data aiding the formation and justification of your conclusions are found in the results section. A summary statement of the results obtained (e.g., "Errorless learning was obtained with the experimental group") generally comes near the beginning of the results section. This is followed by an elaboration of the results. Data may be expressed not only verbally, but also in graphs, figures, and tables. One should be careful not to include conclusions or discussion issues in this section. Stick to stating what data were gathered.

*Sample*

> Terminal running speeds averaged over the last 10 days of the experiments are shown in the two panels of Figure 1. Both experiments showed a significant overall effect of delay (Experiment 1: $F = 25.3$, $df = 1/36$, $p < .01$; Experiment 2: $F = 542.5$, $df = 1/32$, $p < .01$). More importantly, however, both experiments also showed a significant interaction between delay and the nature of the motivating conditions (Experiment 1: $F = 7.2$, $df = 1/36$, $p < .02$; Experiment 2: $F = 9.6$, $df = 1/32$, $p < .01$). This interaction can not be attributed to unequal units of measurement or to gross differences in motivation, since the conditions employed were such that the thirsty rats ran somewhat slower under the 1-sec. delay and somewhat faster under the 30-sec. delay.

Notice the definite absence of any inferences, conclusions, or hypotheses. Raw data are merely summarized and explained in detail. Clear and concise observation is needed.

Notice also the advantage of using graphs and tables. These condense

---

3. Such detail as the experimental control, definition of variables, and so on can be placed in the procedure subsection instead.

much valid and important material into a small space and give the reader an opportunity to see a whole procedure or its results at a glance. Let us examine in more detail the acceptable form for figures and graphs.

**Figures and tables.** Within the results section, you may want to include a graph of the data gathered. The *raw* data are often not included, however; neither are the calculations.[4] Figures, tables, or both serve as a *summary* of the data: a condensation of the major finding of the study in numerical and tabular form. These data are used as support for the conclusions and must be presented as systematically and accurately as possible. Main points of the data pertinent to the conclusion should be readily apparent in the table. Taken from another study, the table in Figure 14–2 is an example of a well-organized tabular presentation of data.

A figure is commonly a graph, a chart, or a photograph. Certain kinds of data are best shown by a figure. Again, the criteria for a figure are much like that for a table: be accurate, readable, and systematic. In experimental research figures are most often similar to the illustrations in Figure 14–3.

**FIGURE 14–2**

Example of a well-organized table

(From Weiss, Stone, & Harrell [1970], p. 158. Copyright 1970 by the American Psychological Association. Reprinted by permission.)

TABLE 2

BRAIN NOREPINEPHRINE LEVELS
IN EXPERIMENT 2

| Triplet | Brain norepinephrine level (ng/g) | | |
|---|---|---|---|
| | Avoidance-escape | Yoked | Nonshock[a] |
| 1 | 475 | 372 | 395 |
| 2 | 496 | 359 | 410 |
| 3 | 360 | 329 | 345 |
| 4 | 393 | 357 | 358 |
| 5 | 466 | 451 | 477 |
| 6 | 309 | 226 | 300 |
| 7 | 400 | 333 | 372 |

$$p < .01 \quad p < .02$$
$$p < .05$$

[a] Lower NE values in this experiment than in Experiment 1 were due to use of a catecholamine-specific method (see text).

4. For student reports, the professor may often ask that an appendix be added in which raw data is placed and can be easily evaluated.

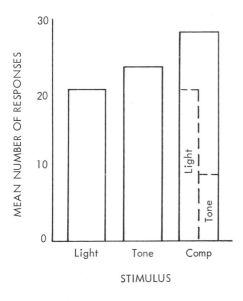

Fig. 2. Mean number of responses emitted during presentations of the single and compound $S^D$s by Subjects 13 to 18 for the two test days combined. Each $S^D$ was correlated with its own lever and both levers were always extended. That portion of compound responses emitted on the light- and tone-correlated levers is indicated by the dotted lines within the bar graph denoting compound responding.

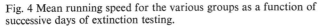

Fig. 4 Mean running speed for the various groups as a function of successive days of extinction testing.

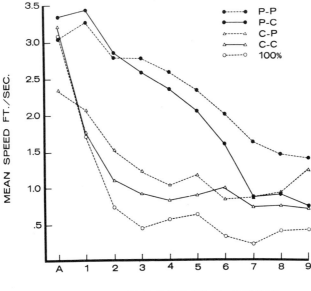

**FIGURE 14–3**

Two examples of typical graphs in research articles

(*Top:* Miller [1973], Figure 2. Reprinted with permission from the author and the *Journal of the Experimental Analysis of Behavior. Bottom:* Rudy, Homzie, Cox, Graeber, & Carter [1970], Figure 4. Copyright 1970 by the American Psychological Association. Reprinted by permission.)

A general rule of thumb when drawing a table or a graph is to make it three units high for every four units wide.

Labeling and captioning a figure is important both for identification and for understanding. What the figure shows should also be reviewed in the body of the results section. Thus, in referring to the bottom graph in Figure 14–3, the results of the data could be written as follows:

> As Figure 14–3 (*bottom*) reveals, there were differences in extinction performance among the five groups. . . .

When reviewing the journals, the reader may note that there is a trend toward using line graphs instead of tables. Over the years psychologists have become aware of the fact that line graphs show data more quickly at a glance than tables, which require the reader to study them more carefully. Relationships between groups stand out better with line graphs. This trend illustrates an important point about journal publications: their objective is to make articles clearer and easier to read. If one type of presentation does this better than another, it is adopted into report formats.

The results section of an unpublished report does not actually include the figures or tables. The author indicates in the manuscript where the figure or graph should be inserted in the published article, but actually places the figures on separate pages at the end of the report. An example is shown below.

> There were a total, then, of four different testing conditions:
> (*a*) weekly exams given which counted toward the students' grades,
> (*b*) weekly exams given which did not count toward the students' grades,
> (*c*) monthly exams given which counted toward the students' grades, and
> (*d*) monthly exams given which did not count toward the students' grades.
> Table 1 shows how the students were rotated through the four testing conditions.
> ---------------------------------------------------------------
> Insert Table 1 about here
> ---------------------------------------------------------------
> The term was divided into four time periods, each terminated with the administration of the monthly exam, the first time period was actually three weeks long with each of the remaining three periods four weeks long.

## Discussion

Now that the facts are stated and the statistics gathered and presented, interpretation of those facts and data becomes necessary. Of what value are bare facts without some discussion or explanation of them and of their relation to other studies? It is here, in the discussion section, that the explanation of the presented data is expected. In no other section of the report should any attempt be made at interpretation or discussion of data.

Other literature relating to the study may be brought into the writeup at this point. The present results may be related to previously stated ones; concurrent research or related studies may provide new insights into your study. Other studies may confirm your hypothesis; or if other findings run counter to yours, alternate explanations can be pointed out or a slightly altered hypothesis may be advanced for possible future investigation. If some unexpected incongruence appears in your results, an unforeseen bump in a graph or line, do not hesitate to question, examine, and maybe offer a hypothesis on that fluctuation.

Every experiment has limitations, so it is not in any way degrading to the work done to point these out. Usually such limitations are valid and provide the reader with valuable information. It is wise for the researcher to determine the extent to which conclusions and hypotheses may be generalized. Can you safely generalize your study using rats as subjects to a human population or human behavior? Note and state to what extent the uncontrolled variables hinder generalization of that particular study. This is the place to discuss every crucial uncontrolled variable. It is in this section also where you may state possible modification of design and/or procedure. Also, review additional problems uncovered by the study that were obscure before and that now need to be changed in future study.

Consider for a moment the possibility of obtaining a negative relationship and inferences. Some experimenters mistakenly find this to be humiliating and embarrassing. As was mentioned previously, this is *not* a "bad" possibility; in fact, it is not uncommon to find negatively corresponding results. They can even be valuable for possible future studies. In such cases, a long dissertation on the possible reasons why such results were obtained is *not* recommended. Instead, a brief discussion with some speculation as to why the results were obtained and possible changes for future investigations is appropriate.

### Conclusions and/or Summary

Although the abstract has usurped the place of the summary, often the abstract is limited in scope. It may be wise to end the report with a brief formal statement of the problem, the results, and the conclusions.

Final compilation is next. This general format or order will prove to be helpful:

1. Abstract (also title, author, affiliation of the author)
2. Text
3. References (start on a new page)
4. Footnotes (start on a new page)
5. Tables (each on a separate page)
6. Figures (each on a separate page)

Study examples in journals and texts to determine similarities and differences in good and poor examples of figures and tables. You will find the best are those that are easy to discern and read.

## DRY FACTS AND SOME REQUIREMENTS OF STYLE

Style is the culmination of many techniques, but the best and easiest is adherence to elementary rules of good grammar and sentence structure. The following portion of the chapter is subdivided for quick reference to some of the more commonl helpful hints and rules for effective report writing.

### Accuracy

Of major importance is the completeness and accuracy of references and citations. Careful checking of the original publication should be routine.

### Length

Because of the number of articles being submitted to journals daily, conciseness is mandatory. Length varies with each study and the amount of comment needed. In general, however, rewrite and condense that which is necessary. The upper limit over which special permission from the journal editorial staff is needed for publication is approximately 16,000 words. Many times the journal for which you are writing will specify the precise length of the report.

### Typing

Typing the manuscript is considered a common and expected procedure. Double spacing with margins of one inch or more on top, sides, and bottom of the page is the rule. Avoid block-style typing by using paragraphs and headings accurately. The only copy to be typed in all capital letters is the title, centered, at the top of the first page of the manuscript, with a deep margin above it.

### Tense and Person

Since the research has already been done, the description of procedure as well as statements concerning the review of literature should be stated in the past tense. Of course, this generalization is not rule of law; however, it should be used in context with clarity and understanding as the criteria. The present tense may be used to discuss the results (e.g., "Rats do work harder for more food"), whereas a description of the results may be in the past tense (e.g., "Twelve rats ran the maze with fewer than six errors").

In scientific writing, the third person is more effective than "I," "me," or "we" to establish an objective tone. Generally, use of the third person is preferred, although the first person may be used by the author to state what he did (e.g., "To control that secondary variable, I employed a matched group design").

*Sample*

> *Poor:*    I found that whenever my difference obtained was significant, the mean score of the total student population fell between the mean scores of the experimental groups.
>
> *Better:*    Whenever a significant difference appeared, the mean score of the total student population fell between the mean scores of the experimental groups.

## Headings

The headings should indicate clearly the organization of the paper. In the APA requirements, three types of headings are usually employed. Main headings, used for identifying the method, results, discussion, and summary sections, are centered and typed with major words capitalized. Do not use all capitals or any end punctuation. Main headings are not underlined. Side headings are typed flush to the left margin and are italicized (underlined). To continue the text, double space, then indent for continuation. Paragraph headings are indented, and only the initial letter of the first word is capitalized. They should be italicized and followed by a period. Continue the text directly with no special spacing. Use side and paragraph headings when making subsections. Side headings are generally used for identifying subsections such as subjects, apparatus, procedure, and design, although paragraph headings can be used for these if no subdivisions are required within them. For further helpful hints, refer to the APA *Publication Manual* and other journal articles, and study the example shown below, as well as Figure 14–1.

*Sample*

Main Heading

Side Heading
    Paragraph heading.

## Footnotes

Footnotes may sometimes prove more of a hindrance than a help to clear, concise writing. They should be used primarily for citations to supporting evidence. Footnotes may also acknowledge help in the preparation of the manuscript or give the author's address. In general, try to avoid putting tangential material or parenthetical discussions in footnotes.

*Sample*

[1]The literature on the nature and bodily mechanism of emotion is extensive. The following works contain discussions and references: Ruckmick [1936], Lund [1939], Young [1943], Woodworth and Schlosberg [1954].

## *Abbreviations and Symbols*

Abbreviations are used sparingly in psychological journals. Longer technical terms or names of specific techniques may be initially spelled out, then followed by the abbreviation in parentheses. The abbreviations are then used alone throughout the report. The use of abbreviations such as S (subject), E (experimenter), and I (investigator) is discouraged. In APA journals and most psychology writings, researchers have established a general vocabulary that includes certain abbreviations (e.g., $t$, $N$, $df$), which are acceptable in reports.

## *References*

References to other studies or authors commonly appear both in the text and in a list at the end of the manuscript. In the text, references should be cited by enclosing in brackets the author's surname and the year of the publication. For example, if we were referring to a certain study, we would say "Jones [1953] said. . . ." If a reference has more than two authors, include the surnames of all authors the first time, and thereafter use only the surname of the senior author and the abbreviation et al.

*Sample*

A recent study [Salvador, Fuentes, Smith, and Black, 1968] shows. . . . The study previously cited [Salvador et al., 1968] shows. . . .

If the author has completed many works relevant to the data you wish to support, place the dates in sequence by year of publication.

*Sample*

Recent studies [Jones, 1973, 1974, 1976] have shown. . . .

## PEER COMMUNICATION

As you recall from Chapter One, the psychologist requires five basic skills. The first, analytical prowess, describes the ability of the psychologist to analyze a situation accurately. The second skill is knowledge of psychological principles. The third and fourth skills deal with the ability to communicate. Last is the skill of evaluation and of interpretation.

Let us go back to the second skill, knowledge of principles, and look at it more closely. As an authority in his field, the psychologist's familiarity with the major works as well as with the newest discoveries should be both deep and broad. Like a medical doctor, the psychologist is looked upon as one having solutions to many problems because of his wide range of knowledge. If he does not know the answer from his background, he does know where to go to find the answer in a book, journal, or from colleagues having close connections with that particular problem. To examine that last statement further, let us look at an example.

Remember the last time you felt queasy inside, experienced dizzy spells, and your hands were cold, wet, and shaky? After making the decision to go to the doctor, you made your way to his office. When the nurse took you to the back room and ordered you to undress, you complied slowly. Remember waiting for the doctor, twiddling your thumbs (only too aware of your appearance)? The doctor arrives and inquires in a very businesslike way about your health. After finishing the examination, he turns, tells you to dress, and leaves the room. Did you ever wonder what the doctor was doing while you dressed? Your guess is probably right. He most likely was off to his library to look up possible answers to your particular symptoms. By the time you are through dressing, he has a diagnosis (a solution to the problem) and three prescriptions with the appropriate medicine, dosage, and price. The doctor demonstrated his knowledge of his field both with the accuracy of his analysis and with his knowledge of where and how to look up the answer quickly. A thorough and up-to-date knowledge of the field is required of an authority, in this example, a doctor, as it is of a psychologist.

Psychology is not a "stand-still" science. New principles are being discovered and old principles are being built upon everyday. With information arriving at such a rapid pace, effective communication is a problem. How can this information be transmitted to those who need it? Consider for a moment the problem faced by researchers in the field. New areas being opened have had research started but are by no means considered to have solutions yet. If this initial information is given to another authority working on the same or similar information, the addition of this new input could mean an earlier solution. Each small advance of a particular subject may also be a clue to later studies. One small step found by a colleague somewhere else in the world may prove to be the missing key to the solution to another's problem. The distribution of this material must be continuous and rapid, and a book requires years in writing, compilation, printing, and distributing. By the time it is finished, the information it contains may be obsolete. This problem is currently being solved by the use of journals and conventions.

### The Journal

As a source of quick reference and up-to-date discoveries, the journal is an invaluable aid to both the medical doctor and the psychologist. The journal solves many dilemmas.

Journals provide a record of recent significant advances in the field so that at any time the psychologist can easily refer back to that study to enhance his newest research. Another hurdle partly overcome by the journal is sheer reading load. To keep abreast of current research, the psychologist must read a great amount of current material. In view of the fact that thousands of articles are published in over a hundred journals in psychology alone; reading everything is physically impossible. The authority in whatever field reads only that material pertaining to his area of expertise or specific problem. Knowing where to look as well as how to look up a particular study) is a great advantage. We will look at how to approach the guides to journals later in the chapter.

Journals assist the professional since they must be selective of the information sent to them. Often journals are known for their particular content coverage. This helps the professional narrow his reading to those topics that deal most closely with his field. For instance, a clinical psychologist would most likely refer often to journals dealing mainly with human subjects, whereas the experimental psychologist would want to read mainly journals carrying experimental articles with more emphasis on nonhuman subjects. Table 14–1 lists the major psychology journals along with what types of investigations (e.g., EPF, large or small $N$ experiments, and so on) they specialize in reporting, the types of subjects used in the investigations they report, the content areas they emphasize, and whether or not they publish review and/or theoretical articles.

Psychologists are not the only professionals plagued with the problem of how to keep up with the field. Most areas of research have an information pool much like psychology, where some journals are devoted just to reviews of the latest findings and publications. The professional can quickly scan what is available and can more easily choose those articles and journals most applicable to his particular field of study.

Another advantage of the journal is the assistance it gives the professional in problem areas lying *outside* his field of expertise. Remember the example in Chapter One in which the psychologist's behavioral principles did not work with the girl using obscene language. It was obvious that the psychologist was not an expert on behavior modification. The area was out of his field of expertise. Perhaps, if he had been more widely read on the subject and been more familiar with the details, he could have discovered that certain rewards are not effective because of a principle called individual reward hierarchy. He could also have found out how to remedy the problem and find a more effective reward rather than giving up. Psychologists, like other professionals, often rely on colleagues who may themselves be authorities in similar fields. If no peer is available for consultation, journals may also fill this need for an information source.

## TABLE 14–1

*Major psychology journals and the types of investigations, subjects, and content areas they emphasize*

| Journal | Ex post facto studies | Experiments—large N | Experiments—small N | Animal subjects | Human subjects | Theory and systems | Research technology and statistics | Perception and sensation | Motivation and emotion | Learning and thinking | Physiological psychology | Pharmacology | Genetics | Developmental and child psychology | Educational psychology | Social psychology | Personality | Mental retardation | Clinical psychology | Review articles | Theoretical articles |
|---|---|---|---|---|---|---|---|---|---|---|---|---|---|---|---|---|---|---|---|---|---|
| American Behavioral Scientist | × | × | × |  | × | × |  | × | × | × |  |  |  | × | × | × | × |  | × | × | × |
| American Journal of Mental Deficiency | × | × | × |  | × |  |  | × | × | × | × |  | × | × | × | × | × | × | × | × | × |
| American Journal of Psychiatry | × |  |  |  | × |  |  |  |  |  | × | × | × | × | × | × | × |  | × |  | × |
| American Journal of Psychology | × | × |  | × | × |  |  | × | × | × | × | × | × | × |  |  |  |  |  |  |  |
| American Psychologist | × |  | × | × | × | × | × | × | × | × | × | × | × | × | × | × | × | × | × | × | × |
| American Scientist | × | × |  | × | × |  |  | × | × | × | × | × |  | × | × | × | × | × |  | × |  |
| American Statistical Association Journal | × | × |  | × | × |  | × |  |  |  |  |  |  |  |  |  |  |  |  | × | × |
| American Statistician | × | × |  |  | × | × |  |  |  |  |  |  |  |  | × |  |  |  |  |  |  |
| Animal Behavior | × | × |  | × |  | × |  | × | × | × |  | × | × |  |  | × |  |  |  |  |  |
| Annual Review of Psychology | × | × | × | × | × | × | × | × | × | × | × | × | × | × | × | × | × | × | × | × |  |
| Archives of General Psychiatry | × |  | × | × | × |  | × |  | × |  | × | × | × | × |  | × | × | × | × | × | × |
| Behavior |  | × |  | × |  |  |  | × | × | × | × | × | × |  |  |  |  |  |  |  | × |
| Behavior Research and Therapy |  | × | × | × | × |  |  | × | × | × |  | × |  |  |  | × |  | × |  |  |  |
| Behavioral Science | × | × |  | × | × | × |  |  | × | × |  |  |  |  |  | × | × | × |  |  | × |
| Biometrics | × | × |  |  |  |  | × |  |  |  |  |  |  |  |  |  |  |  |  |  |  |
| British Journal of Educational Psychology | × | × | × |  | × |  | × |  | × | × |  |  |  |  | × | × | × |  |  | × | × |
| British Journal of Medical Psychology | × | × | × |  | × |  |  | × | × | × | × |  |  |  | × | × | × | × | × | × | × |
| British Journal of Psychology | × | × |  | × | × |  |  | × | × |  | × | × |  |  | × |  |  |  | × | × | × |
| Canadian Journal of Psychology | × | × | × | × | × | × |  | × | × | × | × | × |  |  |  | × | × | × | × |  | × |

TABLE 14–1   Continued

| Journal | Ex post facto studies | Experiments—large N | Experiments—small N | Animal subjects | Human subjects | Theory and systems | Research technology and statistics | Perception and sensation | Motivation and emotion | Learning and thinking | Physiological psychology | Pharmacology | Genetics | Developmental and child psychology | Educational psychology | Social psychology | Personality | Mental retardation | Clinical psychology | Review articles | Theoretical articles |
|---|---|---|---|---|---|---|---|---|---|---|---|---|---|---|---|---|---|---|---|---|---|
| Canadian Psychologist | × |  | × |  | × | × | × | × | × | × | × |  |  | × | × | × | × | × | × | × |  |
| Child Development | × | × | × |  | × |  |  |  |  |  |  |  |  | × |  |  |  |  |  |  |  |
| Cognitive Psychology |  | × |  |  | × | × |  | × |  | × |  |  |  | × | × |  |  |  |  | × | × |
| Counseling Psychologist |  | × |  |  | × |  |  |  |  |  |  |  |  |  |  |  |  |  | × | × | × |
| Developmental Psychology | × | × |  | × | × | × |  |  | × | × | × |  |  | × | × | × | × | × | × |  |  |
| Dissertation Abstracts | × | × | × | × | × | × | × | × | × | × | × | × | × | × | × | × | × | × | × | × | × |
| Educational and Psychological Measurement | × | × |  |  |  |  | × |  |  |  |  |  |  | × | × |  |  | × |  |  |  |
| Genetic Psychology Monographs |  | × |  |  | × |  |  |  |  |  |  |  |  | × | × |  |  | × | × | × | × |
| Journal of Abnormal Psychology |  | × |  |  | × | × |  |  | × | × |  |  |  | × |  | × | × | × | × | × | × |
| Journal of Applied Behavioral Analysis | × | × | × |  | × | × | × | × | × | × | × | × |  | × | × | × |  |  | × | × | × |
| Journal of Applied Psychology | × | × |  |  | × |  | × | × |  | × |  |  |  | × | × | × | × | × | × |  |  |
| Journal of Biological Psychology | × | × |  | × |  | × |  |  | × | × | × | × | × |  |  |  |  |  |  |  |  |
| Journal of Child Psychology and Psychiatry | × | × | × | × | × |  |  |  |  |  |  |  |  | × | × | × | × | × | × | × | × |
| Journal of Clinical Psychology | × | × |  |  | × |  |  |  |  |  |  |  |  |  |  |  |  | × | × |  |  |
| Journal of Comparative and Physiological Psychology | × | × |  | × | × |  |  | × | × | × | × | × | × | × |  |  |  |  |  |  |  |
| Journal of Consulting and Clinical Psychology | × | × |  |  | × |  |  |  |  |  |  |  |  | × | × |  |  |  | × | × | × |
| Journal of Educational Measurement | × | × | × |  | × |  | × |  |  |  |  |  |  |  | × |  |  |  |  |  |  |
| Journal of Educational Psychology | × | × |  |  | × | × |  |  | × | × | × |  |  | × | × | × |  | × |  |  |  |

**TABLE 14–1 Continued**

| Journal | Ex post facto studies | Experiments—large N | Experiments—small N | Animal subjects | Human subjects | Theory and systems | Research technology and statistics | Perception and sensation | Motivation and emotion | Learning and thinking | Physiological psychology | Pharmacology | Genetics | Developmental and child psychology | Educational psychology | Social psychology | Personality | Mental retardation | Clinical psychology | Review articles | Theoretical articles |
|---|---|---|---|---|---|---|---|---|---|---|---|---|---|---|---|---|---|---|---|---|---|
| Journal of Experimental Child Psychology | × | × | | | × | | | × | | × | | | | × | | × | | | × | | |
| Journal of Experimental Psychology | × | × | | × | × | | | × | × | × | | | | × | | | | | | × | × |
| Journal of Experimental Research in Personality | × | × | | × | × | | | | | | | | | | | | × | | | | |
| Journal of Experimental Social Psychology | × | × | | | × | | | | | | | | | × | | × | | | | | |
| Journal of General Psychology | × | × | | × | × | | × | × | | × | × | | | | | | | | | | |
| Journal of Genetic Psychology | × | × | | | × | | | | | | | × | × | | | | | × | × | × | × |
| Journal of Mathematical Psychology | | | | | | | × | | | | | | | | | | | | | × | × |
| Journal of Mental Deficiency Research | × | × | | × | × | | | | | | × | × | × | × | | | | × | | | |
| Journal of Personality | × | × | × | | × | × | | | | | | | | × | | × | × | | × | | × |
| Journal of Personality and Social Psychology | × | × | | × | × | | | × | | | | | | × | | × | × | | | | |
| Journal of Social Psychology | × | × | | | × | | | | | | | | | | | × | × | | | | |
| Journal of the Experimental Analysis of Behavior | × | | | × | × | × | × | × | × | × | × | × | × | | | × | × | | | × | × |
| Journal of Verbal Learning and Verbal Behavior | | × | | | × | | | | × | | | | | × | | | | | | | |
| Perception and Psychophysics | | × | | × | × | × | | × | × | | | | | | | | | | | × | × |
| Perceptual and Motor Skills | × | × | | × | × | × | × | × | | | | × | × | | | | | | | × | × |
| Physiology and Behavior | | × | | × | × | | | | × | × | × | × | × | × | | | | | | × | × |
| Psychological Abstracts | × | × | | × | × | × | × | × | × | × | × | × | × | × | × | × | × | × | × | | × |

**TABLE 14–1    Continued**

| Journal | Ex post facto studies | Experiments—large N | Experiments—small N | Animal subjects | Human subjects | Theory and systems | Research technology and statistics | Perception and sensation | Motivation and emotion | Learning and thinking | Physiological psychology | Pharmacology | Genetics | Developmental and child psychology | Educational psychology | Social psychology | Personality | Mental retardation | Clinical psychology | Review articles | Theoretical articles |
|---|---|---|---|---|---|---|---|---|---|---|---|---|---|---|---|---|---|---|---|---|---|
| Psychological Bulletin | X | X |  | X | X | X | X | X | X | X | X | X | X | X | X | X | X | X | X |  | X |
| Psychological Record | X | X | X | X | X | X | X | X | X | X | X | X | X | X | X | X | X | X | X | X | X |
| Psychological Reports | X | X | X | X | X | X | X | X | X | X | X | X | X | X | X | X | X | X | X | X | X |
| Psychological Review | X | X |  | X | X | X |  | X | X | X | X | X | X | X | X | X | X | X | X |  |  |
| Psychology Today | X | X | X | X | X | X |  | X | X | X | X | X | X | X | X | X | X | X | X |  | X |
| Psychometrika |  | X |  | X | X | X | X |  |  |  |  |  |  |  |  |  |  |  |  |  |  |
| Psychonomic Science | X | X | X | X | X | X | X | X | X | X | X | X | X | X | X | X | X | X | X | X | X |
| Psychopharmacologica | X | X |  | X | X |  |  | X | X | X | X | X |  |  |  |  |  |  |  |  |  |
| Psychophysiology |  | X |  | X | X |  | X |  |  | X | X | X |  | X |  |  |  |  |  |  |  |
| Quarterly Journal of Experimental Psychology |  | X |  | X | X |  | X | X | X | X |  |  |  | X |  |  |  |  |  |  |  |
| Review of Educational Research | X | X |  |  | X | X | X |  |  | X |  |  |  | X | X | X |  | X | X | X |  |
| Science | X | X | X | X | X | X |  | X | X | X | X | X | X | X |  | X | X | X |  |  |  |
| Scientific American | X | X | X | X | X | X |  | X | X | X | X | X | X | X |  |  |  | X | X |  |  |

Note: The information in this table was obtained from questionnaires sent to each journal by the author.

### Locating Journal Articles

One of the most frustrating tasks for the undergraduate student is looking up published material from which to make a report. He is often faced with rows and rows of volumes of journals, all in chronological order instead of by title, author, or subject. The confused student sees no possible route to finding the one article he needs in those thousands of books. The student is not alone; even professionals are often confused about how to search for that one tiny but vital article in the mass of published material.

The best guide to the journals is *Psychological Abstracts*, a tool to help find that hidden article the psychologist or student needs. *Psychological Abstracts* contains summaries of technical reports, journal articles, and books. Some have likened it to a small catalog of directions. Compiled into two volumes each year, *Psychological Abstracts* has a cumulative index for each. Each index lists the national and international journals regularly reviewed in the *Abstracts*.

In using *Psychological Abstracts*, you will notice that it provides summaries of journal articles. It also refers the searcher to books and specific chapters in books. A code is used for easier searching. Near the front of each issue is a table of general area content. However, a subject index is also provided (Figure 14–4). For the recent unbound issues, similar information can be found using the brief subject index found usually at the end of each monthly issue (Figure 14–5).

## SUBJECT INDEX

Hodgkin's disease, psychosomatics of, 4439
Holism, psychologists' attitudes toward, 7212
Holland (*See* Cultures)
Holland Vocational Preference Inventory, as personality inventory, 9955
Hollingsworth, H. L., obituary, 179
Home (*See* Family)
    running away from (*See* Runaways)
Home Environment Diagnosis Test, & Effort Quotient, 2165
Homemaker service, for family stability, 8306
Homeostasis (*See also* Equilibrium)
    activity level &, rat, 9470
    concept analysis, 2425
    consolation &, 7187
    normality concept &, 10269
    in puberty, 5832
    in schizophrenia, 8767
Homer, Odyssey, Penelope, psychoanalysis, 864
Homing, bats, 542
    in fish, California rocky shore, 567
    magnetic theory, pigeons, 2988
    in nonmigratory bats, 5483
    rodents, 5493
Homogeneity, factor analysis vs. analysis of variance in, 9287
    test of, item selection methods, 5070
        by item-test regression, 3833
        for normal distribution, 7265
Homosexuality (*See also* Lesbianism)
    avoidance learning of rat &, 523
    in college students, 10457
    diagnosis & treatment of, 10610
    in drug addiction, 3921
    effeminate passive obligatory, 10596
    etiological theories of, male, 8695
    fetishism, case study, 1699
    group, behavior, male, 4211
        therapy, 6366
    impotence & frigidity, 1824
    inversion vs., term distinction, 8692

Howard Ink Blot Test, 6289
"How I Feel About Things" Test, validity of, childhood, 7947
How Supervise?, Supervisory Practices Test vs., 11124
H-Technique scales (*See* Stauffer's H-Technique)
Hull, C., motor performance theory of, 7683
Human (*See* Man)
Human engineering (*See* Engineering psychology)
Human figure drawing (*See* Drawing)
Human relations, 4872
    attitude change in, 8407
    cases, 4866
    changing technology, 2336
    classification & typology, 5055(a)
    concepts of, 4762
    faith as basis of, 4887
    in growing company, 2326
    inservice program, 7152
    international, 8172
    inventory of problems in, 4860
    on-the-job, 2346
    & management principles, 2328
    manipulating vs. understanding approach to, 10105
    in officers, test for, 2304, 2305, 8407
    science of, 7039
    supervision &, 9105, 9136
    supervisor selection &, 4871
    test construction, user's role, 2305
    training evaluation method, 11142
Human Relations Inventory, vs. MMPI, social conformity, 3491
Humanism, & scientific training, 5054
Humidity (*See also* Air; Climate; Temperature)
    peripheral vision in, 9559
    suicide notes &, 10605
Humm-Wadsworth Temperament Scale, critique of, 9102

**FIGURE 14–4**

Section of a page from the subject index in *Psychological Abstracts*
(*Psychological Abstracts*, 1959, vol. 33, no. 6, p. 1179.)

The *Abstracts* contain a summary or a statement representing each of the areas of a research report: introduction, method, results, and conclusion. The first sentence of the summaries also tells whether it is a research article,

*BRIEF SUBJECT INDEX*

**Physiological Correlates** (see also Stress/Physiological)
13718, 13961, 14144, 14151, 14157, 14246, 14395, 14399, 14946, 14974, 14980, 14982, 14998, 15449

**Physiological Psychology**
13709, 13736, 13851, 13857, 13951, 14157, 15369

**Physiology** (see also Electrophysiology)
13644, 13645, 13843, 13847, 13852, 13855, 13867, 14565, 15089

**Physiology/Sensory** (see also Vision/Physiology of)
13855, 13952, 13976, 13983

**Physique** (SEE Body)

**Piaget/J.**
14318, 14324, 14325, 14329, 14332, 15504

**Picture**
13672, 14157, 14346, 15179, 15308, 15485

**Picture-Frustration** (SEE Projective Technique)

**Pigeon**
13910, 13931, 14081, 14184, 14185, 14201, 14210, 14219, 14220, 14231, 14247, 14249, 14252

**Pilot** (SEE Aviation. Personnel/Military)

**Pitch** (SEE Sound. Audition)

**Pituitary** (SEE Gland. Hormone)

**PK** (SEE Parapsychology)

**Placebo** (SEE Drug Effects)

**Play** (SEE Game. Recreation)

**Play Therapy** (SEE Therapy)

**Pleasure** (SEE Emotion)

**Poisson Distribution** (SEE Mathematics)

**Police** (SEE Crime & Criminals. Law)

**Political Behavior**

**Problem Solving** (see also Choice Behavior, Decision Making, Childhood/Concept Formation & Problem Solving in)
13656, 13832, 13833, 13905, 14162, 14332, 14427, 14505, 14597, 14613, 14672, 14901, 15066, 15135, 15228, 15509

**Profile** (SEE Score & Scoring)

**Programed Instruction** (see also Teaching Aids)
13782, 15158, 15346, 15484, 15501, 15502, 15503, 15504, 15505, 15506, 15507, 15508, 15509, 15510, 15511

**Programing** (SEE Computer)

**Projection** (SEE Defense Mechanism, Cerebral Cortex, Visual Cortex)

**Projective Technique** (see also Rorschach Test)
13841, 14366, 14374, 14389, 14393, 14425, 14564, 14578, 14640, 14646, 14654, 14666, 14883, 14894, 15084, 15282, 15283

**Propaganda** (SEE Communication, Communication/Mass, Persuasion)

**Proprioception** (SEE Kinesthesis, Somesthesia)

**Prostitution** (SEE Occupation, Sexual Behavior)

**Protestantism** (SEE Religion)

**Psychedelic Experience** (SEE Drug Effects–Human)

**Psychiatric Diagnosis** (SEE Psychodiagnosis)

**Psychiatric Hospital** (SEE Mental Hospitalization)

**Psychiatric Patient** (see also Patient)
14591, 14637, 14654, 14659, 14666, 14668, 14673, 14689, 14705, 14745, 14754, 14757, 14760, 14835, 14836, 14840, 14845, 14850, 14869, 14870, 14871, 14873, 14875, 14885, 14896, 14920, 14921, 14932, 15035, 15037,

**Psychology**
13581, 13582, 13593, 13596, 13597, 13598, 13599, 13600, 13601, 14437, 14889, 14895, 15069, 15199

**Psychology Abroad**
13590, 13594, 13640, 13843, 13855, 14401, 14606, 14626, 14639, 15254

**Psychology/History of**
13563, 13564, 13565, 13648, 13720, 13855, 14401, 14671, 14843, 14938, 15065, 15068, 15232

**Psychometrics** (SEE Test & Testing, Psychophysics, Statistics)

**Psychomotor Performance** (SEE Motor Performance)

**Psychoneurosis** (SEE Neurosis)

**Psychopathology**
13562, 13593, 14154, 14464, 14575, 14624, 14660, 14664, 14674, 14692, 14710, 14722, 14798, 14836, 14878, 14896, 14962, 15003, 15042, 15089

**Psychopathy** (SEE Mental Disorder)

**Psychopharmacology** (SEE Drug Effects, Drug Therapy, Biochemistry)

**Psychophysics**
13655, 13658, 13711

**Psychophysiology** (SEE Physiological Psychology)

**Psychosis & Psychotics** (see also Mental Disorder, specific psychoses)
14740, 14773, 14795, 14798, 14807, 14810, 14820, 14874, 14880, 14931, 14932, 14939, 15003, 15017, 15020, 15023, 15024, 15027, 15214, 15215

**Psychosis/Children** (SEE Childhood/Psychosis in)

**FIGURE 14–5**

Section of a page from the brief subject index in *Psychological Abstracts*

(*Psychological Abstracts*, 1970, vol. 44, no. 9, p. xi.)

SOCIAL PSYCHOLOGY

5886. **Abramson, E., Cutter, H. A., Kautz, R. W., & Mendelson, M.** (Pennsylvania State U.) **Social power and commitment: A theoretical statement.** *Amer. sociol. Rev.,* 1958, **23,** 15–22.—A statement and analysis of a general theory of the relationship of social power and social interaction.—*G. H. Frank.*

5887. **Adler, H. G. Ideas toward a sociology of the concentration camp.** *Amer. J. Sociol.,* 1958, **63,** 513–522,—Indicates possible methods for studying the concentration camp sociologically. The concentration camp reached its most extreme and cruel stage of development in the totalitarian state. One of the primary dangers of contemporary life is the concentration camp.—*R. M. Frumkin.*

**FIGURE 14–6**

Two summaries from *Psychological Abstracts*

a review article, or a theoretical discussion (Figure 14–6). *Psychological Abstracts* is a time-saving device. By using it, you can decide whether or not to take the time and trouble to go to the original source. An author index for the names of the authors whose articles you have previously found helpful is also available.

Let us go through a simulated search. Suppose you noted a significant effect on the behavior of your rat when you delayed the reinforcement he received. You first would go to the cumulative index and look for a reference. Maybe "reinforcement, delay" or "reinforcement schedules" will lead you to the right reference article. You decide to look under "reinforcement, delay" and you find it has the number 14224 after it. You search then for the number 14224 in the volume describing that year, 1970, and the approximate month, July–December, and soon find the material shown in Figure 14–7. The running head at the top corner of the page includes the number 44: 14217–14225. The title, author, journal, volume, number, and page are all listed there. You then can choose to discard it after reading the abstract or go to the stacks and look up the article itself.

### Conventions

A second way of disseminating newly discovered information is through conventions. The United States is divided into geographical regions. Within these regions, psychological conventions are held, usually annually. A large national convention is also held. At these conventions, speakers present papers, and smaller discussion groups present the most recent developments within their topic area.

Two basic objectives are accomplished by conventions. This convening by either shock-level group. Under the present conditions, fear conditioning to visual cues in a 1-trial passive-avoidance situation could not be demonstrated. —*Journal abstract.*

14217. **Nagy, Z. Michael, Misanin, James R., & Newman, Judith A.** (Susquehanna U.) **Anatomy of escape behavior in neonatal mice.** *Journal of Comparative & Physiological Psychology,* 1970, **72**(1), 116–124.—6 groups of Swiss-Webster albino mice (N = 96), 5–15 days of age, were given 25 trials in a straight-alley shock-escape task to examine the possibility of instrumental learning at these ages. Several different measures reflected improved escape behavior by the end of the training session for Ss as young as 5 days of age. By comparing performance measures, it was possible to rule out maturation, fatigue, and habituation as factors leading to the improved escape behavior. The data are interpreted as providing evidence that 5-day-old Ss are capable of learning instrumental escape responses. (20 ref.)—*Journal abstract.*

### Reinforcement

14218. **Birkimer, John C. & Aylworth, Charles E.** (U. Louisville) **Rapid extinction of conditioned reinforcement effects in the signaled absence of primary reinforcement.** *Psychonomic Science,* 1970, **18**(1), 31–32.—Trained 6 male albino Sprague-Dawley rats on a multiple schedule involving intermittent white noise and sucrose solution for bar-pressing in the presence of 1 stimulus and extinction in the presence of the 2nd. When responding in the 2nd stimulus context reached a low level, the noise was made available for each response in that context. The noise functioned as a conditioned reinforcer, temporarily raising response rates in the 2nd stimulus context above their earlier level. The reinforcing effects of the noise quickly extinguished, suggesting procedural and species-specific differences between the current study and recent research by J. R. Thomas with pigeons.—*Journal abstract.*

14219. **Brownstein, Aaron J. & Hughes, Ronald G.** (U. North Carolina, Greensboro) **The role of response suppression in behavioral contrast: Signaled reinforcement.** *Psychonomic Science,* 1970, **18**(1), 50–52. —After responding was maintained on multiple variable-interval schedules of reinforcement, a signaling procedure was added to 1 component. 4 adult white Carneaux pigeons served as Ss. The signaling procedure consisted of illuminating the key, the only source of illumination in the chamber, only when responding would be reinforced. Rate of responding in the unaltered component increased. When the signaling procedure was removed, rate of responding decreased in the component in which reinforcement had never been signaled. Obtained rates of reinforcement in both components were equal throughout the experiment.—*Journal abstract.*

14220. **Brownstein, Aaron J. & Newsom, Crighton.** (U. North Carolina, Greensboro) **Behavioral contrast in multiple schedules with equal reinforcement rates.** *Psychonomic Science,* 1970, **18**(1), 25–26.—After responding was maintained on multiple fixed-interval schedules of reinforcement, with 4 Silver King pigeons, a cuing procedure was added to 1 component. Cuing was accomplished by illuminating a lamp just prior to reinforcement availability. This procedure produced positive behavioral contrast. The rate of responding in the cued component decreased, and the rate in the uncued component increased. When the cue was removed, negative behavioral contrast occurred. Rate of responding in the component from which the cue had been removed increased, and in the other component decreased. Throughout the experiment, rates of reinforcement in both components were held constant. —*Journal abstract.*

14221. **Capaldi, E. J., Ziff, D. R., & Godbout, R. C.** (Purdue U.) **Extinction and the necessity or nonnecessity of anticipating reward on nonrewarded trials.** *Psychonomic Science,* 1970, **18**(1), 61–63.—Male Holtzman rats receiving nonrewarded trials but not previous rewarded trials showed a PRE. These data are similar to those produced in initial nonreward effect studies, except that fewer nonrewards were employed here. Results are not consistent with the hypothesis that at least 1 rewarded trial must precede nonrewarded trials in order to obtain a PRE, nor do they support the idea that reward must be expected on nonrewarded trials in order to obtain a PRE. Reinforcing this view are the results of studies that did not attempt to eliminate expectancy, as here, but rather manipulated its strength prior to extinction. (17 ref.)—*Journal abstract.*

14222. **Farrell, Walter M.** (U. Miami) **Some motivating and reinforcing functions of an auditory stimulus.** *Dissertation Abstracts International,* 1969, **30**(5-B), 2435.

14223. **Logan, Frank A. & Spanier, Douglas.** (U. New Mexico) **Chaining and nonchaining delay of reinforcement.** *Journal of Comparative & Physiological Psychology,* 1970, **72**(1), 98–101.—Exp. I pitted a differential in amount of reward against a comparable differential in nonchaining delay of reward, at 2 different lengths of chaining delay accomplished by different runway lengths. 28 male albino rats served as Ss. Ss tended to choose the smaller more immediate reward in short runways and the larger delayed reward in long runways. Exp. II pitted a short chaining delay combined with a nonchaining delay against a long chaining delay. Ss tended to choose the short chaining delay even when the added nonchaining delay resulted in a longer total time of delay of reward. Results indicate that Ss combine both sources of delay in choosing between alternatives, with chaining delay more deleterious than nonchaining delay. This latter finding is interpreted in terms of immediacy of secondary reinforcement.—*Journal abstract.*

14224. **Logan, Frank A. & Spanier, Douglas.** (U. New Mexico) **Relative effect of delay of food and water reward.** *Journal of Comparative & Physiological Psychology,* 1970, **72**(1), 102–104.—Gave 76 hungry or thirsty male hooded rats the appropriate reward after 1- or 30-sec time of delay in a between-groups 2 × 2 design. In 1 experiment, delay was imposed in the goal box; in another experiment, delay was imposed in the straight alley just before the goal box. In both experiments, the thirsty S ran somewhat slower at the short delay and somewhat faster at the long delay, producing significant interactions. Hence, delay of water reward was found to be relatively less detrimental than delay of food reward. This finding may be related to the degree to which incompatible responses are elicited by the different drive stimuli during the time of delay.—*Journal abstract.*

14225. **McHewitt, Earl R. & McHose, James H.** (Southern Illinois U.) **Role of nonreward in differential conditioning.** *Journal of Experimental Psychology,* 1970,

1455

---

**FIGURE 14–7**

The page from *Psychological Abstracts* containing the summary for the Logan and Spanier article shown in Figure 14–1.

(*Psychological Abstracts,* 1970, vol. 44, no. 9, p. 1455.)

of professionals from often great distances allows each authority to tell the others of the most recent studies. This is a great help, since even with the journal an author has to deal with what is called publication lag, the time it takes to publish and review the material.[5] Conventions also allow professionals to get together for personal discussion of their research. Since some may be working on the same or similar fields, this personal interaction is a valuable information source.

## SUMMARY

The report is the final effort to communicate all facets of the experiment undertaken: the reasons for the experiment, the method used in carrying it out, the precise measurements taken, and the conclusions drawn from the results. In writing, the researcher seeks to communicate to both the professional and the layman. In doing so he uses precise definitions and wording so that everyone will interpret the words similarly. Often the researcher uses operational definitions to make his meaning clear. This scientific writing, though "boring" to many unfamiliar with the style, is precise and aimed at exact understanding. The objective of the report is to transmit the exact information so that another researcher doing the same experiment can replicate the previously derived results. Organization, accuracy, clarity, and readability are the vital elements in a good report.

The universally accepted form of the report is as follows:

Abstract
Text
    Introduction
    Method
        Subjects
        Apparatus
        Procedure
        Design
    Results
    Discussion
References
Footnotes
Tables and Figures

5. Traditionally for a journal, the publication lag ranges from twelve to eighteen months. Though some journals take only three to four months, they are usually review journals specifically for the purpose of giving an introduction to a certain study in hopes that it will be elaborated on in a future article. The latter situation described may be found in *Psychonomic Science* and *Science*, two journals specifically having brief (two-page) research reports. Articles in those journals are characterized by a short time period from submission to publication.

The psychologist, considered to be an authority in his field, faces the ever-present problem of keeping up with the masses of new material being published every day. One solution to the problem is the journal. Journals are subdivided and categorized according to subjects, content areas, and the types of investigations they publish. A psychologist can refer to that journal most applicable to his particular current problem or field of expertise. Thus the journal assists the professional by narrowing his reading spectrum. Another advantage is the assistance journals give as sources of information to the professional in problem areas lying outside his field of expertise. In the absence of authorities, the journal plays another important role as an information source.

Finding journal articles poses yet another hurdle. *Psychological Abstracts*, containing summaries of journal articles, is a time-saving device and an invaluable tool for finding material.

Besides the journal, another solution to the problem of distribution of new information is the convention. Conventions aid professionals by side-stepping the publication lag to the newest information and by allowing personal discussion of problems so that data can be compared and other authorities can be consulted on particular research problems.

# Appendix

**TABLE A**
Table of $t$

| df | P | 0.9 | 0.8 | 0.7 | 0.6 | 0.5 | 0.4 | 0.3 | 0.2 | 0.1 | 0.05 | 0.02 | 0.01 |
|----|---|-----|-----|-----|-----|-----|-----|-----|-----|-----|------|------|------|
| 1  |   | 0.158 | 0.325 | 0.510 | 0.727 | 1.000 | 1.376 | 1.963 | 3.078 | 6.314 | 12.706 | 31.821 | 63.657 |
| 2  |   | 0.142 | 0.289 | 0.445 | 0.617 | 0.816 | 1.061 | 1.386 | 1.886 | 2.920 | 4.303 | 6.965 | 9.925 |
| 3  |   | 0.137 | 0.277 | 0.424 | 0.584 | 0.765 | 0.978 | 1.250 | 1.638 | 2.353 | 3.182 | 4.541 | 5.841 |
| 4  |   | 0.134 | 0.271 | 0.414 | 0.589 | 0.741 | 0.941 | 1.190 | 1.533 | 2.132 | 2.776 | 3.747 | 4.604 |
| 5  |   | 0.132 | 0.267 | 0.408 | 0.559 | 0.727 | 0.920 | 1.156 | 1.476 | 2.015 | 2.571 | 3.365 | 4.032 |
| 6  |   | 0.131 | 0.265 | 0.404 | 0.553 | 0.718 | 0.906 | 1.134 | 1.440 | 1.943 | 2.447 | 3.143 | 3.707 |
| 7  |   | 0.130 | 0.263 | 0.402 | 0.549 | 0.711 | 0.896 | 1.119 | 1.415 | 1.895 | 2.365 | 2.998 | 3.499 |
| 8  |   | 0.130 | 0.262 | 0.399 | 0.546 | 0.706 | 0.889 | 1.108 | 1.397 | 1.860 | 2.306 | 2.896 | 3.355 |
| 9  |   | 0.129 | 0.261 | 0.398 | 0.543 | 0.703 | 0.883 | 1.100 | 1.383 | 1.833 | 2.262 | 2.821 | 3.250 |
| 10 |   | 0.129 | 0.260 | 0.397 | 0.542 | 0.700 | 0.879 | 1.093 | 1.372 | 1.812 | 2.228 | 2.764 | 3.169 |
| 11 |   | 0.129 | 0.260 | 0.396 | 0.540 | 0.697 | 0.876 | 1.088 | 1.363 | 1.796 | 2.201 | 2.718 | 3.106 |
| 12 |   | 0.128 | 0.259 | 0.395 | 0.539 | 0.695 | 0.873 | 1.083 | 1.356 | 1.782 | 2.179 | 2.681 | 3.055 |
| 13 |   | 0.128 | 0.259 | 0.394 | 0.538 | 0.694 | 0.870 | 1.079 | 1.350 | 1.771 | 2.160 | 2.650 | 3.012 |
| 14 |   | 0.128 | 0.258 | 0.393 | 0.537 | 0.692 | 0.868 | 1.076 | 1.345 | 1.761 | 2.145 | 2.624 | 2.977 |
| 15 |   | 0.128 | 0.258 | 0.393 | 0.536 | 0.691 | 0.866 | 1.074 | 1.341 | 1.753 | 2.131 | 2.602 | 2.947 |

| | | | | | | | | | | | |
|---|---|---|---|---|---|---|---|---|---|---|---|
| 16 | 0.128 | 0.258 | 0.392 | 0.535 | 0.690 | 0.865 | 1.071 | 1.337 | 1.746 | 2.120 | 2.583 | 2.921 |
| 17 | 0.128 | 0.257 | 0.392 | 0.534 | 0.689 | 0.863 | 1.069 | 1.333 | 1.740 | 2.110 | 2.567 | 2.898 |
| 18 | 0.127 | 0.257 | 0.392 | 0.534 | 0.688 | 0.862 | 1.067 | 1.330 | 1.734 | 2.101 | 2.552 | 2.878 |
| 19 | 0.127 | 0.257 | 0.391 | 0.533 | 0.688 | 0.861 | 1.066 | 1.328 | 1.729 | 2.093 | 2.539 | 2.861 |
| 20 | 0.127 | 0.257 | 0.391 | 0.533 | 0.687 | 0.860 | 1.064 | 1.325 | 1.725 | 2.086 | 2.528 | 2.845 |
| 21 | 0.127 | 0.257 | 0.391 | 0.532 | 0.686 | 0.859 | 1.063 | 1.323 | 1.721 | 2.080 | 2.518 | 2.831 |
| 22 | 0.127 | 0.256 | 0.390 | 0.532 | 0.686 | 0.858 | 1.061 | 1.321 | 1.717 | 2.074 | 2.508 | 2.819 |
| 23 | 0.127 | 0.256 | 0.390 | 0.532 | 0.685 | 0.858 | 1.060 | 1.319 | 1.714 | 2.069 | 2.500 | 2.807 |
| 24 | 0.127 | 0.256 | 0.390 | 0.531 | 0.685 | 0.857 | 1.059 | 1.318 | 1.711 | 2.064 | 2.492 | 2.797 |
| 25 | 0.127 | 0.256 | 0.390 | 0.531 | 0.684 | 0.856 | 1.058 | 1.316 | 1.708 | 2.060 | 2.485 | 2.787 |
| 26 | 0.127 | 0.256 | 0.390 | 0.531 | 0.684 | 0.856 | 1.058 | 1.315 | 1.706 | 2.056 | 2.479 | 2.779 |
| 27 | 0.127 | 0.256 | 0.389 | 0.531 | 0.684 | 0.855 | 1.057 | 1.314 | 1.703 | 2.052 | 2.473 | 2.771 |
| 28 | 0.127 | 0.256 | 0.389 | 0.530 | 0.683 | 0.855 | 1.056 | 1.313 | 1.701 | 2.048 | 2.467 | 2.763 |
| 29 | 0.127 | 0.256 | 0.389 | 0.530 | 0.683 | 0.854 | 1.055 | 1.311 | 1.699 | 2.045 | 2.462 | 2.756 |
| 30 | 0.127 | 0.256 | 0.389 | 0.530 | 0.683 | 0.854 | 1.055 | 1.310 | 1.697 | 2.042 | 2.457 | 2.750 |
| ∞ | 0.12566 | 0.25335 | 0.38532 | 0.52440 | 0.67449 | 0.84162 | 1.03643 | 1.28155 | 1.64485 | 1.95996 | 2.32634 | 2.57582 |

Source: Reprinted from Table 4 of Fisher, *Statistical methods for research workers*, 14th ed. Copyright © 1972 by Hafner Press. Used by permission of the publisher.

## TABLE B
### Table of F

| $df$ Associated with Denominator | $P$ | \[df Associated with Numerator\] 1 | 2 | 3 | 4 | 5 | 6 | 8 | 12 | 24 | ∞ |
|---|---|---|---|---|---|---|---|---|---|---|---|
| 1 | 0.01 | 4052 | 4999 | 5403 | 5625 | 5764 | 5859 | 5981 | 6106 | 6234 | 6366 |
|   | 0.05 | 161.45 | 199.50 | 215.71 | 224.58 | 230.16 | 233.99 | 238.88 | 243.91 | 249.05 | 254.32 |
|   | 0.10 | 39.86 | 49.50 | 53.59 | 55.83 | 57.24 | 58.20 | 59.44 | 60.70 | 62.00 | 63.33 |
|   | 0.20 | 9.47 | 12.00 | 13.06 | 13.73 | 14.01 | 14.26 | 14.59 | 14.90 | 15.24 | 15.58 |
| 2 | 0.01 | 98.49 | 99.00 | 99.17 | 99.25 | 99.30 | 99.33 | 99.36 | 99.42 | 99.46 | 99.50 |
|   | 0.05 | 18.51 | 19.00 | 19.16 | 19.25 | 19.30 | 19.33 | 19.37 | 19.41 | 19.45 | 19.50 |
|   | 0.10 | 8.53 | 9.00 | 9.16 | 9.24 | 9.29 | 9.33 | 9.37 | 9.41 | 9.45 | 9.49 |
|   | 0.20 | 3.56 | 4.00 | 4.16 | 4.24 | 4.28 | 4.32 | 4.36 | 4.40 | 4.44 | 4.48 |
| 3 | 0.01 | 34.12 | 30.81 | 29.46 | 28.71 | 28.24 | 27.91 | 27.49 | 27.05 | 26.60 | 26.12 |
|   | 0.05 | 10.13 | 9.55 | 9.28 | 9.12 | 9.01 | 8.94 | 8.84 | 8.74 | 8.64 | 8.53 |
|   | 0.10 | 5.54 | 5.46 | 5.39 | 5.34 | 5.31 | 5.28 | 5.25 | 5.22 | 5.18 | 5.13 |
|   | 0.20 | 2.68 | 2.89 | 2.94 | 2.96 | 2.97 | 2.97 | 2.98 | 2.98 | 2.98 | 2.98 |
| 4 | 0.01 | 21.20 | 18.00 | 16.69 | 15.98 | 15.52 | 15.21 | 14.80 | 14.37 | 13.93 | 13.46 |
|   | 0.05 | 7.71 | 6.94 | 6.59 | 6.39 | 6.26 | 6.16 | 6.04 | 5.91 | 5.77 | 5.63 |
|   | 0.10 | 4.54 | 4.32 | 4.19 | 4.11 | 4.05 | 4.01 | 3.95 | 3.90 | 3.83 | 3.76 |
|   | 0.20 | 2.35 | 2.47 | 2.48 | 2.48 | 2.48 | 2.47 | 2.47 | 2.46 | 2.44 | 2.43 |
| 5 | 0.01 | 16.26 | 13.27 | 12.06 | 11.39 | 10.97 | 10.67 | 10.29 | 9.89 | 9.47 | 9.02 |
|   | 0.05 | 6.61 | 5.79 | 5.41 | 5.19 | 5.05 | 4.95 | 4.82 | 4.68 | 4.53 | 4.36 |
|   | 0.10 | 4.06 | 3.78 | 3.62 | 3.52 | 3.45 | 3.40 | 3.34 | 3.27 | 3.19 | 3.10 |
|   | 0.20 | 2.18 | 2.26 | 2.25 | 2.24 | 2.23 | 2.22 | 2.20 | 2.18 | 2.16 | 2.13 |

| | | | | | | | | | | | |
|---|---|---|---|---|---|---|---|---|---|---|---|
| 6 | 0.01 | 13.74 | 10.92 | 9.78 | 9.15 | 8.75 | 8.47 | 8.10 | 7.72 | 7.31 | 6.88 |
| | 0.05 | 5.99 | 5.14 | 4.76 | 4.53 | 4.39 | 4.28 | 4.15 | 4.00 | 3.84 | 3.67 |
| | 0.10 | 3.78 | 3.46 | 3.29 | 3.18 | 3.11 | 3.05 | 2.98 | 2.90 | 2.82 | 2.72 |
| | 0.20 | 2.07 | 2.13 | 2.11 | 2.09 | 2.08 | 2.06 | 2.04 | 2.02 | 1.99 | 1.95 |
| 7 | 0.01 | 12.25 | 9.55 | 8.45 | 7.85 | 7.46 | 7.19 | 6.84 | 6.47 | 6.07 | 5.65 |
| | 0.05 | 5.59 | 4.74 | 4.35 | 4.12 | 3.97 | 3.87 | 3.73 | 3.57 | 3.41 | 3.23 |
| | 0.10 | 3.59 | 3.26 | 3.07 | 2.96 | 2.88 | 2.83 | 2.75 | 2.67 | 2.58 | 2.47 |
| | 0.20 | 2.00 | 2.04 | 2.02 | 1.99 | 1.97 | 1.96 | 1.93 | 1.91 | 1.87 | 1.83 |
| 8 | 0.01 | 11.26 | 8.65 | 7.59 | 7.01 | 6.63 | 6.37 | 6.03 | 5.67 | 5.28 | 4.86 |
| | 0.05 | 5.32 | 4.46 | 4.07 | 3.84 | 3.69 | 3.58 | 3.44 | 3.28 | 3.12 | 2.93 |
| | 0.10 | 3.46 | 3.11 | 2.92 | 2.81 | 2.73 | 2.67 | 2.59 | 2.50 | 2.40 | 2.29 |
| | 0.20 | 1.95 | 1.98 | 1.95 | 1.92 | 1.90 | 1.88 | 1.86 | 1.83 | 1.79 | 1.74 |
| 9 | 0.01 | 10.56 | 8.02 | 6.99 | 6.42 | 6.06 | 5.80 | 5.47 | 5.11 | 4.73 | 4.31 |
| | 0.05 | 5.12 | 4.26 | 3.86 | 3.63 | 3.48 | 3.37 | 3.23 | 3.07 | 2.90 | 2.71 |
| | 0.10 | 3.36 | 3.01 | 2.81 | 2.69 | 2.61 | 2.55 | 2.47 | 2.38 | 2.28 | 2.16 |
| | 0.20 | 1.91 | 1.94 | 1.90 | 1.87 | 1.85 | 1.83 | 1.80 | 1.76 | 1.72 | 1.67 |
| 10 | 0.01 | 10.04 | 7.56 | 6.55 | 5.99 | 5.64 | 5.39 | 5.06 | 4.71 | 4.33 | 3.91 |
| | 0.05 | 4.96 | 4.10 | 3.71 | 3.48 | 3.33 | 3.22 | 3.07 | 2.91 | 2.74 | 2.54 |
| | 0.10 | 3.28 | 2.92 | 2.73 | 2.61 | 2.52 | 2.46 | 2.38 | 2.28 | 2.18 | 2.06 |
| | 0.20 | 1.88 | 1.90 | 1.86 | 1.83 | 1.80 | 1.78 | 1.75 | 1.72 | 1.67 | 1.62 |
| 11 | 0.01 | 9.65 | 7.20 | 6.22 | 5.67 | 5.32 | 5.07 | 4.74 | 4.40 | 4.02 | 3.60 |
| | 0.05 | 4.84 | 3.98 | 3.59 | 3.36 | 3.20 | 3.09 | 2.95 | 2.79 | 2.61 | 2.40 |
| | 0.10 | 3.23 | 2.86 | 2.66 | 2.54 | 2.45 | 2.39 | 2.30 | 2.21 | 2.10 | 1.97 |
| | 0.20 | 1.86 | 1.87 | 1.83 | 1.80 | 1.77 | 1.75 | 1.72 | 1.68 | 1.63 | 1.57 |
| 12 | 0.01 | 9.33 | 6.93 | 5.95 | 5.41 | 5.06 | 4.82 | 4.50 | 4.16 | 3.78 | 3.36 |
| | 0.05 | 4.75 | 3.88 | 3.49 | 3.26 | 3.11 | 3.00 | 2.85 | 2.69 | 2.50 | 2.30 |
| | 0.10 | 3.18 | 2.81 | 2.61 | 2.48 | 2.39 | 2.33 | 2.24 | 2.15 | 2.04 | 1.90 |
| | 0.20 | 1.84 | 1.85 | 1.80 | 1.77 | 1.74 | 1.72 | 1.69 | 1.65 | 1.60 | 1.54 |

**TABLE B Continued**

| df Associated with Denominator | P | \multicolumn{10}{c}{df Associated with Numerator} | | | | | | | | | |
|---|---|---|---|---|---|---|---|---|---|---|---|
| | | 1 | 2 | 3 | 4 | 5 | 6 | 8 | 12 | 24 | ∞ |
| 13 | 0.01 | 9.07 | 6.70 | 5.74 | 5.20 | 4.86 | 4.62 | 4.30 | 3.96 | 3.59 | 3.16 |
| | 0.05 | 4.67 | 3.80 | 3.41 | 3.18 | 3.02 | 2.92 | 2.77 | 2.60 | 2.42 | 2.21 |
| | 0.10 | 3.14 | 2.76 | 2.56 | 2.43 | 2.35 | 2.28 | 2.20 | 2.10 | 1.98 | 1.85 |
| | 0.20 | 1.82 | 1.88 | 1.78 | 1.75 | 1.72 | 1.69 | 1.66 | 1.62 | 1.57 | 1.51 |
| 14 | 0.01 | 8.86 | 6.51 | 5.56 | 5.08 | 4.69 | 4.46 | 4.14 | 3.80 | 3.43 | 3.00 |
| | 0.05 | 4.60 | 3.74 | 3.34 | 3.11 | 2.96 | 2.85 | 2.70 | 2.53 | 2.35 | 2.13 |
| | 0.10 | 3.10 | 2.73 | 2.52 | 2.39 | 2.31 | 2.24 | 2.15 | 2.05 | 1.94 | 1.80 |
| | 0.20 | 1.81 | 1.81 | 1.76 | 1.78 | 1.70 | 1.67 | 1.64 | 1.60 | 1.55 | 1.48 |
| 15 | 0.01 | 8.68 | 6.36 | 5.42 | 4.89 | 4.56 | 4.32 | 4.00 | 3.67 | 3.29 | 2.87 |
| | 0.05 | 4.54 | 3.68 | 3.29 | 3.06 | 2.90 | 2.79 | 2.64 | 2.48 | 2.29 | 2.07 |
| | 0.10 | 3.07 | 2.70 | 2.49 | 2.36 | 2.27 | 2.21 | 2.12 | 2.02 | 1.90 | 1.76 |
| | 0.20 | 1.80 | 1.79 | 1.75 | 1.71 | 1.68 | 1.66 | 1.62 | 1.58 | 1.53 | 1.46 |
| 16 | 0.01 | 8.53 | 6.23 | 5.29 | 4.77 | 4.44 | 4.20 | 3.89 | 3.55 | 3.18 | 2.75 |
| | 0.05 | 4.49 | 3.63 | 3.24 | 3.01 | 2.85 | 2.74 | 2.59 | 2.42 | 2.24 | 2.01 |
| | 0.10 | 3.05 | 2.67 | 2.46 | 2.33 | 2.24 | 2.18 | 2.09 | 1.99 | 1.87 | 1.72 |
| | 0.20 | 1.79 | 1.78 | 1.74 | 1.70 | 1.67 | 1.64 | 1.61 | 1.56 | 1.51 | 1.43 |
| 17 | 0.01 | 8.40 | 6.11 | 5.18 | 4.67 | 4.34 | 4.10 | 3.79 | 3.45 | 3.08 | 2.65 |
| | 0.05 | 4.45 | 3.59 | 3.20 | 2.96 | 2.81 | 2.70 | 2.55 | 2.38 | 2.19 | 1.96 |
| | 0.10 | 3.03 | 2.64 | 2.44 | 2.31 | 2.22 | 2.15 | 2.06 | 1.96 | 1.84 | 1.69 |
| | 0.20 | 1.78 | 1.77 | 1.72 | 1.68 | 1.65 | 1.63 | 1.59 | 1.55 | 1.49 | 1.42 |

| | | | | | | | | | | | |
|---|---|---|---|---|---|---|---|---|---|---|---|
| 18 | 0.01 | 8.28 | 6.01 | 5.09 | 4.58 | 4.25 | 4.01 | 3.71 | 3.37 | 3.00 | 2.57 |
| | 0.05 | 4.41 | 3.55 | 3.16 | 2.93 | 2.77 | 2.66 | 2.51 | 2.34 | 2.15 | 1.92 |
| | 0.10 | 3.01 | 3.62 | 2.42 | 2.29 | 2.20 | 2.13 | 2.04 | 1.93 | 1.81 | 1.66 |
| | 0.20 | 1.77 | 1.76 | 1.71 | 1.67 | 1.64 | 1.62 | 1.58 | 1.53 | 1.48 | 1.40 |
| 19 | 0.01 | 8.18 | 5.93 | 5.01 | 4.50 | 4.17 | 3.94 | 3.63 | 3.30 | 2.92 | 2.49 |
| | 0.05 | 4.38 | 3.52 | 3.13 | 2.90 | 2.74 | 2.63 | 2.48 | 2.31 | 2.11 | 1.88 |
| | 0.10 | 2.99 | 2.61 | 2.40 | 2.27 | 2.18 | 2.11 | 2.02 | 1.91 | 1.79 | 1.63 |
| | 0.20 | 1.76 | 1.75 | 1.70 | 1.66 | 1.63 | 1.61 | 1.57 | 1.52 | 1.46 | 1.39 |
| 20 | 0.01 | 8.10 | 5.85 | 4.94 | 4.43 | 4.10 | 3.87 | 3.56 | 3.23 | 2.86 | 2.42 |
| | 0.05 | 4.35 | 3.49 | 3.10 | 2.87 | 2.71 | 2.60 | 2.45 | 2.28 | 2.08 | 1.84 |
| | 0.10 | 2.97 | 2.59 | 2.38 | 2.25 | 2.16 | 2.09 | 2.00 | 1.89 | 1.77 | 1.61 |
| | 0.20 | 1.76 | 1.75 | 1.70 | 1.65 | 1.62 | 1.60 | 1.56 | 1.51 | 1.45 | 1.37 |
| 21 | 0.01 | 8.02 | 5.78 | 4.87 | 4.37 | 4.04 | 3.81 | 3.51 | 3.17 | 2.80 | 2.36 |
| | 0.05 | 4.32 | 3.47 | 3.07 | 2.84 | 2.68 | 2.57 | 2.42 | 2.25 | 2.05 | 1.81 |
| | 0.10 | 2.96 | 2.57 | 2.36 | 2.23 | 2.14 | 2.08 | 1.98 | 1.88 | 1.75 | 1.59 |
| | 0.20 | 1.75 | 1.74 | 1.69 | 1.65 | 1.61 | 1.59 | 1.55 | 1.50 | 1.44 | 1.36 |
| 22 | 0.01 | 7.94 | 5.72 | 4.82 | 4.31 | 3.99 | 3.76 | 3.45 | 3.12 | 2.75 | 2.31 |
| | 0.05 | 4.30 | 3.44 | 3.05 | 2.82 | 2.66 | 2.55 | 2.40 | 2.23 | 2.03 | 1.78 |
| | 0.10 | 2.95 | 2.56 | 2.35 | 2.22 | 2.13 | 2.06 | 1.97 | 1.86 | 1.73 | 1.57 |
| | 0.20 | 1.75 | 1.73 | 1.68 | 1.64 | 1.61 | 1.58 | 1.54 | 1.49 | 1.43 | 1.35 |
| 23 | 0.01 | 7.88 | 5.66 | 4.76 | 4.26 | 3.94 | 3.71 | 3.41 | 3.07 | 2.70 | 2.26 |
| | 0.05 | 4.28 | 3.42 | 3.03 | 2.80 | 2.64 | 2.53 | 2.38 | 2.20 | 2.00 | 1.76 |
| | 0.10 | 2.94 | 2.55 | 2.34 | 2.21 | 2.11 | 2.05 | 1.95 | 1.84 | 1.72 | 1.55 |
| | 0.20 | 1.74 | 1.73 | 1.68 | 1.63 | 1.60 | 1.57 | 1.53 | 1.49 | 1.42 | 1.34 |
| 24 | 0.01 | 7.82 | 5.61 | 4.72 | 4.22 | 3.90 | 3.67 | 3.36 | 3.03 | 2.66 | 2.21 |
| | 0.05 | 4.26 | 3.40 | 3.01 | 2.78 | 2.62 | 2.51 | 2.36 | 2.18 | 1.98 | 1.73 |
| | 0.10 | 2.93 | 2.54 | 2.33 | 2.19 | 2.10 | 2.04 | 1.94 | 1.83 | 1.70 | 1.53 |
| | 0.20 | 1.74 | 1.72 | 1.67 | 1.63 | 1.59 | 1.57 | 1.53 | 1.48 | 1.42 | 1.33 |

| df Associated with Denominator | P | \$df\$ Associated with Numerator | | | | | | | | | |
|---|---|---|---|---|---|---|---|---|---|---|---|
| | | 1 | 2 | 3 | 4 | 5 | 6 | 8 | 12 | 24 | ∞ |
| 25 | 0.01 | 7.77 | 5.57 | 4.68 | 4.18 | 3.86 | 3.63 | 3.32 | 2.99 | 2.62 | 2.17 |
| | 0.05 | 4.24 | 3.38 | 2.99 | 2.76 | 2.60 | 2.49 | 2.34 | 2.16 | 1.96 | 1.71 |
| | 0.10 | 2.92 | 2.53 | 2.32 | 2.18 | 2.09 | 2.02 | 1.93 | 1.82 | 1.69 | 1.52 |
| | 0.20 | 1.73 | 1.72 | 1.66 | 1.62 | 1.59 | 1.56 | 1.52 | 1.47 | 1.41 | 1.32 |
| 26 | 0.01 | 7.72 | 5.53 | 4.64 | 4.14 | 3.82 | 3.59 | 3.29 | 2.96 | 2.58 | 2.13 |
| | 0.05 | 4.22 | 3.37 | 2.98 | 2.74 | 2.59 | 2.47 | 2.32 | 2.15 | 1.95 | 1.69 |
| | 0.10 | 2.91 | 2.52 | 2.31 | 2.17 | 2.08 | 2.01 | 1.92 | 1.81 | 1.68 | 1.50 |
| | 0.20 | 1.73 | 1.71 | 1.66 | 1.62 | 1.58 | 1.56 | 1.52 | 1.47 | 1.40 | 1.31 |
| 27 | 0.01 | 7.68 | 5.49 | 4.60 | 4.11 | 3.78 | 3.56 | 3.26 | 2.93 | 2.55 | 2.10 |
| | 0.05 | 4.21 | 3.35 | 2.96 | 2.73 | 2.57 | 2.46 | 2.30 | 2.13 | 1.93 | 1.67 |
| | 0.10 | 2.90 | 2.51 | 2.30 | 2.17 | 2.07 | 2.00 | 1.91 | 1.80 | 1.67 | 1.49 |
| | 0.20 | 1.73 | 1.71 | 1.66 | 1.61 | 1.58 | 1.55 | 1.51 | 1.46 | 1.40 | 1.30 |
| 28 | 0.01 | 7.64 | 5.45 | 4.57 | 4.07 | 3.75 | 3.53 | 3.23 | 2.90 | 2.52 | 2.06 |
| | 0.05 | 4.20 | 3.34 | 2.95 | 2.71 | 2.56 | 2.44 | 2.29 | 2.12 | 1.91 | 1.65 |
| | 0.10 | 2.89 | 2.50 | 2.29 | 2.16 | 2.06 | 2.00 | 1.90 | 1.79 | 1.66 | 1.48 |
| | 0.20 | 1.72 | 1.71 | 1.65 | 1.61 | 1.57 | 1.55 | 1.51 | 1.46 | 1.39 | 1.30 |
| 29 | 0.01 | 7.60 | 5.42 | 4.54 | 4.04 | 3.73 | 3.50 | 3.20 | 2.87 | 2.49 | 2.03 |
| | 0.05 | 4.18 | 3.33 | 2.93 | 2.70 | 2.54 | 2.43 | 2.28 | 2.10 | 1.90 | 1.64 |
| | 0.10 | 2.89 | 2.50 | 2.28 | 2.15 | 2.06 | 1.99 | 1.89 | 1.78 | 1.65 | 1.47 |
| | 0.20 | 1.72 | 1.70 | 1.65 | 1.60 | 1.57 | 1.54 | 1.50 | 1.45 | 1.39 | 1.29 |

| $v_2$ | $\alpha$ | | | | | | | | | | |
|---|---|---|---|---|---|---|---|---|---|---|---|
| 30 | 0.01 | 7.56 | 5.39 | 4.51 | 4.02 | 3.70 | 3.47 | 3.17 | 2.84 | 2.47 | 2.01 |
|  | 0.05 | 4.17 | 3.32 | 2.92 | 2.69 | 2.53 | 2.42 | 2.27 | 2.09 | 1.89 | 1.62 |
|  | 0.10 | 2.88 | 2.49 | 2.28 | 2.14 | 2.05 | 1.98 | 1.88 | 1.77 | 1.64 | 1.46 |
|  | 0.20 | 1.72 | 1.70 | 1.64 | 1.60 | 1.57 | 1.54 | 1.50 | 1.45 | 1.38 | 1.28 |
| 40 | 0.01 | 7.31 | 5.18 | 4.31 | 3.83 | 3.51 | 3.29 | 2.99 | 2.66 | 2.29 | 1.80 |
|  | 0.05 | 4.08 | 3.23 | 2.84 | 2.61 | 2.45 | 2.34 | 2.18 | 2.00 | 1.79 | 1.51 |
|  | 0.10 | 2.84 | 2.44 | 2.23 | 2.09 | 2.00 | 1.93 | 1.83 | 1.71 | 1.57 | 1.38 |
|  | 0.20 | 1.70 | 1.68 | 1.62 | 1.57 | 1.54 | 1.51 | 1.47 | 1.41 | 1.34 | 1.24 |
| 60 | 0.01 | 7.08 | 4.98 | 4.13 | 3.65 | 3.34 | 3.12 | 2.82 | 2.50 | 2.12 | 1.60 |
|  | 0.05 | 4.00 | 3.15 | 2.76 | 2.52 | 2.37 | 2.25 | 2.10 | 1.92 | 1.70 | 1.39 |
|  | 0.10 | 2.79 | 2.39 | 2.18 | 2.04 | 1.95 | 1.87 | 1.77 | 1.66 | 1.51 | 1.29 |
|  | 0.20 | 1.68 | 1.65 | 1.59 | 1.55 | 1.51 | 1.48 | 1.44 | 1.38 | 1.31 | 1.18 |
| 120 | 0.01 | 6.85 | 4.79 | 3.95 | 3.48 | 3.17 | 2.96 | 2.66 | 2.34 | 1.95 | 1.38 |
|  | 0.05 | 3.92 | 3.07 | 2.68 | 2.45 | 2.29 | 2.17 | 2.02 | 1.83 | 1.61 | 1.25 |
|  | 0.10 | 2.75 | 2.35 | 2.13 | 1.99 | 1.90 | 1.82 | 1.72 | 1.60 | 1.45 | 1.19 |
|  | 0.20 | 1.66 | 1.63 | 1.57 | 1.52 | 1.48 | 1.45 | 1.41 | 1.35 | 1.27 | 1.12 |
| $\infty$ | 0.01 | 6.64 | 4.60 | 3.78 | 3.32 | 3.02 | 2.80 | 2.51 | 2.18 | 1.79 | 1.00 |
|  | 0.05 | 3.84 | 2.99 | 2.60 | 2.37 | 2.21 | 2.09 | 1.94 | 1.75 | 1.52 | 1.00 |
|  | 0.10 | 2.71 | 2.30 | 2.08 | 1.94 | 1.85 | 1.77 | 1.67 | 1.55 | 1.38 | 1.00 |
|  | 0.20 | 1.64 | 1.61 | 1.55 | 1.50 | 1.46 | 1.43 | 1.38 | 1.32 | 1.23 | 1.00 |

# References

ALEXANDER, R. D. Aggressiveness, territoriality, and sexual behavior in field crickets. *Behavior*, 1961, **71,** 2–3.

AMERICAN PSYCHOLOGICAL ASSOCIATION, Ad Hoc Committee on Ethical Standards in Psychological Research. *Ethical principles in the conduct of research with human participants.* Washington, D.C.: American Psychological Association, 1973.

BARNETT, S. A. *The rat.* Chicago: Aldine, 1963.

BARRY, H. Prolonged measurements of discrimination between alcohol and non-drug states. *Journal of Comparative Physiological Psychology*, 1968, **65,** 349–352.

BELLVILLE, R. E. Control of behavior by drug-produced internal stimuli. *Psychopharmicologia* (Berl.), 1964, **5,** 95–105.

BERGIN, A. E., & GARFIELD, S. L. (Eds.) *Handbook of psychotherapy and behavior change: an empirical analysis.* New York: Wiley, 1971.

BERKOWITZ, L., & LEPAGE, A. Weapons as aggression-eliciting stimuli. *Journal of Personality and Social Psychology*, 1967, **7** (2), 202–207.

BRADY, J. V. Ulcers in "executive" monkeys. *Scientific American*, 1958, **199,** 95–100.

BRELAND, K., & BRELAND M. *Animal behavior.* New York: Macmillan, 1966.

BUDZYNSKI, T., STOYVA, J., & ADLER, C. Feedback-induced muscle relaxation: application to tension headache. *Journal of Behavioral, Therapeutic, and Experimental Psychiatry*, 1970, **1,** 205–211.

BURKE, R. L., & BENNIS, W. G. Changes in perception of self and others during human relations training. *Human Relations*, 1961, **14,** 165–182.

BURKS, B. S. The relative influence of nature and nurture upon mental development: a comparative study of foster parent-child resemblance and true parent-child resemblance. 27th Yearbook, Part 1, National Society for the Study of Education. Chicago: Univ. of Chicago Press, 1928.

BUTLER, J. M., & HAIGH, C. V. Changes in the relation between self-concepts and ideal concepts consequent upon client-centered counseling. In C. R. Rogers and

F. R. Dymond (Eds.), *Psychotherapy and personality change*. Chicago: Univ. of Chicago Press, 1954.

CAMPBELL, D. T., & STANLEY, J. C. *Experimental and quasi-experimental designs for research*. Skokie: Rand McNally, 1966.

CATTELL, R. B. *The scientific analysis of personality*. Baltimore: Penguin, 1965.

CIEUTAT, V. J., STOCKWELL, F. E., & NOBLE, C. E. The interaction of ability and amount of practice with stimulus and response meaningfulness (m, m) in paired-associate learning. *Journal of Experimental Psychology*, 1958, **56**, 193–202.

COHEN, E., MOTTO, J. A., & SEIDEN, R. H. An instrument for evaluating suicide potential: a preliminary study. *American Journal of Psychiatry*, 1966, **22** (8), 886–891.

COLLMANN, R. D., & STROLLER, A. A survey of mongoloid births in Victoria, Australia, 1942–1957. *American Journal of Public Health*, 1962, **52**, 813–829.

———. Virus aetiology for Down's syndrome. *Nature*, 1965, **208**, 903–904.

CONRAD, H. S. Clearance of questionnaires with respect to "invasion of privacy," public sensitivities, ethical standards, etc. *American Psychologist*, 1967, **22** (5), 356–359.

CRONBACH, L. J., & GLESER, G. C. *Psychological tests and personnel decisions*. Urbana: Univ. of Illinois Press, 1957.

CUMMINGS, W. W. A bird's eye glimpse of men and machines. In *Control of human behavior*, Vol. I. Chicago: Scott, Foresman, 1966.

DEMBER, W. N. *The psychology of perception*. New York: Holt, Rinehart and Winston, 1963.

DODWELL, P. C., & BESSANT, D. E. Learning without swimming in a water maze. *Journal of Comparative Physiological Psychology*, 1960, **54**, 422–425.

DUNCAN, C. P. Habit reversal induced by electroshock in the rat. *Journal of Comparative and Physiological Psychology*, 1948, **41**, 11–16.

EYSENCK, H. J. The effects of psychotherapy: an evaluation. *Journal of Consulting Psychology*, 1952, **16**, 319–324.

FERGUSON, G. A. *Statistical analysis in psychology and education*. New York: McGraw-Hill, 1966.

FERSTER, C. B., & SKINNER, B. F. *Schedules of reinforcement*. New York: Appleton-Century-Crofts, 1957.

GAZZANIGA, M. S. *The bisected brain*. New York: Appleton-Century-Crofts, 1970.

GIBSON, E. J., & WALK, R. D. The "visual cliff." *Scientific American*, 1960, **202**, 64–71.

GIRDEN, E., & CULLER, E. A. Conditioned responses in curarized striate muscle in dogs. *Journal of Comparative Psychology*, 1937, **23**, 261–274.

GOLDSCHMIDT, W. The brideprice of the Sebei. *Scientific American*, 1973, **229** (1), 74–85.

GOODWIN, D. W., POWELL, B., BREMER, D., HOINE, H., & STERN, J. Alcohol and recall: state dependent effects in man. *Science*, 1969, **163**, 1358–1360.

GUTTMAN, N., & KALISH, H. I. Discriminability and stimulus generalization. *Journal of Experimental Psychology*, 1956, **51**, 79–88.

HALACY, D. S. *Man and memory*. New York: Harper & Row, 1970.

HAYS, W. L. *Statistics for psychologists.* New York: Holt, Rinehart and Winston, 1973.

HEISTAD, G. T., & TORRES, A. A. A mechanism for the effect of a tranquilizing drug on learned emotional responses. *Univ. of Minnesota Medical Bulletin,* 1959, **30,** 518–527.

HELD R., & HEIN, A. Movement-produced stimulation in the development of visually guided behavior. *Journal of Comparative and Physiological Psychology,* 1963, **56,** 872–876.

HINDE, R. A. *Animal behavior.* New York: McGraw-Hill, 1970.

HOLMGREN, B. *Drug dependent conditioned reflexes.* Paper read at the international symposium on cortical-subcortical relationships in sensory regulation. Havana, Cuba, 1965.

HYDÉN, H. The question of a molecular basis for the memory trace. In K. H. Pribram and D. E. Broadbent (Eds.), *Biology of memory.* New York: Academic Press, 1970.

JEFFRY, R. The psychologist as an expert witness on the issue of insanity. *American Psychologist,* 1964, **19,** 838–843.

JENKINS, J. G., & DALLENBACH, K. M. Oblivescence during sleep and waking. *American Journal of Psychology,* 1924, **35,** 605–612.

JOHNSON, R. C., & MEDINNUS, G. R. *Child psychology.* New York: Wiley, 1969.

KELMAN, H. C. Humane use of human subjects: the problem of deception in social psychological experiments. *Psychological Bulletin,* 1967, **67** (1), 1–11.

KEPPEL, G. *Design and analysis: a researcher's handbook.* Englewood Cliffs: Prentice-Hall, 1973.

KERLINGER, F. N. *Foundations of behavioral research.* New York: Holt, Rinehart and Winston, 1973.

KIRK, R. E. *Experimental design: procedures for the behavioral sciences.* Monterey: Brooks-Cole, 1968.

KLING, J. W., & RIGGS, L. A. *Experimental psychology.* New York: Holt, Rinehart and Winston, 1971.

KOPP, O. O., BOHDANECKY, O. O., & JARVICK, O. O. Long temporal gradient of retrograde amnesia for a well discriminated stimulus. *Science,* 1966, **153,** 1547–1549.

KORNHAUSER, A., & SHEATSLEY, P. Questionnaire construction and interview procedure. In C. Selltiz *et al.* (Eds.), *Research methods in social relations.* New York: Holt, Rinehart and Winston, 1959.

LEAHY, A. M. Nature-nurture and intelligence. *Genetic Psychological Monographs,* 1935, **17,** 236–308.

LEVINE, S., CHEVALIER, J. A., & KORCHIN, S. J. The effects of shock and handling in infancy on later avoidance learning. *Journal of Personality,* 1956, **25,** 475–493.

LOGAN, F. A., & SPANIER, D. Relative effect of delay of food and water reward. *Journal of Comparative and Physiological Psychology,* 1970, **72** (1), 102–104.

LOVELL, V. R. The human use of personality tests: a dissenting view. *American Psychologist,* 1967, **22** (5), 383–393.

MANOSEVITZ, M. Hoarding—an exercise in behavioral genetics. *Psychology Today,* August 1970.

MATHESON, D. W., BRUCE, R. L., & BEAUCHAMP, K. L. *Introduction to experimental psychology*. New York: Holt, Rinehart and Winston, 1970.

MAXWELL, A. E. *Basic statistics in behavioural research*. Baltimore: Penguin, 1970.

McGUIGAN, F. J., & WOODS, P. J. *Contemporary studies in psychology*. Englewood Cliffs: Prentice-Hall, 1972.

MICHAEL, J. *Laboratory studies in operant behavior*. New York: McGraw-Hill, 1963.

MILLER, N. E. Some recent studies of conflict behavior and drugs. *American Psychologist*, 1961, **16**, 12–24.

MOORE, R., & GOLDIAMOND, I. Errorless establishment of visual discrimination using fading procedures. *Journal of Experimental Analysis of Behavior*, 1964, **7**, 269–272.

MURCH, G. M. *Visual and auditory perception*. New York: Bobbs-Merrill, 1973.

MURDOCK, B. B., Jr. The serial position effect of free recall. *Journal of Experimental Psychology*, 1962, **64**, 482–488.

OVERTON, D. A. State-dependent or "dissociated" learning produced with pentobarbital. *Journal of Comparative Physiological Psychology*, 1964, **57**, 3–12.

PARTEN, M. *Surveys, polls, and samples*. New York: Harper & Row, 1950.

PAUL, G. L. *Insight versus desensitization in psychotherapy*. Palo Alto: Stanford Univ. Press, 1966.

PENFIELD, W. The interpretive cortex. *Science*, **129**, 1959, p. 1721.

PETTIGREW, T. Regional differences in anti-Negro prejudice. *Journal of Abnormal Psychology*, 1959, **59**, 28–36.

*Publication manual*. Washington, D.C.: American Psychological Association.

REESE, E. P. *Experiments in operant behavior*. New York: Appleton-Century-Crofts, 1964.

ROBINSON, H. B., & ROBINSON, N. M. Mental retardation. In P. H. Mussen (Ed.), *Manual of child psychology*. New York: Wiley, 1970.

ROBINSON, P. W., & SHELLEY, M. F. The effects of total darkness on schedule control. *Journal of Experimental Analysis of Behavior*, 1974, **22**, 391–400.

ROSENTHAL, R. *Experimenter effects in behavioral research*. New York: Appleton-Century-Crofts, 1966.

ROSENZWEIG, M. R., BENNETT, E. L., & DIAMOND, M. C. Brain changes in response to experience. *Scientific American*, 1972, **226** (2), 22–29.

ROSS, S., & LOCKMAN, R. F. *A career in psychology*. Washington, D.C.: American Psychological Association, 1963.

RUEBHAUSEN, O. M., & BRIM, O. G. J. Privacy and behavioral research. *American Psychologist*, 1966, **21** (5), 423–437.

RYAN, T. A. Multiple comparisons in psychological research. *Psychological Bulletin*, 1959, **56**, 26–47.

SAINSBURY, P., & BARRACLOUGH, B. Differences between suicidal rates. *Nature*, 1968, **220**, 1252.

SASSON, R., & NELSON, T. M. The human experimental subject in context. *Canadian Psychologist*, 1969, **10** (4), 409–437.

SEEMAN, J. Deception in psychological research. *American Psychologist*, 1969, **24** (11), 1025–1028.

SEIDEN, R. H. Campus tragedy: a study of student suicide. *Journal of Abnormal and Social Psychology*, 1966, **71,** 389–399.

SHELDON, W. H. (with S. S. Stevens and W. B. Tucker). *The varieties of human physique: an introduction to constitutional psychology.* New York: Harper & Row, 1940.

SIDMAN, M. *Tactics of scientific research.* New York: Basic Books, 1960.

SIDMAN, M., & STODDARD, L. T. The effectiveness of fading in programming simultaneous form discrimination for retarded children. *Journal of Experimental Analysis of Behavior*, 1967, **10,** 3–15.

SISSON, R. F. Aha! It really works! *National Geographic*, 1974, **145** (1), 142–147.

SKINNER, B. F. Pigeons in a pelican. *American Psychologist*, 1960, **19,** 28–37.

SMITH, D. E., KING, M. B., HOEBEL, B. G. Lateral hypothalamic control of killing: evidence for a cholinoceptive mechanism. *Science*, 1970, **167,** 900–901.

SPERRY, R. W. Hemisphere deconnection and unity in conscious awareness. *American Psychologist*, 1968, **23,** 723–733.

SULZBACHER, S. I., & HOUSER, J. E. A tactic to eliminate disruptive behaviors in the classroom: group contingent consequences. *American Journal of Mental Deficiency*, 1966, **1,** 182–187.

TERRACE, H. S. Discrimination learning with and without errors. *Journal of Experimental Analysis of Behavior*, 1963, **6,** 1–27.

THOMAS, A., CHESS, S., & BIRCH, H. G. The origin of personality. In *Contemporary psychology: readings from Scientific American*. San Francisco: Freeman, 1971.

THORNDIKE, E. L., MCCALL, W. A., & CHAPMAN, J. C. Ventilation in relation to mental work. *Teachers College Contributions in Education*, 1916, 78.

WALK, R. D., & GIBSON, E. J. A comparative and analytical study of visual depth perception. *Psychological Monographs*, 1961, **75,** Whole No. 519.

WARWICK, D. P., & OSHERSON, S. *Comparative research methods.* Englewood Cliffs: Prentice-Hall, 1973.

WHALEY, D. L., & MALOTT, R. W. *Elementary principles of behavior.* New York: Appleton-Century-Crofts, 1971.

WHALEY, D. L., & SURRATT, S. L. *Attitudes of science.* Kalamazoo: Behaviordelia, 1968.

WINER, B. J. *Statistical principles in experimental design.* 2nd ed. New York: McGraw-Hill, 1971.

WIXEN, B. N. *Children of the rich.* New York: Crown, 1973.

WOLF, M. M., RISTEY, T., & MEES, H. Application of operant conditioning procedures to the behavior problems of an autistic child. *Behavior Research and Therapy*, 1964, **1,** 305–312.

*Index*